Starting an Online Business

FOR DUMMIES®
A Wiley Brand

7th Edition

by Greg Holden

FOR DUMMIES®
A Wiley Brand

Starting an Online Business For Dummies®, 7th Edition

Published by:
John Wiley & Sons, Inc.
111 River Street
Hoboken, NJ 07030-5774
www.wiley.com

Contents at a Glance

Table of Contents

Introduction

You've been thinking about starting your own business for a while now. You've heard about the woman whose Julie/Julia Project blog was turned into a book and a popular movie. You've heard about young entrepreneurs who've made billions creating popular websites such as Facebook. But you've been slow to jump on the bandwagon. You're a busy person, after all. You have a full-time job, whether it's running your home or working outside your home. Or perhaps you've been laid off or are going through some other life-changing event and are ready to take off in a new direction, but the economic upheavals of recent years leave you understandably reluctant to make a big career change.

Well, I have news for you: *Now* is the perfect time to turn your dream into reality by starting your own online business. More individuals than ever before — regular folks just like you — are making money and enriching their lives by operating businesses online. The clock and your location are no longer limiting factors. Small business owners can now work any time of the night or day in their spare bedrooms, local libraries, or neighborhood coffee shops.

If you like the idea of being in business for yourself but don't have a particular product or service in mind, relax and keep yourself open to inspiration. Many different kinds of commercial enterprises can hit it big on the Internet. Among the entrepreneurs I interviewed for this book are a woman who sells her own insect repellent, a husband and wife who sell items from their native Europe, a woman who provides office services for the medical community, a housewife who sells sweetener and coffee on eBay, a sculptor and painter, a young man who started selling electronics online at age 16, and several folks who create web pages for other businesses. With the help of this book, you can start a new endeavor and be in charge of your own cyberbusiness, too.

You Can Do It!

What's that? You say you wouldn't know a merchant account, a profit and loss statement, or a clickthrough advertising rate if it came up to you on the street and introduced itself? Don't worry: The Internet (and this book) levels the playing field so that a novice has just as good a chance at succeeding as MBAs who love to throw around business terms at cocktail parties.

The Internet is a pervasive and everyday part of the business landscape these days. Whether you've been in business for 20 years or 20 minutes, the keys to success are the same:

- ✔ **Having a good idea:** If you have something to sell that people have an appetite for, and if your competition is slim, you have a strong chance of being successful.

- ✔ **Working hard:** When you're your own boss, you can make yourself work harder than any of your former bosses ever could. If you put in the effort and persist through the inevitable ups and downs, you'll be a winner.

- ✔ **Believing in yourself:** One of the most surprising and useful things I discovered from the online businesspeople I interviewed was that if you believe that you'll succeed, you probably will. Believe in yourself and proceed as though you'll be successful. Together with your good ideas and hard work, your confidence will pay off.

If you're the cautious type who wants to test the waters before you launch your new business on the Internet, let this book lead you gently up the learning curve. After you're online, you can master techniques to improve your presence. This book includes helpful hints for doing market research and reworking your website to achieve success.

Jump In, the Water's Fine

When I first started revising this new edition in early 2013, I was not surprised to find that many businesses had rebounded five years after the serious economic crash. I *was* surprised to find that so many new ways of doing business had either appeared or become commonplace (mobile shopping and Facebook stores, for example). It turns out that *any time* is a good time to start an online business as long as you have a good idea and a smart business plan.

New resources, many of which didn't exist when I wrote the previous edition, present entrepreneurs with opportunities to market themselves and their products and services. Tablets make selling easier than ever, and smartphones make mobile shopping an everyday occurrence. Standards such as Pinterest, Fulfillment By Amazon, and Square Payments were either just emerging or hadn't yet come to fruition only a few years ago. Well-known marketplaces such as eBay give businesspeople a solid foundation on which to start a new business. Other well-known web-based service providers such as Yahoo!, PayPal, and Amazon.com give you a way to reach millions of potential customers. Bloggers are an everyday part of the cyberspace landscape, and some are making a regular source of income from their online diaries. Google and Yahoo! are making it easier than ever to gain advertising revenue.

As the web becomes more of a way of life and broadband Internet connections become widespread around the world, doing business online isn't considered unusual anymore. Still, you may have reasonable concerns about the future of e-commerce and for the entrepreneurs this book seeks to help — individuals who are starting their first businesses on the web. Your fears will quickly evaporate when you read this book's case studies of my friends and colleagues who conduct business online. They're either thriving or at least keeping their heads above water, and they enthusiastically encourage others to jump right in.

Where This Book Is Coming From

Online business isn't just for large corporations, or even just for small businesses that already have a storefront in the real world and simply want to supplement their marketability with a website.

The Internet is a perfect venue for individuals who are comfortable using computers, and who want to start their own business and believe that cyberspace is the place to do it. You don't need much money to get started. If you already have a computer as well as an Internet connection and can create your own web pages (something this book helps you with), making the move to your own business website may cost only $100 or less. After you're online, the overhead is pretty reasonable, too: You may pay only $10 to $75 per month to a web hosting service to keep your site online — or pay nothing, if you sign up with one of the specialty marketplaces that give you a platform for creating web pages and selling products, and charge a fee only if you make a sale.

With each month that goes by, the number of Internet users increases exponentially. The growth is greatest outside the United States. To be precise, in summer 2012, Internet World Stats released data indicating that the number of Internet users worldwide was nearing 2.5 billion — double the number of users five years before. Asia had by far the largest number of users, with more than 1 billion individuals online, a full 44 percent of the world's total. Amazingly, that still means only 27.5 percent of the Asian population has Internet access at home, setting the stage for continued growth in that continent. We have long since reached that critical mass where *most* people are using the Internet regularly for everyday shopping and other financial activities. The Internet is already becoming a powerhouse for small businesses.

How to Use This Book

Want to focus on what's new and different in e-commerce? Jump right in to Chapter 1. Looking for an overview of the whole process of going online and being inspired by one man's online business success story? Zip ahead to Chapter 2. Want to find out how to accept credit card payments? Flip ahead to Chapter 7. Feel free to skip back and forth to chapters that interest you. I've made this book into an easy-to-use reference tool that you'll be comfortable with, no matter what your level of experience with computers and networking. You don't have to scour each chapter methodically from beginning to end to find what you want. The Internet doesn't work that way, and neither does this book!

If you're just starting out and need to do some essential business planning, see Chapter 2. If you want to prepare a shopping list of business equipment, see Chapter 3. Chapters 4–9 are all about the essential aspects of creating and operating a successful online business, from organizing and marketing your website to providing effective online customer service and sourcing merchandise to sell. Chapters 10–13 examine the many ways to market your business cost effectively online. Chapters 14–16 explore a variety of marketplaces and services you can exploit, including eBay, Amazon.com, Google, and Facebook. Later chapters get into legal issues and accounting. The fun thing about being online is that it's easy to continually improve and redo your presentation. So start where it suits you and come back later for more.

What This Book Assumes about You

This book assumes that you've never been in business before but that you're interested in setting up your own commercial site on the Internet. I also assume that you're familiar with the Internet, have been surfing for a while, and may even have put out some information of your own in a home page.

This book also assumes that you have or are ready to get the following:

- **Some sort of computing device, either handheld or desktop, and a way to get online:** Don't worry; Chapters 3 and 4 explain exactly what hardware and software you need.

- **Instructions on how to think like a businessperson:** I spend a lot of time in this book encouraging you to set goals, devise strategies to meet those goals, and do the sort of planning that successful businesspeople need to do.

- **Just enough technical know-how:** You don't have to do it all yourself. Plenty of entrepreneurs decide to partner with someone or hire an expert to perform design or technical work. This book can help you understand your options and gives you a basic vocabulary so that you can work productively with any consultants you may hire.

What's Where in This Book

This book is divided into six parts. Each part contains chapters that discuss stages in the process of starting an online business: launching your business, and combining a website, social marketing, and multiple storefronts to reach customers from three different angles.

Part I: Launching Your Online Business

In Part I, I describe what you need to do and how you need to *think* so that you can start your online business. The first chapter summarizes what's new in e-commerce, so you can get up to speed right away. Chapter 2 describes several Internet success stories, including a programmer who turned his career around and a mapmaker turned entrepreneur. In subsequent chapters I describe how other entrepreneurs started their online businesses. I also describe the software you need to create web pages and perform essential business tasks, along with any computer upgrades that help your business run more smoothly. You also discover how to choose a web host and find exciting new ways to make money online.

Part II: Creating a Business Website

Even if you only sell on eBay or make money by placing affiliate ads, at some point you need to create a *website* — a series of interconnected web pages that everyone in cyberspace can view with a web browser. A website is a home base where people can find you and see what you have to offer. This part explains how to create a compelling website that attracts paying customers around the world and keeps them coming back to make more purchases. This part also includes options for attracting and keeping customers, making your site organized and easy to navigate, sourcing inventory, and updating and improving your online business.

Part III: Social Networking and Marketing

Some of the most exciting options for starting a business online are building a name for yourself and attracting customers to your products and services through word-of-mouth advertising, social networking, and other advertising strategies. In this part, you find out all about those options and discover the ins and outs of advertising online. You improve your visibility by keeping up with your customers through e-mail and newsletters, and optimizing your catalog listings and website for search engines such as Google and Bing. You also see how to spread the word on Facebook, Twitter, and your own blog, and find out how to reach customers in your local area. Many of these sites enable budding businesspeople to conduct a cost-effective and highly targeted form of online advertising called *search engine optimization (SEO)*, which I describe in detail in Chapter 11.

Part IV: Expanding Beyond Your Website

You can generate sales revenue without setting up your own website from scratch. Rather than go it alone, you can sign up with one of the many well-established business marketplaces on the web that enable individuals just like you to create storefronts or sell individual items. In this part, you find out about creating websites or storefronts on Amazon and eBay, among other venues. You also learn about the third part of triangulation: reaching customers through one or more specialty marketplaces. Finally, you learn how to manage a business with multiple channels through special software and tools provided by Google.

Part V: Keeping Your Business Legal and Fiscally Responsible

This part delves into some essential activities for any online business. Find out about general security methods designed to make commerce more secure on the Internet. I also discuss copyrights, trademarks, and other legal concerns for anyone wanting to start a company in the increasingly competitive atmosphere of the Internet. Finally, you get an overview of basic accounting practices for online businesses and suggestions for accounting tools that you can use to keep track of your e-commerce activities.

Part VI: The Part of Tens

Filled with tips, cautions, suggestions, and examples, the Part of Tens presents many tidbits of information you can use to plan and create your own business presence on the Internet, including ten e-commerce marketplaces worth exploring.

Conventions Used in This Book

In this book, I format important bits of information in special ways to make sure you notice them right away:

- ✔ **In This Chapter lists:** Chapters start with a list of the topics I cover in that chapter. This list is like a miniature table of contents.

- ✔ **Numbered lists:** When you see a numbered list, follow the steps in that order to accomplish a given task.

- ✔ **Bulleted lists:** Bulleted lists (like this one) indicate things you can do in any order, or they list related bits of information.

- ✔ **Web addresses:** When I describe activities or sites of interest on the World Wide Web, I include the address, or Uniform Resource Locator (URL), in a special typeface, like this: `http://www.wiley.com`. Because the newer versions of popular web browsers don't require you to enter the entire URL, this book uses shortened addresses. For example, if you want to connect to the Wiley Publishing site, simply enter the following in your browser's Go To or Address box: `www.wiley.com`.

  Don't be surprised if your browser can't find an Internet address you type or if a web page shown in this book no longer looks the same. Although the sites were current when the book was written, web addresses (and sites themselves) can be pretty fickle. Try looking for a missing site by using an Internet search engine. Or try shortening the address by deleting everything after the `.com` (or `.org` or `.edu`).

Icons Used in This Book

Starting an Online Business For Dummies, 7th Edition, uses special graphical elements — *icons* — to get your attention. Here's what they look like and what they mean:

This icon points out some technical details that may be of interest to you. A thorough understanding, however, isn't a prerequisite to grasping the underlying concept. Non-techies are welcome to skip items marked by this icon.

This icon calls your attention to interviews I conducted with online entrepreneurs who provided tips and instructions for running an online business.

This icon flags practical advice about particular software programs or issues of importance to businesses. Look to these tips for help with finding resources quickly, making sales, or improving the quality of your online business site. This icon also alerts you to software programs and other resources that I consider to be especially good, particularly for the novice user.

This icon points out potential pitfalls that can develop into more-major problems if you're not careful.

This icon alerts you to facts and figures that are important to keep in mind when you run your online business.

This icon alerts you to find related information elsewhere in the book or in another book.

Beyond the Book

This edition of *Starting an Online Business For Dummies* isn't just what you see within the book you're holding. Here's a glimpse at this book's companion content, which you can reference online at any time:

✔ **Cheat Sheet:** Go to www.dummies.com/cheatsheet/starting anonlinebusiness, and you'll find lists, charts, and summaries that serve as an easy-to-use reference when you don't have the book at hand. You'll find a chart matching specific business goals with the three components of online business triangulation (website, social marketing, and storefronts); a second chart that matches the many types of website/storefront hosts you can choose with the types of merchandise you want to sell; a checklist to help you boost your search engine placement; and a sample calendar you can modify to help you fit all your e-commerce tasks into a weekly schedule.

✔ **Extras:** On several of the pages that open each of this book's Parts, you'll find links to web extras — articles that expand on some of the concepts discussed in that part. The web extra for Part II summarizes some essential tasks you need to perform to get your new business off the ground. In the web extra for Part III, you get three social marketing tips. In Part IV's web extra, you discover more about expanding your business beyond your website. You'll find the web extras at www.dummies.com/extras/startinganonlinebusiness.

We're In It Together

Improving communication is the whole point of this book. My goal is to help you express yourself in the dynamic medium of the Internet and to remind you that you're not alone. I'm a businessperson myself, so I hope you'll let me know what you think about this book by contacting me directly if you have questions or comments. Visit my personal web page at www.gregholden.com or e-mail me at greg@gregholden.com.

Part I
Launching Your Online Business

getting started
with
an online
business

In this part . . .

- ✔ Be inspired by stories of successful online businesspeople and how they are connecting with customers and followers.

- ✔ Follow ten essential steps for opening your own online business.

- ✔ Plan out your e-business and get the essential software and hardware you need to get started.

- ✔ Find hosting services for your domain name and website.

- ✔ Learn about shopping cart and Web editing software you need to build your online presence.

Chapter 1

New Tools and Strategies for Your Online Business

*N*ew technologies and ways of shopping and selling are always popping up in the world of online commerce. One of the biggest new developments is the proliferation of devices like the ones in your own pocket or on your work table. Buyers — the people you want to connect with online — are finding new ways to shop and make purchases. Consumers can shop wherever they are in the world. They're surfing with small screens, using mobile apps, and taking charge of the e-commerce experience more than ever before.

At the same time, those who seek to start or grow an online business have new opportunities to help them along. They can get help from the same engaged customers with whom they engage on social marketing sites like Facebook and Twitter. They can find the funding they need by turning to new resources like Kickstarter. And they can follow the example of the many ambitious small business owners who are triangulating their business processes — using websites, social media, and storefronts to connect with customers from many different angles.

Keeping up with all the new trends in online commerce is getting harder because it's a constantly moving target. This chapter gives you an overview of some of the many new and exciting ways to conduct e-commerce. If you've heard about e-commerce before and weren't attracted by the thought of creating a website and sales catalog, take a look at these innovative options for generating revenue.

E-Commerce Is Goin' Mobile

As I was working on this chapter, I covered eBay's Analyst Day event, in which eBay describes the trends it is seeing in e-commerce and made projections about future growth. CEO John Donahoe focused his opening remarks on the rise of mobile commerce.

Consumers now shop with smartphones in hand in brick-and-mortar stores. They compare prices and research the products they see in front of them. They don't always follow through and make purchases with their mobile devices. But more and more shoppers throughout the world are going through the purchase process on the small screen. But you can increase the chances that they will, as described in the sections that follow.

eBay reported $13 billion in sales volume in 2012; that represents 13.5 percent of its entire volume of $175 billion. The company projects that its mobile commerce figures will grow 20 percent annually through 2015. Find out more at www.ebayinc.com/investor_relations/analyst_day_2013.

Designing for the small screen

The first way to attract mobile shoppers is to make sure your website or online store loads quickly and is easy to navigate. For big companies that have their own IT and web design staff, that means adapting the site they've designed to appear on a big desktop monitor so that it works on a 5-inch or smaller smartphone screen.

If you don't have a designer on staff, you can get your own mobile site by signing up with a hosting service that provides you one for free. You can also turn to a company like Mobify (www.mobify.com), which specializes in creating mobile sites for online sellers. Three versions of one home page are shown in the image on Mobify's home page, shown in Figure 1-1.

See Chapter 19 for ten ways to reach mobile shoppers.

Figure 1-1: Make sure your website or store is adapted for mobile users.

Selling mobile, selling local: Two examples

There are many ways to sell online, but some of the newest involve mobile technology and reaching local customers online. Here are just two examples of entrepreneurs who are taking advantage of these approaches.

Lisa Bettany, a professional photographer (not a programmer), spent a year and a half creating an app for the iPhone called Camera+. She was pretty much destitute while she was doing this. She hired a programmer to help make her idea a reality. Since it was released, she has generated $4 million by selling 4 million of her apps in iTunes and other locations. You can find more about Lisa at www.MostlyLisa.com.

What if you aren't technologically savvy, but you have a great deal of knowledge, even passion, for a particular subject? Dean Pettit was a worker for NASA in Florida when he

was laid off. He loves the outdoors, especially the area called the Space Coast. He created a aggregation website called Space Coast Outdoors (www.spacecoastoutdoors.net), which collects information about a single topic in one place so it's easy to find. It's the kind of aggregation of information that has worked since Yahoo! started back in the 1990s.

You're probably wondering how this kind of site makes money when all you're providing is information. You build as much traffic as you can, and when you get to a certain number of visitors, you can start to sell ads.

Dean Pettit isn't getting rich from his site, at least not yet. But the extra spending money helps while he's between day jobs, and he's hoping to build enough monthly income so eventually he won't need a day job.

Facilitating purchases and searches

You need to list yourself where mobile shoppers hang out. Make sure you're on the local directory Google Places for Business (www.google.com/business/placesforbusiness) and places like the review site Yelp (www.yelp.com), for example. List your products on venues like eBay Local Shopping (www.ebay.com/local). People love to look up reviews on their mobile devices, so make sure you're there.

Mobile commerce is also about making it easy for shoppers to tap the Buy button on their touch screens. Here again, the choice of service provider is critical. Some specifically focus on making shopping and purchasing as easy as possible for mobile buyers.

Find out more about organizing both desktop and mobile websites in Chapter 5.

Businesses Processes Are Becoming Social

Those who believe in political or human rights know the power a group of people can have. In the online business world, some forward-looking companies have enlisted the participation of the "crowd."

I'm not talking about using social marketing sites like Facebook to build brand loyalty and boost sales. (That subject is discussed in Chapter 13, by the way.) Rather, these innovative companies are letting customers participate in the process of manufacturing and designing products.

Choosing merchandise with customers' help

At the women's vintage and retro clothing site ModCloth (www.modcloth.com), enthusiastic buyers use their smartphones and an internal app developed by the company to provide real-time feedback on how much they like sweaters, other clothing, and accessories that have just been made. The site invites users to "be the buyer," as shown in Figure 1-2.

Figure 1-2:
ModCloth makes buying decisions based on user ratings.

ModCloth can gauge the sentiment of its customer base within minutes and use that information to do strategic purchasing. If the clothing vendor is in its facility while the feedback is being registered, ModCloth can tell the vendor immediately whether it wants an item, and whether it wants to purchase 50, 100, or 500 of that item.

Instead of making such decisions by intuition or by the gut feeling of a few sample shoppers, ModCloth can back up such decisions with user data. The community has even suggested new dress designs and new colors for sweaters, for example.

The coupon and deal company RetailMeNot (www.retailmenot.com) was developed in part on recommendations from community members who suggested deals, coupons, and other ways to save money on shopping.

Bringing end-users into the development process

At Quirky (www.quirky.com), the user community participates in many critical aspects of creating new products for sale. Customers submit ideas for products; they vote on and rate one another's products, as shown in Figure 1-3; they name items; they even photograph products. The company can get merchandise online that much quicker because of the use of crowdsourcing.

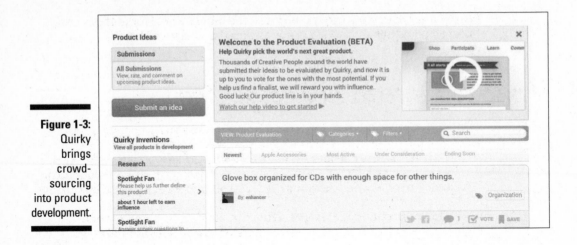

Figure 1-3:
Quirky
brings
crowd-
sourcing
into product
development.

Bringing the "crowd" into your operations is among the latest and most exciting developments as I write this edition of *Starting an Online Business For Dummies*. It goes beyond selling merchandise. Author Hugh Howey (www.hughhowey.com) brings his audience into the process of writing his highly popular series of novels. He expanded his bestselling *Wool* from a story to a novel because readers urged him for more. He wrote the novel as a serial, releasing a bit at a time, and responding to feedback as he went along. He encourages others to write "fan fiction" based on his work.

Howey himself participates in a huge reader community he has created on his website. On his home page (which doubles as his blog, as shown in Figure 1-4), he posts progress bars showing how far along he is with writing his books.

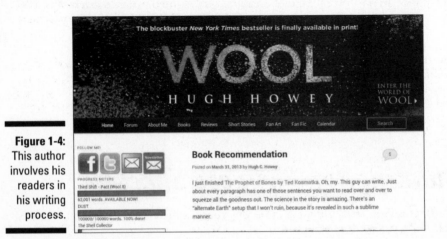

Figure 1-4:
This author
involves his
readers in
his writing
process.

Howey has created his own platform — the ultimate goal for authors and businesspeople alike, and a subject explored in Chapter 20.

Venture Capital Is Social, Too

You've probably already heard one of the success stories coming out of a crowd-funding website called Kickstarter (www.kickstarter.com). According to Business Insider (www.businessinsider.com/kickstarter-success-stories-2013-1), in 2012 about 18,000 projects were funded on this site by people who contributed $320 million. Here are some examples:

- Pebble, a watch that uses Bluetooth to connect to a smartphone, received $10.3 million (its developers originally sought $100,000).
- Singer Amanda Palmer raised more than $1.1 million to fund her new album, art book, and tour after breaking from her record label.
- Two MIT Media Lab researchers raised $2.9 million to create an "affordable, professional 3-D printer."

As venture capitalist Josh Goldman of Northwest Venture Partners said in an interview on EcommerceBytes in 2012 (www.ecommercebytes.com/cab/abn/y12/m08/i27/s01), venture capital is more readily available now than it was five or ten years ago for those with good ideas and a well-developed plans for an online businesses. Goldman suggested sites like AngelList (https://angel.co) for matching investors whose area of focus meshes with what you want to do.

Small, mom-and-pop businesses can secure venture capital just like high-tech startups. Capital Access Network (CAN) targets small- and medium-size businesses for funding. Most grants are for $500 to $1,000, although they can go up to $250,000.

Indiegogo (www.indiegogo.com) also provides funding to individuals and businesses in search of funds. Kabbage (www.kabbage.com) specializes in providing loans and cash advances to small online business owners. Typically, the financing costs between 2 and 7 percent of the loan amount, according to the company.

Triangulating for Business Success

One trend I've been following in recent years is the rise of online businesses that sell through three venues:

- ✔ A website as your "home base"

- ✔ A presence on social media sites, most notably Facebook and Twitter, to connect with potential customers and keep up with your fans, friends, and buyers

- ✔ One or more online storefronts on sites like eBay, Amazon, Bonanza, eCRATER, or Etsy

Together, these three components of an online business combine to drive traffic to one another and to drive customers to your website. The fact is, a single store or standalone website is not enough. I've been covering e-commerce since the 1990s, and when I started out, someone with a great idea or a terrific product could make a killing with one website. It's not quite as easy these days. There is so much competition, and so many people have become so sophisticated about marketing, that the most successful entrepreneurs are triangulating these three components.

Maintaining a presence in all these sites is a lot of work, to be sure, but the rewards include a better search engine placement and increased sales. The following sections explore this trend and how you can take advantage of it.

Creating a home page that's a "home base"

There are more ways than ever before to pop up online, especially when you consider resources like Twitter, YouTube, and the photo-sharing site Pinterest. But the thing that ties all these together is still a website.

If there's a trend pertaining to websites in 2013, it's the merger of websites with blogs. For many people, their website *is* their blog. That's the case with my own website (www.gregholden.com). It's run on the blogging site WordPress, which enables anyone to not only create a blog, but also design web pages and post photos and other contents. Business sites that sell products are a natural fit with blogs, too.

Creating a blog to support your business is a powerful way of reaching potential customers and strengthening connections with current ones. The word-of-mouth marketing that results from successful blog publishing is effective while also being cost-effective: Advertising costs are miniscule compared to a traditional marketing effort.

What's the first step in creating a blog? I usually advocate thinking before clicking. Think about the kind of blog you want to create. An article titled "Create a Blog to Boost Your Business" in *Entrepreneur* magazine describes several different types of blogs created by Denali Flavors to promote its

Moose Tracks line of ice cream flavors. Each blog took a different approach to promoting the same product:

- ✔ **Entertainment:** The blog *Moosetopia* is (or was; it was discontinued but is still online) written by the Moose Tracks Moose, the product mascot.

- ✔ **Useful advice:** The blog *Free Money Finance* provides something that everyone needs — advice on how to handle their money. The connection to the product is a "sponsored by" Moose Tracks ice cream logo to the right of the blog, as shown in Figure 1-5.

- ✔ **Public relations:** Another blog, *Team Moose Tracks,* concerns efforts of the company's cycling team to raise money for an orphanage in Latvia. It reflects positively on the company and the brand.

- ✔ **Behind the scenes:** A fourth blog, *Denali Flavors,* takes a look at what goes on in the company.

The article (www.entrepreneur.com/article/80100-2) reports that site visits went up 25.7 percent after the blogs went online; the company spent less than $700 on all four blogs, too. You can take any or all of these approaches in your own blog, depending on the product you're trying to sell and your available resources. If you're selling a "fun" product, you might decide to take the entertainment approach; if you work for a big company, you might take the behind-the-scenes approach.

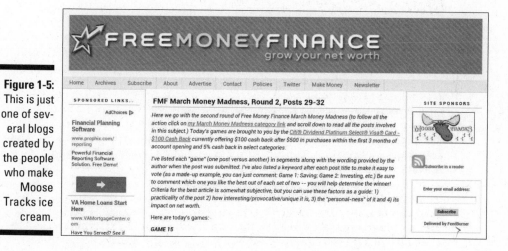

Figure 1-5: This is just one of several blogs created by the people who make Moose Tracks ice cream.

After you have a general idea of the approach you want to take, it's time to get started. The first step is to choose your blog host. You don't necessarily have to pay to do this; most of the best-known blog hosts offer hosting for free. They include

- ✔ **Blogger** (www.blogger.com) doesn't have as many features as other blog utilities, but it's free.

- ✔ **WordPress** (www.wordpress.com) is software you download and install to create and manage your blog. WordPress offers free hosting for blogs and is very popular; find out more in the latest edition of *WordPress For Dummies,* by Lisa Sabin-Wilson.

- ✔ **TypePad** (www.typepad.com) has lots of features, but it costs anywhere from $8.95 to $29.95 per month. The Unlimited plan, at $14.95 per month, should be sufficient for most online business owners.

Take some time to look at other business blogs and examine how they use type and color. Often, for a purely personal blog, it doesn't matter whether it's carefully designed. But for a blog that has a business purpose, you need to make it look professional.

Next, determine who will do the blogging. You may not want to do it all yourself. If you can gather two or three contributors, you increase the chances that you can post entries on a daily basis, which is important for blogs. That way, if someone needs time off, you'll have backup contributors available.

When you configure your blog, no matter which host you choose, the main features tend to be more or less the same. Figure 1-6 shows the Clean Air Gardening Blog, one of the many blogs created by expert marketer Lars Hundley, whom I profile in the sidebar "Blogs plant seeds, gardening business blooms," later in this chapter. The blog includes some Google AdSense ads to drum up extra revenue; a link for visitors to post comments; categories that organize past blog posts; a chronological archive of posts; and links to other relevant sites, including Hundley's main Clean Air Gardening website (www.cleanairgardening.com).

For detailed instructions on how to create a business blog, turn to *Buzz Marketing with Blogs For Dummies,* by Susannah Gardner.

Perhaps the most difficult aspect of blogging isn't actually creating the blog, but maintaining it. Developing a schedule in which you publish regular blog posts is important. It's also important to measure how many visits your blog and your business website get so that you can measure results. Be sure to do a benchmark test — a test done before a process or procedure that gives you baseline data — so that you can judge results afterward. Adjust your site as needed to attract more visitors, but remember to stay on topic so that you don't drive away the audience you already have.

A business website needs to have the elements described in Chapter 5; an overview follows.

Figure 1-6:
Make your
blog attrac-
tive, well
organized,
and
interactive.

Domain name

You need a domain name: something short and catchy that you can register with a domain name registrar, one of the companies that keeps track of
such things, like GoDaddy (www.godaddy.com). Your name can suggest
what you sell, but it doesn't have to. It can be a word that doesn't necessarily mean anything, like Skype, the videoconferencing service, or Timbuk2
(www.timbuk2.com), the shoulder-bag company that took off because of
the Internet. One of the biggest sellers on eBay used to be called Inflatable
Madness, for example. The name is so nutty that you tend to remember it.

Logo

When you're surfing a succession of web pages that seem to flash by on your
monitor like stores passing through a car window, you need a landmark or
indicator that lets you know what's there for you. On the street, you scan
signs. On the Internet, you look at logos.

A logo gives visitors an indication, in a single glance, of what your business
is all about. It's an essential part of your online identity and something you
can carry through to your Facebook page and other sites where you have a
presence. Ultimately, they'll help you to build a platform, a subject covered
in Chapter 20. You'll find out more about logos in Chapter 5.

Hosting service

In exchange for a monthly or yearly fee, a website host gives you space on a web server, a computer that is always connected to the Internet and is reliable and fast. You share the server with other businesses (although you can pay more and get your own server if you want a really fast connection). You *upload* (or move) your photos and web page files from your computer to the server, and you are given an address or URL so everyone can find them.

Beyond that, a host can do a lot more. It's helpful to break hosting services into two general types: a general website host and an e-commerce host, sometimes called a shopping cart service.

Shopping cart

At the core of the store is a shopping cart: a utility that makes it easy for you to create individual product listings that include photos, descriptions, and a button labeled Buy Now or Add to Cart. A shopping cart also gives you:

- A secure server
- A payment method
- Search engine optimization (SEO), a way of improving your placement in search engine results, as well as your marketing
- Consultation on your store/business

A shopping cart generally costs more than a general website host. Volusion (www.volusion.com), for example, offers five different hosting packages ranging from $49 to $149 per month. But the consultation, customer support, and marketing assistance offered by shopping cart packages makes them well worth the expense, especially when you're just starting out.

Design

You don't always need to hire a designer, especially if you sell on Amazon.com, where design hardly matters and you place only brief product listings. Some e-commerce hosting services provide templates that you can adapt to your own site. (A *template* is a predesigned web page that you can fill with your own words and images. You don't have to do any design.) Since you're just starting out and are on a shoestring, sign up with a host and use its templates to get your site started. Once you get some income flowing, you might want to hire someone to create a distinctive design and help you with more advanced store features.

Promotions

Whether you're selling products on a blog or promoting your services, your goal is to entice visitors to click your website, explore it, stay for as long as possible, and come back on a regular basis. You want your website or your store to have a "stickiness" factor. Promotions can go a long way toward making your site sticky. These include

- Coupons
- Sales
- Free shipping
- Deals for returning customers

Free shipping is a big deal on the web. Studies have shown that people are more likely to click the Add to Cart or Buy button if they don't have to pay for shipping — even if the price is higher because you, the seller, have built the shipping cost into the price. This is controversial. On eBay, sellers get a higher seller rating if they offer free shipping. But with the higher price, you become less competitive compared to other sellers who might be offering similar items. You might consider doing an experiment and offering some items with free shipping as a promotion, and see what happens.

How do you create these kinds of promotions? That's where the choice of shopping cart service becomes critical; it can help you with creating and distributing such deals.

Once you have a website in place, you can branch out to link it to other promotional sites, videos, or photo collections, just as entrepreneur Lars Hundley does in the nearby sidebar. Or you might open storefronts and social media sites as described in the sections that follow.

Connecting with customers via social marketing

When I wrote the first edition of this book back in 1998, you could advertise your online business in a few ways: through a website, through postings on online discussion boards, through placing banner ads, and by exchanging links to other sites. Now you can do *viral marketing* (word-of-mouth advertising) on social networking sites.

Blogs plant seeds, gardening business blooms

Lars Hundley is an expert with blogs, photo-sharing, and social networking sites to market his products. His Dallas, Texas–based business, Clean Air Gardening (www.cleanairgardening.com), posted sales of $1.2 million in 2012, down from $1.5 million in 2006. A site related to the main one, the yo-yo site Yoyoplay.com, posted sales of $750,000 and $500,000 in sales came from listings on Amazon.com. "Amazon and its shipping prices on oversized items like composters and rain barrels are killing us!" commented Hundley. But he continues to market multiple websites enthusiastically with the optimism of the successful entrepreneur.

Products occasionally receive the attention of traditional media. A few years ago, for example, Clear Air Gardening was mentioned in *The New York Times* as well as on *Good Morning America*.

Hundley uses a variety of blogs and online video sites to promote his Clean Air Gardening online business:

- ✔ **Practical Environmentalist** (www.practicalenvironmentalist.com): This blog isn't branded for Clean Air Gardening or directly linked to the company, but it is intended to attract the same kind of environmentally aware person who is its typical customer. This blog is more a free service than it is a hard-selling kind of blog.

- ✔ **Reel Mowers** (www.reelmowers.org): This blog bills itself as the ultimate guide to reel push lawn mowers.

- ✔ **Compost guide** (www.compostguide.com): This blog promotes several different companies. It's designed to generate a lot of composting-related educational information as well as keyword-rich pages and product promotion pages that give Air Gardening a growing body of search engine–friendly composting content over time.

- ✔ **Flash-based video on Clean Air Gardening:** Flash-based video helps sell products. Hundley films the videos with his Canon PowerShot S1 digital camera, which also shoots video. Then he edits them with his Mac mini and converts them to Flash so that people can watch them with their web browser directly on the page. One example is at www.cleanairgardening.com/patdesaustum.html.

- ✔ **Videos on YouTube.com:** Hundley uploads videos so that he doesn't have to pay for the bandwidth. Then he embeds the YouTube video on his product page. That also allows people to find the products on the YouTube site and click through to Clean Air Gardening. "When we add a video to a web page, we can increase our conversion rate for that product by up to 20 percent," comments Hundley. Find the company's videos at www.youtube.com/cleanairgardening.

- ✔ **Product and testimonial photos at Flickr:** Hundley puts his customer testimonial photos on Flickr and links to them from his testimonials page on his website. People can access these photos directly on Flickr (www.flickr.com/photos/cleanairgardening). They can then use a link to return to the Clean Air Gardening page.

"If you're thinking about starting your own Internet business, just do it!", says Hundley. "Start a small site and do it in your spare time to test the waters. I kept my day job for the first year when I started this business, until it started to take off and make money. Now, 11 years later, it is a multimillion-dollar-a-year company with 14 employees and a large, 14,000-square-foot warehouse and office. You can do it too, if you try!"

Social networking sites are the modern-day equivalent of the town square. When you go to a social networking site, you strike up a personal relationship with a merchant; after you do, you're that much more likely to buy something from that person. Social networking sites give potential customers another place where they can find you and get to know you. The best-known sites are

- ✔ **Twitter** (www.twitter.com)
- ✔ **Facebook** (www.facebook.com)
- ✔ **MySpace** (www.myspace.com)
- ✔ **Pinterest** (www.pinterest.com)

If you want to reach a younger generation of consumers, places like Pinterest and Facebook are among the best ways to find them. If you sell services that depend on personal contact with a customer, such as a group of musicians that plays for weddings or a wedding planner, people sometimes hire you as much for your personality and personal approach as for your actual work. In these kinds of fields, social networking sites are even more important.

Another networking site, LinkedIn (www.linkedin.com), lets you build a network of business contacts who can get in touch with one another and build a community.

Facebooking your business

Facebook wasn't started with the idea of business in mind. It is primarily a site where you connect with friends, family, and others on a regular basis. You sign up for a Facebook account and create a page where you post information about yourself and (optionally) a photo. You then decide whether that information is available to the public at large or only to people you invite to see it. That's the nice thing about Facebook: You control who communicates with you because you "invite" or "approve" them as needed. If you are approached by someone you don't know, you simply decline to approve that person's access.

For me, Facebook is a terrific way to keep in touch with friends I don't see often enough and family members who live far away. Recently, I used Facebook to write a story that I share with my Facebook friends. I write an episode of the story on my blog and then announce it via Facebook. One of these announcements is shown in Figure 1-7.

As often happens, this popular online resource has become a place to do business for a few early adopters. With more than 1 billion registered users, 60+ percent of whom log in every day, it's a natural for businesspeople to advertise themselves and even offer items for sale.

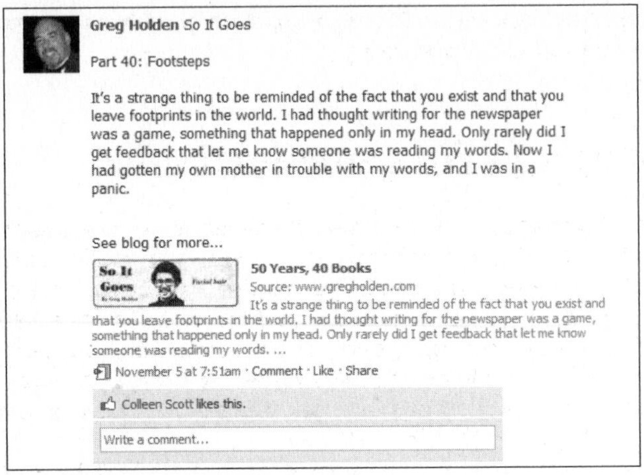

> **Greg Holden** So It Goes
>
> Part 40: Footsteps
>
> It's a strange thing to be reminded of the fact that you exist and that you leave footprints in the world. I had thought writing for the newspaper was a game, something that happened only in my head. Only rarely did I get feedback that let me know someone was reading my words. Now I had gotten my own mother in trouble with my words, and I was in a panic.
>
> See blog for more...
>
> **50 Years, 40 Books**
> Source: www.gregholden.com
> It's a strange thing to be reminded of the fact that you exist and that you leave footprints in the world. I had thought writing for the newspaper was a game, something that happened only in my head. Only rarely did I get feedback that let me know someone was reading my words. ...
>
> November 5 at 7:51am · Comment · Like · Share
>
> Colleen Scott likes this.
>
> Write a comment...

Figure 1-7: You can use Facebook to keep in touch or promote a story or a cause.

The statistics about Facebook come from the site itself: `newsroom.fb.com/Key-Facts`.

A marketplace for artists called ArtFire (`www.artfire.com`) allows its members to display items from its sales catalogs on their Facebook pages. Not only that, but if you shop in one of these Facebook "kiosks," you can make a purchase there without having to go to ArtFire or another site. The utility is available to ArtFire members as part of their $12.95 per month hosting fee. In Chapter 13, you can read about one enterprising seller who's sold items through Facebook.

Tweeting for fun and profit

Twitter is a true Internet phenomenon. It distinguishes itself from other social networking sites by limiting users to posting comments that contain no more than 140 characters. Despite this restriction, many businesspeople as well as public figures have latched on to Twitter as a convenient and simple way to spread the word about anything. That includes senators posting "tweets" about upcoming votes in Congress, Sarah Palin talking about herself, and stars like Ashton Kutcher (Twitter name: @aplusk), who at this writing has 14 million people around the world "following" his Twitter posts. Every time he posts a tweet, 14 million people get the message.

With that kind of platform, anyone can promote him- or herself or a business online. Kutcher, to his credit, regularly promotes social change and peace. But my colleague Ina Steiner, who runs a website called EveryPlaceISell, uses

Twitter as a platform for sellers. Sellers regularly post tweets about sales and promotions. See Chapter 13 for more.

Blogging to build your business

In the late 1990s, web pages were where it was at as far as e-commerce goes. As of this writing, the blog is the tool of choice for many online entrepreneurs. On the surface, a blog doesn't seem like something that can make you money. A *blog* is a web page, but one that is updated frequently with content to which readers can quickly respond with comments. Many blogs take the form of an online diary: a running commentary that the blogger adds to as often as possible — every few days, every day, or perhaps even several times a day.

Blogs do make money, however. When you have a dependable number of viewers, you can generate revenue from your blog by using these methods:

- ✔ **Placing ads:** You can use a service such as Blogads (`www.blogads.com`) or Google's AdSense (`adsense.google.com`).

- ✔ **Placing affiliate ads:** You sign up for well-known programs that steer potential buyers to Amazon.com or eBay.

- ✔ **Building interest in your website:** By talking about yourself, your knowledge, or your services, you encourage customers to commit to them.

See Chapter 13 for more about blogs and how they can help your business.

Sharing your work with Flickr

If you're lucky, your products sell themselves. But for some products, photos are a necessity. If you have a big piece of furniture, such as a couch or a rare antique or a work of art, a description that consists solely of words just doesn't cut it. Photos give you a real selling point. You can post photos on your own website, of course. But the cool and trendy place for them to appear is at the popular photo-sharing site Flickr (`www.flickr.com`).

Flickr is free and easy to use. I can't think of a better business use for the site than the Clean Air Gardening customer photos, shown in Figure 1-8. Lars Hundley (whom I profile in the sidebar earlier in this chapter) invites his customers to submit photos of the products they've purchased, such as push reel lawn mowers and weathervanes.

Figure 1-8:
Use photo-sharing sites to publish photos of your products in action.

Diversifying sales with multiple storefronts

An online storefront is a site you don't own yourself. It's one you set up with a marketplace that charges you a monthly fee for e-commerce hosting. The e-commerce hosts I mention in the previous sections let you set up your own website. The ones I mention in this section are marketplaces. Some marketplaces, like eBay and Amazon, let you sell all kinds of merchandise. Others are set up for people who sell a particular kind of item. They attract people who are looking for just that kind of item:

- ✔ **Etsy** (www.etsy.com) is set up for handmade arts and crafts.
- ✔ **Ruby Lane** (www.rubylane.com) is for antiques and collectibles.
- ✔ **AbeBooks** (www.abebooks.com) is for used books; this is where all those booksellers you used to see around are going now.
- ✔ **Planet Diecast** (www.planetdiecast.com) is for, as you might expect, diecast toys.
- ✔ **iOffer** (www.ioffer.com) gives buyers the chance to make an offer for what you have to sell.

Some storefronts don't focus on any particular type of sales items; they are general interest marketplaces. Some of the most popular are eCRATER and Bonanza. They are popular alternatives for people who are looking for an alternative to eBay in particular, who want lower fees and fewer regulations.

After you go through the effort of creating your own website, why should you open another storefront on someone else's site and pay another rental fee? It's not something you have to do right away. You might want to get one store up and running and get some income flowing before you open a second one.

The big thing a storefront does is give you a ready-made source of potential customers. A site like eBay, with its many millions of visitors a month, is bound to bring attention to your sales catalog. In fact, most people, when they start an online business, start with a site like eBay, not their own website. A storefront in a marketplace can also:

- ✔ Get your business up and running quickly.
- ✔ Give you other shoppers you can talk to and consult (that is, a user community).
- ✔ Supplement a website.
- ✔ Give you more customers.
- ✔ Give your customers a trustworthy way to buy from you.
- ✔ Come with a shopping cart/shipping system/payment plan.

People who might be reluctant to buy from your website, or who might not find your website, might be more likely to find you in a big, well-known marketplace that attracts millions of customers each day. If you're just starting out, it's a great idea to set up a store with one of the big players. These sites might have lots of rules and they cut into your profits with their fees, but they bring you more customers, too. Once you have customers, you can keep communicating with them to purchase on your website, where you get to keep all the profits.

Find out more about opening storefronts on eBay and Amazon.com in Chapter 14.

Partnering with a service provider

Many sellers who want to maximize their sales volume to the highest degree possible decide to sign up with high-powered professional business services to help them manage multiple online stores.

Moving from doing all the work yourself to signing up with a service provider is like the difference between cleaning your own house and hiring a cleaning service to do the work for you. You do have to pay for a cleaning service, but you'll have less stress in the long run.

By signing up with a company, such as ChannelAdvisor (www.channel advisor.com) or Infopia (www.infopia.com), you can not only create an online store, but also get help with publicizing it and conducting transactions.

You don't have to be a beginner to align with one of these marketing companies. One of the best online sellers I know, David Yaskulka of Blueberry Boutique (www.blueberryboutique.net), signed up with ChannelAdvisor, and he already knows a lot about marketing and selling online.

See Chapter 16 for more about services that help businesspeople manage multiple sales channels.

Chapter 2

Opening Your Online Business

....

In This Chapter

▶ Finding a unique niche for your business

▶ Identifying a need and targeting your customers

▶ Turning your website into an indispensable resource

▶ Finding more than one way to market your business

▶ Generating interest in your business

....

The concept of starting a business online has been around since the 1990s. These days, opening a storefront or a sales channel on the Internet is not the least bit unusual. As time goes on, you have more and more success stories to emulate and be inspired by. Also, new software and services are continually developed to make creating web pages and transacting business online easier than ever. But after you leap a few not-so-high technological hurdles, the basic steps for starting a successful online business haven't really changed. Those steps are well within the reach of individuals like you and me who have no prior business experience.

Online businesses are affected by economic downturns just as offline operations are. But in good times or bad, you can still thrive. All you need are a good idea, a bit of startup money, some computer equipment, and a little help from your friends.

One of my goals in this book is to be one of those friends — someone who provides you with the right advice and support to get your business online and make it a success. In this chapter, I give you a step-by-step overview of the entire process of starting an online business.

Step 1: Identify a Need

"The best of anything hasn't been done yet," says John Moen, the successful founder of the Graphic Maps website (www.graphicmaps.com) I profile in this chapter. "The web isn't over. Someday someone will invent a better

Walmart, and there will be a bigger and better store. As the technology changes, someone will create a business online that makes people say, 'Holy cow, that's cool.'"

In fact, in the course of writing about online business for ECommerceBytes (www.ecommercebytes.com), I've found out about all kinds of new online services, such as:

- ✓ **RIVworks** (www.rivworks.com) lets small businesses affordably add video clips to their websites. RIV stands for Rich Interactive Video.

- ✓ **SteelHouse** (www.steelhouse.com), a "behavioral advertising" company, gives online businesses the ability to display animated or video ads on their sites.

- ✓ **FBAPower** (www.fbapower.com) helps those who sell on Amazon.com boost their profit margin by finding products that sell well on the site and then letting Amazon ship them through its Fulfillment By Amazon service.

- ✓ **FeeFighters** (www.feefighters.com) helps businesspeople shop for the best discount rates from credit companies so they can accept credit card payments from shoppers.

- ✓ **Mobify** (www.mobify.com), helps merchants create mobile versions of their websites so they can pursue "m-commerce."

In addition to these service providers, I've profiled small business websites that sell handmade primitive artwork, elaborate eggshell art, high-quality merchandise from Europe, and lots of other products.

Electronic commerce (e-commerce) and the web have been around for nearly 15 years. But new products and ways to sell those products are identified all the time. Think of the things that didn't exist when the first websites were created: blogs, Twitter, search ads, podcasts, RSS feeds, MP3s, YouTube, DVDs, and eBay. Consider my brother, Mike: For the past couple of years, he has operated an online business — lp2cdsolutions, Inc., which converts scratchy old records to clean and repackaged CDs. Business has remained steady because, like many entrepreneurs, Mike reached a simple conclusion: "If I want this product so much, I bet a lot of other people do, too." He spent thousands of dollars on computer hardware and software, and he got really good at audio restoration. Now he's making a modest but steady extra income and putting his technical talents to good use. Will he succeed because he has me to help him? I don't think success is guaranteed. It depends on you — your energy, dedication, and enthusiasm.

A hotbed of commerce

Statistically, the Internet continues to be a hotbed of commerce — and shopping online is becoming more accepted among consumers. Here's what the experts are saying:

- **Forrester Research** (www.forrester.com) says U.S. online retail sales reached $155 billion in 2009 and are projected to grow to $248 billion by 2014. Business-to-consumer (B2C) e-commerce still grows by double-digit rates each year and is projected to climb 10 percent per year through 2014. By contrast, the National Retail Federation forecasts that traditional retail sales will grow more slowly — a 34 percent increase in 2013.

- **Statistics Canada** (www.statcan.ca), the Canadian government's central statistical agency, reports that e-commerce sales in Canada in 2010 amounted to $15.3 billion, and consumers placed 13.8 million orders online during the year. These sales figures represented a 6.8 percent increase from 2007.

- **The U.S. Department of Commerce** (www.census.gov/retail/mrts/www/data/pdf/ec_current.pdf) reports that e-commerce sales in the United States reached $5.5 billion in the fourth quarter of 2012. This was a 4.4 percent increase from the previous quarter and a continuation of the steady upward trend that e-commerce sales in the United States have posted since 2000.

- **eMarketer** (www.emarketer.com/Webinar/Retail-Ecommerce-ForecastChallenging-Economy-Drives-Online-Shopping/4000055) reports that in the United Kingdom, e-commerce has been relatively immune to the economic slowdown, thanks to the many factors that make e-commerce attractive to shoppers eager to save time and money. These include fuel savings, convenience, and easy and quick ways to comparison-shop. Other countries show a booming online business environment: eMarketer predicts that Asia-Pacific e-commerce sales will surpass those of the United States in 2013, growing more than 30 percent to over $433 billion.

Your first job, accordingly, is to get in touch with your *market* (the people who'll be buying your stuff or using your services) and determine how you can best meet that market's needs and demands. After all, you can't expect web surfers to patronize your online business unless you identify services or items that they really need. For Ryan Hatfield, who sold general merchandise on eBay from 2002 to 2009, a desire to automatically lower his prices to beat the competition served as the impetus to create his own company selling his product, Price Spectre, online. For more on Ryan, see the "Programmer maps plan for success" sidebar, later in this chapter.

Getting to know the marketplace

The Internet is a worldwide interconnected network of computers to which people can connect either from work or home, and through which people can communicate via e-mail, receive information from the web, and buy and sell items with credit cards or by other methods.

Many people decide to start an online business with little more than a casual knowledge of the Internet. But when you decide to get serious about going online with a commercial endeavor, it pays to get to know the environment in which you plan to be working.

One of your first steps is finding out what it means to do business online and determining the best ways for you to fit into the exploding field of e-commerce. For example, you need to realize that the Internet is a personal place; customers are active, not passive, in the way they absorb information; and the Internet was established within a culture of people sharing information freely and helping one another. For another, you need to know that although the marketplace continues to grow, most of the new growth is expected to come from experienced online shoppers rather than people making their first purchases online. That means you must address the needs of experienced shoppers who are becoming more demanding of web-based merchants.

Some of the best places to find out about the culture of the Internet are blogs, social networking sites such as Facebook, chat rooms, and sites such as Twitter where individuals gather and exchange brief messages online. Visiting discussion forums devoted to topics that interest you can be especially helpful, and you're likely to end up participating. Also visit commerce websites such as eBay and Amazon.com for ideas and approaches you may want to use.

"Cee-ing" what's out there

The more information you have about the "four Cs" of the online world, the more likely you are to succeed in doing business online:

- ✔ **Competitors:** Familiarize yourself with other online businesses that already do what you want to do. Don't let their presence intimidate you. You're going to find a different and better way to do what they already do.

- ✔ **Customers:** Investigate the various kinds of customers who shop online and who might visit your site.

- ✔ **Culture:** Explore the special language and style that people use when they communicate.

- ✔ **Content:** Although websites have become far more visually interesting over the years, what truly distinguishes them is their content. Useful information attracts repeat visitors, which leads to increased sales.

When you take a look around the Internet, notice the kinds of goods and services that tend to sell in the increasingly crowded, occasionally disorganized, and sometimes complex online world. The products that sell best in cyberspace include these four Cs:

- **Cheap:** Online items tend to sell at a discount — at least, that's what shoppers expect.

- **Customized:** Anything that's hard to find, personalized, or unique sells well online.

- **Convenient:** Shoppers look for items that are easier to buy online than at a "real" store, such as a rare book that you can order in minutes from Amazon.com (www.amazon.com) or an electronic greeting card that you can send online in seconds (www.greeting-cards.com).

- **Compelling:** Consumers go online to quickly read news stories from sources that are available by subscription, such as newspapers and magazines; content that is exciting and eye-catching or that exists online only, such as homemade videos on YouTube (www.youtube.com) or blogs (a term derived from *web logs)*.

 Visit one of the tried-and-true indexes to the Internet, such as Yahoo! (www.yahoo.com), or the search services Google (www.google.com) or Bing (www.bing.com). Enter a word or phrase in the site's home page search box that describes the kinds of goods or services you want to provide online. Press Enter, and you'll find out how many existing businesses already do what you want to do. Better yet, determine what they *don't* do and set a goal of meeting that specialized need yourself.

Figuring out how to do it better

After you see what's already out there, you want to find ways to make your business stand out from the crowd. Direct your energies toward making your site unique and providing products or services that others don't offer. Offerings that set your online business apart can be as tangible as half-price sales, contests, seasonal sales, or freebies. They can also involve making your business site higher in quality than others. Maybe you can just provide better or more personalized customer service than anyone else.

What if you can't find other online businesses that do what you want to do? Lucky you! In e-commerce, being first often means getting a head start and being more successful than latecomers, even if they have more resources than you do. (Just ask Jeff Bezos and others who founded the online bookstore Amazon.com.) Don't be afraid to try something new and outlandish. It just might work!

CASE STUDY

Programmer maps plan for success

Ryan Hatfield persisted through tough economic times to reinvent himself and achieve his vision for an online business.

Hatfield was laid off from his job as a software engineer at the start of the economic downturn of 2008. Using his experience selling general merchandise on eBay, he set out to develop an app for eBay sellers called Quantity Manager. For the next year he struggled financially, living on unemployment and trying to find a job while promoting his app.

Hatfield formed a company and won an award for one of his apps, but didn't have the money to travel to a developers' conference to pick it up in person. He continued to struggle during 2009, at one point moving in with his mother. During this period he drew up a series of goals:

1. Break even.

2. Avoid bankruptcy.

3. Keep apartment.

4. Earn a livable wage.

5. Afford the lifestyle I was accustomed to while employed.

6. Reach my old salary.

7. Be able to afford a condo in an upscale high-rise building and never have to work again.

His Quantity Manager app began to generate some income. "In April, one of my Quantity Manager subscribers mentioned an idea that eventually turned into Price Spectre," Hatfield says. "The basic concept was an app that would watch a competitor's listing instead of the seller's listing. When a price was changed, it would change the price of the seller's listing."

He kept working on this new software for eBay and for eBay's related marketplace, half.com, and began to offer it on its own website (www.pricespectre.com). He won another software award, and this time a family friend enabled him to fly to San Jose, California, to pick it up. This gave him the opportunity to network with other developers. He received new attention for his apps, and eBay began promoting them. In early 2012 Hatfield reached the sixth goal on his list — he was making as much as his old salary, three years and four months after being laid off.

Hatfield now runs PriceSpectre.com, where he sells and manages his app, enabling sellers to reprice their merchandise automatically so that their price is lower than the competition's. His program is well received by online merchants.

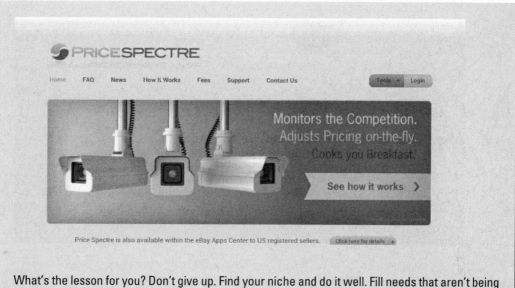

What's the lesson for you? Don't give up. Find your niche and do it well. Fill needs that aren't being addressed. Get to know others in your field, and do everything you can to promote your product.

Step 2: Determine What You Have to Offer

Business is all about identifying customers' needs and figuring out exactly what goods or services you'll provide to meet those needs. It's the same both online and off. (Often, you perform this step before or at the same time you scope out what the business needs are and figure out how you can position yourself to meet those needs, as I explain in "Step 1: Identify a Need.")

To determine what you have to offer, make a list of all the items you have to put up for sale or all the services you plan to provide to your customers. Next, decide not only what goods or services you can provide online, but also where to obtain them. Will you create sale items yourself? Will you purchase them from another supplier? Jot down your ideas and keep them close at hand while you develop your business plan.

The Internet is a personal, highly interactive medium. Be as specific as possible with what you plan to do online. Don't try to do everything; the medium favors businesses that do one thing well. The more specific your business, the more personal the level of service you can provide to your customers.

Step 3: Come Up with a Cyberbusiness Plan

The process of setting goals and objectives and then designing strategies for attaining them is essential when starting a new business. What you end up with is a *business plan*. A good business plan applies not only to the startup phase, but also to a business's day-to-day operation. It can also be instrumental in helping a small business obtain a bank loan.

To set specific goals for your new business, ask yourself these questions:

- ✔ Why do I want to start a business?
- ✔ Why do I want to start it online?
- ✔ What would *I* want to buy online?
- ✔ What would make me buy it?

These questions may seem simple. But many businesspeople never take the time to answer them — to their detriment. And only *you* can answer these questions for yourself. Make sure that you have a clear idea of where you're going so that you can commit to making your venture successful over the long haul. (See Chapter 3 for more on setting goals and envisioning your business.)

To carry your plan into your daily operations, consider these suggestions:

- ✔ Write a brief description of your company and what you hope to accomplish with it.
- ✔ Draw up a marketing strategy. (See Chapter 10 for tips.)
- ✔ Keep track of your finances. (See Chapter 18 for specifics.)

Consider using specialized software to help prepare your business plan. Programs such as Business Plan Pro by Palo Alto Software (www.paloalto.com) lead you through the process by asking you a series of questions to identify what you want to do. The Standard version of the program retails for $99.95. You can find an online version for $19.95 per month.

If you set aside part of your home for business purposes, you may be eligible for tax deductions, depending on how much space you use and whether it is completely dedicated to your business. (You can't work in a corner of the kitchen but then deduct the entire kitchen, for example.) You can depreciate your computers and other business equipment, too. On the other hand, your municipality may require you to obtain a license if you operate a business in a residential area; check with your local authorities to make sure that you're on the up and up. You can find out more about tax and legal issues, including local licensing requirements, in Chapters 17 and 18.

Go to my website (`www.gregholden.com/busplan.doc`) to download information created by business consultant Jeffrey Edelheit about creating a business plan.

Step 4: Assemble Your Hardware and Software

One of the great advantages of opening a store on the Internet rather than on Main Street is money — or, rather, the lack of it. Rather than rent a space and set up furniture and fixtures, you can buy a domain name, sign up with a hosting service, create some web pages, and get started with an investment of only a few hundred dollars or less.

In addition to your virtual storefront, you have to find a real place to do your business. You don't necessarily have to rent a warehouse or other large space. Many online entrepreneurs use a home office or a corner in a room set up with a computer, books, and other business-related equipment.

Finding a host for your website

Although doing business online means you don't have to rent space in a mall or open a real, physical store, you do have to set up a virtual space for your online business. The most common way to do so is by creating a website and finding a company to host it. In cyberspace, your landlord is a web hosting service. A *web host* is a company that, for a fee, makes your site available 24 hours a day by maintaining it on a special computer — a web *server*.

A web host can be as large and well known as America Online, which gives all its customers a place to create and publish their own web pages. Some web-based resources, such as Microsoft Office Live 365 (`www.microsoft.com/en-us/office365/enterprise-home.aspx`) and

Tripod (www.tripod.lycos.com), act as hosting services and provide easy-to-use website creation tools as well. When my brother decided to create his website, he signed up with a company called Webmasters.com, which charges him $9.95 per month. Webmasters offers many features, including the form shown in Figure 2-1, which enables you to create a simple web page without typing any HTML.

In addition, the company that gives you access to the Internet — your Internet service provider (ISP) — may also publish your web pages. Make sure your host has a fast connection to the Internet and can handle the large numbers of simultaneous visits, or *hits,* that your website is sure to get eventually. You can find a detailed description of web hosting options in Chapter 4.

Figure 2-1:
Take the time to choose an affordable web host that makes it easy for you to create and maintain your site.

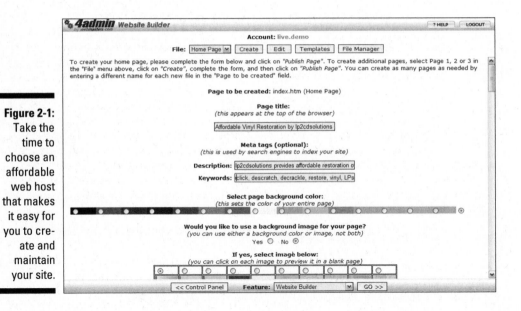

Assembling the equipment you need

Think of all the equipment you *don't* need when you set up shop online. You don't need shelving, a cash register, a parking lot, electricity, a fire protection system, a burglar alarm . . . the list goes on and on. You may need some of those for your home, but you don't need to purchase them especially for your online business.

For doing business online, your most important piece of equipment is your computer, whether it's a laptop, tablet, or desktop machine. Other hardware, such as a scanner, digital camera, and printer, is essential, too. Make sure that your computer equipment is fast enough and has enough memory because you'll spend a lot of time online: answering e-mail, checking orders, revising your website, and marketing your product. Expect to spend anywhere between $800 and $5,000 for equipment if you don't have any to begin with.

Remember that online shoppers expect a higher level of customer service. You don't want substandard equipment to slow down your responses and performance. It pays to shop wisely and get the best setup you can afford up front so that you don't have to purchase upgrades later on. (For more suggestions on buying business hardware and software, see Chapter 3.)

Keeping track of your inventory

It's easy to overlook stocking inventory and setting up systems for processing orders when you're just starting out. But as Lucky Boyd, an entrepreneur who started MyTexasMusic (www.mytexasmusic.com) and other websites, pointed out to me, make sure that you have a "big vision" early in the process of creating your site. In his case, it meant having a site that could handle lots of visitors and make purchasing easy. In other cases, it might mean having sufficient inventory to meet demand. Having too many items for sale is preferable to not having enough. "We operated on a low budget in the beginning, and we didn't have the inventory that people wanted," the entrepreneur commented. "People online get impatient if they have to wait for things too long. Make sure you have the goods you advertise. Plan to be successful."

Jinele Boyd, co-founder of MyTexasMusic, adds that they treat every order with urgency and make an effort to ship the same day the order arrives — or no longer than 36 hours after receiving it. "We also hand-write a note inside every box," she says. "We get e-mails and calls all the time from people telling us how amazed they were that a 'real person' handled their order and took the time to hand-address the boxes."

Many online businesses keep track of their inventory (and thus fulfill orders quickly) by using a database that's connected to their website. When someone orders a product from the website, that order is recorded automatically in the database, which then produces an order for replacement stock. Lucky and his staff originally used a version of Microsoft Excel with database functions to track inventory. They've since moved to a PHP/SQL system according to Boyd. "We still ship the same day, and we never have something for sale on the site that's not in stock. Customers hate to add something to their cart only to find that it's out of stock."

In this kind of arrangement, the database serves as a so-called *back end* or *back office* to the web-based storefront. This is a sophisticated arrangement that's not for beginners. However, if orders and inventory get to be too much for you to handle, consider hiring a web developer to set up such a system for you.

Other "back end" features such as packing and shipping are just as important. Boyd coped with increases in shipping costs by raising shipping costs to his customers by 14 cents on the first item and just 1 cent on all additional items — thus encouraging increased sales. He also found a lighter box that cut shipping charges by 17 cents per order. "It really pays to research the little things," he says. "They add up quickly."

Choosing business software

For the most part, the programs you need in order to operate an online business are the same as the software you use to surf the Internet. You do, however, need to have a wider variety of tools than you would use for simple information gathering.

Because you'll be in the business of information *providing* now, as well as information gathering, you need programs such as the following:

- **A web page editor:** These programs, also called *web page creation tools* or *web page authoring tools,* make it easy for you to format text, add images, and design web pages without having to master HTML.

- **Graphics software:** If you decide to create your business website yourself rather than find someone to do it for you, you need a program that can help you draw or edit images to include on your site.

- **Storefront software:** You can purchase software (or pay a monthly fee) that leads you through the process of creating a full-fledged online business and getting your pages on the web.

- **RSS feed software:** RSS (Real Simple Syndication) is a way of formatting web content in the form of an eXtensible Markup Language (XML) file so it can be read quickly and easily by people who subscribe to it. You can find instructions on how to create an RSS feed and a list of feed creation tools at www.rss-specifications.com/create-rss-feed.htm.

- **Accounting programs:** You can write your expenses and income on a sheet of paper. But it's far more efficient to use software that acts as a spreadsheet, helps you with billing, and even calculates sales tax.

Some businesspeople (such as Judy Vorfeld, whom I profile in Chapter 5) prefer blog software rather than a full-blown web editor to create their website's content. I also use the blogging program WordPress to create content for my personal website (www.gregholden.com).

Step 5: Find People to Help You

Conducting an online business does involve relatively new technologies, but they aren't impossible to figure out. In fact, the technology is becoming more accessible all the time. Many people who start online businesses find out how to create web pages and promote their companies by reading books, attending classes, or networking with friends and colleagues. Of course, just because you *can* do it all doesn't mean that you have to. Often, you're better off hiring help, either to advise you in areas where you aren't as strong or simply to help you tackle the growing workload — and help your business grow at the same time.

Hiring technical experts

Spending some money upfront to hire professionals who can point you in the right direction can help you maintain an effective web presence for years to come. Many businesspeople who usually work alone (myself included) hire knowledgeable individuals to do design or programming work that they would find impossible to tackle otherwise. You'll find many technical experts eager to help you, for a reasonable price, at the freelance marketplace Elance (www.elance.com).

Don't be reluctant to hire professional help to get your business online. The web is full of development firms that perform several related functions: providing customers with web access, helping to create websites, and hosting sites on their servers. The expense for such services may be considerable at first. The programming involved in setting up databases, creating purchasing systems, and programming web pages can run over $10,000 for particularly extensive websites, but the investment can pay off in the long term. Choose a designer carefully and check out sites he or she has done before. Tell the designer your plan for the organization and content, and spell out clearly what you want each page to do. Another area where you may want to find help is in computer and network maintenance. You need someone who knows how to troubleshoot and keep your computer running. Find out whether you have a computer expert in your neighborhood who is available on short notice.

If you do find a business partner, make sure that the person's abilities balance your own. If you're great at sales and public relations, for example, find a writer or web page designer to partner with.

Gathering your team members

Many entrepreneurial businesses are family affairs. A successful eBay business, Maxwell Street Market (www.maxwellstreetmarket.com), is run by a husband-and-wife team as well as family members and neighbors. The husband does the buying, the wife prepares sales descriptions, and the others help with packing and shipping. John Moen found some retired teachers to help answer the geography questions that come into his WorldAtlas.com site. The convenience of the Internet means that these geography experts can log on to the site's e-mail inbox from their respective homes and answer questions quickly.

Early on, when you have plenty of time to do planning, you probably won't feel a pressing need to hire others to help you. Many people don't seek help until they have a deadline to meet or are in a financial crunch. Waiting to seek help is okay — as long as you realize that you *will* need help, sooner or later.

Of course, you don't have to hire family and friends, but you must find people who are reliable and can make a long-term commitment to your project. Keep these things in mind:

- ✔ Pick someone who already exhibits experience with computers and the Internet.

- ✔ Always review a résumé, get at least three references, and ask for samples of the candidate's work.

- ✔ Pick someone who responds promptly and courteously, and provides the talents you need.

- ✔ If your only contact is by phone and e-mail, references are even more important.

Step 6: Construct a Website

Although you can make a living buying and selling full time on eBay, a website is still likely to be the focus of your online business. Fortunately, websites are becoming easier to create. You don't have to know a line of HTML to create an effective web page. Chapter 5 walks you through the specific tasks involved in organizing and designing web pages. Chapter 5 also gives you tips on making your web pages content-rich and interactive.

Make your business easy to find online. Pick a web address (also known as a *URL,* or Uniform Resource Locator) that's easy to remember. You can purchase a short domain-name alias, such as www.company.com, to replace a longer one like www.internetprovider.com/~username/companyname/index.html. If the ideal dot-com (.com) name isn't available, you can choose one of the newer domain suffixes such as .biz. See Chapter 4 for more information on domain name aliases.

If the perfect domain name for your business is already taken, consider adding a short, easy-to-remember prefix or suffix to your existing company name. For example, if your company name is something common, such as Housing Services, try fairly recognizable names such as housing.com and housingservices.com. That way, the web address is still easy to recall and associate with your business. Or create a "cyber" name that's related to your real name. The Art Institute of Chicago can't use www.artinstitute.edu because it's already taken by a group of Art Institutes to which it belongs. So the Art Institute of Chicago created the short abbreviation www.artic.edu — which I, for one, find easy to remember.

Spellings that differ from common English, such as `niteline.com`, are difficult for people to remember — and people who only hear the name spoken
won't know how to type it or search for it properly. Also avoid hyphens in
your domain name, such as in `WBX-TV-Bozo@somestation.com`, because,
again, their placement isn't obvious.

Making your site content-rich

The textual component of a website is what attracts visitors and keeps them
coming back. The more useful information and compelling content you provide, the more visits your site will receive. I'm talking about words, headings,
or images that induce visitors to interact with your site in some way. You can
make your content compelling in a number of ways:

✔ Provide a call to action, such as Click Here! or Buy Now!

✔ Explain how the reader benefits by clicking a link and exploring your
   site. ("Visit our News and Specials page to find out how to win
   500 frequent flyer miles.")

✔ Briefly and concisely state your business and its mission.

✔ Scan or use a digital camera to capture images of your sale items (or of
   the services you provide) as I describe in Chapter 5 and post them on a
   web page called Products.

Don't forget the personal touch when connecting with your customers' needs.
Online shoppers don't get to meet their merchants in person, so anything you
can tell about yourself helps to personalize the process and put your visitors
at ease. For example, one of Lucky Boyd's primary goals for his MyTexasMusic
site (`www.mytexasmusic.com`) is to encourage people to become members
so they're more likely to visit on a regular basis. His photos of music fans (see
Figure 2-2) personalize the site and remind visitors that they're members of a
community of music lovers. Let your cybervisitors know that they're dealing
with real people, not remote machines and computer programs.

Peeking in on other businesses' websites to pick up ideas and see how they
handle similar issues is a natural practice. In cyberspace, you can visit plenty
of businesses that are comparable to yours from the comfort of your home
office, and the trip takes only minutes.

Establishing a graphic identity

When you start your first business on the web, you have to convince customers that you're competent and professional. One factor that helps build trust
is a graphic identity. A site with an identity looks a certain way. For example,
take a look at Figure 2-3 as well as Figure 2-4, later in this chapter. Both pages

are from the Graphic Maps website (www.graphicmaps.com). Notice that each has the same white background, the same distinctive and simple logo, and both have similar heading styles. Using such elements consistently from page to page creates an identity that gives your business credibility and helps viewers find what they're looking for.

Figure 2-2: Personalize your business to connect with customers online.

Figure 2-3: Through careful planning and design, the Graphic Maps site maintains a consistent look and feel, or graphic identity, on each page.

Step 7: Set Up a System for Processing Sales

Many businesses unprepared for success go online. They don't have systems in place for finalizing sales, shipping purchased goods in a timely manner, or tracking finances and inventory.

An excellent way to plan for success is to set up ways to track your business finances and create a secure purchasing environment for your online customers. That way, you can build on your success rather than be surprised by it.

Providing a means for secure transactions

Getting paid is the key to survival as well as success. However, the payment process for an online business isn't always straightforward. Make your website a safe place for customers to pay you. Provide different payment options and build a level of trust any way you can.

Some people are squeamish about submitting their credit card numbers online. And beginning businesspeople are understandably intimidated by the requirements of processing credit card transactions. In the early stages, you can simply create a form for customers to print out and mail to you along with a check. (The Graphic Maps site is successful without having an online credit card system; clients phone in their orders.)

When you can accept credit cards, make your customers feel at ease by explaining what measures you're taking to ensure that their information is secure. Such measures include signing up for an account with a web host that provides a *secure server,* a computer that uses software to encrypt data and uses digital documents, or *certificates,* to ensure its identity. (See Chapters 6 and 7 for more on Internet security and secure shopping systems.)

Becoming a credit card merchant

E-commerce brings to mind visions of online forms and credit card data that's transmitted over the Internet. Do you have to provide such service to run a successful online business? Not necessarily. Being a credit card merchant makes life easier for your customers, to be sure, but it also adds complications and extra costs to your operation.

The traditional way to become a credit card merchant is to apply to a bank. Small and home-based businesses can have difficulty getting their applications approved. Alternatively, you can sign up with a company that provides electronic shopping cart services and credit card payments online to small businesses. See Chapter 7 for suggestions. You can also accept credit card payments through the popular electronic payment service PayPal. Your customers have to have an account with PayPal and have their purchase price debited from their credit card accounts, but the service is popular enough that many of your online shoppers are probably members already.

If you do get the go-ahead from a bank to become a credit card merchant, you have to pay it a *discount rate,* which is a fee (typically 2 to 3 percent of each transaction). You sometimes have to pay a monthly premium charge of $10 to $25 as well. Besides that, you may need special software or hardware to accept credit card payments.

To maximize your sales by reaching users who either don't have credit cards or don't want to use them on the Internet, provide low-tech alternatives (such as toll-free phone numbers and fax numbers) so that your customers can provide you with information using more familiar technologies.

After much searching, Lucky Boyd signed with a company called Goemerchant (www.goemerchant.com), which provides him with the payment systems that many online shoppers recognize when they want to make a purchase. First, Goemerchant has a *shopping cart* — a set of pages that acts as an electronic holding area for items before they are purchased. Next, it has a secure way for people to make electronic purchases by providing online forms, where they can safely enter credit card and other personal information. The note stating that the payment area is protected by Secure Sockets Layer (SSL) encryption tells people that even if a criminal intercepts their credit card data, he can't read it.

Safeguarding your customers' personal information is important, but you also need to safeguard your business. Many online businesses get burned by bad guys who submit fraudulent credit card information. If you don't verify the information and submit it to your financial institution for processing, you're liable for the cost. Strongly consider signing up with a service that handles credit card verification for you in order to cut down on lost revenue.

Keeping your books straight

In the simplest sense, "keeping your books" means recording all financial activities that pertain to your business, including any expenses you incur, all the income you receive, as well as your equipment and tax deductions.

The financial side of running a business also entails creating reports, such as profit and loss statements, that banks require if you apply for a loan. Such reports not only help meet financial institutions' needs, but also provide you with essential information about how your business is doing at any time.

You can record all this information the old-fashioned way, by writing it down in ledgers and journals, or you can use accounting software. (See Chapter 18 for information about easy-to-use accounting packages that are great for financial novices.) Because you're making a commitment to use a computer on a regular basis by starting an online business, it's only natural for you to use a computer to keep your books, too. Accounting software can help you keep track of expenses and provide information that may save you some headaches at tax time.

After you save your financial data on your hard drive, make backups so that you don't lose information you need to do business. See Chapter 6 for ways to back up and protect your files.

Step 8: Provide Personal Service

Because the Internet runs on wires, cables, and computer chips, it may not seem like a place for the personal touch. But technology didn't actually create the Internet and all of its content; *people* did. In fact, the Internet is a great place to provide your clients and customers with outstanding personal customer service.

In many cases, offering customer service on the Internet means you are available and respond quickly to all inquiries. You check your e-mail regularly, you make sure that you respond within a day, you cheerfully solve problems and hand out refunds if needed. By helping your customers, you help yourself, too. You build loyalty as well as credibility among your clientele. For many small businesses, the key to competing effectively with larger businesses is by providing superior customer service. See Chapter 8 for more ideas on how you can do this.

Selling by sharing your expertise

Your knowledge and experience are among your most valuable commodities. So you may be surprised when I suggest that you give them away for free. Why? It's a "try before you buy" concept. Helping people for free builds your credibility and makes them more likely to pay for your services down the road.

When your business is online, you can easily communicate what you know about your field and make your knowledge readily available. One way is to set up a web page that presents the basics about your company and your field of interest in the form of Frequently Asked Questions (FAQs). Another technique is to become a virtual publisher/editor and create your own newsletter in which you write about what's new with your company and topics related to your work. See Chapter 8 for more on communicating your expertise through FAQs, newsletters, and advanced e-mail techniques.

My brother was skeptical when I recommended that he include a page of technical information explaining exactly what equipment he uses and describing the steps involved in audio restoration. He didn't think anyone would be interested; he also didn't want to give away his "trade secrets." *Au contraire, mon frère!* People who surf the Internet gobble up all the technical details they can find. The more you wow them with the names and model numbers of your expensive equipment, not to mention the work you go through to restore their old records, the more they'll trust you. And trust gets people to place an order with you.

Making your site a go-to resource

Many *ontrepreneurs* (online entrepreneurs) succeed by making their websites not only places for sales and promotion, but also indispensable resources full of useful hyperlinks and other information so customers want to visit again and again. For example, the Graphic Maps website mentioned earlier in this chapter acts as a resource for anyone who has a question about geography. To promote the site, John Moen gives away free maps for nonprofit organizations, operates a daily geography contest with a $100 prize to the first person with the correct answer (as shown in Figure 2-4), and answers e-mail promptly. "I feel strongly that the secret on the web is to provide a solution to a problem and, for the most part, to do it for free," he suggests.

The MyTexasMusic site (www.mytexasmusic.com) uses the concept of membership to strengthen its connections with customers. The main purpose of the site is to make money by selling the works of Texas musicians as well as tickets to concerts. But to make money, you need to give people a reason to visit your site on a regular basis. When people are *members* rather than *shoppers,* they feel connected and privileged.

"Memberships work for us in two ways," comments Boyd. "Every vendor who consigns to us is a member. Customers can also be members. Membership invokes the idea of ownership, and everyone likes to feel as though they are a part owner of the process."

Figure 2-4:
This site
uses free
art, a mail-
ing list, and
daily prizes
to drum up
business.

The site encourages music lovers and musicians to become members: They provide information about who they are and where they live, and they create their own usernames and passwords so that they can access special content and perform special functions on the site, such as selling their own CDs or posting song clips. For an online business, the names and addresses of people who visit and who don't necessarily make purchases is a gold mine of information. The business can use the contact information to send members special offers and news releases; the more frequently contact is maintained, the more likely those casual shoppers are to eventually turn into paying customers.

The concept of membership also builds a feeling of community among customers. By turning the e-commerce site into a meeting place for members who love Texas musicians, those members make new friends and have a reason to visit the site on a regular basis. Community building is one way in which commerce on the web differs from traditional brick-and-mortar selling, and it's something you should consider, too.

Another way to encourage customers to congregate at your site is to create a discussion area. In Chapter 8, I show you how to provide a discussion page right on your own website.

Becoming a super e-mailer

E-mail is, in my humble opinion, the single most important marketing tool that you can use to boost your online business. Becoming an expert e-mail user increases your contacts and provides you with new sources of support, too.

The two best and easiest e-mail strategies are the following:

✔ Check your e-mail as often as possible.

✔ Respond to e-mail inquiries immediately.

Additionally, you can e-mail inquiries about co-marketing opportunities to other websites similar to your own. Ask other online business owners if they will provide links to your site in exchange for you providing links to theirs. And always include a signature file with your message that includes the name of your business and a link to your business site. See Chapter 8 for more information on using e-mail effectively to build and maintain relations with your online customers.

I encourage you to use e-mail primarily for one-to-one communication. The Internet excels at bringing individuals together. Mailing lists and newsletters can use e-mail effectively for marketing, too.

I'm *not* encouraging you to send out mass quantities of unsolicited commercial e-mail, a practice that turns off almost all consumers and that can get you in trouble with the law, too. Spam artists have been convicted, and the sentences are getting more severe. In April 2005, a man was sentenced to nine years in prison for masking his identity while bombarding Internet users with millions of unsolicited e-mail messages (www.pcworld.com/news/article/0,aid,118493,00.asp). In November 2009, four individuals were sentenced in a Detroit federal court for their roles in an international stock fraud scheme involving the illegal use of spam e-mails, which violated the CAN-SPAM Act.

In November 2009 Alan M. Ralsky, 64, and Scott Bradley, 48, both of West Bloomfield, Michigan, were sentenced to 51 months and 40 months in prison, respectively, for conspiring to commit wire fraud, mail fraud, violating the CAN-SPAM Act, and engaging in money laundering. Ralsky and Bradley were also each sentenced to five years of supervised release following their respective prison terms, and were each ordered to forfeit $250,000 that the United States seized from them in December 2007.

Step 9: Alert the Media and Everyone Else

To be successful, small businesses need to get the word out to the people who are likely to purchase what they have to offer. If this group turns out to be a narrow market, so much the better; the Internet is great for connecting to niche markets that share a common interest. (See Chapter 8 for more on locating your most likely customers on the Internet and figuring out how best to communicate with them.)

The Internet provides many unique and effective ways for small businesses to advertise, including search services, e-mail, newsgroups, and electronic mailing lists. It's encouraging to note, though, that you don't always have to depend on high-tech solutions to get publicity. "We still do not spend money on print advertising — and we have more business than we can handle from word of mouth," says Jinele Boyd of MyTexasMusic.

Listing your site with Internet search services

How, exactly, do you get listed on search engines such as Yahoo! and Lycos? Frankly, it's getting more difficult. Many of the big search services charge for listings (Yahoo!'s fees for commercial listings in its directory are particularly steep). But some let you contribute a listing for free, though there's no guarantee if or when you'll see your site included in their databases.

You can increase the chances that search services list your site by including special keywords and site descriptions in the titles, body text, and HTML commands for your web pages. You place some of these keywords after a special HTML command (the <meta> tag), making them invisible to the casual viewer of your site. Turn to Chapter 11 for details.

Both John Moen and Lucky Boyd have created multiple websites for different purposes. One purpose is to reach different markets. Another is to improve rankings on search engines, such as Google, by linking one site to several other sites; the site is considered more popular, and its ranking rises. See Chapter 11 for more on this and other tips on getting listed by Internet search engines.

Reaching the entire Internet

Your website may be the cornerstone of your business, but if nobody knows it's out there, it can't help you generate sales. Perhaps the most familiar form of online advertising is *banner ads,* those little electronic billboards that seem to show up on every popular web page.

But banner advertising can be expensive and may not be the best way for a small business to advertise online. In fact, the most effective marketing for some businesses hasn't been traditional banner advertising or newspaper/magazine placements. Rather, the e-marketers who run those businesses target electronic bulletin boards and mailing lists where people already discuss the products being sold. You can post notices on the bulletin boards where your potential customers congregate, notifying them that your services are now available. (Make sure that the board in question permits such solicitation before you do so, or you'll chase away the very customers you want.)

This sort of direct, one-to-one marketing may seem tedious, but it's often the best way to develop a business on the Internet. Reach out to your potential customers and strike up an individual, personal relationship with each one.

Chapter 10 has everything you need to know about advertising with mailing lists, newsgroups, and even traditional banner ads.

Step 10: Review, Revise, and Improve

For any long-term endeavor, you need to establish standards by which you can judge its success or failure. You must decide for yourself what you consider success to be. After a period of time, take stock of where your business is and then take steps to do even better.

Taking stock

After 12 months online, Lucky Boyd took stock. His site was online, but he wasn't getting many page views. He redid the site, increased the number of giveaways, and traffic to his site increased. Now he makes music downloads available on his site; he also redid his web pages with the Hypertext Preprocessor (PHP) programming language. He has also expanded to include a business presence on the popular social networking sites MySpace, Facebook, and Twitter.

HTML is a markup language: It identifies parts of a web page that need to be formatted as headings, text, images, and so on. It can be used to include scripts, such as those written in the JavaScript language. But by creating his pages from scratch with PHP, Boyd can make his site more dynamic and easier to update. He can rotate random images, process forms, and compile statistics that track his visitors by using PHP scripts, for example. He can design web pages in a modular way so that they can be redesigned and revised more quickly than with HTML.

Your business may do so well that you can reinvest in it by buying new equipment or increasing your services. You may even be able to give something back to nonprofits and those in need. The young founders of The Chocolate Farm set up a scholarship fund designed to bring young people from other countries to the United States to help them find out about free enterprise. (See the upcoming case study for more.) Perhaps you'll have enough money left over to reward yourself, too — as if being able to tell everyone "I own an online business" isn't reward enough!

Money is only one form of success. Plenty of entrepreneurs are online for reasons other than making money. That said, it *is* important from time to time to evaluate how well you're doing financially. Accounting software, such as the programs I describe in Chapter 18, makes it easy to check your revenues on a daily or weekly basis. The key is to establish the goals you want to reach and develop measurements so that you know when and if you reach those goals.

Updating your data

Getting your business online now and then updating your site regularly is better than waiting to unveil the perfect website all at one time. In fact, seeing your site improve and grow is one of the best things about going online. Over time, you can create contests, strike up cooperative relationships with other businesses, and add more background information about your products and services.

Consider The Chocolate Farm, a business that was owned and operated for ten years by siblings Evan and Elise MacMillan of Denver, Colorado. The business was started when Elise was just 10 years old and Evan was 13. They began by selling chocolates with a farm theme, such as chocolate cows; later, they focused on creating custom chocolates — sweets made to order for businesses, many of which bore the company's logo. Evan and Elise eventually oversaw the work of 50 full- and part-time employees.

Today, Evan reports that he and his sister decided to wrap up their involvement with The Chocolate Farm. It was sold to another chocolate company.

"We considered the exit a success," says Evan. He recalls how much the project brought to their lives: an appearance on *The Oprah Winfrey Show* and coverage in *The Wall Street Journal*. He adds: "And yes, it did help us with college expenses." Elise is a student at Stanford University, studying computer music and art. Evan graduated in the spring of 2009 and began work on his fifth startup company (he co-founded and operated a couple of energy software companies while still a college student). "Though we are out of the business, we still love chocolate, and Elise and I make things together on weekends."

Businesses on the web need to evaluate and revise their practices on a regular basis. Lucky Boyd studies reports of where visitors come from before they reach his site, and what pages they visit on the site, so that he can attract new customers. Online business is a process of trial and error. Some promotions work better than others. The point is that it needs to be an ongoing process and a long-term commitment. Taking a chance and profiting from your mistakes is better than not trying in the first place.

Chapter 3

Choosing and Equipping Your New E-Business

Starting your own online business is like rehabbing an old house — something I've been doing for years. Both projects involve a series of recognizable phases:

✔ **The idea phase:** You tell people about your great idea. They hear the enthusiasm in your voice, nod their heads, and say something like, "Good luck." They've seen you in this condition before and know how it usually turns out.

✔ **The decision phase:** Undaunted, you begin honing your plan. You read books (like this one), ask questions, and shop around until you find just the right tools and materials. Of course, when the project is staring you down in your own workshop, you may start to panic, asking yourself whether you're really up for the task. Don't worry: You are!

✔ **The assembly phase:** Still determined to proceed, you forge ahead. You plug in your tools and go to work. Drills spin, sparks fly, and metal moves.

✔ **The test-drive phase:** One fine day, out of the dust and fumes, your masterpiece emerges. You invite everyone over to enjoy the fruits of your labor. All those who were skeptical before are now full of admiration. You get enjoyment from your project for years to come.

If rehabbing a house doesn't work for you, think about restoring an antique auto, planning an anniversary party, or devising a mountain-climbing excursion in Tibet. The point is that starting an online business is a project like any other — one that you can understand and accomplish in stages. Right now, you're at the first stage of launching your new cyberbusiness. Your creativity is working overtime. You have some rough sketches that only a mother could love.

This chapter helps you get from idea to reality. Your first step is to imagine how you want your business to look and feel. Then you can begin to develop and implement strategies for achieving your dream. You have a big advantage over those who started new businesses a few years ago: You have plenty of models to show you what works and what doesn't.

While you travel along the path from idea to reality, you must also consider properly equipping your online business — just like you would have to equip a traditional brick-and-mortar business. One of the many exciting aspects of launching a business online, however, is the absence of much *overhead* (that is, operating expenses). Many non-cyberspace businesses must take out loans to pay rent, remodel their storefronts, and purchase store fixtures. In contrast, the primary overhead for an online business is computer hardware and software. Although it's great if you can afford top-of-the-line equipment, you'll be happy to know that the latest bells and whistles aren't absolutely necessary to get a business site online and maintain it effectively. But to streamline the technical aspects of connecting to the online world and creating a business presence, some investment may be a wise and profitable idea.

Don't rush into signing a contract to get your online business hosted. I've encountered experienced businesspeople who prepaid for a year's worth of web hosting with nothing else yet in place. Be sure you know your options and have a business strategy, no matter how simple, before you sign anything. Websites are important, but they're not all there is to creating a presence and branding yourself, as you discover throughout this book.

Mapping Out Your Online Business

How do you get to square one? Start by imagining the kind of business that is your ultimate goal. This is the time to indulge in some brainstorming. Envisioning your business is a creative way of asking the all-important questions: Why do I want to go into business online? What are my goals? Table 3-1 illustrates some possible goals and suggests how to achieve them. By envisioning the final result you want to achieve, you can determine your online business goals.

Table 3-1	Online Business Models	
Goal	**Type of Website**	**What to Do**
Make big bucks.	Sales	Sell items/gain paying advertisers.
Gain credibility and attention.	Marketing	Start a blog; start Twittering; put your résumé and samples of your work online.
Become a resource.	Information	Gather and organize information on a specific topic so visitors can find what they want easily.
Create a tech tool.	Technology	Create an app that makes life easier for consumers.
Promote yourself.	Personal	Promote yourself in discussion groups or on your website so that people will hire you or want to use your goods or services.
Turn an interest into a source of income.	Hobby/special interest	Invite like-minded people to share your passion, participate in your site, and generate traffic so that you can gain advertisers.

Looking around

You don't have to reinvent the wheel. Your ultimate destination can be the best source of information on how to get there. Sometimes, spending just half an hour surfing the Internet can stimulate your own mental network. Find sites with qualities you want to emulate. Throughout this book, I suggest business sites you can visit to find good models to follow.

Don't feel obligated to keep moving in the same direction all the time, either. One of the many advantages of starting an online business is the ability to change direction with relative ease.

 Because you're not unlike your target audience, your likes and dislikes have value. Keep a low-tech pencil and pad of paper handy each time you surf for ideas. Make a list as you go of what you find appealing and jot down notes on logos, designs, and text. That way, you'll have raw data to draw upon when you begin to refine what you want to do.

Making your mark

The web and other parts of the online world have undergone a population explosion that shows no signs of slowing. According to the Internet Systems Consortium Domain Survey (www.isc.org/solutions/survey), in July 2012, 908.5 million computers that hosted websites were connected to the Internet, compared with 625.2 million in 2009, 439.3 million in 2006, and 285 million in 2004. Seventeen percent of those computers host web addresses that end with the commercial (.com) designation.

As an *ontrepreneur* (online entrepreneur), your goal is to stand out from the crowd — or to "position yourself in the marketplace," as business consultants like to say. Consider the following tried-and-true suggestions if you want your website to be a go-to place:

- ✔ **Pursue something you know well.** Experience adds value to the information that you provide. In the online world, expertise sells.

- ✔ **Make a statement.** On your website, include a mission statement that clearly identifies what you do, the customers you hope to reach, and how you're different from your competitors. On your blog, give your opinions. On discussion groups, share your knowledge.

- ✔ **Give something away for free.** Giveaways and promotions are surefire ways to gain attention and develop a loyal customer base. In fact, entire websites are devoted to providing free stuff online, such as see FreeNapkin (www.freenapkin.com). Or read the Fox News article describing five sources of freebies (www.foxnews.com). You don't have to give away an actual product; you could also offer words of wisdom based on your training and experience.

- ✔ **Find your niche.** Web space is a great place to pursue niche marketing. In fact, it often seems that the quirkier the item, the better it sells. Some of the most successful sellers I know deal in things like flavored coffee, toy train accessories, fountain pens, women's purses, and the like. Don't be afraid to target a narrow audience and direct all your sales efforts to a small group of devoted followers.

- ✔ **Do something you love.** The more you love your business, the more time and effort you're apt to put into it and, therefore, the more likely it is to be successful. Such businesses take advantage of the Internet's worldwide reach, which makes it easy for people with the same interests to gather at the same virtual location.

Scan through the list of *Inc.* magazine's Top 5000 privately held companies (www.inc.com/inc5000), and you find many examples of businesses that follow all these strategies:

- ✔ The number 11 company for 2012, Nasty Gal (`www.nastygal.com`), was started by a lone entrepreneur selling vintage clothing, shoes, and accessories on eBay.

- ✔ The number 17 company for 2012, CampusBookRentals (`www.campusbookrentals.com`), does what it says, renting textbooks to 50 million students across the country.

- ✔ The number 4 company for 2009, Perfect Fitness (`https://perfectonline.com`), has a niche selling fitness equipment online.

Gather ideas for innovative websites by scouring Google News for the latest business success stories. For example, when I did a search for the term "business success story," I found an article about Tim Brennan, who does "content marketing."

```
www.business2community.com/content-marketing/market-with-
        an-ebook-why-itll-work-and-how-0321290
```

Tim marketed his business by writing and selling an e-book on chess tactics on Amazon.com. Do your own search, and write down ideas for your own sales and marketing efforts.

Evaluating commercial websites

How is your business the same as others? How is it different? Your customers will ask these questions, so you need to ask them also. Commercial websites — those whose Internet addresses end with `.com` or `.biz` — are the fastest-growing segment of the Internet. This is the area you're entering, too. The trick is to be comfortable with the size and level of complexity of a business that's right for you. In general, your options are

- ✔ **A big commercial website:** The web means big business, and plenty of big companies create websites with the primary goal of supplementing a product or business that's already well known and well established. Just a few examples are the Ragu website (`www.ragu.com`), the Pepsi World website (`www.pepsiworld.com`), and the Toyota website (`www.toyota.com`). True, corporations with thousands of dollars to throw into web design created these commercial websites, but you can still look at them to get ideas for your own site.

- ✔ **A midsize site:** Many a small business of 10 to 12 employees makes good use of the web to provide customer service, disseminate information, and post a sales catalog. You may find some features that midsize companies use, such as a Frequently Asked Questions (FAQ) page or a sales catalog, useful to you. Look at the Golfballs.com site (`www.golfballs.com`) for good ideas.

✔ **A site that's just right:** You don't need business experience to guarantee success on the Web. You can also start out as a single person, couple, or family doing business. In fact, the rest of this book is devoted to helping you produce a fine, homegrown entrepreneurial business. This chapter gets you off to a good start by examining the different kinds of businesses you can launch online and some business goals you can set for yourself.

Taste-Testing Flavors of Online Businesses

If you're easily overstimulated, you may feel you need blinders when you comb the Internet for ideas to give your online business a definite shape and form. Use the following brief descriptions of online businesses to create categories of interest and then zero in on the ones that are most useful to you.

Selling consumer products

Leading Internet research firm Forrester Research (www.internetretailer.com) predicts that despite slowdowns in the economy, total e-commerce sales in the United States will continue to grow to $262 billion by the end of 2013, an increase of 13.4 percent over 2012's figures. The online marketplace is a great venue if you have products to sell (such as auto parts, antiques, jewelry, or food). The web has always attracted those looking for unique items or something customized just for them. Consider taking your wares online if any of the following applies to you:

✔ Your products are high in quality.

✔ You create your own products; for example, you design dishes, make fudge, or sell gift baskets of wine.

✔ You specialize in some aspects of your product that larger businesses can't achieve. Perhaps you sell regional foods, such as Chicago deep-dish pizza or live lobsters from Maine.

I have always admired the customization tools available on the site of Timbuk2 (www.timbuk2.com), which manufactures bicycle messenger bags and sells them directly to the public. Other sites don't sell consumer goods directly, but they support consumer goods. For example, ice cream may not be good for my waistline, but I often go to the Ben and Jerry's

Chicago Public Library
Harold Washington Library Center

11/10/2014   1:46:38 PM
-Patron Receipt-

ITEMS RENEWED:

1:
Title: Starting an online business for dummies /
Item #: R0428873934
— **Renewed** —
Number of times renewed: 2
Due Date: 12/1/2014

-Please retain for your records-

IBCOLEMA

website (`www.benjerry.com`) just to drool. These guys are entrepreneurs just like you, and I like their website as well as their products. The website focuses on the unique flavors and the high quality of their ice cream, as well as their personalities and business standards. And on the day this book's editor visited, it was a free cone day; they were doing a giveaway, another promotional strategy mentioned earlier.

So c'mon in, the water's fine. The key is to find your niche, as many small-but-successful businesses have done. Use your web space to declare your love for your products (and, by implication, why your customers will love them, too).

Offering your professional services

Either through a website or through listings in indexes and directories, offering your professional services online can expand your client base dramatically. A web presence also gives existing clients a new way to contact you: through e-mail. Here are just a few examples of professionals who are offering their services online:

- **Attorneys:** Family-law attorney Andrea Lance is based in Boston. Through her website (`http://lancelawmass.com`), she can reach individuals around the Boston metropolitan area and beyond who need legal assistance.

- **Psychotherapists:** Julie Hendrickson uses a simple, nicely designed website (`www.seattlepsychotherapyservices.com`) to pursue a profession you might not think you could do online: psychotherapy. Her site is upfront about her work and her fees, too. My friend Michael Vernon also advertises his counseling services through his The Mindfulness Clinic website (`http://themindfulnessclinic.com`).

- **Physicians:** Dr. Rob Lamberts, a physician in Augusta, Georgia, maintains a blog called "Musings of a Distractible Mind" (`www.distractible.org`) that gives opinions and tips. He is also known as "The House Call Doctor" on the Quick and Dirty Tips website (`http://quickanddirtytips.com`).

- **Consultants:** Experts who keep their knowledge up to date and are willing to give advice to those with similar interests and needs are always in demand. Consultants in a specialized area often find a great demand for their services on the Internet. The Yahoo! Consulting page is crowded with fields in which online consultants are available:

```
dir.yahoo.com/business_and_economy/
        business_to_business/consulting
```

We're busy people who don't always have the time to pore over the fine print. Short and snappy nuggets of information can draw customers to your site and make them feel as though they're getting something for free. One way you can put forth this professional expertise is by starting your own online newsletter. You get to be editor, writer, and mailing-list manager. Plus you get to talk as much as you want, network with people who are interested enough in what you have to say to subscribe to your publication, and put your name and business before lots of people. Judy Vorfeld (whom I profile in Chapter 5) puts out a regular newsletter called *Communication Expressway* that supplements her online business site (`www.ossweb.com/ezine.html`).

Selling your expertise

The original purpose of the Internet was to share knowledge via computers, and information is the commodity that has fueled cyberspace's rapid growth. As the Internet and commercial online networks continue to expand, information remains key.

Finding valuable information and gathering a particular kind of resource for one location online can be a business in itself. People love to get knowledge they trust from the comfort of their own homes. For example, students and parents are eager to pay someone to help them sort through the procedures involved and the data required to apply for college. (See the intriguing School Finder website, `www.princetonreview.com/schoolsearch.aspx`, run by The Princeton Review and *Seventeen* magazine, for example.)

Other online businesses provide gathering points or indexes to more specific areas. Here are just a few examples:

- ✔ **Search engines:** Some businesses succeed by connecting cybersurfers with companies, organizations, and individuals that specialize in a given area. Yahoo! (`www.yahoo.com`) is the most obvious example. Originally started by two college students, Yahoo! has practically become an Internet legend by gathering information in one index so that people can easily find things online.

- ✔ **Links pages:** On her Sweepstakes Crazy website (`www.sweepstakescrazy.com`), Janet Marchbanks-Aulenta gathers links to current contests along with short descriptions of each one. Janet says her site receives as many as 22,000 visits per month and generates income through advertising and affiliate links to other contest websites. She says she loves running her own business despite the hard work involved with keeping it updated. "The key to succeeding at this type of site is to build up a regular base of users who return each day to find new contests — the daily upkeep is very important," she says.

✔ **Personal recommendations:** The personal touch sells. Just look at sites like Lifehacker (`http://lifehacker.com`) and About.com (`www.about.com`). The latter is a guide to the online world that provides web surfers with a central location where they can locate virtually anything. It works because real people do the choosing and provide evaluations (albeit brief) of the sites they list. In Chapter 1, you find out about Dean Pettit, who created an online guide to Florida's Space Coast.

Resource sites such as these can transform information into money in a number of ways. In some cases, individuals pay to become members. Sometimes, businesses pay to be listed on a site; other times, a site attracts so many regular visitors that other companies pay to post advertising on the site. Big successes — such as About.com — carry a healthy share of ads and strike lucrative partnerships with big companies as well.

Finding opportunities with technology or computer resources

What could be more natural than using the web to sell what you need to get and stay online? The online world itself, by the very fact that it exists, has spawned all kinds of business opportunities for entrepreneurs:

✔ **Computer services:** *U.S. News and World Report* listed computer services as one of the best small businesses to start, and mentioned Arlington Virginia Computer Repair (`arlingtonvacomputerrepair.com`) as an example. Owner Alex Chamandy fills a niche by dealing with customers face to face, and by locating his company in the basement of his residence, he saves on overhead and other costs. He is thus able to offer lower rates than repair services of the "big box" computer stores.

✔ **Internet service providers:** These businesses give you a high-speed connection to the Internet. Many ISPs, such as Comcast or AT&T, are big companies with nationwide coverage. But smaller companies are succeeding as well — such as Starpoint Digital (`www.mystarpoint.com`), based in Schaumburg, Illinois, which offers free online web training for its customers.

✔ **Software:** Matt Wright is well known on the web for providing free computer scripts that add important functionality to websites, such as processing information that visitors submit via online forms. Matt's Script Archive site (`www.scriptarchive.com`) includes an advertisement for a book on scripting that he coauthored, as well as a web postcard system for sale and an invitation to businesses to take out advertisements on his site.

Being a starving artist without the starving

Being creative no longer means you have to live out of your flower-covered van, driving from art fairs to craft shows. If you're simply looking for exposure and feedback on your creations, you can put samples of your work online. Consider the following suggestions for virtual creative venues (and revenues):

- ✔ **Host art galleries.** Thanks to online galleries, artists whose sales were previously limited to one region can get inquiries from all over the world. Art-2k.com (`www.art-2k.com`) has been advertising artists' websites since 1999. The personal website created by artist Marques Vickers (`www.marquesv.com`), shown in Figure 3-1, has received worldwide attention.

- ✔ **Publish your writing.** Blogs (web logs, or online diaries) are all the rage these days. One of the most successful, such as The Dish by Andrew Sullivan (`http://dish.andrewsullivan.com`), just went independent and is generating ad or subscription revenue. To find out how to create a blog, check out WordPress (`http://wordpress.com`).

Figure 3-1: A California artist created this website to gain recognition and sell his creative work.

> ✔ **Get your art printed.** Two young men named Jake and Jacob met through a design forum and dropped out of college to start an online T-shirt business. Today, their Threadless T-Shirts (`www.threadless.com`) website rakes in millions.
>
> ✔ **Sell your music.** Singer-songwriter Michael McDermott sells his own CDs, videos, and posters through his online store (`www.michael-mcdermott.com`).

You can, of course, also sell all that junk that's been accumulating in your basement, as well as your relatives' and family members' junk, on eBay; see Chapter 14 for more information on this and Chapter 15 for other exciting niche marketplaces.

Easyware (Not Hardware) for Your Business

Becoming an information provider on the Internet places an additional burden on your computer and peripheral equipment. When you're "in it for the money," you may go online every day, perhaps for hours at a time, especially if you buy and sell on eBay. The better your computer setup, the more e-mail messages you can download, the more catalog items you can store, and so on.

That said, it's easier than ever to find what you need either online or at your local big box store. Rather than going through detailed sections specifying the amount of RAM or bandwidth you need, I suggest you follow a couple of basic common-sense principles:

> ✔ **Look on the Internet for what you need.** You can find just about everything you want to get you started.
>
> ✔ **Be sure to try before you buy!** Don't pull out that credit card until you get the facts on what warranty and technical support your hardware or software vendor provides. Make sure that your vendor provides phone support 24 hours a day, 7 days a week. Also ask how long the typical turnaround time is in case your equipment needs to be serviced.
>
> ✔ **Buy the best equipment you can afford.** Don't scrimp when it comes to imaging, speed, and storage space.

When you do business, you need to take high-quality photos of yourself and your products. A cell phone camera probably won't be up to the task. It pays to spend the money to get a good digital camera.

You'll also be running a higher number of applications, often at the same time, when you're designing web pages, editing images, and the like. Make sure your computing device has enough memory to do the job.

It doesn't matter so much whether you use a tablet or a desktop computer to create and maintain your business. That choice depends on your working style and habits. Just make sure you can type and point easily and that you won't run out of memory. And make sure you have all the ports you need. Your iPad might be slick and fast, but if you need to transfer lots of files to or from another device, you need to be able to do that easily. You might be accustomed to using a portable drive (like a thumb drive) to do this, but you won't find a full-size USB port on the iPad to accommodate it. Consider looking for another option, at least if you want to use USB devices.

If you purchase lots of new hardware and software, remember to update your insurance by sending your insurer a list of your new equipment. Also consider purchasing insurance specifically for your computer-related items from a company such as Safeware (www.safeware.com).

The right computer for your online business

You may already have an existing computer setup that's adequate to get your business online. After all, personal computers and tablets are becoming more powerful and at the same time generally less expensive. Or you may be starting from scratch and looking to purchase a new computer. In either case, it pays to know what all the technical terms and specifications mean. Here are some general terms you need to understand:

- **Gigahertz (GHz) and megahertz (MHz):** These units of measure indicate how quickly a computer's processor can perform functions. The central processing unit (CPU) of a computer is where the computing work gets done. In general, the higher the processor's internal clock rate, the faster the computer.

- **Random access memory (RAM):** This is the memory that your computer uses to temporarily store information needed to operate programs. RAM is usually expressed in millions of bytes, or megabytes (MB). The more RAM you have, the more programs you can run simultaneously. See Table 3-2 for some guidelines.

- **Synchronous dynamic RAM (SDRAM):** Many ultra-fast computers use some form of SDRAM synchronized with a particular clock rate of a CPU so that a processor can perform more instructions in a given time.

- **Double data rate SDRAM (DDR SDRAM):** This is a type of SDRAM that can dramatically improve the clock rate of a CPU.

✔ **Auxiliary storage:** This term refers to physical data-storage space on a hard drive, tape, CD-RW, DVD, or other device.

✔ **Portable storage:** SD, XD, CF, and other memory cards can store data in cell phones, cameras, and other portable devices. And don't forget those little USB flash drives (also called thumb drives) that can help you back up your data in — well, a flash.

✔ **Virtual memory:** This is a type of memory on your hard drive that your computer can "borrow" to serve as extra RAM.

✔ **Wireless network card:** The laptop or desktop computer you purchase almost certainly has a wireless network card installed so that you can connect your wireless modem to another network using Wi-Fi. Chances are you don't need to purchase a network card as an add-on.

The Internet is teeming with places where you can find good deals on hardware. A great place to start is the CNET Shopper.com website (`http://shopper.cnet.com`). Also visit the auction site uBid.com (`www.ubid.com`).

Make sure that you have enough memory to run the types of applications shown in Table 3-2. (Note that these are only estimates, based on the Windows versions of these products that were available at the time of this writing.)

Table 3-2	Memory Requirements	
Type of Application	*Example*	*Amount of RAM Recommended*
Web browser	Internet Explorer	512MB
Web page editor	Adobe Dreamweaver	512MB
Word processor	Microsoft Word	1–2GB (as part of Office 2010)
Graphics program	Corel PaintShop Pro X5	22GB
Professional drawing/ editing software	Adobe Photoshop CS6	1GB
Animation/Presentation	Adobe Flash Professional	23GB

The RAM recommended for the sample applications in Table 3-2 adds up to more than 8–9GB. If you plan to work, be sure to get at least 10GB of RAM — more if you can swing it. Memory is cheap nowadays, so get all the RAM you can afford.

Storage space

RAM is only one type of memory your computer uses; the other kind, the memory in the hard drive, stores information, such as text files, audio files, programs, and the many essential files your computer's operating system needs. Most new computers come with hard drives that store many gigabytes of data. Any hard drive with a few gigabytes of storage space should be adequate for your business needs if you don't do a lot of graphics work. Most new computers come with hard drives that are 500GB or larger.

Whether you use a desktop, laptop, tablet, or smartphone as your primary computing device, you need to consider auxiliary or add-on storage. Nearly all desktops and laptops let you plug in an auxiliary disk drive or a USB thumb drive. But not all tablets or phones are "expandable." In particular, the iPhone and iPad don't include slots for USB drives or mini-SD cards. That's just one reason why I chose an Android phone and tablet. Both can hold a mini-SD that gives me 32GB of extra storage. If you have lots of photos or files you need or want to carry around with you, and you don't want to be constrained by the storage space that comes with your computing device of choice, be sure to buy a device with a storage slot.

There's a third type of storage you should consider that can make thumb drives and SD cards obsolete. It's called cloud storage. The "cloud" is one or more computers on which you have been allocated storage space. Services like Apple's iCloud make up for the fact that its devices don't have ports or disk drives. Rather than storing (or backing up) to a drive you can hold in your hand, you transfer those files to your space on a cloud-based computer via the Internet. (See the "Back-up software" section, later in this chapter.) My own tablet came with cloud storage provided by its manufacturer, Asus; an image of this service is shown in Figure 3-2.

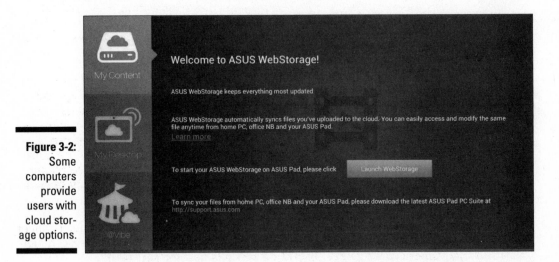

Figure 3-2:
Some computers provide users with cloud storage options.

Use care when posting your sensitive business files in the cloud, including your customer data. You place considerable trust in the company you choose to store your information. Research the company thoroughly; look for online reviews and check newsgroup comments to make sure it hasn't had security breaches.

Be sure to protect your equipment against electrical problems that can result in loss of data or substantial repair bills. At the very least, make sure your home office has grounded three-prong outlets and a *surge suppressor* (also called a surge protector). A common variety is a five- or six-outlet strip that has a protection device built in. Also consider an uninterruptible power supply (UPS), which keeps devices from shutting off immediately in the event of blackouts. Eaton Corp. presents a questionnaire on its website that leads you through the process of selecting just the right UPS device for your device and your needs. Try it out at

```
http://powerquality.eaton.com/UPS/selector/
        SolutionOverview.asp
```

Image capture devices

When you're ready to start creating a web page or putting products up for sale in an online store, think about obtaining a tool for capturing photographic images. (By *capturing,* I mean *digitizing* an image or, in other words, saving it in computerized, digital format.) Photos are often essential elements of business web pages: They attract a customer's attention, they illustrate items for sale, and they can provide before-and-after samples of your work. If you're an artist or a designer, having photographic representations of your work is vital.

Digital displays such as computer monitors and digital cameras display graphic information that consists of little units — *pixels*. Each pixel appears onscreen as a small dot — so small that it's hard to see with the naked eye unless you magnify an image to look at details closely. Together, the patterns of pixels create different intensities of light in an image as well as ranges of color. A pixel can contain one or more bytes of binary information. The more pixels per inch (ppi), the higher a monitor's potential resolution. The higher the resolution, the closer the image appears to a continuous-tone image such as a photo.

Including clear, sharp images on your website greatly increases your chances of selling your product or service. You have two choices for digitizing: a digital camera or a scanner. To decide which is best for you, read on.

Digital camera

Not so long ago, digital cameras cost thousands of dollars. These days, you've probably got a perfectly good one in your pocket, because it comes with your cell phone. Mine has an 8-megapixel camera, which is a high resolution. You can also find a very serviceable camera made by a reputable manufacturer, such as Nikon, Fuji, Canon, Olympus, or Kodak, for around $100 or less. The small investment in this particular tool can pay off for you big time. With the addition of a color printer, you can even print your own photos. Standalone digital cameras often have more controls than cell phone cameras and are worth considering.

Don't hesitate to fork over the extra dough to get a camera that gives you good resolution. Cutting corners doesn't pay when you end up with images that look fuzzy, but you can find many low-cost devices with good features. For example, the Canon PowerShot A2300, which costs about $89, has a resolution of 16 megapixels — fine enough to print on a color printer and enlarge to a size such as 5 x 7 inches — and a zoom feature. Megapixels are calculated by multiplying the number of pixels in an image — for example, 1,984 x 1,488 = 2,952,192 pixels, or 2.9 megapixels. The higher the resolution, the fewer photos your camera can store at any one time because each image file requires more memory.

Having super-high-resolution images isn't critical for web images because they display on computer monitors (which have limited resolution). Before you can display an image on a web browser, you have to compress it by putting it in GIF, PNG, or JPEG format. (See Chapter 5 for more scintillating technical details on GIF, PNG, and JPEG.) Also, smaller and simpler images (as opposed to large, high-resolution graphics) generally appear more quickly on the viewer's screen. If you make your customers wait too long (more than ten seconds or so) for an image to appear onscreen, they're highly likely to go to someone else's online store.

When shopping for a digital camera, look for the following features:

- ✔ The ability to download images to your computer via a FireWire or USB connection
- ✔ Bundled image-processing software
- ✔ The ability to download image files directly to a memory card that you can easily transport to a computer's memory card reader
- ✔ A macro function that enables you to capture clear close-up images
- ✔ An included LCD screen that lets you see your images immediately

Digital photography is a fascinating and technical process, and you'll do well to read more about it in other books, such as *Digital Photography All-in-One For Dummies,* 4th Edition, by David Busch, or *Digital Photography For Dummies,* 6th Edition, by Julie Adair King and Serge Timacheff.

Scanners

Scanning is the process of turning the colors and shapes contained in a photographic print or slide into digital information (that is, bytes of data) that a computer can understand. You place the image in a position where the scanner's camera can pass over it, and the scanner turns the image into a computer document that consists of tiny bits of information — pixels. I find it easiest to use a flatbed scanner. You place the photo or other image on a flat glass bed, just like what you find on a photocopier. An optical device moves under the glass and scans the photo.

The best news about scanners is that they've been around for a while, which, in the world of computing, means that prices are going down while quality is on the rise. Many good scanners are built into printers, so you can buy both in one device. The bargain models sell for under $100, and I've even seen a couple of standalone photo scanners for as low as $59 new.

A type of scanner that has lots of benefits for small or home-based businesses is a multifunction device (also called an all-in-one device). You can find these units, along with conventional printers and scanners, everywhere: at computer outlets, office-supply shops, big-box stores such as Target and Costco, and online through `TigerDirect.com` and many other vendors. I use a multifunction device in my home office that sends and receives faxes, scans images, acts as a laser printer, and makes copies — plus it includes a telephone and answering machine. Now, if it could just make a good cup of espresso. . . .

Getting Online: Connection Options

After computer hardware, Internet connection fees are likely to be the biggest monthly expense you'll encounter in your online business. In the United States (where, unfortunately, it's rare that true fiber-optic connections go to your home or office), the options for most people are cable providers, DSL providers, and wireless networks like 4G LTE systems.

Cable modem

Cable modem connections offer an attractive way to get a high-speed connection to cyberspace. So go ahead and ask your local cable TV providers whether they provide this service. But other options, such as AT&T (`www.att.com`) and EarthLink (`www.earthlink.net`), provide high-speed Internet access through affiliations with cable TV providers in many parts of the country. In my neighborhood in Chicago, a company called RCN Chicago (`www.rcn.com/about-rcn`) offers Internet access via cable modem for $39.99 to $59.99 plus a $5 fee for the cable modem device. AT&T however, offers several U-verse high-speed Internet packages ranging from $4 to $66 per month.

There are many advantages to having a cable modem connection: It's a direct connection, it frees up a phone line, and it's super-fast. Cable modems have the capacity to deliver 4MB or 5MB of data per second. But some providers don't tell you what kind of connection you're getting: You might pay for the speed of the connection instead. Currently, AT&T provides a connection of up to 6.0 Mbps for $24.95 per month, which is a good deal.

Of course, the speed is less than this because you're sharing access with other users. Plus you have to purchase or lease the cable modem, pay an installation fee, and purchase an Ethernet card (if your computer doesn't already have one installed). A cable modem is far faster than a dial-up connection, though.

You can compare cable modem and DSL providers cover your area by visiting the MyRatePlan website:

```
www.myrateplan.com/internet/cable_modem.php
```

DSL

If your telephone company offers its customers Digital Subscriber Line (DSL) connections, you may be able to get a connection that approaches the speed of cable. With DSL, you can use your existing, conventional phone lines rather than have to install a new line to your house. That's because DSLs "borrow" the part of your phone line that your voice doesn't use, the part that transmits signals of 3,000 Hz (hertz) or higher. DSLs can *upload* (send) data to another location on the Internet at up to 6.0 Mbps (megabits per second) and *download* (receive) data at up to 2.560 Mbps. (Yours may get half that speed, though, depending on your location.)

DSL comes in different varieties. Asymmetrical Digital Subscriber Line (ADSL) transmits information at different speeds, depending on whether you're sending or receiving data. Symmetrical Digital Subscriber Line (SDSL) transmits information at the same speed in both directions. As DSL gets more popular, it becomes more widely available and the pricing drops. As of this writing, EarthLink DSL is available for just $14.95 per month (for the first three months) with free DSL modem and installation. Your local phone provider might offer DSL, too. AT&T has a DSL option for just $14.95 per month for the first three months plus 5 percent off a DSL modem.

Smartphone

One of the most convenient ways to get online, when I'm on the road, is through my smartphone, which has 4G LTE web access. Originally, I had unlimited data usage from my provider, Verizon. That service has since been discontinued, and I get 2GB of data per month. I'm on the phone all the time, checking my Gmail, my webmail, and even posting on my blog occasionally.

For an online businessperson, a cell phone is a necessity. A smartphone enables you to respond quickly to queries from customers who visit your website and ask questions about your products and services.

The big phone providers can give you wireless Internet access wherever you are. A portable wireless hotspot like Verizon's MiFi costs $167 on Amazon. com at this writing. If you purchase a new two-year service contract through Amazon Wireless (`http://wireless.amazon.com`), however, the device costs only one cent. It connects to Verizon's 4G LTE network and acts as a wireless modem. You can connect to it with your smartphone, tablet, or any computing device that uses Wi-Fi.

Software Solutions for Online Business

One of the great things about starting an Internet business is that you get to use Internet software. The programs you use online are inexpensive (sometimes free), easy to use and install, and continually being updated.

Although you probably already have basic software to help you find information and communicate with others in cyberspace, the following sections describe some programs that may come in handy when you create your online business.

Don't forget to update your homeowner's or renter's insurance by sending your insurer a list of new software (and hardware) or even by purchasing insurance specifically for your computer-related items from a company such as Safeware. With homeowner's or renter's insurance, some accidents are not covered, and you don't always get replacement coverage for items such as computers. Check with your insurance provider to be sure.

Anyone who uses firewall or antivirus software will tell you how essential these pieces of software are for home or business use. Find out more about such software in Chapter 6. See Chapter 18 for suggestions about accounting software — other important software you need.

Web page editor

HyperText Markup Language (HTML) is a set of instructions used to format text, images, and other web page elements so that web browsers can correctly display them. But you don't have to master HTML to create your own web pages. Plenty of programs — web page editors — are available to help you format text, add images, make hyperlinks, and do all the fun assembly steps necessary to make your website a winner. Among the most popular are Adobe Dreamweaver, Adobe GoLive, and Microsoft Expression Web.

Sometimes, programs that you use for one purpose can also help you create web documents: Software you use to create blogs, such as WordPress, can help you format other types of web content. Microsoft Word enables you to save text documents as HTML web pages, and Microsoft Office enables you to export files in web page format automatically.

Taking e-mail a step higher

You're probably very familiar with sending and receiving e-mail messages. But when you start an online business, make sure that e-mail software has some advanced features:

- **Autoresponders:** Some programs automatically respond to e-mail requests with a form letter or document of your choice.
- **Mailing lists:** With a well-organized address book (a feature that comes with some e-mail programs), you can collect the e-mail addresses of visitors or subscribers and send them a regular update of your business activities or, better yet, an e-mail newsletter.
- **Quoting:** Almost all e-mail programs let you quote from a message to which you're replying so that you can respond easily to questions.
- **Attaching:** Attaching a file to an e-mail message is a quick and convenient way to transmit information from one person to another.
- **Signature files:** Make sure your e-mail software automatically includes a simple electronic signature at the end. Use this space to list your company name, title, and website URL.

Both Outlook (the e-mail component of Microsoft Internet Explorer) and Thunderbird (associated with the web browser Mozilla Firefox) include most or all these features. These functions are essential aspects of providing good customer service; I discuss them in detail in Chapter 8.

Image editors

You need a graphics-editing program either to create original artwork for your web pages or to crop and adjust your scanned images and digital photographs. If you're adjusting or cropping photographic image files, the software you need almost always comes bundled with your scanner or digital camera, so you don't need to buy separate software for that.

If you're creating original artwork, three programs I recommend are Adobe Photoshop Elements (www.adobe.com/products/photoshop-elements. html), LView Pro by Leonardo Haddad Loureiro (www.lview.com), and PaintShop Pro by Corel (www.corel.com). You can download all these programs from the Web to use on a trial basis. After the trial period is over, you pay a small fee to the developer to register and keep the program. Photoshop Elements costs $99.95, LView Pro version 2006 costs $29.95, and PaintShop Pro X5 costs $59.95.

The ability to download and use free (and almost free) software from shareware archives and many other sites is one of the nicest things about the Internet. Keep the system working by remembering to pay the shareware fees to the nice folks who make their software available to individuals like you and me.

Internet phone software

Skype (pronounced *skipe;* rhymes with *snipe)* is the best known of a group of software programs that provide you with Internet phone service. Skype allows you to talk to other computer users over the Internet, provided that you have a microphone connected to your computer and a headset if your built-in speakers aren't loud enough. Skype gives you a highly cost-effective alternative to long-distance or international phone calls. Skype works best if both parties have a high-speed Internet connection. Skype is convenient and a lot of fun. When one Skype member calls another, the connection is free. In addition, you can

- ✔ Type messages to one individual, either in a real-time "chat"-like session or by typing a message that the individual reads when he or she is back online.

- ✔ Put the Skype logo on your website to help market your business by letting people know you'll speak to them personally, for free.

Giving your customers the chance to "meet" you in person, at least virtually, helps build their trust. Find out more at www.skype.com.

Back-up software

Losing copies of your personal documents is one thing, but losing files related to your business can hit you hard in the wallet. That makes it even more important to make back-ups of your online business computer files. Iomega Prestige or eGo drives (http://go.iomega.com) come with software that lets you automatically make backups of your files. If you don't own one of these programs, I recommend you become familiar with the back-up program included with Windows XP or look into Backup Exec 2012 by Symantec Corporation:

```
www.symantec.com/products/data-backup-software
```

Or just buy a USB flash drive that holds 4GB or more of information and use that to back up your files.

Instead of (or along with) purchasing a disk drive to back up your files, you can store your files in an online "cloud." Cloud computing is all the rage these days. A *cloud* is a huge storage space on a server provided by an online provider. Perhaps the best-known example is Google. Google not only gives people access to many gigabytes' worth of e-mail storage space through its Gmail service, but also gives Gmail users free access to a service called Google Docs (`docs.google.com`). Google Docs lets you work on Google's servers, doing word processing and spreadsheet computing while storing your files online so that you can access them from anywhere you have an Internet connection. Some service providers provide space in the cloud (that is, on their servers) specifically for storage and backup. These include Microsoft's SkyDrive (`skydrive.live.com`), which gives you 7GB of free storage space, and Box (`www.box.com`), which has a free option with up to 50GB of space or 1000GB for $15 per month.

Chapter 4

Selecting Your E-Commerce Host and Design Tools

*N*early every business, online or off, needs a storefront where merchandise can be displayed and customers can make purchases. The vast majority of online commercial concerns use their websites as the primary way to attract customers, convey their message, and make sales. Ambitious capitalists use online auction sites such as eBay (www.ebay.com) to make money, but the auctioneers who depend on eBay for regular income often have their own web pages, too — plus storefronts on other hosting sites, where they can gather all the profit without having to pay fees to the auction marketplace.

The success of an online business depends on two important factors: where it's hosted and how it's designed. These factors affect how easily you can create and update your web pages; what special features, such as multimedia or interactive forms, you can have on your site; and even how your site looks. Some hosting services provide web page creation tools that are easy to use but limit the level of sophistication you can apply to the page's design. Other services leave the creation and design up to you. In this chapter, I provide an overview of your storefront hosting options as well as different design approaches that you can implement.

Plenty of web hosting services and software claim they can have your website up and running online "in a matter of minutes" by using a "seamless" process. The actual construction may indeed be quick and smooth — as long as you do all the work beforehand. This preparation work includes identifying your goals for going online, deciding what market you want to reach, deciding what products you want to sell, and writing descriptions and capturing images of those products. Before you jump over to Yahoo! Small Business or Microsoft Small Business Center and start assembling your site, be sure that you do all the groundwork that I discuss in Chapter 2, such as identifying your audience and setting up your hardware.

Getting the Most from Your Storefront Host

An Internet connection and a web browser are all you need if you're primarily interested in surfing through cyberspace, consuming information, and shopping for online goodies. But when you're starting an online business, you're no longer just a consumer; you're becoming a provider of information and consumable goods. Along with a way to connect to the Internet, you need to find a hosting service to make your online business available to prospective customers.

A web hosting service is the online world's equivalent of a landlord. Just as the owner of a building gives you office space or room for a storefront where you can hang your shingle, a hosting service provides you with space online where you can set up shop. A web hosting service may or may not advertise itself as such. On Zazzle (`www.zazzle.com`), for example, you can set up a storefront for free, customize it to your liking, and take advantage of a store-builder utility. Essentially, you're setting up your own website with Zazzle as the host.

Web hosts come in many flavors

Not all web hosting services are intended to help you create your own full-fledged website. They come in different varieties, depending on the type of business you want to run and the amount of control you want to have over your presentation. Here's a look at the most common hosting options.

A big e-commerce marketplace as host

You can operate an online storefront with your business name and a catalog full of browsable items if you sell regularly on eBay, Amazon.com, or another big marketplace that sells a wide variety of merchandise. On eBay, you can create an About Me page or an eBay store; on Amazon, you can open a webstore (`webstore.amazon.com`). In either case, eBay or Amazon itself is your host, and you pay a monthly fee to host your store. See Chapter 14 for more information.

A small specialty marketplace as host

I'm a big fan of small marketplaces that specialize in one type of merchandise. Because they're smaller than the big venues, you generally pay less for hosting, and get more personal support. If you sell handmade crafts, Etsy (www.etsy.com) is an obvious choice. For artists, ArtFire (www.artfire.com) is a good option. Such storefronts are excellent choices for a business that already has a website and wants to expand (or as I say, combine multiple storefronts with social marketing) to improve marketing and reach more customers. See Chapter 15 for more on opening specialty storefronts of this sort.

An e-commerce "shopping cart" service as host

Services like Volusion, Shopify, ZenCart, X-Cart, Ecwid, and other businesses that provide store owners with shopping carts and related services also provide storefronts, hosting, and support for a monthly fee. The term *shopping cart* is somewhat misleading, because these services give you much more than just a system for shopping, making selections, and checking out. You get a full-featured storefront with design templates and phone or e-mail support as well.

A hosting service dedicated to websites as host

If you don't necessarily want to set up an e-commerce storefront (for example, if you do consulting, design, or other professional services rather than individual items), many hosting services are happy to help you create a home page and associated web pages so people can find you online.

What's the difference between a web host like HostGator (www.hostgator.com) and a shopping cart host? Not much. HostGator hosts an e-commerce storefront and gives you a shopping cart. A storefront hosted with Shopify looks just the same as one hosted with HostGator. You might get better customer support and more e-commerce options with a shopping cart host because it specializes in hosting for online businesses. But all these hosts give you space on a web server; a URL so people can find you; and a way to post text, images, and other content online.

You don't need a storefront if you sell by placing ads on Craigslist or if you add merchandise to Amazon.com's marketplace listings, for example.

In all of these cases, a web host provides space on special computers — *web servers* — that are always connected to the Internet. Web servers are equipped with software that makes your web pages visible to people who connect to them by using a web browser. The process of using a web hosting service for your online business works roughly like this:

1. **Decide where you want your site to appear on the Internet.**

Do you want it to be part of a virtual shopping mall that includes many other businesses? Or do you want a standalone site with its own web address that doesn't appear to be affiliated with any other organization?

2. **Sign up with the host.**

   Sometimes you pay a fee. In some cases, no fee is required. In all cases, you're assigned space on a server. Your website gets an address, or *URL,* that people can enter in their browsers to view your pages.

3. **Create your web pages.**

   Usually, you use a web page editor to do this step, although many hosts help by providing a "store builder" or other utility.

4. **Transfer your web page files (HTML documents, images, and so on) from your computer to the host's web server.**

   You generally need special File Transfer Protocol (FTP) software to do the transferring. But many web hosts can help you through the process by providing their own user-friendly software. (The most popular web editors, such as Adobe Dreamweaver, let you do this, too.)

5. **Access your site with your web browser and check the contents to make sure that all images appear correctly and any hypertext links you created go to the intended destinations.**

   At this point, you're open for business — visitors can view your web pages by entering your web address in their web browser's Go To or Address box.

6. **Market and promote your site to attract potential clients or customers, as described in Chapter 10.**

Choose your web host carefully, because the host affects which software you need to use to create your web pages and get them online. The challenge when you're just starting out is to keep an eye on your overall business plan. Think about the site you want to serve as your "home base" and set that up first. Then you can expand to other venues, as described in Chapters 13 and 15.

You can host your own site if you have a direct connection to the Internet, such as through DSL or cable, and are competent with computers (or know someone who is). However, turning your computer into a web server is more complicated than signing up with a hosting service. Your Internet service provider (ISP) may not allow you to set up your own server anyway; check your user agreement first. You need to install server software and set up a domain name for your computer. You also have to purchase a static IP address for your machine. (An *IP address* is a number that identifies every computer that's connected to the Internet; it consists of four sets of numerals separated by dots, such as 206.207.99.1. A *static IP address* is one that doesn't change from session to session.)

If you're just starting a simple home-based or part-time business, hosting your own website is probably more trouble than you care to handle, but you should be aware that it's an option. If you're interested in becoming a webmaster, check out MegaPath (www.megapath.com). This ISP encourages users to set up their own web servers and offers eight static IP addresses with a DSL line for $59.95 per month.

One of the best shortcuts to success is to find a good web servicing host or ISP and then use that company's software tools and service reps when you need help building your website, processing forms, running scripts, and performing similar tasks.

Before you sign up with a host, check out its customer service options. Specifically, find out when the service staff is available by telephone. Also ask whether telephone support costs extra.

A web host called pair Networks (www.pair.com) offers a typical selection of hosting options and has been praised by some technical writers I know. It also provides e-commerce services that go beyond basic hosting arrangements: a *secure server* (a computer that can encrypt sensitive data such as credit card numbers that the customer sends to your site), a shopping card, credit card authorization, and a dedicated server. These services range from $10 to $50 per month.

Instead of getting locked into a long-term contract with a web host, go month to month or sign a one-year contract. Even if you're initially happy with your host, you want a chance to back out if the company takes a turn for the worse or your needs change.

Domain-name registration

Some ISPs also function as domain-name registrars by enabling anyone to purchase the rights to use a domain name for one or more years. Having your own domain name lets you associate the name with your site rather than have to point the name at the server that holds your site.

By *pointing* your domain name at your server, you purchase the rights to a domain name from a registrar. You then need to associate the name with your website so that when people connect to your site, they won't have to enter a long URL such as username.home.earthlink.com. Instead, they'll enter www.mybusiness.com. To do this, you tell the registrar that your domain name should be assigned to the IP address of your server. Your ISP or web host tells you the IP address to give to the registrar.

New domains are available that can provide you an alternative in case your ideal name on the dot-com (.com) domain is unavailable. Even if you do get a dot-com name (.com is still the most recognizable and desirable domain-name extension), you may want to buy the same name with .biz, .info, or .tv at the end so that someone else doesn't grab it.

Marketing utilities

Some people are great at promotion and marketing. Others excel at detail work. If you're not among the lucky people who can do both kinds of business tasks well, find a hosting service that helps you get noticed.

Some hosts, such as Microsoft Office Live 365 (www.microsoft.com/en-us/office365/enterprise-home.aspx), give you access to a variety of marketing services if you sign with it as your host. Not all the services are free, of course.

Catalog creators

Some of the biggest web hosts (such as Yahoo! Small Business) give you software that enables you to create an online sales catalog by using your web browser. You don't have to purchase a web design program, figure out how to use it, and create your pages from scratch.

On the downside, a web-based catalog creation tool doesn't give you ultimate control over how your pages look. You probably can't pull off fancy layout effects with tables or layers. (See Chapter 5 for more on using tables and layers to design your site's web pages.) On the plus side, however, you can use one of these tools to get your pages online quickly.

Database connectivity

If you plan to sell only a few items at a time, your e-commerce site can be a *static* site, which means that every time a customer makes a sale, you manually adjust your inventory. A static site also requires you to update descriptions and revise shipping charges or other details by hand, one web page at a time. By contrast, a *dynamic* e-commerce site presents catalog sales items on the fly (dynamically) by connecting to a database whenever a customer requests a web page.

If you need to create a dynamic website, another factor in choosing a web host is whether it supports the web page and database software you want to use. For Doug Laughter of The Silver Connection, LLC (whom I mention later in this chapter), the choice of host was essential. He wanted to develop his site himself using technologies he was familiar with and regarded highly, such as Microsoft Active Server Pages (ASP) technology. If you use a database program, such as MySQL, you may want to sign up with a web host that allows you to run SQL Server on one of its servers.

Finding a Web Server to Call Home

Hi! I'm your friendly World Wide Web real estate agent. Call me Virtual Larry. You say you're not sure exactly what kind of website is right for you, and you want to see all the options, from a tiny storefront in a strip mall to your own landscaped corporate park? Your wish is my command. Just hop into my 2013-model Mozilla Firefox, buckle your seat belt, and I'll show you around the many different business properties available in cyberspace.

Here's a road map of our tour:

- **Online web-host-and-design-kit combos:** These include Microsoft Office 365, Google Sites, and Yahoo! Small Business, among others.

- **Electronic merchant software that is included with a web hosting package:** One example is ShopSite (discussed later in this chapter).

- **eBay and Amazon:** These two big marketplaces let users create their own About Me web pages or their own stores.

- **Auxiliary companies:** These folks do something that doesn't seem directly related to e-commerce, but they let you build a store online, such as FedEx eCommerce Builder or Chase Instant Storefront.

- **An online marketplace:** You can rent a space on these sites, where you can offer specialty items for sale, such as clothing, artwork, or antiques.

- **Your current Internet service provider (ISP):** Many ISPs are only too happy to host your e-commerce site — for a monthly fee in addition to your access fee.

- **Companies devoted to hosting websites full time:** These are businesses whose primary function is hosting e-commerce websites and providing their clients with associated software, such as web page building tools, shopping carts, and catalog builders.

The first four options combine web hosting with web page creation kits. Whether you buy these services or use them on the web for free, you simply follow the manufacturer's instructions. Most of these hosting services enable you to create your web pages by filling in forms; you never have to see a line of HTML code if you don't want to. Depending on which service you choose, you have varying degrees of control over how your site ultimately looks.

The first two options don't give you a lot of control. You might have to pay fees for hosting or for sales. Online marketplaces give you lower fees, design templates, a shopping cart, and payment methods. But you might not get as many customers as you would on eBay or Amazon.

The last two options (ISPs and full-time web hosts) tend to be do-it-yourself projects. You sign up with the host, choose the software, and create your own site. However, the distinction between this category and the others is blurry. As competition between web hosts grows keener, more and more companies are providing ready-made solutions that streamline the process of website creation for their customers. For you, the end-user, this competition is a good thing: You have plenty of control over how your site comes into being and how it grows over time.

If you simply need a basic website and don't want a lot of choices, go with one of the kits. Your site may look like everyone else's and seem a little generic, but setup is easy, and you can concentrate on marketing and running your business.

Using a marketplace to build your webstore

Virtually all the free web hosting services mentioned in the "Website home-steading for free" sidebar and in the "Finding a Web Server to Call Home" section, both earlier in this chapter, make things easy and affordable for would-be ontrepreneurs (online entrepreneurs). These sites act as both a web host and a web page creation tool. You connect to the site, sign up for service, and fill out a series of forms. Submitting the completed forms activates a script on the host site that automatically generates your web pages based on the data you entered. After you have a site, you can expand to have a storefront in a specialty marketplace. Or you can open a storefront in place of a full-fledged website. Such storefronts include

> ✔ **CafePress** (www.cafepress.com) allows you to easily create and sell music CDs, photos, or artwork online for free. The hard part is deciding what you want to sell, how best to describe your sales items, and how to promote your site.

> ✔ **Babylon Mall** (www.babylonmall.com), which caters to vintage-clothing sellers, charges $15 per month and gives members software that helps them design their storefronts.

Most storefront options provide you with predesigned web pages, called *templates,* that you customize for your particular business. Some types of storefront options provide you with shopping cart systems that enable customers to select items and tally the cost at checkout. Figure 4-1 shows one of the templates offered by PrestaShop, the storefront host used by Paula & Chlo handbags, which is profiled later in this chapter.

You choose a template and customize it with your own photos, store name and logo, and sales information. Figure 4-2 shows the Paula & Chlo home page, which shows a few similarities to the template shown in the preceding image.

Website homesteading for free

Free web hosting is still possible for small businesses. If you're on a tight budget and looking for space on a web server for free, turn first to your ISP, which probably gives you server space to set up a website. You can also check out one of a handful of sites that provide customers with hosting space for no money down and no monthly payments. Instead, you pay in terms of advertising: You may have to include some ads or other things on your site, but if you don't mind that, here are a few good deals you can enjoy:

✔ **Google Apps** (www.google.com/enterprise/apps/index.html): If you have a domain name, you can use Google's services. These include Google's Gmail e-mail service and Google Sites for creating web pages. You can access Google Apps with Internet Explorer, Firefox, and other browsers. You get 10GB of web storage space, too.

✔ **Freeservers** (www.freeservers.com): In exchange for banner ads and pop-up ads, which you're required to display if you set up a website on one of its servers, this site gives you add-ons (such as guest books and hit counters) and an online web page building tool for creating your site — not to mention 50MB of server space.

You can find free web hosting services on Yahoo! here:

```
dir.yahoo.com/Business_and_Economy/Business_to_Business/
      Communications_and_Networking/Internet_and_World_
      Wide_Web/Network_Service_Providers/Hosting/Website_
      Hosting/Free_Hosting
```

Be sure that the site you choose lets you set up for-profit business sites for free.

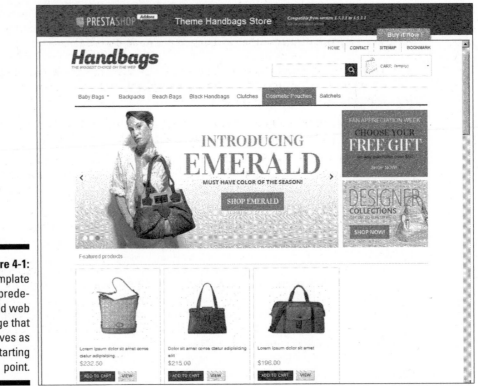

Figure 4-1:
A template is a predesigned web page that serves as a starting point.

Figure 4-2:
The ability to customize a website is a basic feature your host should provide.

Storefront options may also provide an electronic payment option, such as credit card purchases. Usually, you purchase a monthly package and follow a series of steps that mirror the primary aspects of an offline business:

- **The storefront:** This is represented by the web pages that you create. Most options include predesigned web pages that you can copy and customize with your own content.

- **The inventory:** You can stock your virtual storefront shelves by presenting your wares in the form of an online catalog or product list.

- **The delivery truck:** Some storefront packages streamline the process of transferring your files from your computer to the server. Rather than use FTP software, you publish information simply by clicking a button in your web editor or web browser.

- **The checkout counter:** Most electronic storefront packages give you the option of accepting orders by phone, fax, or online with a credit card.

Besides providing you with the software you need to create web pages and get them online, electronic storefronts instruct you on how to market your site and present your goods and services in a positive way. In addition, some programs provide a back room for your business where you can record customer information, orders, and fulfillment. See Chapter 15 for more on setting up shop in one of these specialty marketplaces.

ShopSite

ShopSite, by ShopSite, Inc., isn't software that you purchase and install on your computer. Rather, you find a web hosting service, such as Verio (www. verio.com), that runs ShopSite on its servers. You then set up an account with the host and use the ShopSite software over the Internet, using your web browser. With this kind of setup, which is a *hosted application,* you don't have to worry about having enough memory or hard drive space to run the program yourself. You also don't have to bother with updating or troubleshooting the software; that, too, is the hosting service's responsibility.

To find a hosting service that runs ShopSite, go to the ShopSite website (www.shopsite.com) and scan a list of hosts. You pick a company and arrange for an account. Pricing varies, depending on the host and the version of the service that you want. ShopSite comes in three varieties:

- **Starter:** Lets you create a catalog of only 15 items for sale and 5 web pages. Fees start at $5 per month.

- **Manager:** Gives you an unlimited number of pages, plus templates, themes, a shopping cart, and real-time credit card processing. Fees start at $30 per month.

✔ **Pro:** Adds the ability to track inventory as products are purchased for about $60 per month.

The actual cost for hosting your site plus the additional cost for ShopSite ranges from $5 to $35 per month (Starter) to $60 to $120 per month (Pro).

CASE STUDY

A good host ensures e-commerce success

For Paula Slof, a good e-commerce host provides a business foundation that she can build on. Her hosting service, PrestaShop (www.prestashop.com), gives her the features and platform that she and her web developer can use to customize and develop her Paula & Chlo store (www.paulaandchlo.com).

Developer Stephanie Fredrickson used PrestaShop's templates to design the store and then customized it by using her own code or by installing applications called *modules* that the hosting service makes available to its customers.

"With an online store, the e-commerce host is one of the most important components to running a successful business," says Slof. "Your shopping cart is equivalent to your brick-and-mortar store, your landlord, and your employees. Literally, a good e-commerce host is the difference between success and failure."

A successful online business needs a variety of components to work together, she says:

1. Your e-commerce host

2. Your programmer

3. Your products

4. The appearance and functionality of your site

5. The marketing behind your products and your site

6. Your level of customer service

"I don't think it works without all of these factors in place," says Slof. A host and a good programmer can help you achieve your goals by doing the following, she adds:

✔ **Find a host that sells your products for you.** "You may have great products, but you're online so your customers can't physically touch them. They can't try them on for size or style. They can't feel how soft the leather is on a fabulous handbag you're selling. How do you overcome that? By having great photos and descriptions, and by having a site that sells your product for you. It's like your salesperson."

✔ **Make sure your host drives traffic to your store.** "Even if everything is in place and the site is perfect, without search engine optimization and good marketing, you're goin' nowhere! PrestaShop has built-in SEO, and different modules that we can use to generate SEO. That definitely helps drive traffic to our site."

✔ **Make sure you can customize your site.** "Make sure the host has an open platform that allows you to construct the type of store you're dreaming of."

✔ **Make sure your host has good customer service.** "See if you can talk to a real person who can answer your questions. Some hosts don't even have a phone number; all contact is via the Internet. Often all questions are answered through threads. When you have a 'live' site and you need help immediately, it can be a very bad situation."

✔ **Investigate their payment gateways.** "Verify that they provide you with the methods of payment you want to use."

✔ **Know what it's going to cost you to actually use their service.** "Some hosts charge a fee to use their product and some are free. Even if you are using a free hosting service, there will be additional costs. Make sure you know what they are."

Miva Merchant

Miva Merchant, a competitor of ShopSite, handles all the basics required for an e-commerce storefront, including website templates, a product catalog, electronic payments, inventory tracking, and shipping. It's available on web hosts such as `Hostasaurus.com`. The package lets you go beyond the basics and set up an affiliate program or a mailing list. Find out more at `mivacentral.com`.

Easyhosting

You can also sign up with a host that includes e-commerce software among the services it gives you for a monthly fee. Easyhosting (`easyhosting.com`) includes Easy StoreMaker shopping cart/catalog builder software with its Intermediate and Advanced hosting packages, which start at $49.99 per month.

Moving into an online mall

In addition to website kits, ISPs, and businesses that specialize in web hosting, online shopping malls provide another form of web hosting. You set up your site, either on your own or by using special web page authoring utilities that some malls provide. You pay a monthly fee and transfer your files to the mall's website, and your store appears online. The basic steps are the same with an online mall as with any of the other hosting businesses that I mention in this chapter.

What's the difference, then, between a shopping mall that does web hosting, an ISP that does hosting, and a web hosting service? Their names and the features they offer differ slightly, but they all do essentially the same thing. After you open your virtual business on the web (and as long as you get a custom URL that takes the form www.mybusiness.com), your customers can't always tell whether you're part of America Online, a mall, or a web host such as EarthLink.

What *is* an online shopping mall, anyway? It's a collection of online businesses that are listed in a directory or index provided by a single organization. The directory may be a simple list of stores on a single web page. For larger malls with a thousand stores or more, the online businesses are arranged by category and found in a searchable index.

In theory, an online shopping mall helps small businesses by giving them additional exposure. A customer who shops at one of the mall's stores might notice other businesses on the same site and visit those, too. Some malls function as web hosts that enable their customers to transfer web page files and present their stores online, using one of the mall's web servers. Other malls let people list their business in the mall with a hyperlink, even if the store is actually hosted by another company.

Perhaps the only thing that really distinguishes online malls from other hosting services is presentation:

✔ Some malls, such as Access Market Square (amsquare.com), use the metaphor of a town's market square to organize their businesses. Stores are presented as being on particular parts of the square, but the metaphor is just that; other than the fact that many different owners operate the storefronts, the site is no different from a big marketplace such as Amazon.com.

✔ Another online mall to look into is AOL Shopping (shopping.aol.com), which gathers small and large businesses in one location. You add your products to the shopping area by sending a *feed* — a version of your product catalog that has been converted to the programming language XML (eXtensible Markup Language). Most hosts provide utilities that convert your catalog to a feed so that you can list your products in such areas; make sure that your host does this, too. To find out how to add your products to AOL's shopping area, send an e-mail to AddYourProducts@aol.com.

Consider joining an online mall if you find one that offers an attractive hosting package, particularly if it has web page forms that help you set up your site or create an online catalog quickly. But remember that to web shoppers, it doesn't matter who your host is; what's more important is that you develop compelling content for your site to attract customers and encourage sales.

Amazon.com doesn't look like an online mall, but it has instituted some opportunities for entrepreneurs to sell items on its site. If you don't want to create an entire storefront, you also have the option of selling items individually on the Amazon.com site. You pay fees to list items for sale and for completed sales as well. Find out more by clicking the Selling on Amazon link at the left side of the Amazon.com home page (www.amazon.com).

Turning to your ISP for web hosting

People sometimes talk about ISPs and web hosts as two separate types of Internet businesses, but that's not necessarily the case. Providing users with access to the Internet and hosting websites are two different functions, to be sure, but the same organization may well perform them.

It's natural to ask your ISP first about its web hosting policies for its customers. If you already go online with Comcast, trying out its web hosting facilities makes sense. If you have an Internet access account with the popular ISP EarthLink (www.earthlink.net), by all means consider EarthLink as a web host for your business site.

EarthLink has different web hosting options depending on the kind of account you have. Like most ISPs, however, EarthLink provides web space to its customers so that they can publish web pages that are primarily personal in nature. Yes, you *can* publish a business website, and EarthLink won't complain or cancel your account. But EarthLink really prefers that business users spring for special business services that include oodles of web space; support for forms and *Common Gateway Interface (CGI) scripts* (computer programs that receive the data that someone sends you, such as a customer service request or an order form, and present it in readable form, such as a text file, e-mail message, or an entry in a database); and a "vanity" URL of the www.company.com variety.

EarthLink offers three separate types of web hosting options:

- ✔ **Website Plus** costs $9.97 for the first three months and $19.95 per month thereafter, and gives you 200GB of storage space.
- ✔ **Business Website Plus** costs $17.47 for the first three months and $34.95 per month thereafter, and adds a mobile version of your website.
- ✔ **eCommerce Website Plus** costs $42.47 for the first three months and $84.95 per month thereafter, and adds a mobile site and business phone service.

What should you look for in an ISP web hosting account, and what constitutes a good deal? For one thing, price: A rate of $14.98 per month for 5GB or more of website space is a pretty good deal. Look for a host that doesn't limit the number of web pages that you can create. Also, find one that gives you at least one e-mail address with your account and that lets you add addresses for a nominal fee. Finally, look for a host that gives you the ability to include web page forms on your site so that visitors can send you feedback.

What to expect from an ISP web hosting service

The process of setting up a website varies from ISP to ISP. Here are some general features that you should look for, based on my experience with my own ISP:

- ✓ **Web page editor:** You don't necessarily need to choose a provider that gives you a free web page editor. You can easily download and install the editor of your choice, such as Expression Web or Dreamweaver, to create web pages. (I describe these programs later in this chapter.)

- ✓ **Blog software:** WordPress support should be included so you can create and update your blog if you want to.

- ✓ **Password and username:** When my web pages are ready to go online, I get to use the same username and password to access my website space that I use when I connect to the Internet. Although you don't need to enter a password to view a website through a browser (well, at least at most sites), you do need a password to protect your site from being accessed through an FTP program. Otherwise, anyone can enter your website space and tamper with your files.

- ✓ **FTP software:** When I signed up for a hosting account, I received a CD-ROM containing a basic set of software programs, including a web browser and an FTP program. FTP is the simplest and easiest-to-use software to transfer files from one location to another on the Internet. When I access my website space from my Mac, I use an FTP program — Fetch. From my PC, I have used a program called WS-FTP. CuteFTP (www.cuteftp.com) is another program that many website owners use; it costs $39.99 for Mac users and $59.99 for a Windows version. (I like the free FileZilla even better, however; find it at www.filezilla.com.) Most FTP programs are available for free on the Internet or can be purchased for a nominal fee.

- ✓ **URL:** When you set up a website using your ISP, you're assigned a directory on a web server. The convention for naming this directory is *~username*. The *~username* designation goes at the end of your URL for your website's home page. However, you can (and should) register a shorter URL with a domain-name registrar, such as Network Solutions. You can then "point" the domain name to your ISP's server so that it can serve as an "alias" URL for your site.

After you have your software tools and a user directory on your ISP's web server, it's time to put your website together. Basically, when I want to create or revise content for my website, I open the page in my web page editor, make the changes, save the changes, and then transfer the files to my ISP's directory with my FTP program. Finally, I review the changes in my browser.

What's the ISP difference?

What's the big difference between using a kit, such as Microsoft Office 365 or Yahoo! Small Business, to create your site and using your own inexpensive or free software to create a site from scratch and post it on your ISP's server? It's the difference between putting together a model airplane from a kit and designing the airplane yourself. If you use a kit, you save time and trouble; your plane ends up looking pretty much like everyone else's, but you get the job done faster. If you design it yourself, you have absolute control. Your plane can look just the way you want. It takes longer to get to the end product, but you can be sure that you get what you want.

On the other hand, three differences lie between an ISP-hosted site and a site that resides with a company that does *only* web hosting rather than provides Internet dial-up access and other services:

- ✔ A business that does only web hosting charges you for hosting services, whereas your ISP may not.

- ✔ A web hosting service lets you have your own domain name (www. company.com), whereas an ISP or a service, such as Microsoft Office 365, may not. (Some ISPs require that you upgrade to a business hosting account to obtain the vanity address. See the "What's in a name?" sidebar later in this chapter for more about how web hosting services offer an advantage in the domain-name game.)

- ✔ A web hosting service often provides frills such as super-fast connections, one-button file transfers with your web browser, tons of site statistics, and automatic backups of your web page files.

To find out more about using a real, full-time web hosting service, see the "Going for the works with a web hosting service" section, later in this chapter.

Where to find an ISP

What if you don't already have an ISP, or you're not happy with the one you have? On today's Internet, you can't swing a mouse without hitting an ISP. How do you find the one that's right for you? In general, look for the provider that offers you the least expensive service with the fastest connection and the best options available for your website.

Bigger doesn't necessarily mean cheaper or better; many regional or local ISPs provide good service at rates that are comparable to the giants such as Verio or EarthLink. When you're shopping around for an ISP, be sure to ask the following questions:

✔ What types of connections do you offer?

✔ How many dial-up numbers do you have?

✔ What is your access range? (Do you provide only local coverage, or regional or international coverage as well?)

✔ What type of tech support do you offer? Do you accept phone calls or e-mail inquiries around the clock or only during certain hours? Are real human beings always available on call or are clients sent to a phone message system?

Some websites are well known for listing ISPs by state or by the services they offer. Here are a few starting points in your search for the ideal ISP:

✔ **The List:** This site lists about 8,000 ISPs. You can search the list by area code or by country code, or you can focus on the United States or Canada.

```
thelist.internet.com
```

✔ **Yahoo's List of Internet Access Providers:** This is a good source for directories of national and international ISPs.

```
dir.yahoo.com/Business_and_Economy/Business_to_
     Business/Communications_and_Networking/
     Internet_and_World_Wide_Web/Network_Service_
     Providers/Internet_Service_Providers__ISPs_/
```

Going for the works with a web hosting service

After you've had your site online for a while with a free web host, such as `Freeservers.com`, you may decide you need more room, more services (such as inventory tracking or electronic payments), and a faster connection that can handle many visitors at one time. In that case, you want to locate your online business with a full-time web hosting service.

As the preceding sections attest, many kinds of businesses now host websites. But in this case, I'm defining *web hosting service* as a company whose primary mission is to provide space on web servers for individual, nonprofit, and commercial websites.

What's in a name?

Most hosts assign you a URL that leads to your directory (or folder) on the web server. For example, the typical personal account with an ISP includes space on a web server where you can store your web pages, and the address looks like this:

`http://homepage.speakeasy.net/~gholden`

This is a common form of URL that many web hosts use. It means that your web pages reside in a directory called `~gholden` on a computer named `homepage`. The computer, in turn, resides in your provider's domain on the Internet: `speakeasy.net`.

However, for an extra fee, some web hosts allow you to choose a shorter domain name, provided the one you want to use isn't already taken by another site. For example, if I paid extra for a full-fledged business site, my provider would have let me have a catchier, more memorable address, like this:

`www.gregholden.com`

What to look for in a web host

Along with providing lots of space for your HTML, image, and other files (typically, you get anywhere from 100GB to 500GB of space), web hosting services offer a variety of related services, including some or all of the following:

- **E-mail addresses:** You can likely get several e-mail addresses for your own or your family members' personal use. Besides that, many web hosts give you special e-mail addresses called *autoresponders*. These are e-mail addresses, such as `info@yourcompany.com`, that you can set up to automatically return a text message or a file to anyone looking for information.

- **Domain names:** Virtually all the hosting options that I mention in this chapter give customers the option of obtaining a short domain name, such as `www.mycompany.com`. But some web hosts simplify the process by providing domain-name registration in their flat monthly rates.

- **Web page software:** Some hosting services include web page authoring/editing software, such as Adobe Dreamweaver. Some web hosting services even offer web page forms that you can fill out online to create your own online shopping catalog. All you have to provide is a scanned image of the item you want to sell, along with a price and a description. You submit the information to the web host, which then adds the item to an online catalog that's part of your site.

- **Multimedia/CGI scripts:** One big thing that sets web hosting services apart from other hosts is the ability to serve complex and memory-intensive content, such as RealAudio sound files or RealVideo video clips. They also let you process web page forms that you include on your site by executing CGI scripts. See Chapter 6 for more about how to set up and use forms and other interactive website features.

✔ **Shopping cart software:** If you want to sell specific items online, look for a web host that can streamline the process for you. Most organizations provide web page forms that you can fill out to create sale items and offer them in an online shopping cart, for example.

✔ **Automatic data backups:** Some hosting services automatically back up your website data to protect you against data loss — an especially useful feature because disaster recovery is important. The automatic nature of the backups frees you from the worry and trouble of doing it manually.

✔ **Site statistics:** Virtually all web hosting services also provide you with site statistics that give you an idea (perhaps not a precisely accurate count, but a good estimate) of how many visitors you have received. Even better is access to software reports that analyze and graphically report where your visitors are from, how they found you, which pages on your site are the most frequently viewed, and so on.

✔ **Blogging software:** WordPress is the standard, and your host should make it available to you if you want to operate a business blog.

✔ **Shopping and electronic commerce features:** If you plan to give your customers the ability to order and purchase your goods or services online by credit card, be sure to look for a web host that provides you with secure commerce options. For a more detailed discussion of secure electronic commerce, see Chapter 6.

Having so many hosting options available is the proverbial blessing and curse. It's good that you have so many possibilities and that the competition is so fierce because that can keep prices down. On the other hand, deciding which host is best for you can be difficult. In addition to asking about the preceding list of features, to help narrow the field, here are a few more questions to ask prospective web hosts about their services:

✔ **Do you limit file transfers?** Many services charge a monthly rate for a specific amount of electronic data that is transferred to and from your site. Each time a visitor views a page, that user is actually downloading a few kilobytes of data in order to view it. If your web pages contain, say, 1MB of text and images and you get 1,000 visitors per month, your site accounts for 1GB of data transfer per month. If your host allocates you less than 1GB per month, it probably charges you extra for the amount you go over the limit.

✔ **What kind of connection do you have?** Your site's web page content appears more quickly in web browser windows if your server has a super-fast T1 or T3 connection. Ask your ISP what kind of connection *it* has to the Internet. If you have a DSL line, speeds differ depending on the ISP: You might get a fast connection (1.5Mbps) or a more common, slower one (684Kbps). Make sure that you're getting the fastest connection you can afford.

✔ **Will you promote my site?** Some hosting services (particularly online shopping malls) help publicize your site by listing you with Internet search indexes and search services so that visitors are more likely to find you.

Other obvious questions that you would ask of any contractor apply to web hosting services as well, such as "How long have you been in business?" and "Can you suggest customers who will give me a reference?"

The fact that I include a screen shot of a particular web hosting service's site in this book doesn't mean that I'm endorsing or recommending that particular organization. Shop around carefully and find the one that's best for you. Check out the hosts with the best rates and most reliable service. Visit some other sites that they host, and e-mail the owners of those sites for their opinion of their hosting service.

Finding a host that makes your business dynamic

What kinds of technologies do you need from a web host to run an online business? For Doug Laughter of The Silver Connection, LLC, which sells sterling silver jewelry imported from around the world (www.silverconnection.com), the right technologies help his online store run smoothly. For one thing, a control panel should be available to help you administer your site, he says.

Q. What kinds of questions should small business owners and managers ask when they're shopping for a hosting service? What kinds of features should they be looking for initially?

A. I would first suggest considering how you want to develop your website. Today's business site needs to be dynamic in nature, so the business needs to research and determine what web server application it will use. A web server application consists of the following:

✔ **Server-side technology:** Active Server Pages (ASP, ASP.NET); ColdFusion; Java Server Pages; PHP; XML

✔ **Database solution:** Microsoft SQL Server, MS Access, MySQL, Oracle

✔ **Server application:** IIS, Apache, iPlanet, Sun Java System Web Server

✔ **Operating Platform:** Windows, Unix

So the decision about how the e-commerce website will be developed and in what technology is a key decision to make from the onset. After this is decided, choose a web host that supports your environment of choice.

Q. After the development platform is determined, what features should you look for?

A. Look for essentials that are wholesale elements to develop, maintain, and enhance the web presence. These items are common with most hosting plans but always need attention paid to them. This cursory list includes web disk space, bandwidth limitations, FTP and mail accounts, site statistics, backup plans, merchant applications with payment gateways, and other customary plan offers. Finally, make sure there's an application that can analyze traffic, such as Webtrends.

Competition is tough among hosting services, which means that prices are going down. But it also means that hosting services may seem to promise the moon to get your business. Be sure to read the fine print and talk to the host before you sign a contract, and always get statements about technical support and backups in writing.

What's it gonna cost?

Because of the ongoing competition in the industry, prices for web hosting services vary widely. If you look in the classified sections in the back of magazines that cover the web or the whole Internet, you'll see ads for hosting services costing from $9.95 to $24.95 per month. Chances are, these prices are for a basic level of service: web space, e-mail addresses, domain name, and software. This may be all you need.

The second level of service provides CGI script processing, the ability to serve audio and video files on your site, regular backups, extensive site statistics, and consultants who can help you design and configure your site. This more sophisticated range of features typically runs from $20 to $75 or more per month. At Verio, for example, you can conduct secure electronic commerce on your site as part of hosting packages that begin at $19.95 per month. Its e-commerce packages include the ShopSite software mentioned earlier in this chapter.

Fun with Tools: Choosing a Web Page Editor

A woodworker has a favorite hammer and saw. A cook has an array of utensils and pots and pans. Likewise, a website creator has software programs that facilitate the presentation of words, colors, images, and multimedia in web browsers.

These days, many store owners don't worry about web editors and HTML. They use their storefront's design software or a program like WordPress (which allows you not only to create a blog but to manage and create a full-featured site) to do their editing. But web page editors give you the ultimate amount of control, and even if you use WordPress, you might have to enter some HTML manually once in a while. The "dashboard" view of my own WordPress website is shown in Figure 4-3.

A little HTML is a good thing — but just a little. Knowing HTML comes in handy when you need to add elements that web page editors don't handle. Some programs, for example, don't provide you with easy buttons or menu options for adding `<meta>` tags, which enable you to add keywords or descriptions to a site so that search engines can find them and describe your site correctly.

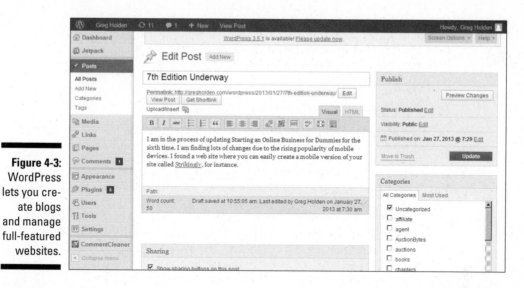

Figure 4-3:
WordPress lets you create blogs and manage full-featured websites.

If you really want to get into HTML or find out more about creating web pages, read *HTML, XHTML & CSS For Dummies,* 7th Edition, by Ed Tittel and Jeff Noble; or *Creating Web Pages For Dummies,* 9th Edition, by Bud Smith.

It pays to spend time choosing a web page editor that has the right qualities. What qualities should you look for in a web page tool and how do you know which tool is right for you? To help narrow the field, I've divided this class of software into different levels of sophistication. Pick the type of program that best fits your technical skill.

For the novice: Use your existing programs

A growing number of word processing, graphics, and business programs are adding HTML to their list of capabilities. You may already have one of these programs at your disposal. By using a program you're already comfortable with, you can avoid having to install a web page editor.

Here are some programs that enable you to generate one type of content and then give you the option of outputting that content in HTML, which means that your words or figures can appear on a web page:

- **Microsoft Word:** The most recent versions of the venerable word processing standby work pretty much seamlessly with web page content. Although most professional web designers would say it generates messy code, it does get the job done for beginners. You can open web pages from within Word and save Word files in web page format.

- ✔ **Adobe PageMaker/Quark Xpress:** The most recent versions of these two popular page layout programs let you save the contents of a document as HTML. Only the words and images are transferred to the web, however; any special typefaces become standard, generic web headings.

- ✔ **Microsoft Office:** The most recent versions of Word, Excel, and PowerPoint give users the option of exporting content to web pages.

- ✔ **WordPerfect and Presentations:** These two component programs within Corel's suite of tools let you save files as an HTML page or a PDF file that you can present on the web. If you chose to present one slide per web page, the program adds clickable arrows to each slide in your presentation so that viewers can skip from one slide to another.

Although these solutions are convenient, they probably won't completely eliminate the need to use a web page editor. Odds are you'll still need to make corrections and do special formatting after you convert your text to HTML.

For intermediate needs: User-friendly web editors

If you're an experienced web surfer and eager to try a simple web editor, make it a program that lets you focus on your site's HTML and textual content, provides you with plenty of functionality, and is still easy to use. Here are some user-friendly programs that are inexpensive (or, better yet, free) and allow you to create a functional website.

The following programs don't include some of the bells and whistles you need to create complex, interactive forms, format a page by using frames, or access a database of information from one of your web pages. These goodies are served up by web page editors that have a higher level of functionality, which I describe in the upcoming section for advanced commerce sites.

BBEdit

If you work on a Mac and you're primarily concerned with textual content, BBEdit is one of the best choices you can make for a web page tool. It lives up to its motto: "It doesn't suck." BBEdit is tailored to use the Mac's highly visual interface, and version 9.2 runs on the Mac OS 10.4 or later. You can use drag-and-drop to add an image file to a web page in progress by dragging the image's icon into the main BBEdit window, for example. Find out more about BBEdit at the Bare Bones Software, Inc., website (`www.barebones.com/products/bbedit/index.html`).

Other good choices of web editors for the Mac are Taco HTML Edit by Taco Software (www.tacosw.com) and PageSpinner by Optima System (www.optima-system.com).

Macromedia HomeSite

HomeSite was an affordable tool for website designers who feel at ease working with HTML code. However, HomeSite is no longer being released or supported by its owner, Adobe Systems. If you can find a copy, though, try it. HomeSite also provides you with step-by-step utilities — *wizards* — to quickly create pages, tables, frames, and JavaScript elements.

CoffeeCup HTML Editor

CoffeeCup HTML Editor, by CoffeeCup Software (www.coffeecup.com), is a popular Windows web page editor that contains a lot of features for a small price ($49). You can begin typing and formatting text by using the CoffeeCup HTML Editor menu options. You can add an image by clicking the Insert Image toolbar button, or use the Forms toolbar to create the text boxes and radio buttons that make up an interactive web page form. You can even add JavaScript effects and choose from a selection of clip art images that come with the software.

CoffeeCup HTML Editor doesn't let you explore database connectivity, add web components, or other bonuses that come with a program like Dreamweaver. But it does have everything you need to create a basic web page.

Nvu

When I read reviews of web page software, I don't often see Nvu included in the list. But to me, it's an ideal program for an entrepreneur on a budget. Why? Let me spell it out for you: F-R-E-E.

Nvu is the successor to Mozilla Composer, a web page editing and authoring tool that came with the full version of the Mozilla browser suite. Although Mozilla no longer supports Composer, you can download Nvu for free at http://net2.com/nvu. The software was developed by using Composer's original source code. With Nvu, you can create sophisticated layout elements, such as tables (which I discuss further in Chapter 5), with an easy-to-use graphical interface. After you edit a page, you can preview it in Firefox with the click of a button. In my opinion, it's worth going through a few extra steps to try this program.

Editors that'll flip your whizzy-wig

Web browsers are multilingual; they understand exotic-sounding languages, such as FTP, HTTP, and GIF, among others. But English is one language browsers don't speak. Browsers don't understand instructions, such as "Put that image there" or "Make that text italic." HyperText Markup Language, or HTML, is a translator, if you will, between human languages and web languages.

If the thought of HTML strikes fear into your heart, relax. Thanks to modern web page creation tools, you don't have to master HTML to create web pages. Although knowing a little HTML does come in handy, you can depend on these special user-friendly tools to do almost all your English-to-HTML translations.

The secret of these web page creation tools is their WYSIWYG (pronounced whizzy-wig) display. WYSIWYG stands for "What You See Is What You Get." A WYSIWYG editor lets you see onscreen how your page looks when it's on the web, rather than force you to type (or even see) HTML commands like this:

```
<H1> This is a Level 1 Heading </H1>
<IMG SRC = "lucy.gif"> <BR>
<P>This is an image of Lucy.</P>
```

A WYSIWYG editor, such as CoffeeCup HTML Editor (www.coffeecup.com), shows you how the page appears even as you assemble it. Besides that, it lets you format text and add images by means of familiar software shortcuts such as menus and buttons.

For advanced commerce sites: Programs that do it all

If you plan to do a great deal of business online or add the title of web designer to your list of talents (as some of the entrepreneurs profiled in this book have done), it makes sense to spend some money upfront and use a web page tool that can do everything you want — today and for years to come.

The advanced programs that I describe here go beyond the simple designation of web page editors. They not only let you edit web pages but also help you add interactivity to your site, link dynamically updated databases to your site, and keep track of how your site is organized and updated. Some programs can even transfer your web documents to your web host with a single menu option. This way, you get to concentrate on the fun part of running an online business — meeting people, taking orders, processing payments, and the like.

Dreamweaver

What's that, you say? You can never have enough bells and whistles? The cutting edge is where you love to walk? Then Dreamweaver, a web authoring tool by Adobe (www.adobe.com), is for you. Dreamweaver is a feature-rich, professional piece of software.

Dreamweaver's strengths aren't so much in the basic features, such as making selected text bold, italic, or a different size; rather, Dreamweaver excels in producing Dynamic HTML (which makes web pages more interactive through scripts) and HTML style sheets. Dreamweaver has ample FTP (File Transfer Protocol) settings, and it gives you the option of seeing the HTML codes you're working with in one window and the formatting of your web page in a second, WYSIWYG window. The latest version is a complex and powerful piece of software. A recent version of Dreamweaver MX is shown in Figure 4-4.

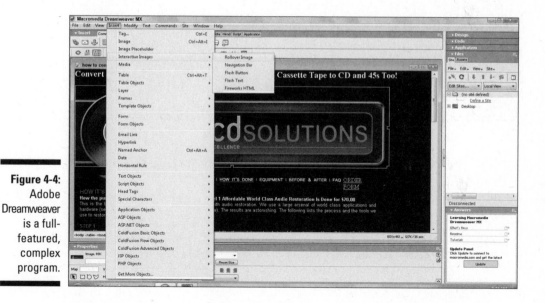

Figure 4-4: Adobe Dreamweaver is a full-featured, complex program.

Dreamweaver lets you create Active Server pages and connect to the ColdFusion database, and it contains lots of templates and wizards. Dreamweaver is available for both Windows and Mac; find out more at the Adobe website (www.adobe.com/products/dreamweaver).

Microsoft Expression Web

Expression Web is a user-friendly yet powerful editor that has strong support for Cascading Style Sheets (CSS), a technology that allows you to format multiple web pages consistently by using standard commands that all web browsers can interpret. The program (`www.microsoft.com/en-us/download/details.aspx?id=36179`) also lets you develop websites with ASP.NET and XML markup. Expression Web includes Dynamic Web Templates — sets of web pages that have master areas that appear on each web page. If you make a change to the master area, the change is carried out through the whole site.

A related program from Microsoft, Silverlight, works in tandem with Expression Web and lets you create sites using Extensible Application Markup Language (XAML). Find Silverlight at `www.microsoft.com/silverlight`. Check out *Silverlight 4 For Dummies*, by Mahesh Krishnan and Philip Beadle, to find out all about Silverlight.

Part II
Creating a Business Website

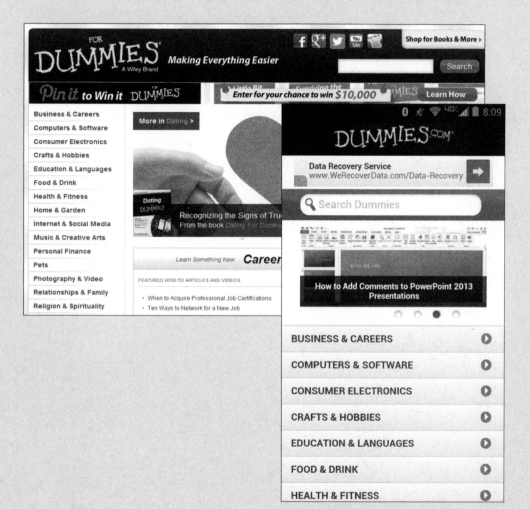

Find out more about website social marketing and storefronts at www.dummies.com/extras/startinganonlinebusiness.

In this part . . .

- ✔ Organize both desktop and mobile websites so customers and clients can easily navigate them.

- ✔ Learn about the essential elements every online storefront needs to make shopping easy.

- ✔ Discover options for accepting credit card and other payments from your customers.

- ✔ Enhance your website or store with customer service and effective communication that builds loyalty and promotes regular visits and sales.

- ✔ Identify the products you want to sell and sources for finding merchandise so you can resell it at a profit.

Chapter 5

Organizing Your Business Presence and Attracting Customers

No matter what you sell or where you sell it — on the web, in a brick-and-mortar store, or even on Facebook — you need to have a home base on the web, a *presence*. Not so long ago, a "home base" on the web automatically meant a website. A website is important, but you can sell online without one. That's why I use the term *presence* instead of *site*.

It's a subtle but significant difference. A presence can include a blog, ads on Craigslist, exposure for your app on iTunes, or storefronts on a variety of marketplaces.

Wherever you do business, the same basic principles work on the web just as well as they do in the brick-and-mortar world. Attracting customers is important, but real success comes from establishing relationships with customers who come to trust you and rely on you for providing excellent products and services.

This chapter focuses on creating an organized website as part of an overall presence to attract not only first-time, but also return customers. In this chapter, you explore ways to achieve these goals, including making your site easy to navigate, creating compelling content, optimizing your images so they appear quickly, and building interactivity into your site so customers want to return on a regular basis.

You might think a single website is your ultimate goal. But if you want your online business to be a source of full-time income or if you hope to be in business for years to come, a website is just the start. Like many ontrepreneurs, you might decide to have multiple presences in different marketplaces, as described in Chapters 14–16. The techniques described in this chapter apply to those storefronts, too.

Feng Shui-ing Your Website

Feng Shui is the art of arranging objects in an environment to achieve (among other things) success in your career, wealth, and happiness. If that's true, try practicing some Feng Shui with your online business environment — that is, your website.

Although you may be tempted to jump right into the creation of a cool website, take a moment to plan. Whether you're setting off on a road trip across the nation or building a new addition on your house, you'll progress more smoothly by first drawing a map of where you want to go. Dig down into your miscellaneous drawer until you find pencil and paper, and make a list of the elements you want to have on your site.

Look over the items on your list and break them into two or three main categories. These main categories will branch off your *home page,* which functions as the grand entrance for your online business site. You can then draw a map of your site similar to the one shown in Figure 5-1.

Note: The page heading Background Information is a placeholder for detailed information about some aspect of your online business. For my brother Mike's audio restoration business, I suggested he include a page of technical information listing the equipment he uses and describing the steps he takes to process audio. You can write about your experience with and your love for what you buy and sell, or anything else that personalizes your site and builds trust.

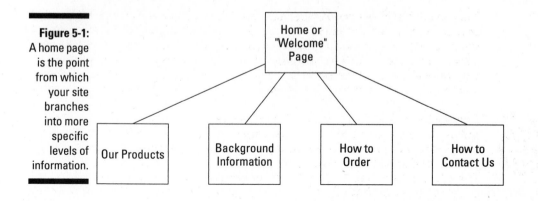

Figure 5-1:
A home page
is the point
from which
your site
branches
into more
specific
levels of
information.

The preceding example results in a very simple website. But there's nothing
wrong with starting out simple. When my brother was creating his first
website, he was intimidated by getting started, and this simple model worked
well. Many other businesses start with a three-layered organization for their
websites. This arrangement divides the site into two sections, one about the
company and one about the products or services for sale, as shown in
Figure 5-2.

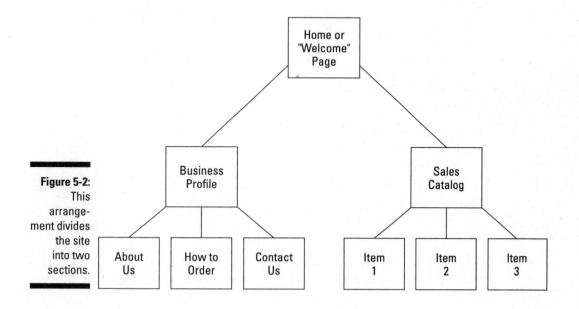

Figure 5-2:
This
arrange-
ment divides
the site
into two
sections.

Think of your home page as the lobby of a museum, where a friendly person at the information desk hands you a list of the special exhibits you can visit that day and shows you a map so you can figure out how you're going to get from here to there. Remember to include the following items on your home page:

✔ The name of the store or business

✔ Your logo, if you have one

✔ Links to the main areas of your site or, if your site isn't overly extensive, to every page

✔ Links to your presences online — your Facebook or Twitter page, or any storefronts you have

✔ Contact information, such as your e-mail address, phone/fax numbers, and (optionally) your business address so that people know where to find you in the Land Beyond Cyberspace

A mobile version of a website strips away most or all of the images and colors and simply presents the content. The presentation needs to be as straightforward as possible so that pages load quickly on a mobile device. Forget about animations or multiple columns. Isolate your most important links in a single one-column page that is easy to read on a smartphone. Figure 5-3 shows a possible arrangement.

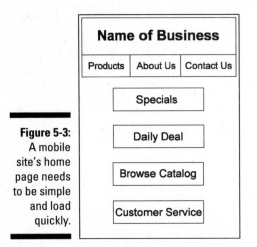

Figure 5-3:
A mobile site's home page needs to be simple and load quickly.

Some sites are "smart" enough to present a limited amount of content depending on whether a touch-enabled device such as an iPad is being used. For example, go to `http://touch2.groupon.com` to see a version of Groupon's mobile site that has fewer links than Groupon's desktop home page (`www.groupon.com`) and only one column. Then go to `http://m.groupon.com` to see an even simpler version with fewer images.

Making them fall in love at first site

First impressions are critical on the web, where shoppers can jump from site to site with a click of their mouse. A few extra seconds of downtime waiting for videos or mini-computer programs — *Java applets* — to download can cause your prospective buyer to lose patience and you to lose a sale. (Keeping your site simple is especially important for mobile device users.)

How do you make visitors to your welcome page feel like they're being greeted with open arms? Here are some suggestions:

- **Remember, less is more.** Don't overload any one page with more than half a dozen images. Keep all images 50KB or less in size. You do this by saving images with a resolution of 72 dpi (dots per inch), as described in "A picture is worth a thousand words," later in this chapter.

- **Find a fast host.** Some web servers have super-fast connections to the Internet and others use slower lines. Test your site; if your pages take 10 or 20 seconds or more to appear, ask your host company why and find out whether it can move you to a faster machine. These days, cable connections of 1MB to 2MB are easy to find and affordable as well.

- **Offer a bargain.** Nothing attracts attention as much as a contest, a giveaway, or a special sales promotion. If you have something you can give away, either through a contest or a deep discount, do it.

- **Provide instant gratification.** Make sure your most important information appears at or near the top of your page. Visitors to the web don't like having to scroll through several screens' worth of material to get to the information they want.

See Chapter 19 for ten ways to make your website ready for mobile devices.

Devising a structure for your website is only one way to organize it — the outer or top-down organizational method, you might say. Organization also comes from the inside — from the content you create. The words, images, and interactive features that help your site get organized are discussed in the following sections.

Creating Content That Attracts Customers

What sells on the web? Look no farther than the search engine you probably use on a regular basis: Google. Google proves that information sells online. Making information easy to find and organizing much of the web's content in one place has helped make this one of the most successful businesses of recent years. When it comes to a business website, you need to present the *right* content in the *right* way to make prospective clients and customers want to explore your site the first time and then come back for more. What, you ask, is the "right" content? The "right" content

- ✔ Helps people absorb information fast
- ✔ Makes it easy for visitors to find out who you are and what you have to offer
- ✔ Is friendly and informal in tone, concise in length, and clear in its organization
- ✔ Helps develop the all-important one-to-one-relationship with customers and clients by inviting dialogue and interaction, both with you and with others who share the same interests

Begin by identifying your target audience. Envision the customers you want to attract and make your site appear to speak directly to them, person to person. Ask around and try to determine what people want from your website. Speak informally and directly to them, by using *you* rather than *we* or *us,* and make sure your site has plenty of action points — links to click, forms to fill out, or product descriptions to view. And follow the general principles outlined in the sections that follow.

Consider doing what professional marketing consultants do and write detailed descriptions of the individuals you're trying to reach. Make your customer profiles complete with fictitious names, ages, job descriptions, type of car they drive, and so on. The more detailed you get, the better you can tailor your content to those people.

Following the KISS principle: Keep it simple, sir (or sister)

Studies of how information on a web page is absorbed indicate that people don't really read the contents from top to bottom (or left to right, or frame to frame) in a linear way. In fact, most web surfers don't *read* in the traditional sense at all. Instead, they browse so quickly you'd think they have an itchy mouse finger. They "flip through pages" by clicking link after link. More and more Internet users are swiping their index fingers on tablets, smartphones, and even cars with Internet-ready computer systems. Because your prospective customers don't necessarily have tons of computing power or hours' worth of time to explore your site, the best rule is to *keep it simple.*

Blogs and Twitter posts are simple and easy to read. They are also ideally suited for harried customers. You can use both to market your products or services. See Chapter 13 for more on these social networking/marketing strategies.

People who are looking for things on the web are often in a state of hurried distraction. Think about a TV watcher browsing during a commercial or a parent stealing a few moments on the computer while the baby naps. Imagine this person surfing while standing on a platform waiting for a train. He isn't in the mood to listen while you unfold your fondest hopes and dreams for success, starting with playing grocery-store cashier as a toddler. Attract him immediately by answering these questions:

- ✔ Who are you, anyway?
- ✔ All right, so what is your main message or mission?
- ✔ Well, then, what do you have here for me?
- ✔ Why should I choose your site to investigate rather than all the others that seem to be about the same?

When it comes to web pages, it pays to put the most important components first: who you are, what you do, how you stand out from any competing sites, and your contact information.

People who visit a website give that site less than a minute (in fact, I've heard only 20 seconds).

If you have a long list of items to sell, you probably can't fit everything you have to offer right on the first page of your site. Even if you could, you wouldn't want to: It's better to prioritize the contents of your site so that the "breaking stories" or the best contents appear at the top, and the rest of what's in your catalog is arranged in order of importance.

Think long and hard before you use features that may scare people away instead of wow them, such as a splash page that contains only a logo or short greeting and then reloads automatically and takes the visitor to the main body of a site. I also don't recommend loading your home page with Flash animations or Java applets that take your prospective customers' browsers precious seconds to load or that might not appear on an iPad, which doesn't support Flash.

Striking the right tone with your text

Business writing on the web differs from the dry, linear report writing of the corporate world. So this is your chance to express the real you: Talk about your fashion sense or your collection of salt and pepper shakers. Your business also has a personality, and the more striking you make its description on your web page, the better. Use the tone of your text to define what makes your business unique and what distinguishes it from your competition.

Satisfied customers are another source of endorsements. Ask your customers whether they're willing to provide a quote about how you helped them. If you don't yet have satisfied customers, ask one or two people to try your products or services for free, and then, if they're happy with your wares, ask permission to use their comments on your site. Your goal is to get a pithy, positive quote that you can put on your home page or on a page specifically devoted to quotes from your clients.

Making your site easy to navigate

Imagine prospective customers arriving at your website with only a fraction of their attention engaged. Making the links easy to read and in obvious locations makes your site easier to navigate. Having a row of clickable buttons at the top of your home page, each pointing to an important area of your site, is always a good idea. Such navigational pointers give visitors an idea of what your site contains in a single glance and immediately encourage them to click a primary subsection of your site and explore further. By placing an interactive table of contents up front, you direct surfers right to the material they're looking for.

The links to the most important areas of a site can go at or near the top of the page on either the left or right side. The Dummies.com home page, as shown in Figure 5-4, has a few links just above the top banner, but also sports links down *both* the left and right sides.

Figure 5-4: Putting at least five or six links near the top of your home page is a good idea.

TECHNICAL STUFF

Navigation can help with marketing: If you want to be ranked highly by search engines (and who doesn't?), you have another good reason to place your site's main topics near the top of the page in a series of links. Some search services index the first 50 or so words on a web page. Therefore, if you can get lots of important keywords included in that index, the chances are better that your site will be ranked highly in a list of links returned by the service in response to a search. See Chapter 11 for more on embedding keywords.

On a tablet or other mobile device, you need to arrange the most important links without flashy graphics. Look at the mobile version of the same Dummies.com home page in Figure 5-5. You don't have to design a simplified mobile version of your home page from scratch (although you can do so at `www.striking.ly`). Just make sure the marketplace or hosting service you choose automatically creates a mobile version of your site for you, as described in Chapter 4.

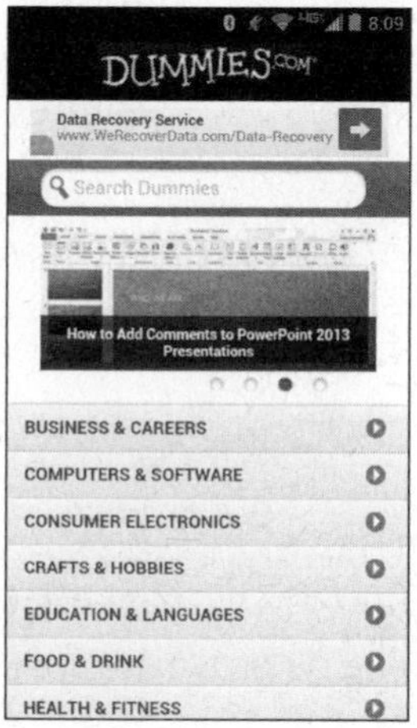

Figure 5-5:
Simple navigation on a mobile site helps you reach visitors who are on the go.

Open the web page you want to edit and follow these steps to create links to local files on your website by using Dreamweaver, the powerful and popular website creation software by Adobe Systems, Inc. (`www.adobe.com`):

1. **Select the text or image on your web page that you want to serve as the jumping-off point for the link.**

2. **Choose Insert⇨Link or press Ctrl+L.**

   The Link Properties dialog box appears, as shown in Figure 5-6.

3. **In the box in the Link Location section, enter the name of the file you want to link to if you know the filename.**

Figure 5-6:
Enter the
name of
the file you
want to
link to.

If the page you want to link to is in the same directory as the page that contains the jumping-off point, enter only the name of the web page. If the page is in another directory, enter a path relative to the web page that contains the link. Or click the Choose File button, locate the file in the Open HTML File dialog box, and click the Open button.

4. **Click OK.**

   You return to the Composer window. If you made a textual link, the selected text is underlined and in a different color. If you made an image link, a box appears around the image.

Presenting the reader with links up front doesn't just help your search engine rankings, but also indicates that your site is content-rich and worthy of exploration.

CASE STUDY

Building an online presence takes time

Judy Vorfeld, who goes by the *nom de Net* Webgrammar, knows all about finding different ways to attract regular clientele. And she knows how important it is to have good content in a business website. She started the online version of her business, Office Support Services (www.ossweb.com), from her home in Arizona in early 1998. She now has a second business site (www.editingandwritingservices.com) and a third (www.webgrammar.com), which serve as resources for students, educators, writers, and web developers.

I've been following Judy for several years now, and I noticed that she's followed a popular business trend: She started her own blog. Her home page, which is also her blog page, displays photos of flowers, wildlife, and other scenes from her personal life. She knows that on the web, getting personal lets you strike up a relationship with potential clients and builds interest as well as trust. "It's difficult to separate who I am from what I do, and almost everything I do in terms of work is based on some kind of presentation or communication," she comments. "Thus, the photos."

Q. What would you describe as the primary goal of your online business?

A. To help small businesses achieve excellent presentation and communication by copyediting their print documents, books, and websites.

Q. How many hours a week do you work on your business sites?

A. Three to six hours, which includes my syndicated writing tips, surveys, and newsletter, *Communication Expressway* (`www.ossweb.com/ezine-archive-index.html`).

Q. How do you promote your site?

A. I participate in newsgroups, write articles for Internet publications, add my URLs to good search engines and directories, moderate discussion lists and forums for others, offer free articles and tips on my sites, and network locally and on the web.

Q. Has your online business been profitable financially?

A. Yes, although slowly. I rarely raise my rates because my skills seem best suited to the small business community, and I want to offer fees these people can afford.

Q. Who creates your business's web pages?

A. Basic design is done by a web designer, and I take over from there. I want the ability to make extensive and frequent changes in text and design. I do hire someone to format my e-zine pages, graphics, and programming.

Q. What advice would you give to someone starting an online business?

A. I have a bunch of suggestions to give, based on my own experience:

- **Network.** Network with small business people who have complementary businesses and with those who have similar businesses. Also, network by joining professional associations participating in the activities. Volunteer time and expertise. Link to these organizations from your site.

- **Join newsgroups and forums.** Study netiquette first. Lurk until you can adequately answer a question or make a comment. Also, keep on the lookout for someone with whom you can build a relationship, someone who might mentor you and be willing to occasionally scrutinize your site, news releases, and so on. This person must be brutally honest, and perhaps you can informally offer one of your own services in return.

- **Learn web development and the culture.** Get a Twitter account (`www.twitter.com`). Subscribe to some blogs at Blogger (`www.blogger.com`). Learn the lingo. Even if you don't do the actual design, you have to make decisions on all the offers you receive regarding how to make money via affiliate programs, link exchanges, hosts, web design software, and so on. Keeping active online and making those judgments yourself is vital unless you thoroughly trust your webmaster. Find online discussion lists that handle all areas of web development, and keep informed.

- **Include a web page that shows your business biography or profile.** Mention any volunteer work you do, groups to which you belong, and anything else you do in and for the community. You need to paint as clear a picture as possible in just a few words. Avoid showcasing your talents and hobbies on a business site unless they're directly related to your business.

(continued)

(continued)

✔ **In *everything* you write, speak to your visitors.** Use the word *you* as much as possible. Avoid the words *I, we,* and *us*. You, as a businessperson, are there to connect with your visitors. You can't give them eye contact, but you can let them know that they matter, that they're (in a sense) the reason for your being there.

✔ **Become known as a specialist in a given field.** Be someone who can always answer a question or go out and find the answer. Your aim is to get as many potential clients or customers to your site as possible, not to get millions of visitors. Forget numbers and concentrate on creating a site that grabs the attention of your target market.

✔ **Get help.** If you can't express yourself well with words (and/or graphics), and know little about layout, formatting, and so on, hire someone to help you. You'll save yourself a lot of grief if you get a capable, trustworthy editor or designer.

She concludes, "Don't start such a business unless you are passionate about it and willing to give it some time and an initial investment. But when you do start, resources are everywhere — many of them free — to help people build their businesses successfully."

Pointing the way with headings

Every web page needs to contain headings that direct the reader's attention to the most important contents. This book provides a good example. The chapter title (I hope) piques your interest first. Then the section headings and subheadings direct you to more details on the topics you want to read about.

Most graphics designers label their heads with the letters of the alphabet: A, B, C, and so on. In a similar fashion, most web page–editing tools designate top-level headings with the style Heading 1. Beneath this, you place one or more Heading 2 headings. Beneath each of those, you may have Heading 3 and, beneath those, Heading 4. (Headings 5 and 6 are too small to be useful, in my opinion.) The arrangement may look like this (I've indented the following headings for clarity; you don't have to indent them on your page):

```
Miss Cookie's Delectable Cooking School (Heading 1)
    Kitchen Equipment You Can't Live Without (Heading 2)
    The Story of a Calorie Counter Gone Wrong (Heading 2)
    Programs of Culinary Study (Heading 2)
        Registration (Heading 3)
        Course Schedule (Heading 3)
            New Course on Whipped Cream Just Added! (Heading 4)
```

You can energize virtually any heading by telling your audience something specific about your business. Instead of "Ida's Antiques Mall," for example, say something like "Ida's Antiques Mall: The Perfect Destination for the Collector and the Crafter." Instead of simply writing a heading like "Stan Thompson, Pet Grooming," say something specific, such as "Stan Thompson: We Groom Your Pet at Our Place or Yours."

Becoming an expert list maker

Lists are simple and effective ways to break up text and make your web content easier to digest. They're easy to create and easy for your customer to view and absorb. Suppose that you import your own decorations and want to offer certain varieties at a discount during various seasons. Rather than bury the items you're offering within an easily overlooked paragraph, why not divide your list into subgroups so that visitors find what they want without being distracted by holidays they don't even celebrate?

Lists are easy to implement. If you're using Microsoft Expression Web (a trial version is available at www.microsoft.com/en-us/download/details.aspx?id=36179), open your web page and follow these steps:

1. **Type a heading for your list and then select the entire heading.**

   For example, you might type and then select the words *This Month's Specials.*

2. **Choose a heading style from the Style drop-down list.**

   Your text is formatted as a heading.

3. **Click anywhere in Expression Web's Design View (the main editing window) to deselect the heading you just formatted.**

4. **Press Enter to move to a new line.**

5. **Type the first item of your list, press Enter, and then type the second item on the next line.**

6. **Repeat Step 5 until you enter all the items of your list.**

7. **Select all the items of your list (but not the heading).**

8. **Choose Format➪Bullets and Numbering.**

   The List Properties dialog box appears.

9. **Choose one of the four bullet styles and click OK.**

   A bullet appears next to each list item, and the items appear closer together onscreen so that they look more like a list. That's all there is to it! Figure 5-7 shows the result.

Figure 5-7:
A bulleted
list is an
easy way
to direct
customers'
attention to
special pro-
motions or
sale items.

Most web editors let you vary the appearance of the bullet. For example, you can make the bullet a hollow circle rather than a solid black dot, or you can choose a rectangle rather than a circle.

Leading your readers on with links

I mean for you to interpret the preceding heading literally, not figuratively. In other words, I'm not suggesting that you make promises you can't deliver on. Rather, I mean that you should do anything you can to lead your visitors to your site and then get them to stay long enough to explore individual pages. You can accomplish this goal with a single hyperlinked word that leads to another page on your site:

More . . .

I see this word all the time on web pages that present a lot of content. At the bottom of a list of their products and services, businesses place that word in bold type: **More . . .** I'm always interested in finding out what more they could possibly have to offer me.

Magazines use the same approach. On their covers you find phrases that refer you to the kinds of stories you find inside. You can do the same kind of thing on your web pages. For example, which of the following links is more likely to get a response?

Next

Next: Paragon's Success Stories

Your web page title: The ultimate heading

When you're dreaming up clever headings for your web pages, don't overlook the "heading" that appears in the narrow title bar at the very top of your visitor's web browser window: the *title* of your web page.

The two HTML tags `<title>` and `</title>` contain the text that appears within the browser title bar. But you don't have to mess with these nasty HTML codes: All web page–creation programs give you an easy way to enter or edit

a title for a web page. Make the title as catchy and specific as possible, but make sure it's no longer than 64 characters, including spaces. An effective title refers to your goods or services while grabbing the viewer's attention. If your business is Myrna's Cheesecakes, for example, you might make your title "Smile and Say Cheese! with Myrna's Cakes" (40 characters, including spaces).

Whenever possible, tell your visitors what they can expect to encounter as a benefit when they click a link. Give them a tease — and then a big payoff for responding.

Enhancing your text with well-placed images

You can add two kinds of images to a web page: an *inline image,* which appears in the body of your page along with your text, or an *external image,* which is a separate file that visitors access by clicking a link. The link may take the form of highlighted text or a small version of the image — a *thumbnail.* You see lots of thumbnails when you do a search for images on Google Images (`http://images.google.com`).

The basic HTML tag that inserts an image in your document takes the following form:

```
<img src="URL">
```

This tag tells your browser to display an image (`<img>`) here. `"URL"` gives the location of the image file that serves as the source (`src`) for this image. Whenever possible, also include `width` and `height` attributes (as follows) because they help speed up graphics display for many browsers:

```
<img height=51 width=48 SRC="target.gif">
```

Most web page editors add the width and height attributes automatically when you insert an image. Typically, here's what happens:

1. **Click the location in the web page where you want the image to appear.**

2. **Click an Image toolbar button or choose Insert⇨Image to display an image selection dialog box.**

3. **Enter the name of the image you want to add and click OK.**

    The image is added to your web page.

A well-placed image points the way to text that you want people to read immediately. Think about where your own eyes go when you first connect to a web page. Most likely, you first look at any images on the page; then you look at the headings; finally, you settle on text to read. If you can place an image next to a heading, you virtually ensure that viewers read the heading.

Making your site searchable

A search box is one of the best kinds of content you can put on your website's opening page. A *search box* is a simple text-entry field that lets a visitor enter a word or phrase. Clicking a button labeled Go or Search sends the search term or terms to the site, where a script checks an index of the site's contents for any files that contain those terms. The script then lists documents that contain the search terms in the visitor's browser window.

Search boxes are not only found, but are expected to be found, on virtually all commercial websites. You usually see them at the top of the home page, near the links to the major sections of the site. Dummies.com, shown in Figure 5-8, includes a search box on the left side of the page.

Search boxes let visitors instantly scan the site's entire contents for a word or phrase. They put visitors in control right away and get them to interact with your site. They're popular for some very good reasons.

 Search boxes require someone with knowledge of computer programming to create or implement a program called a CGI script to do the searching. Someone also has to compile an index of the documents on the website so that the script can search the documents. An application such as ColdFusion works well, but it's not a program for beginners.

Figure 5-8:
Many surf-
ers prefer
using a
search box
to clicking
links.

But you can get around having to write CGI scripts to add search capabilities to your site. Choose one of these options:

✔ **Let your web host do the work.** Some hosting services do the index-ing and creation of the search utility as part of their services. Nearly all shopping carts and e-commerce storefront hosting services do.

✔ **Use a free site search service.** The server that does the indexing of your web pages and holds the index doesn't need to be the server that hosts your site. Some services make your site searchable for free. In exchange, you display advertisements or logos in the search results you return to your visitors.

✔ **Pay for a search service.** If you don't want to display ads on your search results pages, pay a monthly fee to have a company index your pages and let users conduct searches. FreeFind (`www.freefind.com`) has some economy packages, a free version that forces you to view ads, and a professional version that costs $19 per month for a site of 3,000 pages or less and $39 per month for a site of 6,000 pages or less. SiteMiner (`http://siteminer.mycomputer.com`) charges $19.95 per month and lets you customize your search box and re-index your site whenever you add new content.

Make a map of your website

Maps are especially important when navigating the information superhighway. When it comes to your e-commerce website, a map can make your site easier to navigate. A *site map* is a graphical representation of your website — a diagram that graphically depicts all the pages in the site and how they connect to one another. Some web page editing programs, such as the now-defunct Microsoft FrontPage, had a site map function built into them. When you create pages and link them to one another, a site map is created. The following figure shows the site map on the left side of the window and a list of files on the right.

You don't have to invest in a fancy (and expensive) software program to create a site map. You can create one the old-fashioned way, with a pencil and paper. Or you can draw boxes and arrows using a computer graphics program. The point is that your site map can be a useful design tool for organizing the documents within your site.

If your sales are sluggish, make sure that your customers can actually find what they're looking for. Take a typical product in your sales catalog and then visit your own site to see how many clicks someone would need to make to find it. Then see how many clicks that person would need to make to complete the purchase. Eliminating any unnecessary navigational layers (such as category opening pages) makes your site easier to use.

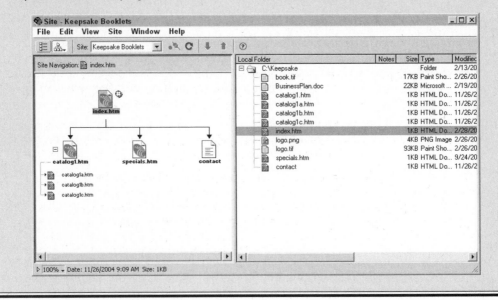

You say you're up to making your site searchable, but you shudder at the prospect of either writing your own computer script or finding and editing someone else's script to index your site's contents and actually do the searching? Then head over to Atomz Site Search (www.atomz.com) and check out its site search hosted application. Other organizations that offer similar services include FreeFind (www.freefind.com), PicoSearch (www.picosearch.com), and Webinator (www.thunderstone.com/texis/site/pages/webinator.html).

Nip and Tuck: Establishing a Visual Identity

The prospect of designing a website may be intimidating if you haven't tried it before. But it really boils down to a simple principle: *effective visual communication that conveys a particular message.* The first step in creating graphics is not to open a painting program and start drawing, but to plan your page's message. Next, determine the audience you want to reach with that message and think about how your graphics can best communicate what you want to say. Some ways to do this are

- **Gather ideas from websites that use graphics well.** Award-winning sites and sites created by designers who are using graphics in new or unusual ways can help you. To find some award winners, check out The Webby Awards (www.webbyawards.com) and the WebAward Competition (www.webaward.org).

- **Use graphics consistently from page to page.** You can create an identity and convey a consistent message.

- **Know your audience.** Create graphics that meet visitors' needs and expectations. If you're selling fashions to teenagers, go for neon colors and out-there graphics. If you're selling financial planning to senior citizens, choose a distinguished and sophisticated typeface.

How do you become acquainted with your customers when it's likely you'll never actually meet them face to face? Find newsgroups and mailing lists in which potential visitors to your site discuss subjects related to what you plan to publish on the web. Read the posted messages to get a sense of the concerns and vocabulary of your intended audience.

Choosing wallpaper that won't make you a wallflower

The technical term for the wallpaper behind the contents of a web page is its *background*. Most web browsers display the background of a page as light gray or white unless you specify something different. In this case, leaving well enough alone isn't good enough. If you choose the wrong background color (one that makes your text hard to read and your images look like they've been smeared with mud), viewers are likely to get the impression that the page is poorly designed or the author of the page hasn't put a great deal of thought into the project.

Most web page–creation programs offer a simple way to specify a color or an image file to serve as the background of a web page. For example, in the free editor Komodo Edit, you Ctrl-click the value next to the background-color command in the style sheet for the page you're working on (the section between the `<style>` and `</style>` tags). When the Color dialog box opens, click the color you want and then click OK. The hexadecimal code for your chosen color is added to the style sheet.

Color your website effective

You can use background and other colors to elicit a particular mood or emotion and convey your organization's identity on the web. The right choice of color can create impressions ranging from elegant to funky.

The basic colors chosen by the United Parcel Service website (www.ups.com) convey to customers that it is a staid and reliable company, and the U.S. Postal Service (www.usps.com) sticks to the patriotic choice of red, white, and blue. In contrast, the designers of the nearly 20-year-old HotHotHot hot sauce site (www.hothothot.com) combine fiery colors to convey a site that sizzles.

When selecting colors for your web pages, consider the demographics of your target audience. Do some research on what emotions or impressions are conveyed by different colors and which colors best match the mission or identity of your business. Refer to resources, such as the online essay "How to Get a Professional Look With Color" by Webdesigner Depot (www.webdesignerdepot.com/2009/12/how-to-get-a-professional-look-with-color), which examines how color choices make web surfers react differently.

The colors you use must have contrast so that they don't blend into one another. For example, you don't want to put purple type on a brown or blue background, or yellow type on a white background. Remember to use light type against a dark background and dark type against a light background. That way, all your page's contents show up.

Tile images in the background

You can use an image rather than a solid color to serve as the background of a page. You specify an image in the style sheet code of your web page, and browsers automatically *tile* the image, reproducing it over and over to fill the current width and height of the browser window.

The fact is that few, if any, professional designers use background images any more. Background images worked only when they were subtle and didn't interfere with the page contents. Often, they were distracting. The emphasis these days is on easily accessible and readable content. Focus on that and make sure the background complements rather than interferes with your page's design. Choose an image with no obvious lines that create a distracting pattern when tiled. The effect you're trying to create should literally resemble wallpaper. Go to Google Images (http://images.google.com) and search for examples of background images that add something to a page's design.

Using web typefaces like a pro

If you create a web page and don't specify that the text be displayed in a particular font, the browser that displays the page uses its default font — which is usually Times New Roman or Helvetica (although individual users can customize their browsers by picking a different default font).

If you want to specify a typeface, the simplest option is to pick a generic font that is built into virtually every computer's operating system. This convention ensures that your web pages look more or less the same no matter what web browser or what type of computer displays them. A few choices available to you are Arial, Courier, Century Schoolbook, and Times New Roman.

However, you don't have to limit yourself to the same-old/same-old. As a web page designer, you can exercise a degree of control over the appearance of your web page by specifying that the body type and headings be displayed in a particular nonstandard font. You have to own the font you want to use; you save it on your computer and identify the font and location in the cascading style sheets (CSS) for your website.

You can copy unusual fonts from dafont.com (www.dafont.com). Its creators sometimes ask for donations for their work. You can generate CSS commands for such typefaces with the aid of Font Squirrel's Webfont Generator (www.fontsquirrel.com/tools/webfont-generator). You then copy and paste the CSS into the style sheet for your page so you can use the font for either headings or body text.

Where do you specify type fonts, colors, and sizes for the text? Again, special HTML tags or CSS commands tell web browsers what fonts to display, but you don't need to mess with these tags yourself if you're using a web page creation tool. The specific steps you take depend on what web design tool you're using. In Dreamweaver, you can specify a group of preferred typefaces rather than a single font in the Properties inspector, as shown in Figure 5-9. If the viewer doesn't have one font in the group, another font displays. Check the Help files with your own program to find out how to format text and what typeface options you have.

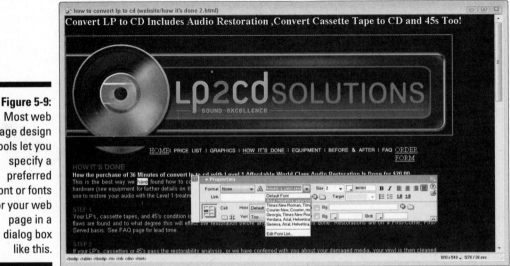

Figure 5-9:
Most web page design tools let you specify a preferred font or fonts for your web page in a dialog box like this.

Not all typefaces are equal in the eye of the user. Serif typefaces, such as Times New Roman, are considered more readable (at least, for printed materials) than sans-serif fonts, such as Helvetica. However, an article on the Web Marketing Today website (`http://webmarketingtoday.com/articles/html-email-fonts`) found that by a whopping 2:1 margin, the sans serif font Arial is considered more readable on a web page than Times New Roman.

If you want to make sure that a heading or block of type appears in a specific typeface (especially a nonstandard one that isn't displayed as body text by web browsers), scan it or create the heading in an image-editing program and insert it into the page as a graphic image. But make sure it doesn't clash with the generic typefaces that appear on the rest of your page.

Using clip art is free and fun

Not everyone has the time or resources to scan photos or create original graphics. But that doesn't mean you can't add graphic interest to your web page. Many web page designers use clip-art bullets, diamonds, or other small images next to list items or major web page headings that they want to call special attention to. Clip art can also provide a background pattern for a web page or highlight sales headings, such as Free!, New!, or Special!.

When I first started in the print publications business, I bought catalogs of illustrations, literally clipped out the art, and pasted it down. It's still called clip art, but now the process is different. In keeping with the spirit of exchange that has been a part of the Internet since its inception, some talented and generous artists have created icons, buttons, and other illustrations in electronic form and offered them free for downloading.

Here are some suggestions for tried-and-true sources of clip art on the web:

- ✔ Clipart.com (`www.clipart.com/en`)
- ✔ Clip Art Universe (`http://clipartuniverse.com`)
- ✔ The Yahoo! page full of links to clip art resources (`http://dir.yahoo.com/computers_and_internet/graphics/clip_art`)

If you use Microsoft Office, you have access to plenty of clip art images that come with the software. In Word, choose Insert⇨Clip Art to open the Insert Clip Art dialog box. If these built-in images aren't sufficient, you can connect to the Microsoft Clip Gallery Live website by clicking the Clips Online toolbar button in the Insert Clip Art dialog box. Web page editors — such as CoffeeCup HTML Editor — come with their own clip art libraries, too.

Be sure to read the copyright fine print *before* you copy graphics. All artists own the copyright to their work. It's up to them to determine how they want to give someone else the right to copy their work. Sometimes, the authors require you to pay a small fee if you want to copy their work, or they may restrict use of their work to nonprofit organizations.

A picture is worth a thousand words

Some customers know exactly what they want from the get-go and don't need any help from you. But most customers love to shop around or could use some encouragement to move from one item or catalog page to another. This is where images can play an important role.

Even if you use only some basic clip art, such as placing spheres or arrows next to sale items, your customer is likely to thank you by buying more. A much better approach, though, is to scan or take digital images of your sale items and provide compact, clear images of them on your site. Here's a quick step-by-step guide to get you started:

1. **Choose the right image to capture.**

   The original quality of an image is just as important as how you scan or retouch it. Images that are murky or fuzzy in print are even worse when viewed on a computer screen.

2. **Preview the image.**

   Digital cameras let you preview images so that you can decide whether to keep or delete individual pictures before downloading to your computer. If you're working with a scanner, some scanning programs let you make a quick *preview scan* of an image so that you can get an idea of what it looks like before you do the actual scan. When you click the Preview button, the optical device in the scanner captures the image. A preview image appears onscreen, surrounded by a *marquee box* (a rectangle made up of dashes), as shown in Figure 5-10.

Figure 5-10:
The mar-
quee box
lets you
crop a pre-
view image
to make it
smaller and
reduce the
file size.

Marquee box

3. **Crop the image.**

   Cropping means that you resize the box around the image to select the portion of the image that you want to keep and leave out the parts of the image that aren't essential. Cropping an image is a good idea because it highlights the most important contents and reduces the file size. Reducing the file size of an image should always be one of your most important goals — the smaller the image, the quicker it appears in some-one's browser window.

Almost all scanning and graphics programs offer separate options for cropping an image and reducing the image size. By cropping the image, you eliminate parts of the image you don't want, and this *does* reduce the image size. But it doesn't reduce the size of the objects within the image. Resizing the overall image size is a separate step, which enables you to change the dimensions of the entire image without eliminating any contents.

4. Select an input mode.

Tell the scanner or graphics program how you want it to save the visual data — as color, line art (used for black-and-white drawings), or grayscale (used for black-and-white photos).

5. Set the resolution.

Digital images are made up of little bits (dots) of computerized information called *pixels*. The more pixels per inch, the higher the level of detail. When you scan an image, you can tell the scanner to make the dots smaller (creating a smoother image) or larger (resulting in a more jagged image). This adjustment is called *setting the resolution* of the image. (When you take a digital photo, the resolution of the image depends on your camera's settings.)

When you're scanning for the web, your images appear primarily on computer screens. Because many computer monitors can display resolutions only up to 72 dpi, 72 dpi — a relatively rough resolution — is an adequate resolution for a web image. Using this coarse resolution has the advantage of keeping the image's file size small. Remember, the smaller the file size, the more quickly an image appears when your customers load your page in their web browsers. (Alternatively, many designers scan at a fine resolution such as 300 dpi and reduce the file size in a graphics program.)

6. Adjust contrast and brightness.

Virtually all scanning programs and graphics editing programs provide brightness and contrast controls that you can adjust with your mouse to improve the image. If you're happy with the image as is, leave the brightness and contrast set where they are. (You can also leave the image as is and adjust brightness and contrast later in a separate graphics program, such as Paint Shop Pro X5, which you can try out by downloading it from the Corel website, www.corel.com/corel.) Or if you're working on the iPhone, check out the Clarity app (http://campl.us/feature/clarity), which dramatically improves so-so images.

7. Reduce the image size.

The old phrase "Good things come in small packages" is never more true than when you're improving your digital image. If you're scanning an image that is 8" x 10" and you're sure that it needs to be about 4" x 5" when it appears on your web page, scan it at 50 percent of the original size. This step reduces the file size and makes the file easier to transport, whether it's from your camera to your computer or your computer to your hosting service. Even more important, it appears more quickly in someone's web browser.

8. **Scan away!**

   Your scanner makes a beautiful whirring sound as it turns those colors into pixels. Because you're scanning only at 72 dpi, the process shouldn't take too long.

9. **Save the file.**

   Now you can save your image to disk. Most programs let you do this by choosing File➪Save. In the dialog box that appears, enter a name for your file and select a file format. (Because you're working with images to be published on the web, remember to save either in GIF or JPEG format.)

Be sure to add the correct filename extension. Web browsers recognize only image files with extensions such as `.gif`, `.jpg`, or `.jpeg`. If you name your image product and save it in GIF format, call it `product.gif`. If you save it in JPEG format and you're using a PC, call it `product.jpg`. On a Mac, call it `product.jpeg`.

For more details on scanning images, check out *Scanners For Dummies,* 2nd Edition, by Mark L. Chambers.

Creating a logo

An effective logo establishes your online business's graphic identity in no uncertain terms. A logo can be as simple as a rendering of the company name that imparts an official typeface or color. Whatever text it includes, a *logo* is a small, self-contained graphic object that conveys the group's identity and purpose. Figure 5-11 shows an example of a logo.

A logo doesn't have to be a fabulously complex drawing with drop shadows and gradations of color. A simple, type-only logo can be as good as gold. Pick a typeface, choose your graphic's outline version, and fill the letters with color.

Figure 5-11:
A good logo effectively combines color, type, and graphics to convey an organization's identity or mission.

GIF, JPEG, and PNG

Website technology and HTML may have changed dramatically over the past several years, but for the most part, there are still only three types of images as far as web pages are concerned: GIF, JPEG, and PNG. All three formats use methods that compress computer image files so that the visual information contained within them can be transmitted easily over computer networks. PNG, a third format designed several years ago as a successor to GIF, is slowly becoming more popular and is far superior in terms of compression and image quality, especially when it comes to photos.

GIF (pronounced either *jiff* or *giff*) stands for Graphics Interchange Format. GIF is best suited to text, line art, or images with well-defined edges. Special types of GIF allow images with transparent backgrounds to be *interlaced* (broken into layers that appear gradually over slow connections) and animated. JPEG (pronounced *jay-peg)* stands for Joint Photographic Experts Group, the name of the group that originated the format. JPEG is preferred for large photos and continuous tones of grayscale or color that need greater compression.

If you have a choice, I suggest you try PNG (Portable Network Graphics). Its images are ideal for the web. The quality is so good that I've even blown up images, printed them on a color inkjet printer, and put them on the wall of my office. And PNG is supported by all the major browsers, so you'll have no problem getting your visitors to enjoy them.

Inviting Comments from Customers

Quick, inexpensive, and *personal:* These are three of the most important advantages that the web has over traditional printed catalogs. The first two are obvious pluses. You don't have to wait for your online catalog to get printed and distributed. On the web, your contents are published and available to your customers right away. Putting a catalog on the web eliminates (or, if publishing a catalog on the web allows you to reduce your print run, dramatically reduces) the cost of printing, which can result in big savings for you.

But the fact that online catalogs can be more personal than the printed variety is perhaps the biggest advantage of all. The personal touch comes from the web's potential for *interactivity.* Getting your customers to click links makes them actively involved with your catalog.

Getting positive e-mail feedback

Playing hide-and-seek is fun when you're amusing your baby niece, but it's not a good way to build a solid base of customers. In fact, providing a way for your customers to interact with you so that they can reach you quickly may be the most important part of your website.

Add a simple `mailto` link like this:

> Questions? Comments? Send e-mail to: `info@mycompany.com`

A `mailto` link gets its name from the HTML command that programmers use to create it. When visitors click the e-mail address, their e-mail program opens a new e-mail message window with your e-mail address already entered. That way, they have only to enter a subject line, type the message, and click Send to send you their thoughts.

Most web page–creation programs make it easy to create a `mailto` link. For example, if you use Dreamweaver, follow these steps:

1. **Launch and open the web page to which you want to add your e-mail link.**

2. **Position your mouse arrow and click the spot on the page where you want the address to appear.**

   The convention is to put your e-mail address at or near the bottom of a web page. A vertical blinking cursor appears at the location where you want to insert the address.

3. **Choose Insert➪Email Link.**

The Insert Email Link dialog box appears.

4. **In the Text box, type the text that you want to appear on your web page.**

   You don't have to type your e-mail address; you can also type **Webmaster, Customer Service,** or your own name.

5. **In the E-Mail box, type your e-mail address.**

6. **Click OK.**

   The Insert Email Link dialog box closes, and you return to the Dreamweaver Document window, where your e-mail link appears in blue and is underlined to signify that it is a clickable link.

Other editors work similarly but don't give you a menu command called Email Link. In that case, you have to type the `mailto` link manually. In the WordPress editor, select the text you want to serve as the link and click the link toolbar icon. When the Insert/Edit Link dialog box opens, in the URL box, after `http://` (which is pre-entered), you type **mailto:name@emailaddress**.

The drawback to publishing your e-mail address directly on your web page is that you're certain to get unsolicited e-mail messages (commonly called *spam*) sent to that address. Hiding your e-mail address behind generic link text (such as `Webmaster`) may help reduce your chances of attracting spam.

Web page forms that aren't offputting

You don't have to do much web surfing before you become intimately acquainted with how web page forms work, at least from the standpoint of someone who has to fill them out to sign up for web hosting or to download software.

When it comes to creating your own website, however, you become conscious of how useful forms are as a means of gathering essential marketing information about your customers. They give your visitors a place to sound off, ask questions, and generally get involved with your online business.

Be clear and use common sense when creating your order form. Here are some general guidelines on how to organize your form and what you need to include:

✔ **Make it easy on the customer.** Whenever possible, add pull-down menus with pre-entered options to your *form fields* (text boxes that visitors use to enter information). That way, users don't have to wonder about things such as whether you want them to spell out a state or use the two-letter abbreviation.

✓ **Validate the information.** You can use a programming language — for example, JavaScript — to ensure that users enter information correctly, that all fields are completely filled out, and so on. You may have to hire someone to add the appropriate code to the order form, but the expense is worth it to save you from having to call customers to verify or correct information that they missed or submitted incorrectly.

✓ **Provide a help number.** Give people a number to call if they have questions or want to check on an order.

✓ **Return an acknowledgment.** Let customers know that you have received their order and will be shipping the merchandise immediately or contacting them if more information is needed.

As usual, good web page–authoring and –editing programs make it a snap to create the text boxes, check boxes, buttons, and other parts of a form that the user fills out. The other part of a form, the computer script that receives the data and processes it so that you can read and use the information, is not as simple. And programs like WordPress provide you with a host of add-on applications — *plugins* — that create both the text entry elements and the scripts for you.

Not so long ago, you had to write or edit a scary CGI script to set up forms processing on your website. Now you can use WordPress plugins, or if you use another application, check out a service like Response-O-Matic (www. response-o-matic.com) or FormMail.To (www.formmail.to/formmail. to). These lead you through the process of setting up a form and providing you with the CGI script that receives the data and forwards it to you.

Blogs that promote discussion

Most blogs give readers the chance to respond to individual comments the author has made. On my own blog, for instance, which was created with WordPress, I make comments, and readers can immediately respond. This is a standard feature to give readers the opportunity to comment on what you've written.

On blogs that attract a wide following, like Talking Points Memo (www.talking pointsmemo.com), comments by multiple authors generate long discussions by a community of devoted readers. (Find out more about blogs in Chapter 1.)

The comments that appear at the end of an article or blog post have replaced what web designers used to call a *guestbook* — a place where visitors signed in so they could feel that they're part of a thriving community. If you use

WordPress to create and manage a blog or website, you can easily give visitors the ability to comment on an article. If you have created a blog, each post is automatically "commentable." That's one of the many nice things about WordPress. You just have to make sure commenting is turned on.

Log in to WordPress and click Settings under the heading Admin Options in the narrow column on the left side of the editing window. Then click Discussion, as shown in Figure 5-12, and select the Allow check box so people can post comments on new articles.

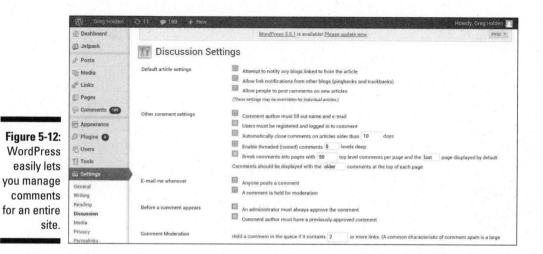

Figure 5-12: WordPress easily lets you manage comments for an entire site.

To enable comments on an individual page, follow these steps:

1. **Click Pages in the Admin settings in the narrow column on the left side of the editing window.**

   The list of pages in your WordPress site appears.

2. **Click the page you want, and if necessary, click Quick Edit.**

   The Quick Edit window for your page opens.

3. **Scroll down to the Discussion section and select the Allow check box.**

After you allow comments, be sure to log in to your site regularly to moderate them. You'll probably have to delete spam comments left by *bots* (programs that perform automated functions such as "scraping" web pages for contents) that post them automatically and respond to legitimate comments that actual human beings have left.

Chit-chat that counts

After visitors start coming to your site, the next step is to retain those visitors. A good way to do this is by building a sense of community by posting a bulletin board–type discussion area.

A discussion area takes the form of back-and-forth messages on topics of mutual interest. Each person can read previously posted messages and either respond or start a new topic of discussion. The comments areas discussed in the preceding section are the most popular ways of promoting this sort of interaction. For a more elaborate example of a discussion area that's tied to an online business, visit the EcommerceBytes (www.ecommercebytes.com) discussion areas, one of which is shown in Figure 5-13. EcommerceBytes is a highly regarded site that provides information about the online auction industry. Its discussion boards give readers a place to bring up questions and issues in a forum that's independent from those provided by auction sites like eBay.

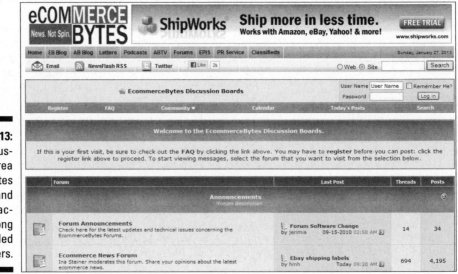

Figure 5-13: A discussion area stimulates interest and interaction among like-minded customers.

The talk doesn't have to be about your particular niche in your business field. In fact, the discussion is livelier if your visitors can discuss concerns about your area of business in general, whether it's flower arranging, boat sales, tax preparation, clock repair, computers, or whatever.

How do you start a discussion area? The basic first step is to install a special computer script on the computer that hosts your website. (Again, discussing this prospect with your web hosting service beforehand is essential.) When visitors come to your site, their web browsers access the script, enabling them to enter comments and read other messages.

Here are some specific ways to prepare a discussion area for your site:

✔ Copy a bulletin board or discussion-group script from either of these sites:

- eXtropia.com (www.extropia.com/applications.html)
- Matt's Script Archive (www.scriptarchive.com)

✔ Start your own forum on a service such as vBulletin (www.vbulletin.com), which is used by the aforementioned EcommerceBytes.

Moving from Website to Web Presence

After you have established a visual identity through colors, images, and a logo, you can "brand" yourself by "popping up" in as many web venues as possible. Make no mistake about it: Tending to your image and building a name for yourself takes time and effort. It might take one, two, or more hours every day. And once you start blogging and building an audience, you need to keep at it every few days, if not *every* day. Otherwise, those fickle web visitors you worked so hard to cultivate will flit away to someone else's website or blog or Facebook page.

How do you "pop up" in places where people will find you? You'll find suggestions throughout this book. Here are a few ideas:

✔ Start up a blog and use it to comment on your area of interest. (See Chapters 1 and 13.)

✔ Twitter as much as possible; short "tweets" can advertise new products or sales you have running. (Again, see Chapter 13.)

✔ Get on Facebook and start cultivating a circle of friends. Use Facebook to point them to your website — and your blog, your tweets, and so on. (You guessed it — see Chapter 13.)

✔ Open a storefront on eBay or on a free site like eCRATER (www.ecrater.com). (See Chapters 5 and 14 for more.)

The art of having a web presence is using all these sites to point to one another, so no matter where you are, shoppers are directed to your products or services, or at least prompted to find out more about you.

Extreme Web Pages: Advanced Layouts

People with some experience creating websites typically use tables for layout. They might be right up the alley of an adventurous type who wants to start an online business.

Setting the tables for your customers

Tables are to designers what statistics are to sports fans. They provide another means to present information in a graphically interesting way. Tables were originally intended to present "tabular" data in columns and rows, much like a spreadsheet. But by using advanced HTML techniques, you can make tables a much more integrated and subtle part of your web page.

Because you can easily create a basic table using web page editors, such as Dreamweaver, GoLive, and Expression Web, starting with one of these tools makes sense. Some adjustments with HTML are probably unavoidable, how-ever, especially if you want to use tables to create blank columns on a web page (as I explain later in this section). Here is a quick rundown of the main HTML tags used for tables:

- ✔ `<table> </table>` encloses the entire table. The `border` attribute sets the width of the line around the cells.

- ✔ `<tr> </tr>` encloses a table row, a horizontal set of cells.

- ✔ `<td> </td>` defines the contents of an individual cell. The `height` and `width` attributes control the size of each cell. For example, the following code tells a browser that the table cell is 120 pixels wide:

```
<td width=120> Contents of cell </td>
```

Cells in a table can contain images as well as text. Also, individual cells can have different colors from the cells around them. You can add a background color to a table cell by adding the `bgcolor` attribute to the `<td>` table cell tag.

TECHNICAL STUFF

A quick HTML primer

Thanks to web page–creation tools, you don't have to master HyperText Markup Language (HTML) to create your own web pages although some knowledge of HTML is helpful when it comes to editing pages and understanding how they're put together.

HTML is a markup language, not a computer programming language. You use it in much the same way that old-fashioned editors marked up copy before they gave it to typesetters. A markup language allows you to identify major sections of a document, such as body text, headings, and title. A software program (in the case of HTML, a web browser) is programmed to recognize the markup language and to display the formatting elements that you have marked.

Markup tags are the basic building blocks of HTML as well as eXtensible Markup Language (XML). Tags enable you to structure the appearance of your document so that, when it is transferred from one computer to another, it looks the way you described it. HTML tags appear within caret-shaped brackets. Most HTML commands require a *start tag* at the beginning

of the section and an *end tag* (which usually begins with a backslash) at the end.

For example, if you place the HTML tags `<b>` and `</b>` around the phrase "This text will be bold," the words appear in bold type on any browser that displays them, whether it's running on a Windows-based PC, a Unix workstation, a Mac, a palm device that's web-enabled, or any other computer.

Many HTML commands are accompanied by *attributes,* which provide a browser with more specific instructions on what action the tag is to perform. In the following line of HTML, `src` is an attribute that works with the `<img>` tag to identify a file to display:

```
<img src="house.jpg">
```

Each attribute is separated from an HTML command by a single blank space. The equal sign (=) is an operator that introduces the value on which the attribute and command functions. Usually, the value is a filename or a directory path leading to a specific file that is to be displayed on a web page. The straight (as opposed to curly) quotation marks around the value are essential for the HTML command to work.

The clever designer can use tables in a hidden way to arrange an entire page, or a large portion of a page, by doing two things:

- **Set the table border to 0.** Doing so makes the table outline invisible, so the viewer sees only the contents of each cell, not the lines bordering the cell.

- **Fill some table cells with blank space.** They act as empty columns that add more white space to a page.

An example of the first approach, that of making the table borders invisible, appears in Figure 5-14: my friend Scott Wills's website, where he advertises his graphic design services. The page appears to be divided into three columns, but the "columns" are cells in a table with borders that aren't visible.

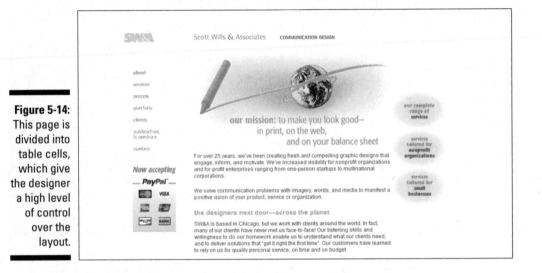

Figure 5-14: This page is divided into table cells, which give the designer a high level of control over the layout.

Breaking the grid with layers

Tables and another set of virtually obsolete layout tools called frames bring organization and interactivity to web pages, but they confine your content to rows and columns. If you feel confined by the old up-down, left-right routine, explore layers for arranging your web page content.

Layers, like table cells and frames, act as containers for text and images on a web page. Layers are unique because they can be moved around freely on the page — they can overlap one another and "bleed" right to the page margin.

Layers carry some big downsides: You can't create them with just any web editor. I recommend Microsoft Expression Web because it lets you create layers using cascading style sheets (CSS) commands so they display accurately by almost all browsers. See the product's website (www.microsoft.com/products/expression/en/web_designer/default.mspx) to find out more about current availability and pricing.

When in doubt, hire a pro

Part of the fun of running your own business is doing things yourself. Most of the ontrepreneurs I interviewed in the course of writing this book do their own web page design work. They discovered how to create websites by reading books or taking classes on the subject. But in many cases, the initial cost of hiring someone to help design your online business can be a good investment. After you pay someone to help you develop a look, you can probably implement it in the future more easily yourself. For example:

✔ If you need business cards, stationery, brochures, or other printed material in addition to a website, hiring someone to develop a consistent look for everything at the beginning is worth the money.

✔ You can pay a designer to get you started with a logo, color selections, and page layouts. Then you can save money by adding text yourself.

✔ If, like me, you're artistically impaired, consider the benefits of having your logo or other artwork drawn by a real artist.

Most professional designers charge $40 to $60 per hour for their work. You can expect a designer to spend five or six hours creating a logo or template, but if your company uses that initial design for the foreseeable future, you're not really paying that much per year.

With either Dreamweaver or Expression Web, you can draw a layer directly on the web page you're creating. You add text or images to the layer, and then resize or relocate it on the page by clicking and dragging it freely. The result is an innovative page design that doesn't conform to the usual grid.

Achieving consistency with Cascading Style Sheets

Cascading style sheets (CSS) are the tools of choice among designers who want to observe standards that have been established on the Internet and who want to make sure their web pages appear the same from browser to browser and from one computer to another. If you have a choice on how to lay out a page, and you want to precisely position items while creating layouts that are easily updatable, I urge you to look into CSS.

CSS is a subject for a book all by itself, so I'm not going to get into any great detail here. Suffice it to say that if you want to create full-featured, cutting-edge layouts, you need to use CSS. The major web design programs — Dreamweaver, GoLive, and Expression Web — all support CSS designs.

Rather than learn CSS from scratch, choose one of these applications and let it do the work for you.

Standards like CSS and XML are important because they enable you to reach the widest set of viewers possible. A *style sheet* is a document that contains the formatting for a web page. By separating the formatting from the content, you quickly apply the same formatting to multiple web pages. You can also update the design of an entire website easily: Rather than change a heading from Arial to Verdana 20 separate times on 20 web pages, for example, you change it once, and all the pages that have the style sheet *attached* to them have their headings updated all at once.

Chapter 6

Making Shopping Easy on Your E-Commerce Site

. . . .

In This Chapter

▶ Knowing what makes online consumers click the Buy button

▶ Sourcing, replenishing inventory, and fulfilling orders

▶ Adding bells and whistles to your site with hosted applications

▶ Protecting your customers' data (and your own) with passwords, firewalls, and back-ups

▶ Letting others know who you really are with a personal certificate

. . . .

*W*alk into any Walmart or other megastore, and you're likely to feel overwhelmed by the sheer size of the place. Not to worry: Walmart makes life (and spending money) easier for its shoppers by having an employee greet you at the door, and by carefully arranging merchandise in aisles where you'll find it easily. Online businesses work much the same; in fact, shoppers want to move even more quickly and easily through an online store than a brick-and-mortar one. Your job is to make your sales items easy to find and purchase, and to make customers feel secure so that you're paid promptly and reliably. You also need to protect yourself financially and guard your business data. In this chapter, I discuss some technologies and strategies that can keep your data secure and make your customers feel at ease, too.

Fostering a good atmosphere for e-commerce is also a matter of presenting your merchandise clearly and making it easy for customers to choose and purchase them. Making changes to your website is relatively easy. You can remake your store's *front door* (your home page) in a matter of minutes. You can revamp your sales catalog in less than an hour. Making regular improvements and updates to your online store doesn't just mean changing the colors or the layout, which is the part of your operation that customers notice, on your website. It also means improving back-office functions that customers don't see, such as inventory management, invoices, labels, packing, and shipping. When you test, check, and revise your website based on its current performance, you can boost your revenue and increase sales as well as make your website more usable.

Here's a short list of what you need to do to be a successful e-commerce businessperson: Set up the right atmosphere for making purchases, provide options for payment, and keep sensitive information private. Oh, and don't forget your main goal is to get goods to the customer safely and on time. In this chapter, I describe ways in which you can implement these essential online business strategies to ensure a positive shopping experience for your customers.

Giving Online Shoppers What They Need

You've heard it before, but I can't emphasize enough the importance of understanding the needs of online shoppers and doing your best to meet them. That's the best way to end up with a healthy balance in your bank account.

Showing what you've got

Customers may end up buying an item in a brick-and-mortar store, but chances are that they saw it online first. Shoppers now routinely assume that legitimate stores have a website and an online sales catalog that is likely to include even more items, accompanied by detailed descriptions, than a shopper would find by going to the store in person.

"It's not enough to just say we have this or that product line for sale. Until we actually add an individual item to our online store, with pictures and prices, we won't sell it," says Ernie Preston, who helped create an 84,000-item online catalog for a brick-and-mortar tool company that I profiled a few years ago for a previous edition of this book. "As soon as you put it in your online catalog, you'll get a call about it. Shopping on the web is the convenience factor that people want."

Suppose you don't have an 84,000-item catalog. Instead, you have only 20–30 items and you're just starting out. What can you do to build trust and encourage shoppers? Observe three basic rules:

- ✔ Make your sales catalog organized so items are easy to find.
- ✔ Talk about yourself and your background.
- ✔ Provide lots of details and good photos.

Here's an example. Nanette Thorell sells egg art (eggshells she has turned into jewelry and other products) on her website, Enchanted Hen Productions (www.enchantedhen.com). She follows the example of "triangulation" that I describe in this book's introduction by selling on eBay, Etsy, and ArtFire, as well as marketing herself with a blog, a newsletter, and on Facebook and Twitter. As you can see from her home page (see Figure 6-1), her links are simple and clearly organized.

Earning trust to gain a sale

Although e-commerce is more and more common, many customers who are relatively new still need to have their fears addressed. They want to be sure that providing their names, phone numbers, and credit card information won't lead to identity theft. And shoppers who are old pros at shopping online want to avoid being flooded with unwanted e-mails. In regard to the sale at hand, many fear that they will pay for merchandise but not receive it.

State your policies clearly and often, providing assurance that you don't give out personal data without consent. If you plan to accept credit card orders, get an account with a web host that provides a *secure server,* which is software that encrypts data exchanged with a browser. And be sure to include comments from satisfied customers. If you run an eBay Store or a store on another marketplace such as Bonanza (www.bonanza.com), your feedback rating provides assurance.

Figure 6-1:
Encourage shoppers with good organization and plenty of product details.

Includes links to her other stores   Link to her blog

Clear links encourage exploration

If you're a member in good standing with the Better Business Bureau (`www.bbb.org`), you may be eligible to apply for the BBB Business Seal for the Web (`www.bbb.org/us/bbb-online-business`) to build credibility and confidence among your clients. Businesses that participate in the BBBOnline program show their commitment to their customers by displaying a BBBOnline Reliability Seal or Privacy Seal on their websites.

One of the best ways to build trust in you and your products is to tell visitors about yourself and your background and experience. Figure 6-2 shows Nanette Thorell's About Me page.

Figure 6-2:
Tell shoppers about your experience and knowledge in your area of business.

Pointing the way with links and graphics

Because most customers are comparison shopping, it's wise to put the cost, measurements, and other important features right next to each item to promote speed and convenience.

TIP

Microsoft Office gives you access to clip art images that help highlight sales items. Figure 6-3 shows an example of how you can edit an HTML web page file with Word by inserting an image from the Clip Art task pane. (You can find more clip art images at the Microsoft Office Clip Art and Media Center, `http://office.microsoft.com/en-us/images`.)

You can also direct shoppers through your site by providing plenty of links from one section to another. Even when they're exploring one section, you should provide links back to the home page or to other areas of your site. In the case of Enchanted Hen Productions (refer to Figure 6-1), if you click Jewelry, you go to a category page with two links: Earrings and Necklaces. Click Earrings, and you see the section opening page shown in Figure 6-4. Even as shoppers are exploring the earrings section of the catalog, clicking a link guides them back to the necklaces section if they wish.

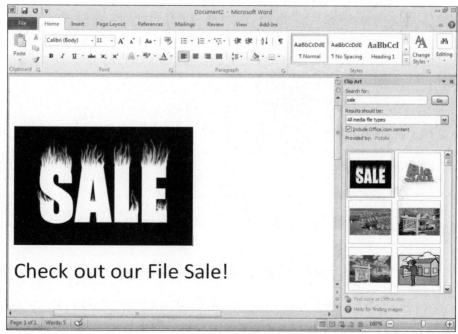

Figure 6-3: Use graphics to call attention to the information your customer wants the most: the price.

Link to other main section of catalog

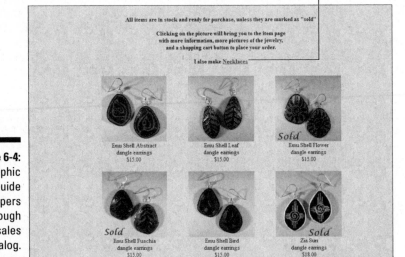

Figure 6-4:
Graphic
links guide
shoppers
through
a sales
catalog.

Giving the essentials

One of the big advantages of operating a business online is space. Not only do you have plenty of room in which to provide full descriptions of your sale items, but you also have no reason to skimp on the details you provide about your business and services. Here are some suggestions on how to provide information that your customer may want:

✔ If you sell clothing, include a page with size and measurement charts.

✔ If you sell food, provide weights, ingredients, and nutritional information.

✔ If you sell programming, web design, or traditional graphic design, provide samples of your work, links to web pages you've created, and testimonials from satisfied clients.

✔ If you're a musician, publish a link to a short sound file of your work.

Don't be reluctant to tell people ways that your products and services are better than others. Visit the Lands' End online catalog (www.landsend.com) for good examples of how this well-established marketer describes the quality of its wares.

The more details you provide about items, the longer someone will stay on your site, and the more likely they'll click Add to Cart or Buy. In your description, try to engage shoppers' imaginations. In Figure 6-5, Nanette Thorell provides a list with specifications, a clear photo, an easy-to-find price, and this phrase: ". . . they [the earrings] will turn and sway as you move your head." The shopper imagines the earrings on her head, which encourages her impulse to purchase.

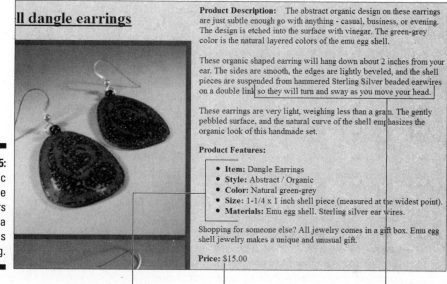

Figure 6-5:
Graphic
links guide
shoppers
through a
sales
catalog.

Provide plenty of details   Make the price easy to find

Get shoppers to envision themselves with the item

Managing Goods and Services

Shoppers on the web are continually in search of The New: the next new product, the latest price reduction or rebate, the latest comment in a blog, or today's headlines. As a provider of content, whether it's in the form of words, images, or products for sale, your job is to manage that content to keep it fresh and available. You also need to replenish stock when it's purchased, handle returns, and deal with shipping options, as I describe in the sections that follow.

Handling returns

Your returns policy depends on the venue where you make your sales. If you sell primarily on eBay or another marketplace, you should accept returns, if only because many of the most experienced and successful sellers do. That doesn't mean you need to accept every single item that is returned. Most businesses place restrictions on when they'll receive a return and send a refund. The items must be returned within 14 days, for example; the packages must be unopened; the merchandise must not be damaged.

Adding shipping rates

These days, when shoppers think about shipping rates, they think about a four-letter word: F-R-E-E. Amazon.com, with its free shipping options, has made sellers expect it as a choice. As a result, sellers on marketplaces like eBay are told to offer free shipping if possible (see www.internetretailer.com/mobile/2011/03/31/ebay-bets-free-shipping). Even if sellers build a $10 shipping cost into a $50 item so the buyer pays $60 with "free shipping," customers are still more likely to buy under such circumstances — or so the conventional wisdom says.

Otherwise, as part of creating a usable e-commerce catalog, you need to provide customers with shipping costs for your merchandise. Shipping rates can be difficult to calculate. They depend on your geographic location as well as the location where you're planning to ship. If you're a small-scale operation and you process each transaction manually, you may want to ship everything a standard way (UPS Ground, FedEx Home Delivery, or the U.S. Postal Service Parcel Post). Then you can keep a copy of your shipper's charges and calculate each package's shipping cost individually.

You can also save time by using the quick shipping calculator provided by iShip (https://iship.com). Just go to the site's home page, enter the origin and destination zip codes, and click Go. You get a set of shipping rates from DHL, UPS, and the U.S. Postal Service so you can pick the most cost-effective option. If you want help with shipping, you can set up your site with the help of a transaction hosting service, such as ChannelAdvisor (www.channeladvisor.com). This company has an agreement with the U.S. Postal Service so that it automatically calculates shipping charges and includes those charges in the invoices it sends to your customers.

If you sell the same type of item all the time, such as a particular type of clothing, you can provide flat-rate shipping using a method such as the U.S. Postal Service's Priority Mail option. You can even add a few dollars to the purchase price to cover the standard shipping charge to most locations in the United States and offer free shipping to your domestic customers.

Maintaining inventory

Shoppers on the web want things to happen instantly. If they discover that you're out of stock of an item they want, they're likely to switch to another online business instead of waiting for you to restock that item. With that in mind, obey the basic principle of planning to be successful: Instead of ordering the bare minimum of this or that item, make sure you have enough to spare. Too much inventory initially is better than running out at some point.

If you have one store with 50–100 items in stock, managing inventory is straightforward. If you manage 13 separate storefronts as well as a brick-and-mortar store, you'd better call in some outside help to keep on top of it all.

Mimi and Peter Kriele operate the website Touch of Europe (www.touchof europe.net) as an Amazon web store, as well as 12 other specialized sites. The Krieles use Miva Merchant to manage their main website. The inventory for all the other stores is taken from Amazon.com and managed using that marketplace's tools for merchants. These are just two approaches. See Chapter 16 for more on different ways to manage multiple storefronts.

Rely on software or management services to help you keep track of what you have. If you feel at ease working with databases, record your initial inventory in an Access or SQL database. A database forces you to record each sale manually so you know how many items are left. You could connect your sales catalog to your database using a program such as ColdFusion from Adobe (www.adobe.com/products/coldfusion). Such a program can update the database on the www.adobe.com/products/coldfusion-family.html when sales are made. But you may need to hire someone with web programming experience to set up the system for you and make sure it actually works.

If you sign up with an online store solution, like Yahoo! Small Business or a sales management provider like Marketplace Advisor Selling Services from ChannelAdvisor (www.channeladvisor.com), inventory is tracked automatically for you. Whether you do the work yourself or hire an outside service, you have to be able to answer basic questions such as these:

- ✔ **When should you reorder?** Establish *reorder points* — points at which you automatically reorder supplies (when you get down to two or three items left, for example).

- ✔ **How many items do you have in stock right now?** Make sure that you have enough merchandise on hand not only for everyday demand but also in case a product gets hot or the holiday season brings about a dramatic increase in orders.

An e-commerce hosting service can also help you with questions that go beyond the basics, such as the purchasing history of customers. Knowing what customers have purchased in the past gives you the ability to suggest *up-sells* — additional items customers might want. But in the early stages, making sure you have a cushion of additional inventory for the time when your site becomes a big success is your primary responsibility.

Keeping Your Website in Top Shape

The job of your hosting service or ISP, of course, is to monitor traffic and make sure your website is up and running. But unless you keep an eye on your site and its availability to your customers, you may not be aware of technical problems that can scare potential business away. If your site is offline periodically or your server crashes or works slowly, it doesn't just waste your customers' time — it can cut into your sales directly.

If your site doesn't work well, a potential customer can find another site whose pages load more quickly just a few mouse clicks away. Outages can be costly, too. The business and technology website Business Insider (www. businessinsider.com) reported that an outage that hit the popular online payment service PayPal in summer 2009 cost businesses between $7 and $32 million. The site was offline for about 4.5 hours. In September 2010, the Virgin Blue airline check-in and online reservations and boarding system went down. The company estimated that the 11-day outage cost it $20 million in profits, which its reservations management company, Navitaire, subsequently paid in compensation (http://m.theaustralian.com.au/business/navitaire-booking-glitch-earns-virgin-20m-in-compo/story-e6frg8zx-1226033624246).

Using software to keep score

Although they take some effort to install, programs are available for between $30 – $200 that continually keep an eye on your website and notify you of any problems. Site24x7 (www.site24x7.com) monitors your website's availability from more than 40 locations around the world. You can try the service for a free 15-day trial period. Three pricing plans are available.

Some companies offer such monitoring as a service. You use the company's software, which resides on its computers, not yours. For example, @Watch (www.atwatch.com) provides an online service that checks your site's images and links periodically to see if everything is working correctly. The company offers several levels of service. The @Watch Advanced version costs $12.99 per month and checks your site once every 30 minutes. For $33.99 per month, the program will check your site every 5 minutes.

Coping when your service goes out to lunch

Ideally, your web host provides a page on its website that keeps track of its network status and records any recent problems. One site monitoring notification (from a program you install yourself or one that you "rent" as a service from an Application Service Provider [ASP] — see the next section, "Outsourcing your business needs") probably isn't cause for concern. However, when you receive a *series* of notifications, call your web-hosting service and tell technical support exactly what the problems are/were.

If the problem with your site is a slow response to requests from web browsers rather than a complete outage, the problem may be that your server is slow because you're sharing it with other websites. Consider moving from shared hosting to a different option. In *co-location,* you purchase the server on which your files reside, but the machine is located at your web host's facility rather than at your own location. Your site is the only one on your machine. You also get the reliability of the host's technical support and high-speed Internet connection.

If you really need bandwidth, consider a *dedicated server.* In this case, you rent space on a machine that is dedicated to serving your site. This arrangement is far more expensive than sharing a web server, and you should choose it only if the number of visits to your site at any one time becomes too great for a shared server to handle. You'll know a shared server is becoming overtaxed if your site is slow to load.

Outsourcing your business needs

One of the most effective ways to save time and money doing business online is to let someone else install and maintain the computer software that you use. *Outsourcing* refers to the practice of having an outside company provide services for your business, such as web hosting, form creation, or financial record keeping, rather than installing software and running it on your own computer.

One of the companies that provides web-based services on an outsourced basis is an *Application Service Provider* (ASP). An ASP makes business or other applications available on the web. For example, when you fill out a form and create a web page on CafePress.com (which I describe in Chapter 15), you're using CafePress.com as an ASP. Rather than create your web page on your own computer, you use an application on the CafePress.com site and store your web page information there.

How ASPs can help your company

You have to pay a monthly fee to use an ASP's services. You may also incur installation fees, and you may have to sign a one- or two-year contract. In return, ASPs provide benefits to your company that include the following:

- ✔ **Shopping cart/store creation:** In addition to a website, open an e-commerce store with shopping cart services like ZenCart, 3D Cart, X-Cart, or one of many other providers.

- ✔ **"Shark tank" feedback:** Concept Feedback (`www.conceptfeedback.com`) provides experts who evaluate your website's design and usability and suggest improvements.

- ✔ **Online form creation:** FormSite.com (`www.formsite.com`) is a leader in creating a variety of forms that can help online shoppers provide essential functions, such as subscribing to newsletters or other publications, asking for information about your goods and services, or providing you with shipping or billing information. The sample pizza order form shown in Figure 6-6 is an example of the type of form that this particular ASP can help you create.

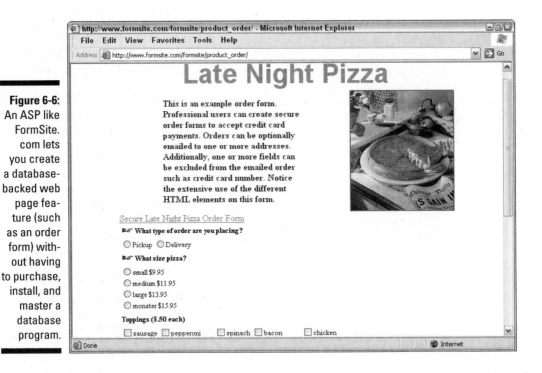

Figure 6-6: An ASP like FormSite. com lets you create a database-backed web page feature (such as an order form) without having to purchase, install, and master a database program.

✔ **Product presentation:** Arqspin (`http://arqspin.com`) lets you create 360-degree "spinning" product photography so customers can see your merchandise from all angles.

✔ **Reduced credit card fees:** All merchants pay fees to credit card processors to receive customers' credit card payments. FeeFighters (`https://feefighters.com`) helps businesses shop for credit card merchant accounts to save money.

Although ASPs can help you in many ways, they require research, interviewing, contract review, and an ongoing commitment on your part. I illustrate the potential pluses and minuses of outsourcing in Table 6-1.

Table 6-1	Outsourcing Benefits and Risks
Pros	*Cons*
Better customer service: By outsourcing scheduling or other functions, businesses give customers increased options for interacting with them online. Customers don't have to call or e-mail the company; in the case of online scheduling, customers can schedule or cancel appointments by accessing the company's online calendar.	**A required contract:** ASPs usually allow customers to try out their services for a while but then offer long-term contracts. The terms of these contracts can range from one to three years. Don't get yourself locked in to a long-term arrangement that prevents you from trying out cheaper or better alternatives down the road.
Greater website functionality: ASPs enable your site to provide better service to your customers and allow you to get more work done.	**ASPs face stiff competition:** Make sure the companies you sign agreements with will be around for a while by talking to current customers and reviewing resumes of senior staff and key employees. Scan the web for any press releases or articles that serve as warning signs about the ASP's financial health.
Expanded scope: You don't have to become proficient in subjects that aren't part of your core business or expertise.	**Security risks:** The moment you hand over your business data to another online firm or give outside companies access to your internal network, you risk theft of data or virus infections from hackers. Make sure the ASPs you work with use encryption and other Internet security measures.

In many cases, ASPs can provide a software solution and customize it to your needs. Outsourcing not only improves your company's bottom line, but also helps you convey your message to potential customers that you might never reach otherwise.

Doing your homework before you sign up

After you try out the software or other service that you want to lease, you usually need to sign a contract. Read the fine print. Contracts can last for 12 to 50 months; make sure you don't get locked in to one that's longer than you need. You have a better chance of getting the service you want if you do the following:

- ✔ **Understand pricing schemes.** Some ASPs charge on a "per-employee" basis while others charge "per-seat" fees based on each registered user. Still others charge "per CPU," which means you're charged for each machine that runs the hosted application.

- ✔ **Pin down start-up fees.** Virtually all ASPs charge a start-up fee, or a service implementation fee, when you sign the contract. Make sure the fee covers installation and any customization that you'll need.

- ✔ **Don't accept just any SLA.** It's essential to obtain a *service level agreement* (SLA), which is a document that spells out what services you expect an ASP (or other vendor) to provide. Don't hesitate to add, delete, or change sections to meet your needs.

- ✔ **Avoid "gotcha" fees.** Pricing arrangements are hardly standard with regard to ASPs. Some of the big hidden costs involve personalizing or customizing the service to adapt to legacy systems. You should ask these questions in order to avoid unpleasant surprises: Is there an additional cost for customizing or personalizing the application? Does it cost extra to back up my company's data and recover it if one of my computers goes down? Is help desk support included in my monthly fee, or will you charge me every time I call with a question or problem?

- ✔ **Make sure your information is secure.** Some huge security risks are associated with transmitting your information across the wide-open spaces of the Internet. Make sure your ASP takes adequate security measures to protect your data by asking informed questions, such as: Is my data protected by SSL encryption? Do you run a virtual private network? How often do you back up your customers' data?

If the answer to any of these questions seems inadequate, move on to the next ASP.

Keeping Your Business Safe

Working at home or in a small office carries its own set of safety concerns for small business owners. Chances are you don't have an IT professional at hand to make sure your files and your network are safe from intrusion. Some safe computing practices, such as using password protection, making regular back-ups, and installing antivirus software, can go a long way toward keeping your data secure, even if you never have to get into more technical subjects such as public key encryption.

Separating the personal and the professional

Many entrepreneurs who run businesses from their homes face a simple logistical problem: Their work takes over their home. Boxes, computers, phones, and other gadgets create disruptions that can drive everyone crazy. Here are some simple steps that can help you set more clearly defined boundaries between work and domestic life.

When the computer is a group sport

A lot to can be said for having at least two separate computers — one for personal use and one for business use. The idea is that you set up your system so that you have to log on to your business computer with a username and password.

If you have only one computer, passwords can still provide a measure of protection. Windows gives you the ability to set up different user profiles, each associated with its own password. User profiles and passwords don't necessarily protect your business files, but they convey to your family members that they should use their own software, stick to their own directories, and not try to explore your company data.

Folder Guard, a program by WinAbility Software3 Corp. (`www.winability.com/folderguard`), enables you to hide or password-protect files or folders on your computer. The software works with Windows 8, 7, Vista, and XP or later. You can choose the Personal version, which is intended for home users, or the Business version, which is designed for business customers. A 30-day trial version is available for download from the WinAbility website; if you want to keep the Personal version of Folder Guard, you have to pay $39.95 (or $79.95 for the Business version).

One phone may not be enough

Having a phone line dedicated to your business not only makes your business seem more serious, but also separates your business calls from your personal calls. If you need a separate line for your online business, consider Google Voice (`www.google.com/voice`). This service gives you voicemail and a phone number that you can route to another phone if needed.

Heading off disasters

An old joke about the telegram from a mother reads, "Worry. Details to follow." When you're lying awake at night, you can be anxious about all sorts of grim disasters affecting your business: flood, fire, theft, computer virus, you name it. Prevention is always better than a cure, so this section covers steps you can take to prevent problems. But should a problem arise, there are also ways to recover more easily.

Insurance . . . the least you can do

I can think of ways to spend money that are a whole lot more fun than paying insurance premiums. Yet there I am every month, writing checks to protect myself in case something goes wrong with my house, car, body, and so on. And yes, there's another item to add to the list: protecting my business investment by obtaining insurance that specifically covers me against hardware damage, theft, and loss of data. You can go a step further and obtain a policy that covers the cost of data entry or equipment rental that would be necessary to recover your business information. Here are some specific strategies:

- ✔ Make a list of all your hardware and software and how much each item cost, and store a copy of it in a secure place, such as a fireproof safe or safe-deposit box.

- ✔ Take photos of your computer setup in case you need to make an insurance claim, and put them in the same safe place.

- ✔ Save your electronic files on CD or DVD and put the disc in a safe storage location, such as a safe-deposit box.

Investigate the many options available to you for insuring your computer hardware and software. Your current homeowner's or renter's insurance may offer coverage, but make sure the dollar amount is sufficient for replacement. You may also want to look into the computer hardware and software coverage provided by Safeware, The Insurance Agency, Inc. (`www.safeware.com`).

Think ahead to the unthinkable

The Gartner Group estimates that two out of five businesses that experience a major disaster go out of business within five years. I would guess that the three that are able to get back up and running quickly already had recovery plans in place. Even if your company is small, be prepared for trouble such as floods, hurricanes, or tornadoes. A recovery effort might include the following strategies:

- ✔ **Back-up power systems:** What will you do if the power goes out, and you can't access the web? You can buy a back-up power system for less than $50 at office supply stores or from Amazon.com.

- ✔ **Data storage:** This is probably the most practical and essential disaster recovery step for small or home-based businesses. Back up your files to the "cloud" using services like Carbonite (`www.carbonite.com`). An article in the IT magazine *Computerworld* compared five of the best-known systems (`www.computerworld.com/s/article/9223805/ 5_online_backup_services_keep_your_data_safewww.computer world.com/s/article/9223805/5_online_backup_services_ keep_your_data_safe`).

- ✔ **Telecommunications:** Having an alternate method of communication available in case your phone system goes down ensures that you're always in touch. The obvious choice is a cell phone. Also set up a voice mailbox so that customers and vendors can leave messages for you even if you can't answer the phone.

Creating a plan is a waste of time if you don't regularly set aside time to keep it up to date. Back up your data on a regular basis, purchase additional equipment if you need it, and make arrangements to use other computers and offices if you need to — in other words, *implement* your plan. You owe it not only to yourself, but also to your customers to be prepared in case of disaster.

Antivirus protection without a needle

As an online businessperson, you download files, receive disks from customers and vendors, and exchange e-mail with all sorts of people you've never met before. Surf safely by installing antivirus programs, such as

- ✔ **Norton Internet Security by Symantec Corp.** (`www.symantec.com/ global/products`): This application, which includes an antivirus program as well as a firewall and lists for $79.99, automates many security functions and is especially good for beginners. A standalone version, Norton AntiVirus, is available for $49.99, but I highly recommend the more full-featured package, which includes a firewall that blocks many other dangerous types of intrusions, such as Trojan horses.

- ✔ **AVG AntiVirus by AVG Technologies** (`www.avg.com`): Many users who find Norton Internet Security too intrusive (it leaves lots of files on your computer and consumes a great deal of memory) turn to this product, which lists for $39.99.

- ✔ **Avira Free Antivirus** (www.avira.com/en/avira-free-antivirus): This is a popular free program.

- ✔ **VirusScan by McAfee** (www.mcafee.com): This is the leading competitor of Norton AntiVirus, which comes bundled with Norton Internet Security. VirusScan is included in McAfee Internet Security, which includes a firewall and costs $67.99.

I love gadgets, and few things get me more excited than handheld devices, laptops, and other portable computing devices. Yet those are the items that I seem to have the most trouble keeping track of, literally and figuratively. At the very least, you should make the device's storage area accessible with a password. You can also install protection software designed especially for mobile devices, such as VirusScan Mobile by McAfee (www.mcafee.com/us/products/mobile-security/index.aspx).

Viruses change all the time, and new ones appear regularly. The antivirus program you install one day may not be able to handle the viruses that appear just a few weeks or months later. You may want to pick an antivirus program that doesn't charge excessive amounts for regular updates (such as every year). Also check the ICSA's Product Testing Reports (go to www.icsalabs.com).

A visible sign that you're trustworthy

Like the office assistant whose work is visible only when he or she is not doing a good job, you may be squeaky clean but nobody will know unless there's a problem . . . or unless you display a "seal of approval" from a reputable online organization. The two best-known seals (which are actually images you add to your web pages to show visitors you're reputable) are TRUSTe and BBBOnline.

The nonprofit organization TRUSTe was created to boost the degree of trust that web surfers have in the Internet. It does this through a third-party oversight "seal" program. If you demonstrate to TRUSTe that you're making efforts to keep your visitors' personal data secure and if you pledge not to share your customers' data and to publish a privacy statement on your site, TRUSTe issues you a seal of approval that you can place on your site's home page. The TRUSTe seal is intended to function as the online equivalent of the Good Housekeeping seal of approval on a product.

By itself, the seal doesn't keep hackers from breaking into your site and stealing your data. That's still up to you. Having the seal just makes visitors feel better about using your services. The TRUSTe site provides you with a wizard that leads you through the process of generating a privacy statement for your site. The statement tells visitors how you protect their information. Find out more by visiting the TRUSTe home page (www.truste.com) and clicking the Business Products header link.

BBBOnline, the web-based arm of the Better Business Bureau, has a similar program for commercial websites. The BBBOnline Reliability Seal Program has several eligibility requirements, including a physical location in the United States or Canada, a business record for at least a year, a satisfactory complaint-handling record, membership in the Better Business Bureau, and a commitment to resolve disputes and respond promptly to consumer complaints. Find out more at `www.bbb.org`.

Low- and high-tech locks

If you play the word game with a web surfer or website and say "Security," you're likely to get a response such as "Encryption." But security doesn't need to start with software. The fact is, all the firewalls and passwords in the world won't help you if someone breaks into your home office and trashes or makes off with the computer that contains all your files.

Besides insuring your computer equipment and taking photos in case you need to replace it, you can invest in locks for your home office and your machines. They might not keep someone from breaking into your house, but they'll at least make it more difficult for intruders to carry off your hardware.

Here are some suggestions for how to protect your hardware and the business data your computers contain:

- **Lock your office.** Everyone has locks on the outer doors of their house, but go a step further and install a deadbolt lock on your office door.

- **Lock your computers.** Innovative Security Products (`www.wesecure.com`) offers several varieties of computer locking systems. It also sells ultraviolet pens that you can use to mark your equipment with your name and the serial number of your computer in case the police recover it.

- **Get a security app.** Software to recover a lost or stolen computer used to come in just a few varieties. Now, with the proliferation of easily lost smartphones and tablets, a new generation of apps is available. Install them before your device goes AWOL, and when the device is lost or stolen, the app will respond in different ways. Find My iPhone for iOS works with iPads as well as phones. If one iOS device goes missing, install Find My iPhone on another one and log in with your Apple ID to remotely erase the device, lock it, play a warning sound, or locate it. Lost for Android devices will perform similar functions. Absolute Computrace (`www.absolute.com`) will do the same with Computrace Plus (offered by Absolute Software Corp.), which costs home office users $49.95 for one year of monitoring.

- **Make back-ups.** Be sure to regularly back up your information on Zip drives, USB drives, CDs, or similar storage devices. Also consider signing up with a web-based storage service where files can be transferred from your computer. That way, if your computers and your extra storage disks are lost, you have an online back-up in a secure location. Look into Norton Online Backup (`www.symantec.com`), which gives you 25GB of storage space for $24.99.

Installing firewalls and other safeguards

You probably know how important a firewall is in a personal sense. Firewalls filter out unwanted intrusions, such as executable programs that hackers seek to plant on your file system, so they can use your computer for their own purposes. When you're starting an online business, the objectives of a firewall become different: You're protecting not just your own information, but also that of your customers. You're quite possibly relying on the firewall to protect your source of income as well as the data on your computers.

A *firewall* is an application or hardware device that monitors the data flowing into or out of a computer network and filters that data based on criteria the owner sets up. Like a security guard at the entrance to an apartment building, a firewall scans the packets of digital information that traverse the Internet, making sure the data is headed for the right destination and that it doesn't match known characteristics of viruses or attacks. Authorized traffic is allowed into your network. Attack attempts or viruses are either deleted automatically or cause an alert message to appear to which you must respond with a decision to block or allow the incoming or outgoing packets.

Keeping out Trojan horses and other unwanted visitors

A *Trojan horse* is a program that enters your computer surreptitiously and then attempts to do something without your knowledge. Some folks say that such programs enter your system through a "back door" because you don't immediately know that they've entered your system. Trojan horses may come in the form of an e-mail attachment with the filename extension .exe (which stands for *executable*). For example, I once received an e-mail that purported to be from Microsoft Corp. and claimed to contain a security update. The attachment looked innocent enough, but had I saved the attachment to my computer, it would have used my computer as a staging area for distributing itself to many other e-mail addresses.

I didn't run into trouble, however. My firewall program recognized the attachment and alerted me to the danger. I highly recommend that anyone who, like me, has a cable modem, DSL, or other direct connection to the Internet install one right away. You can try out the shareware program ZoneAlarm by Zone Labs, Inc. (www.zonealarm.com), that provides you with basic firewall protection, though more full-featured programs like Norton Internet Security (http://us.norton.com/internet-security) are probably more effective.

Cleaning out spyware

Watch out for software that "spies" on your web surfing and other activities and then reports these activities to advertisers, potentially invading your privacy. Ad-Aware isn't a firewall, exactly, but it's a useful program that detects and erases any advertising programs you may have downloaded from the Internet without knowing it. Such advertising programs might be running on your computer, consuming your processing resources and slowing down operations. Some spyware programs track your activities when you surf the web; others simply report that they have been installed. Many users regard these spyware programs as invasions of privacy because they install themselves and do their reporting without your asking for it or even knowing they're active.

When I ran Ad-Aware the first time, it detected a whopping 57 programs I didn't know about that were running on my computer and that had installed themselves when I connected to various websites or downloaded software. As you can see in Figure 6-7, when I ran Ad-Aware while I was working on this chapter, sure enough, it found four suspicious software components running.

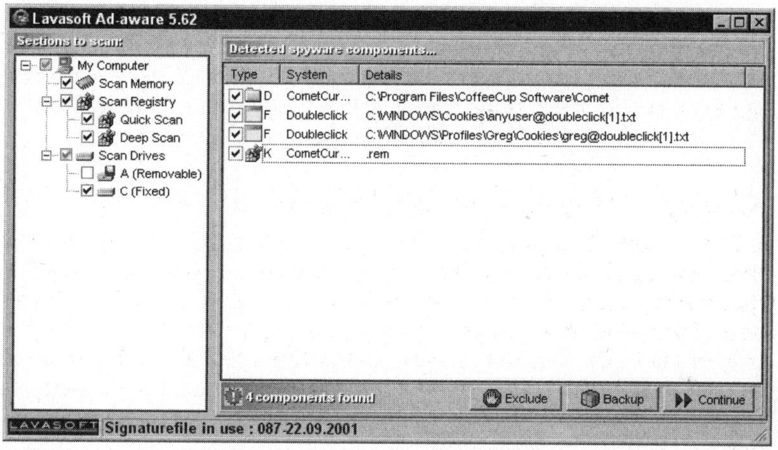

Figure 6-7: Ad-Aware deletes advertising software that, many users believe, can violate your privacy.

I highly recommend Ad-Aware; you can download a version at `www.lava soft.com` and try it for free. You can pay for their Personal or Pro Security versions as well. One of this book's editors personally recommends a free antispyware tool called SpyBot Search & Destroy (`www.safer-networking.org`).

Positioning the firewall

These days, most home networks are configured so that the computers on the network can share information as well as the same Internet connection. Whether you run a home-based business or a business in a discrete location, you almost certainly have a network of multiple computers. A network is far more vulnerable than a single computer connected to the Internet: A network has more entry points than a single computer, and more reliance is placed on each of the operators of those computers to observe good safety practices. And if one computer on the network is attacked, others can be attacked as well.

You probably are acquainted with software firewalls, such as Norton Personal Firewall or Zone Alarm. Software firewalls protect one computer at a time. In a typical business scenario, however, multiple computers share a single Internet connection through a router that functions as a gateway. Many network administrators prefer a *hardware firewall* — a device that functions as a filter for traffic both entering and leaving it. A hardware firewall may also function as a router, but it can also be separate from the router. The device is positioned at the perimeter of the network where it can protect all the company's computers at once. One example of this type of hardware is the WatchGuard Firebox X20e, which costs $572, by WatchGuard (`www.watch guard.com`).

REMEMBER

Companies that want to provide a website the public can visit as well as secure e-mail and other communications services create a secure sub-network of one or more specially *hardened* (in other words, secured because all unnecessary services have been removed from them) computers. This kind of network is a *demilitarized zone* (DMZ).

Keeping your firewall up to date

Firewalls work by means of *attack signatures* (or *definitions*), which are sets of data that identify a connection attempt as a potential attack. Some attacks are easy to stop: They've been attempted for years, and the amateur hackers who attempt intrusions don't give much thought to them. The more dangerous attacks are new ones. These have signatures that emerged after you installed your firewall.

You quickly get a dose of reality and find just how serious the problem is by visiting one of the websites that keeps track of the latest attacks, such as the Distributed Intrusion Detection System or DShield (`www.dshield.org`). On the day I visited, DShield reported that the "survival time" for an unpatched computer (a computer that has security software that isn't equipped with the latest updates called *patches)* after connecting to the Internet was only 16 minutes. Therefore, such a computer only has 16 minutes before someone tries to attack it. If that doesn't scare you into updating your security software, I don't know what will.

Providing security with public keys

The conversations I overhear while I drive my preteen daughters and their friends to events leave no doubt in my mind that different segments of society use code words that only their peers can understand. Even computers use encoding and decoding to protect information exchanged on the Internet. The schemes used online are far more complex and subtle than the slang used by kids, however. This section describes the security method most widely used on the Internet, and the one you're likely to use yourself: Secure Sockets Layer (SSL) encryption.

The keys to public-key/private-key encryption

Terms like *SSL* and *encryption* might make you want to reach for the remote. But don't be too quick to switch channels. SSL is making it safer to do business online and boosting the trust of potential customers. And anything that makes shoppers more likely to spend money online is something you need to know about.

The term *encryption* is the process of encoding data, especially sensitive data, such as credit card numbers. Information is encrypted by means of complex mathematical formulas — *algorithms*. Such a formula may transform a simple-looking bit of information into a huge block of seemingly incomprehensible numbers, letters, and characters. Only someone who has the right formula, called a *key* (which is a complex mass of encoded data), can decode the gobbledygook.

Here's a very simple example. Suppose that my credit card number is `12345`, and I encode it by using an encryption formula into something like the following: `1aFgHx203gX4gLu5cy`.

The algorithm that generated this encrypted information may say something like "Take the first number, multiply it by some numeral, and then add some letters to it. Then take the second number, divide it by x, and add y characters to the result," and so on. (In reality, the formulas are far more complex than this, which is why you usually have to pay a license fee to use them. But this is the general idea.) Someone who has the same formula can run it in reverse, so to speak, to decrypt the encoded number and obtain the original number, `12345`.

In practice, the encoded numbers that are generated by encryption routines and transmitted on the Internet are very large. They vary in size depending on the relative strength (or *uncrackability)* of the security method used. Some methods generate keys that consist of 128 bits of data; a *data bit* is a single unit of digital information. These formulas are *128-bit keys.*

Encryption is the cornerstone of security on the Internet. The most widely used security schemes, such as the Secure Sockets Layer (SSL) protocol, the Secure Electronic Transactions (SET) protocol, and Pretty Good Privacy (PGP), all use some form of encryption.

With some security methods, the party that sends the data and the party that receives it both use the same key (this method is *symmetrical encryption*). This approach isn't considered as secure as an asymmetrical encryption method, such as public-key encryption, however. In public-key encryption, the originating party obtains a license to use a security method. (In the upcoming section, "Obtaining a certificate from Verisign," I show you just how to do this yourself.) As part of the license, you use the encryption algorithm to generate your own private key. You never share this key with anyone. However, you use the private key to create a separate public key. This public key goes out to visitors who connect to a secure area of your website. When they have your public key, users can encode sensitive information and send it back to you. Only you can decode the data — by using your secret, private key.

Getting a certificate without going to school

When you write a check at a retail store, the cashier is likely to make sure you're preregistered as an approved member and also asks to see your driver's license. But on the Internet, how do you know people are who they say they are when all you have to go on is a URL or an e-mail address? The solution in the online world is to obtain a personal certificate that you can send to website visitors or append to your e-mail messages.

How certificates work

A *certificate,* which is also sometimes dubbed a Digital ID, is an electronic document issued by a certification authority (CA). The certificate contains the owner's personal information as well as a public key that can be exchanged with others online. The public key is generated by the owner's private key, which the owner obtains during the process of applying for the certificate.

In issuing the certificate, the CA takes responsibility for saying that the owner of the document is the same as the person actually identified on the certificate. Although the public key helps establish the owner's identity, certificates do require you to put a level of trust in the agency that issues it.

A certificate helps both you and your customers. A certificate assures your customers that you're the person you say you are, plus it protects your e-mail communications by enabling you to encrypt them.

Obtaining a certificate from VeriSign

Considering how important a role certificates play in online security, obtaining one is remarkably easy. You do so by applying and paying a licensing fee to a CA. One of the most popular CAs is VeriSign, Inc., now part of Symantec, which lets you apply for a certificate called a *Class 1 Digital ID.*

A Class 1 Digital ID is only useful for securing personal communications. As an e-commerce website owner, you may want a business-class certificate called a 128-bit SSL Global Server ID (`www.verisign.com/products-services/index.html`). This form of Digital ID works only if your e-commerce site is hosted on a server that runs *secure server software* — software that encrypts transactions — such as Apache Stronghold. Check with your web host to see whether a secure server is available for your website.

A VeriSign personal certificate, which you can use to authenticate yourself in e-mail, news, and other interactions on the Internet, costs $22.95 per year, and you can try out a free certificate for 60 days. Follow these steps to obtain your Digital ID:

1. **Go to the VeriSign, Inc. Digital IDs for Secure E-Mail page at** `www.symantec.com/verisign/digital-id`.

2. **Click Buy Online.**

   The Step 1: Certificate Data page appears.

3. **Type your e-mail address and choose a validity period (25 days or one year); then click Next.**

   If you pick the one-year option, you will be prompted to enter your billing information. Otherwise, the Confirmation page appears.

4. **Read the terms and conditions, click Yes to accept the terms, and then click Submit.**

   The Completion page appears with instructions on how to pick up your Digital ID.

5. **Check the e-mail address you entered in Step 3.**

   You'll receive two e-mails. Click the link in the first one to go to the Verisign self-service page. Log in to the page with the password that was sent in the second e-mail.

6. **The Digital ID for Secure Email login page appears after you click the link in the first e-mail you received. Type the password you received and click Log in.**

   A page appears reviewing your request status for generating a key pair.

7. **Review the key information and then click Generate Key and Install.**

   Allow a few minutes for the key to generate. When your key is generated, you see the message `Successfully generated the private key and installed the certificate to your key store` at the top of the window.

8. **Click the Install Certificate button.**

9. **When a dialog box appears saying the certificate has been installed, click OK.**

10. **To view your certificate, in Microsoft Internet Explorer, choose Tools⇨Internet Options, click Content, and then click Certificates.**

    The Certificate dialog box appears.

11. **Double-click the name of the certificate listed in the Personal tab.**

    The certificate appears. Figure 6-8 shows my certificate for Internet Explorer. (Copying this ID, or anyone else's, is pointless because this is only your public key; the public key is always submitted with your private key, which is secret.)

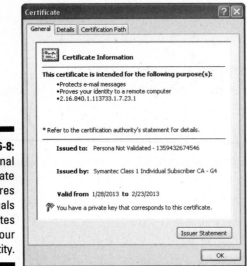

Figure 6-8:
A personal certificate assures individuals or websites of your identity.

After you have your Digital ID, what do you do with it? For one thing, you can use it to verify your identity to sites that accept certificate submissions. Some sites that require members to log in use secure servers that give you the option of submitting your certificate rather than entering the usual user-name and password to identify yourself. You can also attach your Digital ID to your e-mail messages to prove that your message is indeed coming from you. See your e-mail program's Help files for more specific instructions.

You can't encrypt or digitally sign messages on any computer other than the one to which your certificates are issued. If you're using a different computer from the one you used when you obtained your certificates, you must contact your certificate issuer and obtain a new certificate for the computer you're currently using. Or, if your browser allows transfers, you can export your cer-tificate to the new computer.

As far as e-mail security goes, rather than going through the cumbersome process of encrypting individual e-mail messages, the two best tips I can give you are very simple. First, use a secure password. A secure password con-tains at least seven or eight characters and is a mix of capital and lowercase letters, numbers, and punctuation marks. Second, if you use Gmail, enable two-factor authentication. You can Google the subject or read Google's help instructions at http://support.google.com/accounts/bin/answer.py?hl=en&answer=180744.

Chapter 7

Accepting Payments

· ·

· ·

Starting a new business and getting it online is exciting, but believe me, the real excitement occurs when you get paid for what you do. Nothing boosts your confidence and tells you that your hard work is paying off like receiving the proverbial check in the mail or having funds transferred to your business account.

The immediacy and interactivity of selling and promoting yourself online applies to receiving payments, too. You can get paid with just a few mouse clicks and some important data entered on your customer's keyboard. But completing an electronic commerce (*e-commerce* for short) transaction doesn't work the same way as in a traditional retail store. Online, customers can't personally hand you cash or a check. You, the seller, can't verify the user's identity by looking at a signature or photo ID.

In e-commerce, both buyers and sellers have the same concerns they've always had. Customers need a reliable way to pay you securely without worrying that their credit card information might be stolen. The seller needs to know that the customer isn't using a stolen credit card. Luckily, online payments are safer than ever, and more options exist than ever before.

To get paid promptly and reliably online, you have to go through some extra steps to make the customer feel secure — not to mention protecting yourself, too. Successful e-commerce is about setting up the right atmosphere for making purchases, providing options for payment, and keeping sensitive information private. It's also about making sure the goods get to the customer safely and on time. In this chapter, I describe how you can implement these essential online business strategies.

Sealing the Deal: The Options

As anyone who sells online knows, the point at which payment is transferred is one of the most eagerly awaited stages of the transaction. It's also one of the stages apt to produce the most anxiety. Customers and merchants who are used to dealing with one another face to face and personally handing over identification and credit cards suddenly feel lost. On the web, they can't see the person they're dealing with.

For customers, the good news is that paying for something purchased over the Internet is getting to be a matter-of-fact thing. Security has improved dramatically. For merchants like you, there are some basic concerns: You want to make sure that checks don't bounce and purchases aren't made with stolen credit cards.

In giving your customers the ability to make payments online, your goal is to accomplish the following:

- ✔ **Give the customer options.** Online shoppers like to feel that they have some degree of control. Give them a choice of payment alternatives: Phone, check, and credit cards are the main ones. Some also like a choice of online payment services; they want to see that you accept Google Checkout as well as PayPal, for example.

- ✔ **Keep payments secure.** Pay an extra fee to your web host, if necessary, to have your customers submit their credit card numbers or other personal information to a secure server — a server that uses Secure Sockets Layer (SSL) encryption to render personal data unreadable if stolen.

- ✔ **Make payments convenient.** Shoppers on the web are in a hurry. Give them the web page forms and the phone numbers they need so that they can complete a purchase in a matter of seconds.

Though the goals are the same, the options are different if you sell on eBay or on another website that functions as an e-commerce marketplace. If you sell on eBay, either through an auction or an eBay Store, you can take advantage of eBay's fraud protection measures: a feedback system that rewards honesty and penalizes dishonesty, fraud insurance, an investigations staff, and the threat of suspension. Of course, you might still run into buyers who try to cheat you. But the safeguards mean it's feasible to accept cash and personal checks or money orders from buyers. If you don't receive the cash, you don't ship the merchandise. If you receive checks, you can wait until they clear before you ship.

On the web, you don't have a feedback system or an investigations squad to ferret out dishonest buyers. You can accept checks or money orders, but credit cards are the safest and quickest option, and accordingly, they're what buyers expect. It's up to you to verify the buyer's identity as best you can to minimize fraud.

Enabling Credit Card Purchases

Having the ability to accept and process credit card transactions makes it especially easy for your customers to follow the impulse to buy something from you. You stand to generate a lot more sales than you would otherwise.

But although credit cards are easy for shoppers to use, they make *your* life as an online merchant more complicated. You have two options:

- ✔ **Let your customers pay with a credit card through an online payment service.** This requires them to sign up with the same online payment service. But they gain protection from the payment service's security methods.

- ✔ **Sign up with your own merchant account.** This lets you shop around and choose the service with the lowest fees or the best service. But you have to jump through some hoops to get such an account.

I don't want to discourage you from becoming credit card–ready by any means, but you need to be aware of the steps (and the expenses) involved, many of which may not occur to you when you're just starting out. For example, you may not be aware of one or more of the following:

- ✔ **Merchant accounts:** You have to apply and be approved for a special bank account called a *merchant account* for a bank to process the credit card orders that you receive. If you work through traditional banks, approval can take weeks. However, a number of online merchant account businesses are providing hot competition, which includes streamlining the application process.

- ✔ **Fees:** Fees can be high, but they vary widely, and it pays to shop around. Some banks charge a merchant application fee ($300–$800). On the other hand, some online companies, such as 1st American Card Service (www.1stamericancardservice.com), charge no application fee. But other fees do apply (see the next bullet point).

- ✔ **Discount rates:** All banks and merchant account companies (and even payment companies such as PayPal) charge a usage fee, deceptively called a *discount rate*. Typically, this fee ranges from 1 to 4 percent of each transaction. Plus, you may have to pay a monthly premium charge in the range of $30–$70 to the bank. Although 1st American Card Service saves you money with a free application, it charges Internet businesses a 2.19 percent fee that it calls a discount rate, plus 25 cents for each transaction, an $8 monthly statement fee, and a minimum charge of $15 per month.

- ✔ **American Express and Discover:** If you want to accept payments from American Express and Discover cardholders, you must make arrangements through the companies themselves. You can apply online to be an American Express card merchant by going to the American Express

Merchant Homepage (https://merchant.americanexpress.com/accept-card/accepting-american-express-cards?inav=merch_ga_acceptcards) and click Apply Now (or something similar) link. At the Discover Card Network merchant site (www.discovernetwork.com/merchants) click the Start Accepting link and find your existing "acquirer" or bank that you use for other credit cards, so you can expand your account with that bank to accept Discover.

✔ **Software and hardware:** Unless you depend on a payment service such as PayPal, you need software or hardware to process transactions and transmit the data to the banking system. If you plan to accept credit card numbers online only and don't need a device to handle actual "card swipes" from in-person customers, you can use your computer modem to transmit the data. 1st American Card Service lets you use software dubbed Virtual WebLink for processing transactions with your browser, but you have to purchase the software for $39.95 and pay the usual discount rate and fees. This particular package includes a Virtual WebTerminal that lets you enter information manually and send it to the credit card network. Other systems require you to get a hardware terminal or phone line, which you can either purchase for $200 or more or lease for anywhere from $17 to $26 per month, depending on the length of the lease.

New payment systems provide more options

As we move farther into the web's second decade, the payment landscape hasn't changed dramatically. But things have shifted a bit. The changes actually give buyers and sellers more options:

✔ **More and more people are paying bills online.** This change has been taking place over several years and consumers are increasingly at ease with the process.

✔ **PayPal is not the only game in town.** This payment service is owned by eBay, but it can be used by anyone who wants to send or receive money online. PayPal is used by millions of auction sellers every month, but e-commerce store owners can use it, too.

✔ **Google is gaining.** Google Payments charges fees that are no lower than PayPal. Yet, shoppers and sellers alike flock to it. It provides an alternative to PayPal, which isn't popular with many buyers and sellers.

✔ **In-person payments are a square deal.** Lots of sellers also sell at flea markets and art fairs. They can now accept face-to-face credit card payments thanks to a device that connects to a smartphone and processes the payment by connecting to a credit card service. The best-known of these services is called Square Register (`https://squareup.com/`). But other, similar options are springing up, such as LevelUp, Bank of America Mobile Pay on Demand, and PayPal Here.

✔ **Overseas consumers are using new and innovative payment systems.** At some point, if you accept payments from overseas, you might be asked to accept Western Union money transfers or other payment schemes. It's the wave of the future as e-commerce becomes globalized.

The steps in the upcoming section, in which I explain how to create your own merchant account, are useful if you run a brick-and-mortar business that is tied to your online store. But if you don't want to go through the trouble, you might consider a payment service such as PayPal or Google Payments.

Watch for credit card fraud — criminals using stolen numbers to make purchases. You, the merchant, are liable for most of the fictitious transactions. Cardholders are responsible for only $50 of fraudulent purchases. To combat this crime, before completing any transaction, verify that the shipping address supplied by the purchaser is the same (or at least in the same vicinity) as the billing address. If you're in doubt, you can phone the purchaser for verification — it's a courtesy to the customer as well as a means of protection for you. (See the upcoming section "Verifying credit card data.") You can do this check yourself or pay a service to do it for you.

Setting up a merchant account

The good news is that getting merchant status is becoming easier for e-commerce enterprises because banks have accepted the notion that businesses don't have to have a physical storefront to be successful. Getting a merchant account approved, however, still takes a long time, and some hefty fees are involved as well. Banks look more favorably on companies that have been in business for several years and have a proven track record.

Traditional banks are reliable and experienced, and most are likely to be around for a while. The new web-based companies that specialize in giving online businesses merchant account status welcome new businesses and give you wider options and cost savings, but they're new; their services may not be as reliable and their future is less certain.

You can find a long list of institutions that provide merchant accounts for online businesses at one of the Yahoo! index pages:

```
dir.yahoo.com/Business_and_Economy/Business_to_Business/
        Financial_Services/Transaction_Clearing/Credit_
        Card_Merchant_Services
```

The list is so long that knowing which company to choose is difficult. I recommend visiting Wells Fargo Bank (`www.wellsfargo.com`). which has been operating online for several years and is well established. The Wells Fargo website provides a good overview of what's required to obtain a merchant account.

MyTexasMusic.com, the family-run business I profile in Chapter 2, uses a web-based merchant account company called GoEmerchant.com (`www.goemerchant.com`) to set up and process its credit card transactions. (The site also accepts PayPal payments.) This company offers a shopping cart and credit card and debit card processing to businesses that accept payments online. MyTexasMusic.com chose to use GoEmerchant after an extensive search because it found that the company would help provide reliable processing, while also protecting the business from customers who purchased items fraudulently.

One advantage of using one of the payment options set up by PayPal Payments (`www.paypal.com/webapps/mpp/merchant`) is that the system (which originated with the well-known companies CyberCash and VeriSign) was well known and well regarded before PayPal acquired it. I describe the widely used electronic payment company in the section "Choosing an Online Payment System," later in this chapter.

In general, your chances of obtaining merchant status are enhanced if you apply to a bank that welcomes Internet businesses, and if you can provide good business records proving that you're a viable business that makes money.

Be sure to ask about the discount rate that the bank charges for Internet-based transactions before you apply. Compare the rate for online transactions to the rate for conventional "card-swipe" purchases. Most banks and credit card processing companies charge 1 to 2 extra percentage points for online sales.

Do you use an accounting program, such as QuickBooks or MYOB Accounting? The manufacturers of these programs enable their users to become credit card merchants through their websites.

Finding a secure server

A *secure server* uses some form of encryption, such as SSL (which I describe in Chapter 6), to protect data that you receive over the Internet. Customers know that they've entered a secure area when the security key or lock icon at the bottom of the browser window looks locked.

If you plan to receive credit card payments, you definitely want to find a web hosting service that can protect the area of your online business that serves as the online store. In literal terms, you need secure server software protecting the directory on your site that receives customer-sent forms. Some hosts charge a higher monthly fee for using a secure server; with others, the secure server is part of a basic business website account. Ask your host (or hosts you're considering) whether any extra charges apply.

Verifying credit card data

Unfortunately, the world is full of bad people who try to use credit card numbers that don't belong to them. The anonymity of the web and the ability to shop anywhere in the world, combined with the ability to place orders immediately, can facilitate fraudulent orders, just as it can benefit legitimate orders.

Protecting yourself against credit card fraud is essential. Always check the billing address against the shipping address. If the two addresses are thousands of miles apart, contact the purchaser by phone to verify that the transaction is legit. Even if it is, the purchaser will appreciate your taking the time to verify the transaction.

You can use software to help check addresses. Here are three programs that perform this service:

- ✔ **ClearCommerce** (www.fisglobal.com/EMEA/UK/product-merchant acquiring-clearcommerce): This company sells both an automated payment system and payment authentication software that work with credit cards and banks.

- ✔ **PCCharge, VeriFone Payment Processing Software** (www.verifone. com/products/software/pc-payment-software/pccharge): This software enables individuals who use the VeriFone payment service to accept payments online as well.

- ✔ **Payment Software for Windows** (www.firstdata.com/en_us/ products/merchants/support/payment-software-3.html): Formerly known as ICVERIFY, this software verifies the address of the person making an online purchase as a defense against fraud.

Processing the orders

When someone submits credit card information to you, you need to transfer the information to the banking system. Whether you make this transfer yourself or hire another company to do it for you is up to you.

Do-it-yourself processing

To submit credit card information to your bank, you need point of sale (POS) hardware or software. The hardware, which you either purchase or lease from your bank, is a *terminal* — a gray box of the sort you see at many local retailers. The *software* is a program that contacts the bank through a modem.

The terminal or software is programmed to authorize the sale and transmit the data to the bank. The bank then credits your business or personal checking account. The bank also deducts the discount rate from your account weekly, monthly, or with each transaction.

If you have a small-scale website — perhaps with only one item for sale — you can use an online payment gateway, which enables you to add a Pay button to a catalog page that securely processes a customer's payment information. When you receive the information, you can manually submit it for payment by using a program such as First Data Global Gateway Connect (Virtual Terminal). The transaction is then processed on one of First Data's secure servers. Both you and your customer receive e-mail notifications that the transaction is complete. You can find out more on the First Data website at www.aboutcsi.com/secure-transaction-processing.html.

Automatic processing

You can hire a company to automatically process credit card orders for you. These companies compare the shipping and billing addresses to help make sure that the purchaser is the person who actually owns the card and not someone trying to use a stolen credit card number. If everything checks out, the company transmits the data directly to the bank.

You can look into the different options provided by VeriFone, Inc. (www.verifone.com), or AssureBuy (www.otginc.com) for such services.

Automatic credit card processing works so fast that your customer's credit card can be charged immediately, whether or not you have an item in stock. If a customer receives a bill and is still waiting for an item that is on back order, he or she can get very unhappy. For this reason, some business owners choose not to use this type of service.

Choosing an Online Payment System

Some organizations have devised ways to make e-commerce secure and convenient for shoppers and merchants alike. These alternatives fall into one of three general categories:

- ✔ Organizations that help you complete credit card purchases (for example, VeriSign Payment Services).

- ✔ Escrow services that hold your money for you in an account until shipment is received and then pay you, providing security for both you and your customers.

✔ Organizations that provide alternatives to transmitting sensitive information from one computer to another. A number of attempts to create "virtual money" have failed. However, companies such as PayPal let customers make payments by directly debiting their checking accounts.

To use one of these systems, you or your web host sets up special software on the computer that actually stores your website files. This computer is where the transactions take place. The following sections provide general instructions on how to get started with setting up each of the most popular electronic payment systems.

To work smoothly, some electronic payment systems require you to set up programming languages such as Perl, C/C++, or Visual Basic on your site. You also have to work with techy documents called *configuration files*. This is definitely an area in which paying a consultant to get your business set up saves time and headaches. It also gets your new transaction feature online more efficiently than if you tackle it yourself. PayPal, for example, provides support in setting up systems for its merchants; you can find an affiliate to help you or call the company directly. Visit the PayPal Payments page (`www.paypal.com/webapps/mpp/merchant`) for links and phone numbers.

Shopping cart software

When you go to the supermarket or another store, you pick goodies off the shelves and put them in a shopping cart. When you go to the cash register to pay for what you've selected, you empty the cart and present your goods to the cashier.

Shopping cart software performs the same functions on an e-commerce site. Such software sets up a system that allows online shoppers to select items displayed for sale. The selections are held in a virtual shopping cart that "remembers" what the shopper has selected before checking out.

Shopping cart programs are pretty technical for nonprogrammers to set up, but if you're ambitious and want to try it, you can download and install a free program — Perlshop (`www.waveridersystems.com/perlshop4/`). Signing up with a web host that provides you with shopping cart software as part of its services, however, is far easier than tackling this task yourself.

A shopping cart is often described as an essential part of many e-commerce websites, and web hosts usually boast about including a cart along with their other businesses services. You don't *have* to use a shopping cart on your site, though. Some shoppers are put off by them; they're just as likely to abandon a purchase than follow through by submitting payment. Plenty of other e-businesses allow users to phone or fax in an order or fill out an online form instead.

Reach for your wallet!

One of the terms commonly thrown around in the jargon of e-commerce is *wallet*. A *wallet* is software that, like a real wallet, stores available cash and other records. You reach into the cyberwallet and withdraw virtual cash rather than submit a credit card number.

The idea is that a cybershopper who uses wallet software, such as Windows Live ID (www.passport.com), can pay for items online in a matter of seconds, without having to transfer credit card data. What's more, some wallets can even "remember" previous purchases and suggest future purchases. It's taken years for the wallet concept to take hold in the United States, but one option is beginning to gain traction: Google Wallet (www.google.com/wallet). This app for Android phones allows consumers to pay at a growing number of retail outlets, including Best Buy, McDonald's, and CVS. If you're a merchant and you want to receive Google Wallet payments, read about it at www.google.com/wallet/business/. You have to apply and then be approved to receive the API (application

programming interface) needed to set up payments on your site.

Credit cards are quick and convenient, and they've proven to be secure enough for most consumers. Consumers who are committed to using Microsoft's services can use Windows Live ID, which offers a "single sign-in" to register or make purchases on sites that support this technology. It also enables consumers to create a wallet that stores their billing and shipping information. (Credit card numbers are stored in an offline database when users sign up for a Windows Live ID.) Customers can then make purchases at participating sites with the proverbial single mouse click. For your online business website to support Windows Live ID, you need to download and install the Windows Live ID Software Development Kit (SDK) on the server that runs your website. You may need some help in deploying this platform. Links to the SDK are included on the Windows Live ID SDK page (msdn.microsoft.com/en-us/library/bb404787.aspx).

PayPal payments

A good deal of this chapter is devoted to PayPal and its solutions for online buyers and sellers. PayPal is becoming a bigger player in the field of e-commerce. When it purchased the security company Verisign's payment services, it became even bigger. That's not necessarily a bad thing: The more users you have who take advantage of the same services, the more routine payments become, and the more customers trust the whole payment process.

PayPal's Payments page (www.paypal.com/webapps/mpp/merchant) includes services such as Payflow, which lets your company accept payments online, and Website Payments, which facilitates payment with either credit cards or a PayPal account. Options include

  ✔ **E-mail Payments:** Your customers pay through e-mail communications; you don't even need to have a website.

✔ **Website Payments Standard:** Your customers choose an item to buy and are sent to PayPal's site, where they can pay with a credit card or their PayPal account, if they have one.

✔ **Website Payments Pro:** Your customers choose an item to buy from a shopping cart you have on your site. They pay with a credit card on the site (PayPal processes the payment in the background) or to PayPal if they prefer to use their PayPal account.

Trying one of the following Payflow Payment Gateway options is free for 30 days to see how it works with your own business, but both options require that you have a merchant account. (If you don't have one, VeriSign suggests several financial institutions to which you can apply.) The Payflow services do carry some charges and require you to do some work, however:

✔ **Payflow Link:** The smallest and simplest of the VeriSign payment options, this service is intended for small businesses that process 500 transactions or fewer each month. You add a payment link to your online business site and you don't have to do programming or other site development to get the payment system to work. You pay a $179 setup fee and a $19.95 monthly fee.

✔ **Payflow Pro:** With this service, you can process up to 1,000 transactions per month, and any additional transactions cost 10 cents each. To use this option, you begin by installing the Payflow software on the server that runs your website. The customer then makes a purchase on your site, and the Payflow software sends the information to VeriSign, which processes the transaction. Payflow Pro carries a $249 setup fee and costs $59.95 per month.

You can sign up for a trial of Payflow Link or Payflow Pro on the Payflow Payment Gateway page (`www.paypal.com/webapps/mpp/payflow-payment-gateway`).

PayPal's personal payment services

PayPal was one of the first online businesses to hit on the clever idea of giving business owners a way to accept credit and debit card payments from customers without having to apply for a merchant account, download software, apply for online payment processing, or some combination of these steps.

PayPal's person-to-person payment services are ideal for transactions on eBay and other sites. In this sense, PayPal is essentially an *escrow service:* It functions as a sort of financial middleman, debiting buyers' accounts and crediting the accounts of sellers — and, along the way, exacting a fee for its services, which it charges to the merchant receiving the payment. The accounts involved can be credit card accounts, checking accounts, or accounts held at PayPal into which members directly deposit funds. In other words, the person making the payment sets up an account with PayPal by identifying which account (credit card or checking, for example) a payment is to be taken from. The merchant also has a PayPal account and has identified which checking or credit card account is to receive payments. PayPal handles the virtual "card swipe" and verification of customer information.

PayPal is best known as a way to pay for items purchased on eBay. eBay, in fact, owns PayPal. But the service is regularly used to process payments both on and off the auction site. If you want to sell items (including through your website), you sign up for a PayPal Business or Premier account. You get a PayPal button that you add to your auction listing or sales web page. (If you sell on eBay, this button is provided automatically.) The customer clicks the button to transfer the payment from his or her PayPal account to yours, and you're charged a transaction fee.

Setting up a PayPal account is free. Here's how you can set up a PayPal Business account:

1. **Go to the PayPal home page (**www.paypal.com**) and click the Sign Up Now button.**

   The PayPal Account Sign Up page appears.

2. **Choose your country of residence and your language, and click the Get Started button beneath PayPal for Business.**

   The Choose a PayPal Payments Solution page appears.

3. **For this example, click the Get Started button beneath Standard.**

   The Sign Up for PayPal Payments Standard page appears.

4. **Click Create New Account, verify your country and language preference, and click Create New Account.**

   The Business Account Sign Up page appears.

5. **Follow the instructions on the two registration form pages and set up your account with PayPal.**

   After you fill out the registration forms, you receive an e-mail message with a link that takes you to the PayPal website to confirm your e-mail address.

6. **Click the link contained in the e-mail message.**

   You go to the Enter Password page.

7. **Enter your password (the one you created during the registration process) in the Password box and then click the login button.**

   You go to the My Business Setup page.

8. **Click the Merchant Services tab at the top of the My Account page.**

9. **Click Create payment buttons for your website link.**

   The PayPal Payments Standard: Setup.

10. **Click Create a Button; then provide some information about the item you're selling, including**

    • Enter a brief description of your sales item in the Item Name box.

    • Enter an item number in the Item ID box.

    • Enter the price in the Price box.

    • Choose a button that shoppers can click to make the purchase. (You can choose either the PayPal logo button or a button that you've already created.)

11. **When you're done, click the Create Button button.**

    You go to the You Are Viewing Your Button Code page, as shown in Figure 7-1.

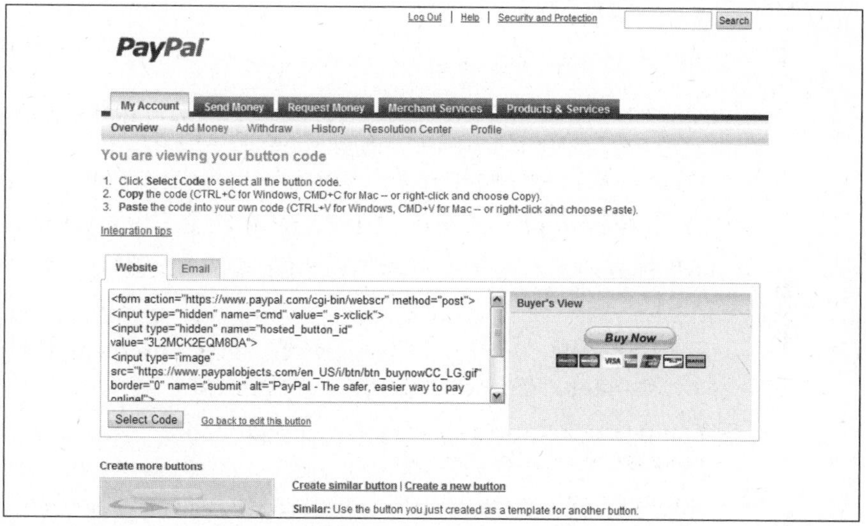

Figure 7-1:
Copy this code to your sales catalog web page to enable other PayPal users to transfer purchase money to your account.

12. **Copy the code in the Website box and paste it onto the web page that holds your sales item.**

    That's all there is to it. When you receive a payment through eBay, you receive an e-mail notification. An example of an e-mail I received is shown in Figure 7-2. When someone sends you money directly through PayPal, you see that, too. You can then verify the payment by logging in to your account on the PayPal website.

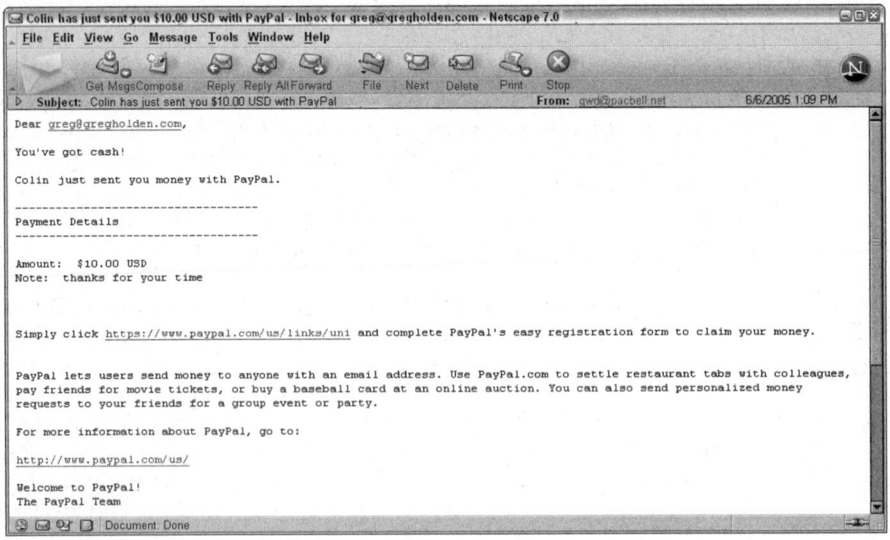

Colin has just sent you $10.00 USD with PayPal - Inbox for greg@gregholden.com - Netscape 7.0

File Edit View Go Message Tools Window Help

Get Msgs Compose   Reply Reply All Forward   File   Next   Delete   Print   Stop

Subject: Colin has just sent you $10.00 USD with PayPal   From: gwdi@pacbell.net   6/6/2005 1:09 PM

Dear greg@gregholden.com,

You've got cash!

Colin just sent you money with PayPal.

Payment Details

Amount: $10.00 USD
Note: thanks for your time

Simply click https://www.paypal.com/us/links/uni and complete PayPal's easy registration form to claim your money.

PayPal lets users send money to anyone with an email address. Use PayPal.com to settle restaurant tabs with colleagues,
pay friends for movie tickets, or buy a baseball card at an online auction. You can also send personalized money
requests to your friends for a group event or party.

For more information about PayPal, go to:

http://www.paypal.com/us/

Welcome to PayPal!
The PayPal Team

Document: Done

Figure 7-2:
When you
receive
payment
through
eBay or
directly
from an
individual,
you receive
a message
like this.

You should realize that accepting money on PayPal is *not* free. Buyers don't pay to use PayPal, but sellers do. I have a Premier account, and every time I receive money from an eBay transaction, PayPal takes its fees off the top. For a purchase of about $23, PayPal takes about $1 in fees, for example. On the plus side, PayPal does make a debit card available that you can use to make your own consumer purchases with the money in your account.

The nice thing about using PayPal is that the system enables you to accept payments through your website without having to obtain a merchant account. The thing to remember is that both you and your customers place a high level of trust in PayPal to handle your money. If fraud is a problem, PayPal investigates it — or is supposed to, anyway. Some former PayPal users detest PayPal because of what they describe as a lack of responsiveness, and they describe their unhappiness in great detail on sites such as www.paypalsucks.com. Be aware of such complaints to have the full picture about PayPal and anticipate problems before they arise.

Google Checkout

Google seems to have a finger in just about every pie when it comes to e-commerce. Payments are no exception. Google Checkout (checkout. google.com) is a convenient and safe way to pay online. The process of signing up for Google Checkout is relatively easy because you probably already have a Google password to check your Gmail or perform other services with Google. If you don't, just go to the Google Checkout home page and click Sign Up Now to obtain one.

Google Checkout was originally seen as a quick payment system for Google itself. If you saw something on a Google search results page and wanted to buy it, you could do so immediately through Google Checkout. But the service also functions as a full-fledged payment system much like PayPal: You sign up for Google Checkout and add "buy" buttons to your sale pages. Buyers can then click these buttons and pay you through Google Checkout. The service registers buyers and their credit card accounts, as well as sellers and their account information. Google Checkout receives payments and passes them on to sellers, and for its efforts, it subtracts a discount rate.

Currently, the rate stands at 2.9 percent plus a 30-cent fee for a purchase under $3,000. Rates are lower for purchases of higher amounts. This is virtually the same as PayPal's rate, at this writing.

One big difference between Google Checkout and PayPal is in the method of payment. Google Checkout accepts only credit card payments. PayPal, on the other hand, also allows withdrawals from bank accounts as well as "eChecks" (payments taken from a buyer's checking account and deposited in the seller's account after a suitable time for the "check" to clear).

Another difference between Google Checkout and PayPal is customer service. You can reach a PayPal service person on the phone, but you can't reach Google Checkout this way.

An article on CNET (`news.cnet.com/8301-30684_3-10348805-265. html`) reported on problems with recurring payments not being processed by Google Checkout for weeks at a time. Trying to reach a human being at Google to discuss the problems seems nearly impossible for the average merchant. (Writers like me can sometimes get a response from a PR person.)

On the plus side, Google Checkout is integrated with Google's popular AdWords system. If you have an active AdWords account, your discount rate is lowered.

An article on the EcommerceBytes website (`www.auctionbytes.com/cab/ abn/y09/m11/i05/s01`) indicates that there may be another advantage to accepting Google Checkout on your website. If you receive payments and then get positive rankings from your customers, you'll get better search placement for your site on Google.

Micropayments

Micropayments are very small units of currency that are exchanged by merchants and customers. The amounts involved may range from one-tenth of one cent (that's $.001) to a few dollars. Such small payments enable sites to provide content for sale on a per-click basis. For users to read articles, listen to music files, or view video clips online, some sites require micropayments in a special form of electronic cash that goes by names such as *scrip* or *eCash.*

Micropayments seemed like a good idea in theory, but they've never caught on with most consumers. On the other hand, they've never totally disappeared, either. The business that proved conclusively that consumers are willing to pay small amounts of money to purchase creative content online is none other than the computer manufacturer Apple, which revolutionized e-commerce with its iPod music player and iTunes Store. Every day, users pay $1.29 to download a song and add it to their iPod selections. But they make such payments with their credit cards, using real dollars and cents.

In other words, iTunes payments aren't true micropayments. But it's just about the only system I know that deals in small payments for items purchased or downloaded online that's really successful. While I was updating this book some news came out about a promising micropayment system called Tinypass (`www.tinypass.com`). It's used by Andrew Sullivan, one of the most successful bloggers around, to move his blog The Dish to a "paywall" system. Regular readers are asked to subscribe for $19.99 per year to read the blog without ads and without restrictions. Visitors are allowed to read a certain amount each month for free; after that, they must subscribe. In just a month, The Dish had collected more than $480,000 in subscriptions, so this is a case where micropayments are working. If you blog or plan to sell content, look into Tinypass.

Other payment options

A number of new online payment options let people pay for merchandise without having to submit credit card numbers or mail checks. Here are some additional options to consider:

- **Dwolla** (`www.dwolla.com`): This relatively new and increasingly popular payment services is great for small-scale sales— for transactions under $10, there are no fees. For a sale of more than $10, the fee is 25 cents.

- **Amazon Payments** (`payments.amazon.com`): Amazon enables users who sell online to accept payments from customers on their websites. Fees start at 2.9 percent plus a 30-cent transaction fee for payments over $10.

- **InspirePay** (`www.inspirepay.com`): Sometimes, shopping cart–based online payments aren't appropriate. Buyers who purchase a group of items from you at wholesale, for example, might prefer an invoice. If that's the case, and if your business also has a payment service in place (such as a merchant account, PayPal, Google Checkout, or Dwolla), consider InspirePay. Users create an InspirePay page, then request payment by sending the buyer a link. For a sale of $60, the link would take the form `https://inspirepay.com/pay/mark/$60.00`. In this case, when the recipient clicks on the link, InspirePay pays the sender $60.

✔ **ClearTran** (`www.bnymellon.com/cleartran/`): This service enables shoppers to make purchases by sending online checks to merchants. The shopper notifies the seller about the purchase and then contacts a special secure website to authorize a debit from his or her checking account. The secure site then transmits the electronic check to the merchant, who can either print the check on paper or save the check in a special format that can be transmitted to banks for immediate deposit.

Which one of these options is right for you? That depends on what you want to sell online. If you're providing articles, reports, music, or other content that you want people to pay a nominal fee to access, consider a micropayment system (see the preceding section). If your customers tend to be sophisticated, technically savvy individuals who are likely to embrace online checks or billing systems, consider ClearTran. The important things are to provide customers with several options for submitting payment and to make the process as easy as possible.

Fulfilling Your Online Orders

Being on the Internet can help when it comes to the final step in the e-commerce dance: order fulfillment. *Fulfillment* refers to what happens after a sale is made. Typical fulfillment tasks include the following:

✔ Packing up the merchandise

✔ Shipping the merchandise

✔ Solving delivery problems or answering questions about orders that haven't reached their destinations

✔ Sending out bills

✔ Following up to see whether the customer is satisfied

Order fulfillment may seem like the least exciting part of running a business, online or otherwise. But from your customers' point of view, it's the most important business activity of all. The following sections suggest how you can use your presence online to help reduce any anxiety your customers may feel about receiving what they ordered.

The back-end (or, to use the Microsoft term, BackOffice) part of your online business is where order fulfillment comes in. If you have a database in which you record customer orders, link it to your website so that your customers can track orders. Dreamweaver or ColdFusion can help you set up a database. (Dreamweaver contains built-in commands that let you link to a ColdFusion database.) Alternatively, if you don't want to go through the effort of setting up the database yourself, you depend on your marketplace's back-end capabilities, which may be more limited.

Providing links to shipping services

One advantage of being online is that you can help customers track packages after shipment. The FedEx online order-tracking feature, shown in Figure 7-3, gets thousands of requests each day and is widely known as one of the most successful marketing tools on the web. If you use FedEx, provide your customers with a link to its online tracking page.

Figure 7-3: Provide links to online tracking services so that your customers can check delivery status.

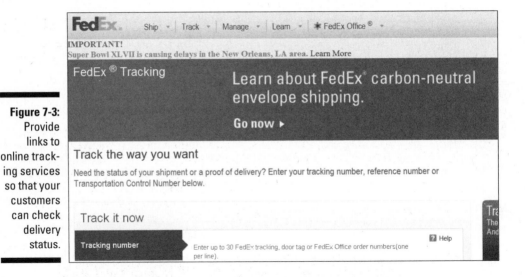

The other big shipping services have also created their own online tracking systems. You can link to these sites, too:

- United Parcel Service (www.ups.com).
- U.S. Postal Service Express Mail (www.usps.gov).
- DHL (www.dhl-usa.com). Be aware that DHL no longer accepts deliveries from the United States to a domestic U.S. address but will ship to/from other countries.

Presenting shipping options clearly

In order fulfillment, as in receiving payment, it pays to present your clients with as many options as possible and to explain the options in detail.

Because you're online, you can provide your customers with as much shipping information as they can stand. Web surfers are knowledge hounds — they can never get enough data, whether it's related to shipping or other parts of your business.

When it comes to shipping, be sure to describe the options, the cost of each, and how long each takes. Here are some more specific suggestions:

- ✔ **Compare shipping costs.** Use an online service, such as InterShipper (`www.intershipper.com`), that allows you to submit the origin, destination, weight, and dimensions of a package that you want to ship via a web page form and then returns the cheapest shipping alternatives.

- ✔ **Make sure you can track a package.** Pick a service that lets you track your package's shipping status.

- ✔ **Be able to confirm receipt.** If you use the U.S. Postal Service, ship the package "return receipt requested" because tracking isn't available — unless you use Priority Mail or Express Mail. You can confirm delivery with Priority Mail (domestic) and Parcel Post.

Many online stores present shipping alternatives in the form of a table or bulleted list of options — or, at the very least, a set of options that resembles a bulleted list. (*Tables,* as you probably know, are web page design elements that let you arrange content in rows and columns, making them easier to read; refer to Chapter 5 for more on adding tables to your site.) You don't have to look very far to find an example; just visit the Dummies.com website (`www.dummies.com`) and order a book from its online store. When you're ready to pay for your items and provide a shipping address, you see the shipping options, which are lined up just like a bulleted list, as shown in Figure 7-4.

Figure 7-4: Tables help shoppers calculate costs, keep track of purchases, and choose shipping options.

DUMMIES Store

Order Summary

Promotion Code

Enter your promotion code, then click the APPLY DISCOUNT button to the right. Your discount will be applied below.   [   ] Apply Code

Shipping Method

- ⦿ Surface, 7-10 business days (First item $6.00 + each additional item $2.00)
- ○ 2-Day, 2-3 business days (First item $12.00 + each additional item $4.00)
- ○ 1-Day, 1-2 business days (First item $25.00 + each additional item $4.00)

Orders submitted after 11:30 am EST will ship the following business day.

Title	Price	Quantity	Total
Investing Online For Dummies, 7th Edition	$24.99	1	$24.99

Joining the International Trade Brigade

International trade may seem like something that only multinational corporations practice. But the so-called little guys like you and me can be international traders, too. In fact, the term simply refers to a transaction between two or more individuals or companies in different countries. If you're a designer living in the United States and you create some stationery artwork and web pages for someone in Germany, you're involved in international trade.

Keeping up with international trade issues

If you really want to be effective in marketing yourself overseas and become an international player in world trade, you need to follow the tried-and-true business strategies: networking, education, and research. Join groups that promote international trade, become familiar with trade laws and restrictions, and generally get a feel for the best marketing practices around the world.

Here are some suggestions for places you can start:

✔ **The Market Access Unit page of the Irish government's Department of Enterprise, Trade, and Employment website** (www.entemp.ie/trade/marketaccess): This page contains links to the European Union's Commercial Policy as well as requirements governing Export Licensing and Import Licensing.

✔ **Small Business Exporters** Association (www.sbea.org): This group of small and midsize business exporters is devoted to networking, assistance, and advocacy.

✔ **globalEDGE** (globaledge.msu.edu/reference-desk): This site is published by Michigan State University and includes hundreds of international trade links.

✔ **Newsletter Access** (www.newsletteraccess.com/subject/intertrade.html): This website has information on how to subscribe to more than 9,000 different newsletters that discuss international trade issues.

Researching specific trade laws

Rather than wait for overseas business to come to you, take a proactive approach. First, do some research into the appropriate trade laws that apply to countries you might do business with. The Internet has an amazing amount of information pertaining to trade practices for individual countries.

You can seek out international business by using one or more message boards designed specifically for small business owners who want to participate in international trade. These message boards let users post *trade leads,* which are messages that announce international business opportunities.

For example, at the TradersCity Import and Export Trade Leads board (www.traderscity.com/board), you may find a message from a Finnish company selling surplus paint, a U.S. company that needs office equipment, or a British company offering X-ray equipment for export. Advertisements on this site typically include the URL for the business's website. The site does not charge a fee to post notices.

If you're in the business of creating computer software or hardware, you need to be aware of restrictions that the U.S. government imposes on the export of some computer-related products. In fact, you may incur a fine of more than $100,000 from the U.S. Treasury Department and the U.S. State Department for exporting just about anything high-tech to a Denied Person, Specially Designated National, or Restricted Country. The list of these people and countries changes frequently. Look for links to the current ones at www.treas.gov/offices/enforcement/ofac/sdn/.

The Buy & Sell Exchange site of the Federation of International Trade Associations (www.worldbid.com) lets you post your own trade leads or search for other leads by keyword. You can find the Trade Leads page of the extensive globalEDGE site (http://globaledge.msu.edu/global-resources/trade-leads) which includes links to sites that post trade leads in countries such as Egypt, India, and Taiwan.

Exploring free trade zones

A *free trade zone* (FTZ) is an officially designated business or industrial area in a country where foreign and domestic goods are considered to be "outside" the territory covered by customs. You don't have to pay customs duty, taxes, or tariffs on merchandise brought into, handled, or stored in an FTZ. You can find FTZs in many countries as well as in many U.S. states.

The purpose of FTZs is to reduce customs costs and make it easier for businesses to send goods into foreign countries. You can store your items in FTZs for a while, exhibit them, and, if necessary, change them to comply with the import requirements of the country in question, until you want to import them into that country.

Shipping Overseas Goods

It never hurts to state the obvious, so here goes: Don't depend on ground mail (appropriately nicknamed *snail mail)* to communicate with overseas customers. Use e-mail and fax to get your message across — and, if you have to ship information or goods, use airmail express delivery. Surface mail can take weeks or even months to reach some regions of some countries — if it gets there at all.

Your customer may ask you to provide an estimate of your export costs by using a special set of abbreviations called incoterms. *Incoterms* (short for *international commercial trade terms)* are standardized acronyms originally established in 1936 by the International Chamber of Commerce. They establish an international language for describing business transactions to prevent misunderstandings between buyers and sellers from different countries. Incoterms thus provide a universal vocabulary that is recognized by all international financial institutions.

Incoterms are most likely to apply to you if you're shipping a large number of items to an overseas factory rather than, for example, a single painting to an individual's home. But just in case you hit the big time, you should be aware of common incoterms, such as

- ✔ **EXW (Ex Works):** This term means that the seller fulfills his or her obligation by making the goods available to the buyer at the seller's own premises (or *works)*. The seller doesn't have to load the goods onto the buyer's vehicle unless otherwise agreed.

- ✔ **FOB (Free on Board):** This term refers to the cost of shipping overseas by ship — not something you're likely to do in this high-tech day and age. But if you sell a vintage automobile to a collector in France, who knows?

- ✔ **CFR (Cost and Freight):** This term refers to the costs and freight charges necessary to transport items to a specific overseas port. CFR describes only costs related to items that are shipped by sea and inland waterways and that go to an actual port. Another incoterm, CPT (Carriage Paid To), can refer to any type of transport, not just shipping, and refers to the cost for the transport (or *carriage)* of the goods to their destination.

You can find a detailed examination of incoterms at the International Chamber of Commerce website (`www.iccwbo.org/products-and-services/ trade-facilitation/incoterms-2010/`).

If the item you're planning to ship overseas by mail is valued at more than $2,500, the United States requires you to fill out and use the Automated Export System (AES) and submit it to a U.S. customs agent. The AES collects

Electronic Export Information (EEI). To use the AES, you need to obtain either filer certification or, if you create computer programs, software certification. You have to file for certification and take a short test. Links to detailed instructions on how to use the AES are available on the U.S. Census Bureau's website (`www.census.gov/foreign-trade/aes/documentlibrary/index.html`). You can file your electronic export data with the AES through the U.S. Customs Service's website (`www.cbp.gov/xp/cgov/trade/automated/aes/`).

Some nations require a certificate of origin or a signed statement that attests to the origin of the exported item. You can usually obtain such certificates through a local chamber of commerce.

Some purchasers or countries may also ask for a certificate of inspection stating the specifications met by the goods shipped. Inspections are performed by independent testing organizations.

Wherever you ship your items, be sure to insure them for the full amount they are worth — and tell your customers about any additional insurance charges upfront. Choose an insurance company that can respond quickly to claims made from your own country *and* from your customer's country.

Getting Paid in International Trade

Having an effective billing policy in place is especially important when your customers live thousands of miles away. The safest strategy is to request payment in U.S. dollars and ask for cash in advance. This approach prevents any collection problems and gets you your money right away.

What happens if you want to receive payment in U.S. dollars from someone overseas but the purchaser is reluctant to send cash? You have a couple of options:

- ✔ You can ask the purchaser to send you a personal check — or, better yet, a cashier's check — but it's up to the buyer to convert the local currency to U.S. dollars.

- ✔ You can suggest that the buyer obtain an International Money Order from a U.S. bank that has a branch in his or her area, and specify that the money order be payable in U.S. dollars.

Suggest that your customers use an online currency conversion utility, such as the Bloomberg Online Currency Calculator (`www.bloomberg.com/markets/currencies/currency-converter`) to do the calculation.

You can also use an online escrow service — such as Escrow.com (www.escrow.com) or Skrill (formerly Moneybookers.com; www.moneybookers.com) — to hold funds in escrow until you and your customer strike a deal. An *escrow service* holds the customer's funds in a trust account so that the seller can ship an item knowing that he or she will be paid. The escrow service transfers the funds from buyer to seller after the buyer has inspected the goods and approved them.

Escrow services usually accept credit card payments from overseas purchasers; this is one way to accept credit card payments even if you don't have a merchant account yourself. The credit card company handles conversion from the local currency into U.S. dollars.

If you're doing a lot of business overseas, consider getting export insurance to protect yourself against loss from damage or delay in transit. Policies are available from the Export-Import Bank of the United States (www.exim.gov) or from other private firms that offer export insurance.

Chapter 8

Communicating with Customers and Building Loyalty

1 once spoke to an antiques dealer who has been selling in a brick-and-mortar store for more than 30 years and several years online. "When someone asks me a question, I am very polite in my answer," said Eva Kertesz. "Good correspondence with customers is very important. I don't use any special gimmick."

Besides having a good idea and lots of chutzpah, the best sellers invariably provide the best customer service. They include extras such as cards and gifts in packages, they make an effort to ship merchandise the same day it's purchased, they have a clear return policy and stick to it, and they answer questions promptly. All of these things help create a positive feedback cycle: You provide good service and get good response from customers, you build more trust, you inspire more people to buy from you, and on and on. When I made an effort to include some "extras" with my packages and to ship quickly and carefully, I received my own glowing comments of appreciation, which proved highly satisfying.

Customer service is one area in which small, entrepreneurial businesses can outshine brick-and-mortar stores and even larger online competitors. Whether you're competing in the areas of e-trading, e-music, or e-tail sales of any sort doesn't matter. Tools such as e-mail, RSS feeds, and interactive forms, coupled with the fact that an online commerce site can provide information 24/7, give you a powerful advantage when it comes to retaining customers and building loyalty. Make no mistake: Giving personal attention to customers who call you on the phone or demand instant shipment is hard work. But it pays off in the long run.

Being responsive and available is only part of the picture, however. This chapter presents ways to succeed with the other essential components: providing information, communicating effectively, and enabling your clientele to talk back to you online.

Keeping Your Customers in the Loop

Satisfaction is all about expectations. If you give your customers what they're expecting or even a little bit more, they'll be happy. But how do you go about setting their level of expectation in the first place? Communication is the key. The more information you can provide upfront, the fewer phone queries or complaints you'll receive later. Printed pamphlets and brochures have traditionally described products and services at length. Online is now the way to go, though.

Say you're talking about a 1,000-word description of your new company and your products, services, or both. If that text were formatted to fit on a 4-x-9-inch foldout brochure, the contents would cover several panels and take at least a few hundred dollars to print.

On the other hand, if those same 1,000 words were arranged on a few web pages and put online, they'd probably be no more than 5KB–10KB in size. The same applies if you distribute your content to subscribers in an e-mail newsletter. In either case, you pay only a little to publish the information.

Online publishing also has the advantage of easier updating. When you add new products or services, or even when you want a different approach, it takes only a little time and effort to change the contents or the look.

Providing FAQs

FAQs (frequently asked questions) can be found on nearly every organization's website. They have worked for many online businesspeople, and they can work for you.

Even the format of FAQ pages is similar from site to site, and this predictability is an asset. FAQ pages are generally presented in Q-and-A format, with topics appearing in the form of questions that have literally been asked by other customers or that have been made up to resemble real questions. Each question has a brief answer that provides essential information about the business.

Just because I'm continually touting communication doesn't mean I want you to bore your potential customers with endless words that don't apply to their interests. To keep your FAQ page from getting too long, I recommend that you list all the questions at the top of the page. This way, by clicking a hyperlinked item in the list, readers jump to the spot on the page where you present the question that relates to them and its answer in detail.

Just having a FAQ page isn't enough. Make sure that yours is easy to use and comprehensive. Take a look at one of the most famous of the genre, the venerable World Wide Web FAQ by Thomas Boutell `www.boutell.com/newfaq` for ideas.

Sure, you could compose a FAQ page off the top of your head, but sometimes getting a different perspective helps. Invite visitors, customers, friends, and family to come up with questions about your business. You may want to include questions on some of the following topics:

- ✔ **Contact information:** If I need to reach you in a hurry by mail, fax, or phone, how do I do that? Are you available only during certain hours?

- ✔ **Instructions:** What if I need more detailed instructions on how to use your products or services? Where can I find them?

- ✔ **Service:** What do I do if the merchandise breaks or doesn't work for some reason? Do you have a return policy?

- ✔ **Sales tax:** Is sales tax added to the cost I see onscreen?

- ✔ **Returns or exchanges:** If I'm not satisfied, can I get my money back or exchange an item? Is there a time limit on this policy?

- ✔ **Shipping:** What are my shipping options?

Nothing makes you look worse than an out-of-date FAQ page. Keep your page up to date as your business grows. Make sure the questions match the sales items and services that you actually provide.

Writing an online newsletter

You may define yourself as an online businessperson, not a newsletter editor. But sharing information with customers and potential customers through an e-mail newsletter is a great way to build credibility for yourself and your business.

For added customer service (not to mention a touch of self-promotion), consider producing a regular publication that you send out to a mailing list. Your mailing list would begin with customers and prospective customers who visit your website and indicate that they want to subscribe.

An e-mail newsletter doesn't happen by magic, but it can provide your business with long-term benefits that include

✔ **Customer tracking:** You can add subscribers' e-mail addresses to a mailing list that you can use for other marketing purposes, such as promoting special sales items for return customers.

✔ **Low bandwidth:** An e-mail newsletter doesn't require much memory. Such newsletters are great for businesspeople who get their e-mail on the road via laptops, Palm devices, or appliances that are designed specifically for sending and receiving e-mail.

✔ **Timeliness:** You can include breaking news in your electronic newsletter much faster than you can put it in print.

The fun part is to name your newsletter and assemble the content you want to include. Then follow these steps to get your publication up and running:

1. **Create your newsletter by typing the contents in plain-text (ASCII) format.**

   Optionally, you can also provide an HTML-formatted version. You can then include headings and graphics, which show up in e-mail programs that support HTML e-mail messages.

   If you use a plain-text newsletter, format it by using capital letters; rules that consist of a row of equal signs, hyphens, or asterisks; or blank spaces to align elements.

2. **Save your file with the proper filename extension: `.txt` for the text version and `.htm` or `.html` if you send an HTML version.**

3. **Attach the file to an e-mail message by using your e-mail program's method of sending attachments — or paste it into the body of the message if your recipients don't receive attachments.**

4. **Address your e-mail to the recipients.**

   If you have lots of subscribers (many newsletters have hundreds or thousands), save their addresses in a mailing list. Use your e-mail program's address book function to do this.

5. **Send your newsletter.**

If you have a large number of subscribers, I recommend sending your publication late at night, when there is generally less traffic on the Internet. I also recommend sending it in several stages — that is, to only so many subscribers simultaneously — rather than all at one time. Those are two good ways to help your words reach their destination quickly and reliably.

Managing a mailing list can be time consuming. You have to keep track of people who want to subscribe or unsubscribe, as well as those who ask for more information. You can save time and trouble by installing a management system such as Lyris ListManager (www.lyris.com) to do the day-to-day list management for you.

The popular e-mail communication service Constant Contact makes it easy to format a publication or message to send to a group. You can insert images from a library you create, and add colors and change type styles as well. The body of a message I'm working on and a menu of text tools with which to edit it is shown in Figure 8-1. The program also makes it easy for recipients to unsubscribe if they wish.

Figure 8-1:
Constant
Contact lets
you format
messages
and manage
an e-mail
list.

 Adobe's Portable Document Format (PDF) enables you to save a publication with the images, special typefaces, and other layout features intact. You can save your file as a PDF document and mail it. Recipients need the widely available program Adobe Reader to open it. You can create PDF files with the CutePDF (www.cutepdf.com) application.

Mixing bricks and clicks

If you operate a brick-and-mortar business as well as a web-based business, you have additional opportunities to get feedback from your shoppers. Take advantage of the fact that you meet customers personally and ask them for opinions and suggestions that can help you operate a more effective website.

When your customers make a purchase, include a message on the receipt asking them to go to your website where they can enter to win a cash prize if they fill out a questionnaire about your website within 24 hours. Consider asking questions like the following:

- ✔ Have you visited this store's website? Are you familiar with it?
- ✔ Would you visit the website more often if you knew there was merchandise or content there that you couldn't find in our physical location?
- ✔ Can you suggest some types of merchandise, or special sales, you'd like to see on the website?

It's also a good idea to include your website's URL on the printed literature in your store. The feedback system works both ways, of course: You can ask online customers for suggestions on how to run your brick-and-mortar store better and what types of merchandise they'd like to see on your real, as opposed to your "virtual," shelves.

Creating an RSS feed

E-mail newsletters and hyperlinks are becoming passé. These days, blogs and RSS feeds are the preferred options for getting the word out. The phrase "send an RSS feed of your website or eBay listings" might sound really high-tech and complex. But it's Really Simple — Really Simple Syndication, or RSS, that is.

RSS converts the contents of a web page to an eXtensible Markup Language (XML) file so that it can be read in a flash by anyone with an *RSS reader* software program. People subscribe to your RSS feed, and they receive it each time your site's contents are updated.

RSS is a marketing tool that is widely used in the world of blogs. Just as a blog publisher can, you can capture an RSS feed of your sales and offer it (you might say, *feed it*) to customers who want to subscribe to it. If you sell through an eBay Store (an option I describe in Chapter 14), it's easy to get started. Follow these steps:

1. **Subscribe to a feeder program, such as FeedBurner (**www.feed burner.com**), or one of the readers I describe in Chapter 1.**

2. **Go to your MyeBay page at** www.ebay.com **and sign in with your User ID and password if needed.**

   The MyeBay page appears.

3. **Hover your mouse pointer over the Account tab and then select Marketing Tools from the drop-down list.**

4. **In the Store Marketing links on the left side of the page, click the RSS Feeds link.**

5. **In the RSS Feeds for eBay Buyers area, select the Activate Your Fixed Price Listings via RSS option.**

6. Click Apply.

eBay creates the file within 12 hours and posts it to a web address (URL) based on your Store's URL. Enter the URL in your web browser to see if the content is available. For example, if your Store's name is "Flashy Shoes," the file is posted to `http://esssl.ebay.com/GetListings/ flashyshoes.`

Once your RSS feed is available, tell your customers they can access it. If you don't sell through eBay, turning your catalog listings into an RSS feed isn't quite as simple. You need to come up with a standard description for your listings: a listing title, description, and hyperlink. You then format each item like this:

```
<item>
<title>Model 101 Widget</title>
<description>Check out the 101, the latest and greatest widget offering ever!</
          description>
<link>http://www.mywidgetcatalog.com/widget101.html</link>
</item>
```

You go to a site, such as Feed Validator (`http://feedvalidator.org`), to make sure that your formatting is correct. Then subscribe to one of the RSS readers mentioned at `http://searchenginewatch.com/article/ 2065637/RSS-Your-Gateway-To-News-Blog-Content` or in Chapter 1 of this book. Copy your feed to the reader and distribute it. Find more info about creating feeds at `http://searchenginewatch.com/article/2065614/ Making-An-RSS-Feed.`

Helping Customers Reach You

I have an unlisted home phone number. But being anonymous is not the way to go when you're running an online business. (I use a different number for business calls, by the way.) Of course, you don't have to promise to be available 24/7 to your customers. But they need to believe that they can get attention no matter what time of the day or night. When you're online, contact information can take several forms. Be sure to include

- ✔ Your snail-mail address
- ✔ Your e-mail address(es)
- ✔ Your phone and fax numbers as well as a toll-free number (if you have one)

My brother recently obtained a toll-free (800) number for his audio restoration business (`www.lp2cdsolutions.com`). He obtained the number for $30 and then had the number assigned to a landline (not a cell phone line). A service called uReach (`www.ureach.com`) can forward a toll-free number to your cell phone. And businesses such as TollFreeNumber.org (`www.tollfreenumber.org`) give you an 800 number that rings on your cell phone. Of course, you also pay for the calls. Ask your local phone company for more information. Google Voice (`www.google.com/voice`) offers voice service, although a nonprofit group I am affiliated with has had trouble getting it to work. Maybe you'll have better luck.

Most web hosting services (such as the types of hosts I describe in Chapter 4) give you more than one e-mail inbox as part of your account. So it may be helpful to set up more than one e-mail address: one for people to communicate with you personally and the other where people go for general information. You can also set up e-mail addresses that respond to messages by automatically sending a text file. (See the "Setting up autoresponders" section, later in this chapter.)

Even though you probably won't meet many of your customers in person, you need to provide them with a human connection. Keep your site as personal and friendly as possible. A contact page is a good place to provide some brief biographical information about the people visitors can contact, namely you and any employees or partners in your company.

Putting your contact information on a separate web page makes your patrons have to wait a few seconds to access it. If your contact data is simple and your website consists of only a few pages, by all means put it right on your home page.

Going upscale with your e-mail

These days nearly everyone I know, including my father, has an e-mail account. But when you're an online businessperson, you need to know more about the features of e-mail than just how to ask about the weather or exchange a recipe. The more you discover about the finer technical points of e-mail, the better you can meet the needs of your clients. The following sections suggest ways to go beyond simply sending and receiving e-mail messages so that you can use e-mail for business publishing and marketing.

Don't forget e-mail basics when it comes to customer service. Tim Nguyen, a former eBay seller who became sales manager at Trumpia (`www.trumpia.com`), told me he learned how to be professional with his e-mails — to respond in a timely manner. "Timing is everything, because you're not dealing with customers face-to-face."

Setting up autoresponders

An *autoresponder*, also called a *mailbot*, is software that you can set up to send automatic replies to requests for information about a product or service, or to respond to people subscribing to an e-mail publication or service.

You can provide automatic responses either through your own e-mail program or your web host's e-mail service. If you use a web host to provide automatic responses, you can usually purchase an extra e-mail address that can be configured to return a text file (such as a form letter) to the sender.

Look for a web host that provides you with one or more autoresponders along with your account. Typically, your host assigns you an e-mail address that takes the form info@mycompany.com. In this case, someone at your hosting service configures the account so that when a visitor to your site sends a message to info@yourcompany.com, a file of your choice, such as a simple text document that contains background information about you and your services, automatically goes out to the sender as a reply. You can do this in Gmail by following these steps:

1. **Click the gear icon in the upper right corner of the Gmail window.**

2. **Click Settings from the drop-down list that appears.**

   The Settings options appear in the main area of the Gmail window.

3. **In the General Settings area (the options that appear beneath the Settings heading), scroll down to Vacation Responder and select the Vacation Responder On option.**

4. **Type a subject and message for your automatic response in the Subject and Message fields, as shown in Figure 8-2.**

5. **(Optional) Select the Only Send a Response to People in My Contacts check box if you don't want everyone who e-mails you to know that you're away from your mail.**

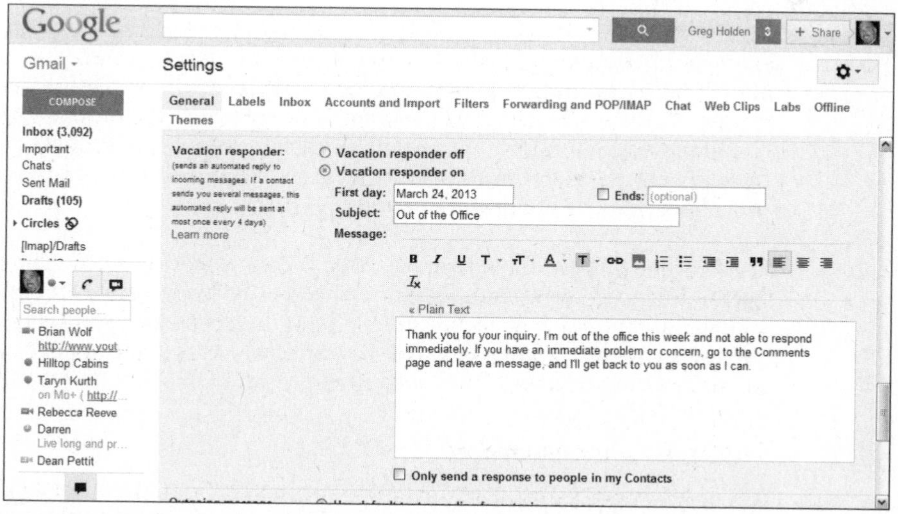

Figure 8-2: Many web hosts and ISPs enable users to create their own auto-response messages.

6. **Click Save Changes when you're done.**

    With the vacation responder turned on, you see a banner across the top of any Gmail page, displaying the subject of your vacation response. To stop Gmail from automatically sending the response, click End Now in the banner.

If the service that hosts your website doesn't provide free autoresponders, look into *SendFree,* an online service that provides you with autoresponder service for free but requires you to display ads along with your automatic response. (An ad-free version is available for $19.97 per month.) Read about it at www.sendfree.com.

Noting by quoting

Responding to a series of questions is easy when you use *quoting* — a feature that lets you copy portions of the message to which you're replying. Quoting, which is available in almost all e-mail programs, is particularly useful for responding to a mailing list or newsgroup message because it indicates the specific topic being discussed.

How do you tell the difference between the quoted material and the body of the new e-mail message? The common convention is to put a greater-than (>) character in the left margin, next to each line of quoted material.

When you tell your e-mail software to quote the original message before you type your reply, it generally quotes the entire message. To save space, you can *snip* (delete) the part that isn't relevant. However, if you do so, it's polite to type the word <snip> to show that you've cut something out.

Attaching files

A quick and convenient way to transmit information is to attach a file to an e-mail message. In fact, attaching files is one of the most useful things you can do with e-mail. *Attaching* — sending a document or file along with an e-mail message — allows you to include material from any file to which you have access. Attached files appear as separate documents that recipients can download to their computers.

Many e-mail clients allow users to attach files with the simple click of a button or other command. Compressing a lengthy series of attachments by using software, such as StuffIt or WinZip, conserves bandwidth. Using compression is also a necessity if you want to send more than one attached file to someone whose e-mail account (such as an AOL account) doesn't accept multiple attachments.

Creating a signature file that sells

One of the easiest and most useful tools for marketing on the Internet is a signature file, or sig file. A *signature file* is a text blurb that your system appends automatically to the bottom of your e-mail messages and newsgroup postings. You want your signature file to tell the readers of your message something about you and your business. You can include information such as your company name and how to contact you.

Creating a signature file takes only a little more time than putting your John Hancock on the dotted line. First, to create the signature file itself, follow these steps:

1. **Open a text-editing program.**

   This example uses Notepad, which comes built in with Windows. If you're a Mac user, you can use SimpleText. With either program, a new blank document opens onscreen.

2. **Press and hold down the hyphen (–) key or the equal sign (=) key to create a dividing line that separates your signature from the body of your message.**

   Depending on which symbol you use, a series of hyphens or equal signs forms a broken line. Don't make this line too long, or it runs onto another line, which doesn't look good; 30 to 40 characters is a safe measure.

3. **Type the information about yourself that you want to appear in the signature, pressing Enter after each line.**

   Include such information as your name, job title, company name, e-mail address, and website URL, if you have one. A three- or four-line signature is the typical length.

   If you're feeling ambitious, you can press the spacebar to arrange your text in two columns. My agent (who's an online entrepreneur) does this with his own signature file, as shown in Figure 8-3.

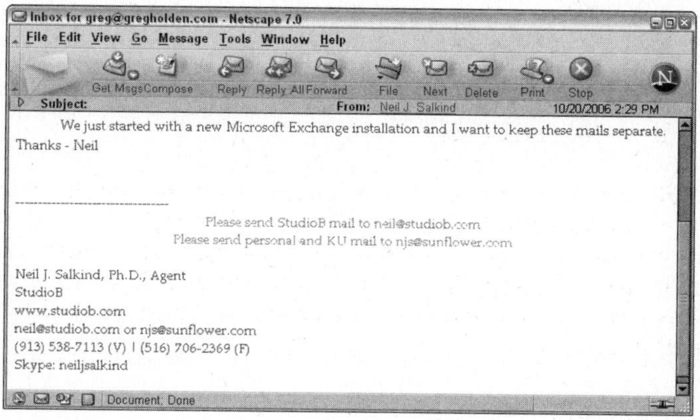

Figure 8-3: A signature file often uses divider lines and a two-column format to occupy less space onscreen.

Always include the URL to your business website in your signature file, and be sure to include it on its own line. Why? Most e-mail programs recognize the URL as a web page by its prefix (`http://`). When your reader opens your message, the e-mail program displays the URL as a clickable hyperlink that, when clicked, opens your web page in a web browser window.

4. **Choose File⇨Save.**

   A dialog box appears, in which you can name the file and save it to a folder on your hard drive.

5. **Type a name for your file that ends in the filename extension** `.txt`.

   This extension identifies your file as a plain-text document.

6. **Click Save.**

   Your text file is saved on your computer's hard drive.

If you created a plain-text version of your electronic signature, the next step is to identify that file to the computer programs that you use to send and receive e-mail and newsgroup messages. Doing so enables the programs to make the signature file appear automatically at the bottom of your messages. The procedure for attaching a signature file varies from program to program; the following steps show you how to do it using Microsoft Outlook Express 6:

1. **Start Outlook Express and choose Tools⇨Options.**

   The Options dialog box opens.

2. **Click the Signatures tab.**

3. **Click New.**

   The options are highlighted in the Signatures and Edit Signature sections of the Signatures tab.

4. **Click File at the bottom of the tab and then click Browse.**

   The Open dialog box appears. This is a standard Windows navigation dialog box that lets you select folders and files on your computer.

5. **Locate the signature file that you created in the preceding set of steps by selecting a drive or folder from the Look In drop-down list.**

6. **When you locate the file, click the filename and then click Open.**

   The Signature File dialog box closes, and you return to the Options dialog box. The path leading to the selected file is listed in the box next to File.

7. **Select the Add Signatures to All Outgoing Messages check box and then click OK.**

   The Options dialog box closes, and you return to Outlook Express. Your signature file is added automatically to your messages.

To test your new signature file, choose File⇨New⇨Mail Message from the Outlook Express menu bar. A new message composition window opens. Your signature file appears in the body of the message composition window. You can compose a message by clicking before the signature and typing.

Signature files, autoresponders, and other techy gimmicks are fine, but the key to making them work is checking your e-mail and phone messages every single day. That includes weekends! If you can't do the job yourself, assign an employee to do it. That's the single most important customer service tip I can give you: Check your messages as frequently as possible, and respond to inquiries as quickly as you can.

Creating forms that aren't formidable

In the old days, people who heard "Here's a form to fill out" usually started to groan. Who likes to stare at a form to apply for a job or for financial aid, or, even worse, to figure out how much you owe in taxes? But as an online businessperson, forms can be your best friends because they give customers a means to provide you with feedback as well as essential marketing information. With forms, you can find out where customers live, how old they are, and so on. Customers can also use forms to sound off and ask questions.

Forms can be really handy from the perspective of the customer as well. The speed of the Internet enables them to dash off information right away. They can then pretty much immediately receive a response from you that's tailored to their needs and interests.

The two components of web page forms

Forms consist of two parts, only one of which is visible on a web page:

- ✔ The *visible* part of the form includes the text-entry fields, buttons, and check boxes that an author creates with HTML commands.
- ✔ The *invisible* part of the form is a computer script that resides on the server that receives the page.

The script, which is typically written in a language such as Perl, AppleScript, or C++, processes the form data a reader submits to a server and presents that data in a format the owner or operator of the website can read and use.

Getting the data

Exactly what happens when customers connect to a page on your site that contains a form? First, they fill out the text-entry fields and other areas you have set up, and select the option (sometimes called radio) buttons. When they finish, they click a button, often marked Submit, to transmit (or *post*) the data from the remote computer to your website.

A computer script called a Common Gateway Interface (CGI) program receives the data submitted to your site and processes it so that you can read it. The CGI may cause the data to be e-mailed to you, or it may present the data in a text file in an easy-to-read format.

Optionally, you can also create a CGI program that prompts your server to send users to a web page acknowledging that you received the information and thanking them for their feedback. This is a nice touch that your customers are sure to appreciate.

Writing the scripts that process form data is definitely the province of webmasters or computer programmers and is far beyond the scope of this book. But you don't have to hire someone to write the scripts: You can use a web page program (such as Microsoft Expression Web or Adobe Dreamweaver) that not only helps you create a form, but also provides you with scripts that process the data for you.

Some clever businesspeople have created really useful web content by providing a way for nonprogrammers, such as you and me, to create forms online. Appropriately enough, you connect to the server's website and fill out a form provided by the service to create your form. The form has a built-in CGI that processes the data and e-mails it to you.

Using Expression Web to create a form

You can use Microsoft Expression Web to create the data-entry parts of forms, such as text boxes and check boxes. You can then link your form to a behind-the-scenes script that processes form data, such as the popular FormMail program provided free online by Matt Wright in Matt's Script Archive (www.scriptarchive.com/formmail.html). Creating your own form gives you more control over how it looks and a greater degree of independence than if you use a ready-made forms service.

You don't have to look far to find FormMail. It's popular enough that many web hosts provide it on their web servers. I found it already up and running on mine. All I had to do was "point" the form to the script to process the data and send it to myself in an e-mail message.

The first step in setting up a web page form is determining what information you want to receive from someone who fills out the form. Your web page creation tool then gives you options to ask for the information you want. Start Expression Web and open the Toolbox by selecting Toolbox from the Task Panes menu. When the Toolbox opens, click the plus sign (+) next to Form Controls. Drag the form object into the page at the spot where you want the form to appear. The Toolbox also gives you a selection of the most commonly used options, including

- ✔ **Text Box:** Creates a single-line box in which someone can type text
- ✔ **Text Area:** Creates a scrolling text box
- ✔ **File Upload:** Lets the user send you a text file
- ✔ **Check Box:** Creates a check box
- ✔ **Input (Radio):** Creates an option (radio) button
- ✔ **Drop-Down Box:** Lets you create a drop-down list
- ✔ **Picture:** Lets you add a graphic image to a form

Figure 8-4 shows the most common form fields as they appear in a web page form that you're creating.

When you add the form control to a page you're designing, Expression Web inserts a dashed, marquee-style box in your document to signify that you're working on web page form fields rather than normal web page text.

You can download Microsoft Expression Web at www.microsoft.com/en-us/download/details.aspx?id=24739.

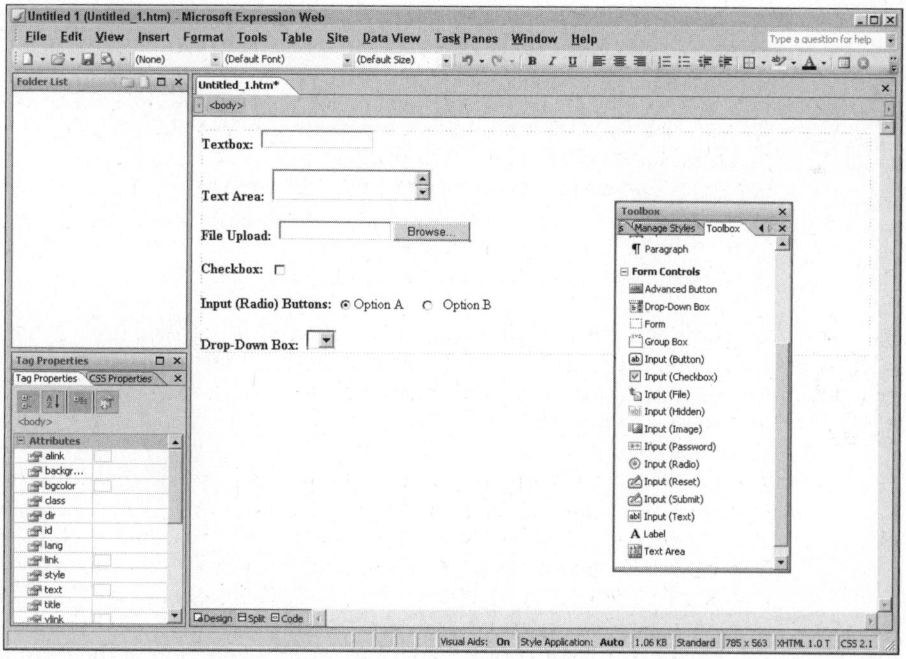

Figure 8-4: Expression Web provides you with a Toolbox for quickly creating form elements.

CASE STUDY

Adding the personal touch that means so much

Sarah-Lou Morris started her business out of an apartment in London, England, in 1997. She developed an herbal insect repellent — Alfresco — while working in a botanical and herbal research center. Since then, sales have grown quickly, often doubling each year. One key to Morris's quick success is her personal approach to serving her customers, who include movie stars on location and other prominent entertainers such as Sir Paul McCartney.

Morris describes her website and operation (www.alfrescoshop.com), shown in the accompanying figure, as "an extremely lively business . . . an ever-growing, 24/7-demanding teenager that could easily drain my resources if I didn't keep a *very* tight shop." Over the years, she stuck to basic business practices and focused on cultivating the customer base she had already developed through selling her product by word of mouth. (The trendy term for this type of publicity is *viral marketing;* see Chapter 10 for more on this topic.) She started a fan club for Alfresco, and she has personally visited some of her best customers. Today, she is expanding her marketing to include social networks and is creating a new product line to reach younger customers.

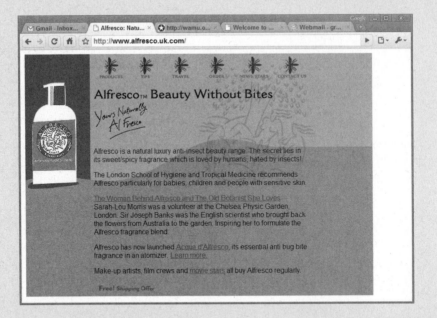

Q. How have you been able to keep a steady flow of business amid the ups and downs of the world economy?

A. We have built a bigger and bigger customer base by constantly giving good service to customers. We send out special editions for frequent buyers, have a fan club, and encourage customers to make recommendations. We listen to our customers — why wouldn't we? Our site could be more automated, making it easier for us to run, but we'd lose the personal touch. It's still rewarding, and

I think profitable in the long term, to take a phone call or e-mail from some VIP in Rome or a badly bitten Chinese customer wanting quickly to buy what a friend just bought. The effort is still geared toward turning the products into a worldwide addiction-by-Internet.

I'm launching a new kids' product, Alfrescokids, that will bring in a new customer age range including young mums and dads, and young families. I decided to turn the concept of "insect repellent" on its head and make the theme for the site "attracting and preserving bugs" as they are part of our food chain. I have gathered good insect-related content and am hoping both children and adults will always think of our site as fun and contemporary.

Q. What are the one or two of the most important things people should keep in mind if they're starting an online business these days?

A. It isn't necessary to spend fortunes setting it up. Find a host that has been in business a number of years. (There *are* experts now.) A clean database that really works for you is vital because your customers are the most precious things a business can have. Keep in touch with them. Treat them with care and respect.

Q. What new approaches are you using to reach your customers?

A. Attracting the interest of search engines is a priority. We have spent enormous time researching our competition as well as the keywords people search for. And we are making sure we are sincere in our ethics. It's important to write intelligently about your products and services in a truthful and interesting way. Search engine robots wander about sites sifting the "worthwhile" from the "not so." If you don't spend time working on getting across clearly and precisely what is being sold, Google Robots will put you at the bottom of the pile.

I realize that including blogs, Twitter posts, newsletters, et al. is going to mean our staff will be extra busy. I have a website that attracts worldwide attention and I am very pleased to put on a good show. Most important is our customers' recommendations and word of mouth. Our Fan Club now enables lots of banter and travel tips, with offers and goodies from all kinds of areas.

Q. What's the single best improvement you've made to your site to attract more customers or retain the ones you've had?

A. Putting on a special code that only special customers or fan club members can access for discounts and so on. For example, Royal Bank of Scotland employees have a special code dedicated to them.

Q. Is this a good time to start an online business?

A. It's a great time to start an e-commerce biz for a number of reasons, not the least being that the technical support is now well and truly in place. Let's just say more people know what they're doing than in earlier years. Secondly, most new customers aren't as concerned about credit card security, as there really has been hardly any fraud.

Q. What advice would you give to someone thinking of starting a new business on the Web?

A. Your customer is king, queen, prince, and princess. Whatever you would like yourself is what you should aim to offer. "Do as you would like to be done by" should be your motto. Expose yourself any which way and as often as is acceptable to as many well-targeted customers as possible. Most of all, keep a positive attitude. Sir Paul McCartney once said to me when I felt depressed and almost ready to give up, "Always have faith." I'm glad I listened to him!

Making Customers Feel They Belong

In the old days, people went to the market often, sometimes daily. The shop-keeper often set aside items for a customer's consideration based on individual tastes and needs. More likely than not, the business transaction followed a discussion of families, politics, and neighborhood gossip.

Good customer service can make your customers feel like members of a community who frequent a mom-and-pop store on the corner of their block — the community of satisfied individuals who regularly use your goods and services. In the following sections, I describe some ways to make your customers feel like members of a group who return to your site on a regular basis to interact with a community of individuals with similar interests.

Putting the "person" into personal service

How often does an employee personally greet you when you walk through the door of a store? On the web as well as in real life, people like a prompt and personal response. Your challenge is to provide live customer support on your website.

Some websites do provide live support so that people can e-mail a question to someone in real time (or close to real time) by using Internet technologies, such as chat and message boards. The online auction giant eBay has a New to eBay message board, for example, where beginners can post questions for eBay support staff, who post answers in response.

Chat, in which individuals type messages to one another over the Internet in real time, provides an even more immediate type of customer support. One way to add chat to your site is to start a Yahoo! Group, which I describe in the "Starting a Yahoo! Group" section, later in this chapter.

LivePerson (www.liveperson.com) provides a simpler alternative that allows small businesses to provide chat-based support. LivePerson is software that enables you to see who is connected to your site at any time and instantly lets you chat with them, just as if you're greeting them at the front door of a brick-and-mortar store.

LivePerson works like this: You install the LivePerson Pro software on your own computer (not the server that runs your site). With LivePerson, you or your assistants can lead the customer through the process of making a purchase. For instance, you might show customers what individual sale items look like by sending them an image file to view with their web browsers. You can try LivePerson Pro for free for 30 days and then pay $99.99 per month thereafter.

Overcoming business barriers

You're probably familiar with terms such as *global village* and *international marketplace*. But how do you extend your reach into the huge overseas markets? It's important to describe your products clearly and objectively, with words as well as images and diagrams, where necessary. You can effectively overcome language and cultural barriers in other ways, some of which are common sense while others are less obvious.

Shoppers in many developing nations still prefer to shop with their five senses. So that foreign customers never have a question on how to proceed, it's essential to provide them with explicit descriptions of the shopping process. Make information on ordering, payment, execution, and support available at every step.

Customer support in Asia is, in many ways, a different creature from in the West. Although personalization still remains critical, language and translation give an e-commerce site a different feel. A Western site that might work well by looking clean and well organized might have to be replaced with the more chaotic blitz of characters and options that's often found more compelling by Eastern markets. In Asia, websites tend to place more emphasis on color and interactivity. Many e-commerce destinations choose to dump all possible options on the front page instead of presenting them in an orderly, sequential flow.

Enhancing your site with a discussion area

Can we talk? Even my pet birds like to communicate by words as well as squawks. A small business can turn its individual customers into a cohesive group by starting its own discussion group on the Internet. Discussion groups work particularly well if you're promoting a specific type of product or if you and your customers are involved in a controversial area of interest.

The three kinds of discussion groups are

- ✔ **A local group:** Some universities create discussion areas exclusively for their students. Other large companies set aside groups that are restricted to their employees. Outsiders can't gain access because the groups aren't on the Internet but rather are on a local server within the organization.

- ✔ **A Usenet newsgroup:** Individuals are allowed to create an Internet-wide discussion group in the `alt` or `biz` categories of Usenet without having to go through the time-consuming application and approval process needed to create other newsgroups. Although Usenet was originally one of the most popular parts of the Internet, my sense is that web-based groups such as Google Groups (`https://groups.google.com`) are more frequently used these days.

✔ **A web-based discussion group:** You can start a Yahoo! Group, which I describe in the upcoming section named (surprise!) "Starting a Yahoo! Group."

Of these three alternatives, the first isn't appropriate for your business purposes. So what follows focuses on the last two types of groups.

In addition to newsgroups, many large corporations host interactive chats moderated by experts on subjects related to their areas of business. Small businesses can also hold chats, most easily by setting up a chat room on a site that hosts chat-based discussions. However, the most common way to build goodwill and establish new connections with customers and interested parties is an interactive web-based diary — a *blog* (short for *web log)*. Find out more about blogs in Chapter 1.

Starting an alt discussion group

Usenet is a system of communication on the Internet that enables individual computer users to participate in group discussions about topics of mutual interest. Internet newsgroups have what's referred to as a hierarchical structure. Most groups belong to one of seven main categories: `comp`, `misc`, `news`, `rec`, `sci`, `soc`, or `talk`. The category name appears at the beginning of the group's name, such as `rec.food.drink.coffee`. In this section, I discuss the `alt` category, which is just about as popular as the seven other categories and enables individuals to establish their own newsgroups.

In my opinion, the `biz` discussion groups aren't taken seriously because they're widely populated by unscrupulous people promoting get-rich-quick schemes and egomaniacs who love the sound of their own voices. The `alt` groups, although they can certainly address some wild and crazy topics, often address serious topics and are at least as well known as the seven main categories mentioned above. Plus the process of setting up an `alt` group is well documented.

The prefix `alt` didn't originally stand for *alternative,* although it has come to mean that. The term was an abbreviation for Anarchists, Lunatics, and Terrorists, which wasn't so politically incorrect back when newsgroups were young. Now `alt` is a catch-all category in which anyone can start a group, if others show interest in the creator's proposal.

The first step to creating your own `alt` discussion group is to point your web browser to Google Groups (`https://groups.google.com`) and access the `alt.config.newgroups` group. This area contains general instructions on starting your own Usenet newsgroup. Also look in `news.answers` for the How to Start a New Usenet Newsgroup message.

To find out how to start a group in the `alt` category, go to Google (`www.google.com`) click Groups, and search for the How to Start an Alt Newsgroup message. Follow the instructions to set up your own discussion group. Basically, the process involves the following steps:

1. **Write a brief proposal describing the purpose of the group you want to create and include an e-mail address where people can respond with comments.**

   The proposal also contains the name of your group in the correct form (`alt.groupname.moreinfo.moreinfo`). Try to keep the group name short and professional if it's for business purposes.

2. **Submit the proposal to the newsgroup `alt.config`.**

3. **Gather feedback to your proposal through e-mail.**

4. **Send a special message, or a *control message*, to the news server that gives you access to Usenet.**

   The exact form of the message varies from server to server, so consult with your ISP on how to compose the message correctly.

5. **Wait a while (a few days or weeks) as *news administrators* (the people who operate news servers at ISPs around the world) decide whether to adopt your request and add your group to their list of newsgroups.**

Before you try to start your own group, look through the seven categories (`comp`, `misc`, `news`, `rec`, `sci`, `soc`, and `talk`) to make sure someone else isn't already covering your topic.

Starting a Yahoo! Group

When the Internet was still fresh and new, Usenet was almost the only game in town. These days, the web is pretty much (along with e-mail) the most popular way to communicate and share information. That's why starting a discussion group on the web makes perfect sense. A web-based discussion group is somewhat less intimidating than others because it doesn't require a participant to use newsgroup software.

Yahoo! Groups are absolutely free to set up. (To find out how, just go to the FAQ page, `help.yahoo.com/kb/index?locale=en_US&page=product&y=PROD_GR`; click Create and Manage Groups; and click the How to Start a New Yahoo! Group link.) They enable users not only to exchange messages, but also to communicate in real time by using chat. And as the list operator, you can send e-mail newsletters and other messages to your participants.

Simply operating an online store isn't enough. You need to present yourself as an authority in a particular area of interest. The discussion group needs to concern itself primarily with that topic and give participants a chance to exchange views and tips on the topic. If people have questions about your store, they can always e-mail you directly — they don't need a discussion group to do that.

Moving to customer service 2.0

Once you've covered the basics, you can make your online business really responsive to your clientele by adopting some approaches that might be described as "Customer Service 2.0." There's nothing dramatically new here. You're taking the basics and being proactive about them by monitoring your reputation, looking for any negative comments, and responding to issues immediately.

An article in *Computerworld* (www.computerworld.com/s/article/ 9090398/Customer_Service_2.0_Clients_become_brand_managers) describes how big businesses are doing 2.0. Comcast, for example, was able to respond to a single post on a microblog about a service outage within 15 minutes because it has people dedicated to looking for such comments and complaints online.

One aspect of "new" customer service is actively looking for potential problems and heading them off before they become big issues. It might mean creating a comment area or discussion feature as mentioned in the preceding section so customers can complain directly to you, and having someone dedicated to monitoring for such comments and arranging for responses. Comcast created a Comcast Cares program that watches for comments on Twitter about its service.

An art and decorating site called The Artful Home, based in Madison, Wisconsin, responds to customer comments gathered by Networked Insights (www. networkedinsights.com), which gathers customer data from social networking sites and other locations to analyze how a brand is being received.

Suppose you're just a one- or two-person operation and you don't have the resources to hire a company to monitor what people are saying about you on Twitter or other sites. Just Google your own business name periodically to see what's being said, or search Twitter or other sites.

A field called "reputation management" helps businesses keep track of what's being said about them online. You can get an overview of the topic at www. cio.com/article/727144/How_to_Avoid_Online_Reputation_ Management_Nightmares.

Chapter 9

Sourcing Worldwide for Your Business

I occasionally get questions from budding entrepreneurs just like you who are wondering how to get started selling online. The question that comes up most often is simple: "What should I sell online?" A variation on this question that I hear almost as frequently goes like this: "What's the single best thing I can possibly sell online?" (Translation: "What can I sell on the web that will make me the most money?")

Everyone who asks this question wants a simple answer, and so do you. But no single item sells better than anything else on the web. Rather, people are hunting for thousands of things while they stare at their laptops and desktop computers. Your challenge is to find a connection between one of those things and you: You need to find something that's desirable that (1) you can find easily and inexpensively, (2) you're interested in, and (3) is easy to photograph, pack, and ship.

The list of desirable items changes all the time as new products catch the fancy of consumers. As I write this, the "hot" items are those with an *i* in front of their names (iPhone 5, iPad, iPad mini) and the Samsung Galaxy line of products. No matter what the hot item is, you want to find something that consumers want and that you can sell for a profit. Sites such as Alibaba (www.alibaba.com) make sourcing in China more feasible to small businesses and individual sellers, too. This chapter describes your options for finding such merchandise in a steady supply and presenting it in a way that will cause web surfers to click your Buy button.

Knowing What Sells Well Online

My first job was as a clerk in my neighborhood pharmacy. Much of my time was spent on the look of the store and the merchandise in it, whether that involved cleaning, arranging items on shelves, creating signs, or rearranging window presentations. All traditional brick-and-mortar store owners take care to show off their merchandise in a way that attracts attention. You should do the same, even though you're dealing in clicks rather than bricks. This isn't a complicated subject. The section that follows examines one basic aspect of a good online sales presentation: choosing desirable merchandise. See Chapter 6 for the other: presenting it in its best light.

These are the kind of sales approaches that apply, whether you're selling on a website, putting an ad on Craigslist, or setting up a storefront in a marketplace such as ArtFire (www.artfire.com) or Etsy (www.etsy.com) — or all of these.

It's hard to predict what kinds of items can attract good profits. But if you can think of a hot product that's in short supply, you can realize such profits yourself. On a much smaller scale, I'm amazed to find merchandise that sold on eBay for far more than I paid for it. Here are a few examples:

- ✔ I found a pair of women's ballet-style slippers by designer Taryn Rose secondhand for $2 and sold them for $132. (I don't have an image of these slippers, but Figure 9-1 shows a pair of sandals by the same designer that I bought for $4 and sold for $51.)

- ✔ I sold a Cedar electronic device, a "de-clicker" for cleaning up audio files, for my brother for $1,500.

- ✔ My mother bought a set of antique wooden-shafted Spalding golf clubs for $10, and I sold them for more than $100.

Does a common thread run through these tales? Two threads, actually. You need to look for merchandise that's desirable, that's in new or near-new condition, and that is either difficult to find or sells for a high amount to begin with. The Cedar device normally sells for several thousand dollars; the ballet slippers sell at retail for $335; the golf clubs are hard to find because they're antique. Online shoppers, in fact, typically flock to two kinds of merchandise:

- ✔ Things that are rare and unusual

- ✔ Things that are very expensive when sold at retail

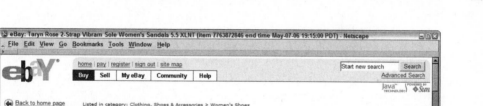

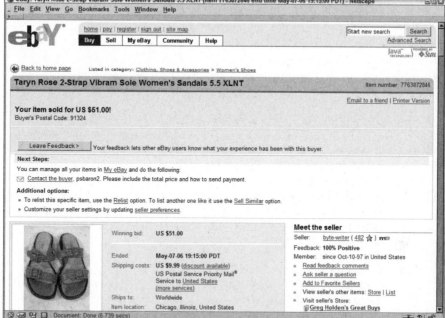

Figure 9-1:
Shoppers
online crave
either a
bargain or a
rare find.

They're looking on the web either to find something they'd have trouble locating anywhere else or to find something at a much lower price than they'd pay anywhere else. Some enterprising sellers can deal in a variety of rare and desirable items. However, the majority of successful online entrepreneurs build their business by settling on a reliable source of desirable merchandise that they can buy in quantity from a wholesale supplier. They realize much slimmer profit margins than they might get from rare antiques. But they can sell a more-or-less predictable quantity of items each month, and what they don't get in profits, they make up for in the quantity and reliability of sales.

Finding Products Yourself

One of the many nice things about running an online business is the extent to which you can perform important functions no matter what your level of experience. However, this is both a blessing and a curse. Finding merchandise to sell is something you have to do on your own, for the most part — yet it's a subject that takes experienced retailers years to figure out. It can be a matter of trial and error, and it can be time-consuming and difficult. But if you succeed with the central objective — finding a steady and reliable source for merchandise you can resell online at a profit — you've taken a huge step toward making your online business a success. I describe the most common options for do-it-yourself sourcing in the following sections.

Cleaning out your closets

Time and again, I interview successful online merchants (especially those who make a living selling on eBay) who began by selling what they found at hand. This kind of online commerce, in fact, is most practical when you're trying to sell on eBay: You start by cleaning your closets, attic, garage, and other storage areas. It's a sort of online garage sale: You get started and whet your appetite for future sales. Rummaging through your closets only takes you so far, though.

eBay isn't the only online marketplace for closet cleaners. If you find textbooks, CDs, DVDs, or other common household items, you can add them to Amazon.com's marketplace. Your items appear alongside the same items offered for sale by "Earth's Biggest Bookstore." Selling in the marketplace is easier and quicker than on eBay; you don't even have to take photos. Find out more about Amazon.com and other specialty book marketplaces like Alibris in Chapter 15.

As a general rule, I tell budding sellers not to take a scattershot approach to sourcing and to avoid selling anything and everything. But in the beginning, when your primary goal is to clean out your house and make a few extra dollars, this approach has an advantage. When you're selling lots of different things, you might just discover one thing that interests you that you can sell in greater quantity. I know one eBay seller (a male, by the way) who sold a purse he found in his closet. It fetched a huge profit. He realized that certain brands of designer purses are eagerly sought on eBay. He has since gone on to become a leading seller of women's purses, items he's never actually used.

Outsourcing your sourcing

Your closets are cleaned out; your attic is bare; you don't have a valuable antique to your name. How can you find merchandise to sell on the web when you don't have anything of your own to start with? You sell other peoples' merchandise, that's how. In other words, you become a consignment seller — someone who puts items up for sale on behalf of the owner, who has given (or *consigned)* them to you to sell. This phenomenon is eBay-centric. In fact, finding eBay sellers who sell on behalf of friends, relatives, or total strangers is pretty common. I've never encountered a businessperson who sells on consignment through a website. The following sections, then, apply to eBay sellers, though they might be relevant to website or brick-and-mortar store owners as well.

Somewhere in the world, a consignment seller probably sells through a conventional e-commerce website rather than an auction venue. But there are well-known consignment sellers who operate their own websites. The top dog among eBay trading assistants for many years, Adam Hersh, had his own website (www.adamhershauctions.com), which included a link to his eBay Store. (See the sidebar for more about Hersh.) As a consignment seller, you need to market and present yourself as effectively as people who are selling their own merchandise directly to customers.

Becoming a trading assistant

I'm using the term *trading assistant* loosely to refer to anyone who sells merchandise on eBay on behalf of the owners of the merchandise. The owner gets most of the profits; the seller earns a fee and does the work of photographing, listing, packing, and shipping the goods. Lots of eBay sellers occasionally peddle objects given to them by friends and family. eBay uses the term *trading assistant* (TA) to designate someone approved by eBay to conduct consignment sales and who is listed in eBay's Trading Assistant Directory (pages.ebay.com/tahub/index.html). In other words, you can become either an informal trading assistant or a formally designated one.

To become an informal trading assistant, you only have to find people who want to sell on eBay but who are unwilling to go through the work involved in conducting actual transactions. Chances are they'll find you and you won't have to do much asking around. When word gets out that you're selling on eBay, you may well find that people come to you with boxes full of mementoes. You can also find clients by posting notices in your neighborhood stores or on your local version of Craigslist (www.craigslist.org), the popular classified-ad service.

The advantage of taking on consignment sales is the ability to boost your feedback and your monthly gross sales figures in a relatively short amount of time. On eBay, a user's feedback rating is very important. *Feedback* is a numeric measurement of the comments left for you by people with whom you've done business. Someone who is satisfied with your performance as a buyer or seller can leave a positive feedback comment, which counts for 1 point. A negative comment counts for –1 point, and a neutral comment counts as 0 (zero). eBay sellers generally find that their sales go up if their feedback rating reaches into the hundreds, if they have good Detailed Seller Ratings (DSRs), which are given anonymously by buyers, and if they can achieve a Top Rated Seller or PowerSeller designation.

A *PowerSeller* has at least $3,000 in annual sales to U.S. buyers and 100 annual transactions; DSRs of at least 4.60; a 98 percent positive feedback rating over the past year; and a good standing record as a seller. *Top-Rated Sellers* must have a positive feedback rating of at least 100 percent, at least 100 transactions and $1,000 in sales with U.S. buyers in the past year, and send package tracking to their buyers.

By turning around a substantial number of transactions for other people in a short amount of time and shipping quickly, you can build both your feedback rating and your potential as a Top-Rated Seller or PowerSeller. You can make some extra money, to boot. (The merchandise is sold under your User ID, and buyers don't need to know that their objects belonged to someone other than you.) Find out more about the criteria at `http://pages.ebay.com/sellerinformation/sellingresources/powerseller_requirements.html`. **Top-Rated Seller** requirements are listed at `http://pages.ebay.com/help/sell/top-rated.html#what`.

Just how much money can you make? That depends on your time and energy. Whether you're a formally designated TA or an informal consignment seller, you get to set your own payment terms. It's wise to look around eBay's Trading Assistant Directory to see what others are charging. The terms vary widely. Some TAs buy their customers' items outright and put them up for sale; others charge a flat fee of $10 per sale; most charge a fee for shipping and handling and a percentage of the sale price (perhaps 40–50 percent).

CASE STUDY

Young trading assistant: No inventory, no worries

What do you do when you're too young to have a storehouse of antiques and collectibles you can sell on eBay? You invite the owners of those valuable items to come to you, and you offer to sell them on eBay on their behalf. That's what Adam Hersh decided to do when he was a communications major at Northeastern University. "At the time, I had no idea what I was going to do with my life. Then I started taking night classes so I could be certified in e-commerce." (He was still in college and didn't have venture capital funding or funds from previous occupations.) "I said to myself, I can either buy or resell slowly or find another way to get inventory. I started as a trading assistant because it was a free way to have thousands of sales items at the same time."

In 2001, Hersh became an eBay trading assistant before there was a formal entity by that name. (eBay now has a program through which it certifies such sellers, as described earlier in this chapter.) Although he was a pioneer in the field, Hersh already had a history of entrepreneurship. At age 12, he formed a corporation buying and selling baseball cards. He later did nightclub and concert promotions.

As a trading assistant, Hersh handled auction sales for some big-name entities, including MTV, Viacom, and the government of South Korea. He ran a charity auction for the New York Public Library. "When I met with the South Korean government, they were satisfied with my presentation, but they flat-out told me, 'I can't believe how young you are.'"

Hersh acknowledged that being a trading assistant can be more difficult and complex than selling for himself. "It is difficult, but it works well if you learn how to perfect it," he says. "If you perfect something that is difficult, you can be at the top."

At this writing, Hersh is around 33 years old. His company was acquired at age 28, and acquired for a second time at age 33 by Gotham City Online. He is still an officer of the Professional eBay Sellers Association (PeSA) and is one of the few people to have made 1 million transactions on eBay.

To find out more about the program, go to the Trading Assistants Program page (`pages.ebay.com/tahub/index.html`). To join the program, you need to have a feedback score of more than 100, have at least 98 percent positive feedback comments, have sold at least 10 items in the past three months, and maintain 10 sales per three-month period. After you're a TA, you can create a profile about yourself and your area of interest, which is then included in a searchable database of such sellers.

Running a drop-off store

A few enterprising eBay sellers have taken consignment selling to a new level and opened brick-and-mortar outlets called *Registered eBay Drop Off Locations (REDOLs)*. This is a big step that you should attempt only if you're an experienced PowerSeller and have a steady sales stream to cover the slowdowns and complications you'll inevitably encounter from opening a real physical store. On the other hand, with a physical location, you have lots of storage, a loading dock, and a location where wholesalers can ship to you. Depending on the location you choose, customers find you in the form of foot traffic. Choosing a good location (at an intersection, on a main street, or in a strip mall with plenty of parking) is only one consideration. Here are some others:

✔ You need lots of storage space to handle the increased sales volume you'll experience.

✔ You need to know how to say no to people whose merchandise just won't attract bids (or high-enough bids; you might want to set a minimum of $50 per sale).

✔ You need a computer network for your employees and possibly for customers who need to see the same search results you're conducting.

Some drop-off store owners used to get a jump start by signing up for a franchise with one of the big chains, such as iSOLD It, although today many of those franchise chains no longer exist. But drop-off stores are risky whether you open your own from scratch or join a franchise. I once interviewed a drop-off store owner in northwest Illinois who grew tired of the complaints, nonpaying bidders, and expenses associated with running a brick-and-mortar store. He bought a signmaking machine from a customer and decided to try his hand at that. The last I heard, he was enjoying making signs even more than he had liked selling on eBay.

Garage sales and flea markets

Garage sales and flea markets are the traditional ways to start selling, on eBay or Amazon.com, at least. You scrounge through your neighborhood garage sales, estate sales, house sales, rummage sales, and flea markets. You pick up some goodies at a bargain and put them up for sale. I know some PowerSellers who still get their merchandise this way. I'm thinking of a hus-band-and-wife team who sell on eBay under the User ID mrmodern. At this writing, their feedback rating is more than 9,900.

They don't waste their time with small-scale garage sales. Rather, they pick out big estate sales with care, and they show up before the sun rises so that they can be among the first in line. (Some sellers also pay students to wait in line for them until just before the sale opens.) Then they practically run through the sale, grabbing items that seem valuable in a frenzy, trying to beat the competition. This is a perfectly viable way to run an eBay business — for some people, though not for me. If you're an incurable bargain hunter and you love the thrill of the hunt — and you have lots of time to spend — start looking in your local paper or online at sites like Craigslist for sales in your area.

A smartphone app called Garage Sale Rover helps you locate garage and estate sales in your area, no matter what the time of year. It's available for iOS and Android; search for it in iTunes and Google Play.

Secondhand stores

Everyone has a thrift store, dollar store, or other secondhand shop in the immediate vicinity. These can be good sources of merchandise, provided that you can go there during the day when new stock is put out and competi-tion is low. You have to be prepared to spend lots of time driving or walking from one venue to another, and you have to enjoy the hunt. Personally, I love the search and the thrill of discovering something that's like a hidden trea-sure. But I realize that for most sellers, finding a reliable wholesale supplier is a more practical option that carries lower stress with it as well.

Working with Wholesale Suppliers

Secondhand stores (such as those mentioned in the preceding section) are, in fact, wholesale suppliers. Getting to know the proprietors of your second-hand stores is a good idea; you can strike up relationships and let the owners know what you're looking for. If you're lucky, you might find they put aside items you want because they value your repeat business. These aren't the only kinds of wholesalers around, however. I give you some tips for finding and working with other sorts of suppliers in the following sections.

Finding wholesalers

If good wholesale suppliers were easy to find, everyone would use them. But finding good suppliers takes time and effort. One problem is that wholesalers don't advertise themselves in the places you're used to looking. Another is that they tend to want to deal with traditional, brick-and-mortar businesses. Some wholesalers look down on eBay or e-commerce sellers. They still don't understand that the web is a legitimate marketplace.

What can you do to overcome these challenges? Other sellers have done the following:

- ✔ Rented a booth in an antiques mall and used that as a business address so that wholesalers could ship merchandise there
- ✔ Listed themselves in the phone book for added credibility
- ✔ Had a tax ID and a business license ready in case these items are requested

To find wholesalers, look around. The web is the logical place to start. The Chinese wholesale marketplace Alibaba (www.alibaba.com) is an increasingly popular venue for sellers seeking merchandise. Another possibility is on eBay through the sales category Wholesale Lots. Another excellent resource is Worldwide Brands (www.worldwidebrands.com), which maintains a database of wholesale suppliers organized by the type of merchandise they provide.

But ask around, too. Often, you find wholesalers by word of mouth. Sometimes, you find products you like and that you're reasonably sure you can sell online. Going directly to the manufacturers is worth a try, but chances are the manufacturer won't sell directly to you. I tried this once. I frequently sell a desirable line of high-end shoes for men that's manufactured in Wisconsin. When I called the company and talked to a sales rep, I was politely rebuffed. Producers are used to selling to wholesalers and not directly to eBay sellers. By selling to you at wholesale, they undercut their wholesalers as well as the retailers who sell their products to the public. You're much better off approaching the wholesalers.

Lots of online businesses advertise themselves as wholesale sellers. Many say they *drop-ship* their merchandise — in other words, they ship what's purchased directly from their wholesale facility so they never actually have to handle the merchandise and may never see it.

Sound too good to be true? In many cases it is, and you should always exercise a healthy dose of caution when you're looking for wholesale suppliers. The eBay sellers I've talked to who have faithful, reliable wholesalers guard the identities of those suppliers jealously. They usually find such suppliers only by word of mouth: Rather than answer an ad or visit a website, they ask someone who knows someone who . . . you get the idea.

If you aren't in the business of selling goods or services that you manufacture yourself, find a steady stream of merchandise that you can sell online. Your goal is to find a wholesaler who can supply you with good-quality items at rock-bottom prices. You can then mark up the prices and make a profit while keeping the prices low enough to make them attractive. Generally, the best wholesale items are small objects that can be packed and shipped inexpensively. On eBay, things like figurines, ornaments, stationery, and other small gift items are commonly sold by PowerSellers along with the occasional antiques and collectibles. Here are a few rules for finding items to resell:

- ✔ **Try them out yourself.** Purchase a few items yourself to start with or ask the wholesaler for samples. (Resist any attempts by the wholesaler to sell you, say, 10,000 items at a supposedly dirt-cheap price right off the bat.) Take a few of the items for a test drive. It's easier to convince others to buy what you like yourself.

- ✔ **Try to sell many small, low-priced items rather than a few large ones.** Rather than computers or printers, consider selling computer memory chips or printer ink cartridges, for example.

- ✔ **Ask for references.** Talk to businesspeople who have already worked with the supplier. Ask how reliable the supplier is and whether the prices are prone to fluctuate.

Giving your business a tax ID

Proper documentation is essential to ensure that wholesalers and other suppliers take your fledgling business seriously. One of the most important pieces of documentation you can provide them is a tax ID. Another is a business license. In either case, you need to apply to the proper authorities to obtain the designation. You may need to obtain a business license from your city, county, or state agency.

A tax ID tells a tax agency that you collect sales tax. That tax agency might be your state tax department or the Internal Revenue Service (IRS). To get a tax ID (or Employer Identification Number, or EIN), fill out a form designated for that purpose. To get one from the IRS, go to `www.irs.gov/Businesses/Small-Businesses-&-Self-Employed/` `Employer-ID-Numbers-(EINs)-`. To get one from the state, contact your state's tax department.

You then need to turn over the sales tax you collect to your state. When the state sends you the forms needed for this purpose, your tax ID number (this might also be called your Business Tax ID or your Employer Identification Number, or EIN) is somewhere on the form. This is the number you can supply to wholesalers.

You can find a page full of links to state departments of revenue, where you can apply for a state tax ID, at `www.aicpa.org/Research/` `ExternalLinks/Pages/Taxes` `StatesDepartmentsofRevenue.aspx`.

When looking for merchandise to sell, try to build on your own hobbies and interests. If you collect model cars, try to develop a sideline selling parts, paints, and components online. You'll find the process more enjoyable when you deal in products you love and know well.

Approaching wholesalers

When you approach wholesalers, it helps to have a business address and a phone number dedicated to your business. Little things, such as an answering service or an assistant to answer your phone, can make a good impression on suppliers who aren't yet on board with the idea of individual entrepreneurs working at home and imagine them padding around their computer-laden offices in their bathrobe and slippers.

When you first talk to a wholesaler, don't immediately mention that you're creating your first website or that you're starting to sell on eBay and are hoping to build your feedback rating. Tell the sales rep your business name, your tax ID, and your address and then tell him or her what you're interested in doing. If the words *e-commerce* and *eBay* never come up in the conversation, so much the better. If they do, don't apologize for wanting to sell online: Be confident and straightforward. If the wholesaler is skeptical and doesn't want to sell to you, just move on to the next supply candidate.

Your first purchase from a wholesaler should be a small trial run. Tell the wholesaler you want to buy a small quantity of what he or she offers to see what sells best. When you make a real purchase from a wholesaler, you'll have to buy a much larger quantity. You might have to take out a home-equity loan or otherwise borrow to cover the initial cost, if you don't have funds to begin with.

Turning to the Far East: Alibaba, brokers, and more

China is known worldwide as a supplier of cheap consumer goods, and online sellers big and small are turning to China as an option for finding merchandise to resell at a profit. As you might expect, there are some potential pitfalls to keep in mind when you turn your attention to the Far East and some special considerations that don't come into play when you are dealing with a wholesaler in the United States or in your own home country.

First, keep in mind that a number of trade laws apply. You have to fill out forms to meet your import and export requirements. You have to pay duty and customs fees as well.

You can find out more about trade laws in Chapter 7.

But you need to keep some subtler issues in mind as well. For starters, you are hardly the first person to think about approaching the Chinese to buy wholesale. Many big-time sellers, including some of the biggest PowerSellers on eBay, have already been there. According to one of them, John Jacobs, a longtime seller on eBay and now CEO of ArtFire (www.artfire.com), China tends to give preferential treatment to bigger sellers. "Typically, when you buy from China, you find that the profit margins are higher the more you buy," he says. In other words, the more you buy, the lower the price you're charged.

How do you compete with the big sellers? You have several options:

- **Make a personal appearance.** If you can go to China and meet factory owners yourself, the personal connection will help. That's what one eBay PowerSeller, Alan Warshauer, found out. He went to China and established connections that enabled him to sell charms on eBay.

- **Find a broker.** A broker functions as a middleman — someone who connects you with factories. Jacobs recommends this option. "Some brokers in China deal with as many as 200 different factories," he says. "They can offer you a wider selection than you would find on your own."

- **Go to trade shows.** You might meet Chinese manufacturers or brokers there. See the following section, "Working the Trade Shows," for more details.

- **Search for a broker or supplier on Alibaba.** I explain this site (www.alibaba.com) further right after this list.

- **Look on eBay.** According to Jacobs, eBay is increasingly becoming a place where goods from China are sold at low prices — in some cases, low enough that you can resell the merchandise elsewhere.

Alibaba is a business-to-business marketplace: It brings together Chinese wholesale suppliers and overseas merchants. Go to the home page (www.alibaba.com), and you see listings for products that include health and beauty supplies, industrial materials, luggage, office supplies, printing and publishing, footwear and accessories, sports and entertainment items, cell phones, jewelry, and toys. The Chinese sellers make these products available to anyone who wants to meet their terms. You might be able to buy cell phone chargers, as long as you meet the minimum order quantity of 100 pieces. You don't always see the price on the site; you might have to contact the seller for that.

Alibaba is a convenient doorway into Chinese suppliers. Founded by former English teacher Jack Ma in 1999, it has grown to be the second-largest

Internet company in China. Alibaba is also moving into the U.S. market. As of this writing, it is planning to set up a marketplace to directly compete with Amazon.com and Walmart.

What are some potential pitfalls in working with suppliers on Alibaba? Testing the merchandise yourself isn't possible. Getting one or two sample items isn't always feasible, either — unless you use the company's new AliExpress site (`www.aliexpress.com`), which is designed for small wholesaler orders.

Stories circulate about suppliers who aren't always trustworthy. Research sellers as much as you can, and try to deal with only those designated as Gold Suppliers. These are Alibaba sellers who have applied for this designation and who have been verified by a third-party security service provider. Find out more at `alibaba.com`.

Working the Trade Shows

A *trade show* is a mass gathering where buyers and sellers meet in the hope of making business connections. For many entrepreneurs, trade shows are a mysterious thing — it seems that they're only for those "in the trade" and not amateurs like you. You need to get over this attitude and realize that you *are* in the trade. In fact, you're on the cutting edge. By selling online, you have something to offer that wholesale suppliers are eager to know about. I highly recommend that after you settle on the kind of merchandise you want to sell, you find trade shows in that area so that you can go on the hunt for wholesale suppliers.

Don't travel all the way to a trade show without registering first and making sure that you're qualified to attend. Saying that you have a website or an eBay Store might not be enough. You might have to provide a tax ID number, a business phone number, or a business address to convince those in charge that you're a legitimate businessperson.

Trade shows aren't always easy to find. Very few are likely to advertise in the local media. Looking online is a better bet. Try the following possibilities:

- The website TSNN.com (`www.tsnn.com`), which calls itself "The Ultimate Trade Show Directory" and gathers information about upcoming trade shows

- Your local convention bureau, which probably has a list of upcoming events

- Trade journals in your chosen field

When you get to an event such as the L.A. Shoe Show, Coffee Fest Chicago, or the Jersey Shore Home Show, you may be overwhelmed with the sheer size of the venue and the large number of people involved, especially if you've traveled a long way to attend. Make sure you go with someone so you can take a team approach and divide the searching. It's also a good idea for one person to "work the floor" while the other is stationed at a computer, either in a hotel room or at home. The person at the show can describe brand names and models, and the computer operator can look them up online to gauge the level of demand for such items.

Part III
Social Networking and Marketing

Explore three essential social marketing approaches for connecting with current and potential customers at www.dummies.com/extras/startinganonline business.

In this part . . .

- ✔ Get to know cost-effective marketing strategies that can spread the word about your products and services including newsletters, mailing lists, discussion groups, contests, and online ads.

- ✔ Understanding search engine optimization (SEO) and how to use it to help search engines return your site in response to queries.

- ✔ Learn how to optimize your business to take advantage of location-based marketing options that can help local shoppers find your brick-and-mortar facility.

- ✔ Connect with "likers" and customers on Facebook, Twitter, Pinterest, and other social media sites.

Chapter 10

Advertising and Publicity: The Basics

*E*very month — sometimes every week, it seems — the Internet spawns a new superstar. As I write this, the stars of the moment are featured in the "Two Girls and a Puppy" Facebook page. After losing their dog to cancer and asking their reluctant father for a new one, he challenged them to get a million Likes on a Facebook page. They posted a cute photo that had a simple message, a call to action, and provoked emotion. Within just seven hours, they managed to achieve their goal. (The puppy followed soon after.)

An article on Entrepreneur.com called "What Makes Your Video Shareable — and Viral" identified some traits common to things that get a lot of attention on the Internet: They generate emotion; they involve something that is startling and attention getting. The article suggested that to get attention, you need to "1. Be true, 2. Don't waste our time, 3. Be unforgettable, and 4. Ultimately, it's all about humanity."

Marketers and businesspeople who try to attract attention online hope to create a gesture or slogan that becomes a *meme* — something easily imitated after being distributed on a web page or in a video.

Meme or not, the web can be a cost-effective way for a small business owner such as yourself to get a potential customer's attention. Targeted, personalized public-relations efforts work online because cyberspace is a personal place where intimate communication is possible. Blanketed advertising strategies of the sort you see in other media (most notably display ads, commercials, or billboards) are expensive and don't always work for online businesses.

Why? They lack the personal edge you get with e-commerce. The web is a one-to-one communications medium. In this chapter, I describe cost-effective, do-it-yourself advertising techniques for the online entrepreneur who has a fledgling business on a tight budget.

Coming Up with a Marketing Strategy

Half the battle with running a successful online business is developing a plan for what you want to do. The next step is to get noticed. For many businesses, the plan frequently involves getting people to talk about you — to promote "viral marketing" in which consumers sing your praises. The following sections describe two strategies for making your company name more visible to online customers and promoting word-of-mouth publicity.

Choosing a brand that speaks for you

In business-speak, *branding* has nothing to do with cattle roundups and everything to do with jacking up your profits. Branding is the process of raising awareness of a company's name and logo through advertising, public relations, or other means (for example, getting people to say, "Did you hear about . . .?" and then mentioning you, your products, your website, and so on).

Despite recent economic crises, the web is a great place for developing a business brand. A study by the Interactive Advertising Bureau (www.iab.net) reported that advertising revenue (the amount that businesses spend to advertise online) reached $9.26 billion for the third quarter of that year — a substantial increase of 18 percent over the same period in the previous year. The report states that the figures are a "testament to the value marketers get from using digital media.

Online advertising works because you don't have to get potential shoppers to dress up, drive across town, and find a parking spot. Web users sit only a foot or two from the screen (or only inches away, if they're using a handheld device), which means your web page can easily get a user's undivided attention — if your content is compelling enough, that is. Don't be shy about providing links to click, thumbnail images to view, and the like. (Just be sure to place these items where they work best; see Chapter 11 for more about that.) Previous studies have found that web advertising that doesn't seem like advertising — that is, it's interactive and entertaining — is supported and liked by consumers. These studies also showed that brands advertised on the web were seen as forward thinking.

But don't rely on your web page alone to spread your name. Use the whole Internet — including e-mail, online communities, contests, and promotions.

These days you have plenty of options to get the word out about your online business, such as the following:

- **Blogs:** These are online diaries that you can create to encourage connections with your customers and other interested individuals; you can use them to build visibility and generate advertising revenue.

- **Social networking:** More and more businesses are using popular places such as Facebook, Twitter, and Pinterest to promote themselves and their products.

- **Banner ads:** This type of ad is similar to the traditional print ads you place in a newspaper. See the "Waving a banner ad" section, later in this chapter, for more information.

- **Classifieds:** You can advertise your goods on a classified ad site such as Craigslist (www.craigslist.org).

- **Interstitials:** These pop-up ads appear in a separate window while a web page is loading.

    Pop-ups are fairly common on the web, but many users strongly dislike them and set their browsers to disallow them. Such ads also slow down the browsing/shopping process, which dampens the enthusiasm of impulse buyers. Before you use them, consider both the upside and downside, as described in the "Pop-up (and under, and over) ads" section, later in this chapter.

- **Keyword searches:** You can learn how search services work so that you can make your site appear more prominently in search results.

- **Newsletters:** You can generate goodwill and drive business to your website by distributing an e-mail newsletter.

- **Partnerships:** Find businesses whose goods and services complement yours and create links on each other's websites.

A website can also promote a brand that has already become well known through traditional sales and marketing strategies. The click-and-mortar version of Walmart (www.walmart.com) works in conjunction with the giant retailer's many brick-and-mortar stores. The website provides a selection of styles and sizes that's generally wider than what customers can find in stores. The National Retail Federation's Stores magazine (www.stores.org) ranked Wal-Mart number 1 among all retail stores, with almost $454 million in revenue in 2012.

You may not have thousands of dollars to spend on banner ads, but they aren't the most effective forms of online advertising anymore, anyway. It's just as effective to start with some simple, cost-effective techniques like this one: Make sure your signature files, domain name, and e-mail address all refer to your company name as closely as possible. It may take a while for your business to develop name awareness among consumers, but these techniques give you a perfect way to start.

Being selective about your audience

Traditional broadcast advertising, such as commercials or radio spots, works kind of like standing on top of a tall building and screaming, "Hey, everyone, come to my store!" Such ads deliver short bits of information to huge numbers of people — everyone in the coverage areas who happens to be tuned in at a particular time. The Internet has its own form of broadcasting — getting your company mentioned or advertised on one of the sites that draws millions of visitors each day.

But where the Internet really excels is in one-to-one communication of the kind that TV and radio can't touch. I suggest you try your own personalized forms of online advertising before you attempt to blanket cyberspace with banner ads. Often you can reach small, *targeted* groups of people — or even one prospect at a time — through free, do-it-yourself marketing strategies. These strategies include using the right keywords, sending newsletters, and taking part in mailing lists and newsgroups, all of which I discuss in the next section.

CASE STUDY

Painting a new business scenario

Marques Vickers has appeared in this book through several editions when he was primarily an artist based in California. His life has changed dramatically, and though he says he doesn't spend as much time online as he used to, he's an example of someone who has been able to change his life and circumstances profoundly, in part through the web. "I can clearly say that Internet access enabled me to pursue my present course even if it meant shifting directions," he declares.

Through his self-named website (www.marquesv.com), he still markets his own painting, sculpture, and photography, as well as his books on marketing and buying fine art online. In 2009, he became an auction consultant, using eBay to market both paintings and collectible items; his new site is at www.artsinamerica.com. He first went online in November 1999, and his art-related sites have received anywhere from 25,000 to 40,000 visits per month.

Q. What have you done to market your work in a difficult economy?

A. Time is the lone commodity we often have control of, so I am focusing my selling activities on areas that are truly productive, and I pay greater attention to the response from advertising. Essentially, time management is my greatest form of cost control.

Q. What are the costs of running all your websites and doing the associated marketing?

A. Out-of-pocket expense is approximately $29 monthly for a website hosting and Internet access package. New domain name registrations and renewals probably add another $250 because I own more than 20 domain names.

Q. What would you describe as the primary goals of your online business?

A. My initial objective was to develop a personalized, round-the-clock global presence in order to recruit sales outlets, sell directly to the public, and create a reference point for people to access and view my work. I also have an intuitive sense that an online website presence will be a marketing necessity for any future visual artist and a lifelong exposure outlet. Having an online presence builds my credibility as a fine artist and positions me to take advantage of the evolution of the fine-arts industry, too.

Q. Has your online business been profitable financially?

A. Absolutely — but make no mistake, achieving sales volume and revenue is a trial-and-error process and involves a significant time commitment. I'm still perfecting the business model, and it may require years to achieve the optimum marketing plan.

Q. How do you promote your site?

A. With the Internet, you are layering a collective web of multiple promotional sources. Experimentation is essential because recognition is not always immediate but may ultimately be forthcoming because postings in cyberspace are often stumbled across from unforeseen resources. I try multiple marketing outlets including paid ad positioning services, such as Overture and Google, bartered advertising space, and reciprocally traded links. Some have had moderate success, some unforeseen and remarkable exposure. Unlike traditional advertising media that have immediate response times, the Internet may lag in its response. It is a long-term commitment and one that cannot be developed by short-term tactics or media blitzes.

Q. Do you create your web pages yourself or do you work with someone to do that?

A. I'm too particular about the quality of content to subcontract the work out. Besides, I know what I want to say, how I want to say it, and am capable of fashioning the design concepts I want to integrate. The rectangular limitations of HTML design make color a very important component, and the very minimal attention span of most web viewers means that you'd better get to the point quickly and concisely. The more personalized, timely, and focused your content, the more reason an individual has to return to your website and ultimately understand your unique vision of what you're trying to create. A website is an unedited forum for telling your version of a story and a means for cultivating a direct support base.

Q. How are you using the web these days?

A. A few years ago, I uprooted from Northern California with my wife, and we moved to the Languedoc region of southern France. I decided to focus my activities on areas more interesting to me and pursue a completely different direction. Much of the process is detailed in a column I write called "An American in the French Languedoc" (www.the-languedoc-page.com/articles/languedoc-articles01g.htm). I am still doing my artwork, but my primary "work" is buying and renovating houses (www.uniqueseek.com). I've taken a decided step back from the pace of Northern California. I still use the Internet for promoting the houses I renovate, however.

Q. What advice would you give to someone starting an online business?

A. Don't hesitate one minute longer than necessary. Read substantially and from a diverse selection of sources on the subject. Subscribe to e-zines on related subject matter and query the webmasters of sites that impress you with their content. Go to informational seminars; ask questions. Distribute your message to multiple outlets, but focus your time and energy on what works best. Don't be afraid to experiment. Established sales outlets are usually best. The Internet is here to stay, and we have just scratched the surface in terms of potential.

Publicizing Your Online Business Free

In the following sections, I describe some ways you can publicize your online business yourself — for free. Prepare, however, to devote several hours a week to corresponding by e-mail and applying to have your business listed in search services, Internet indexes, or websites that have a customer base similar to yours.

The best way to generate first-time and return visits to your business site is to make yourself useful as well as ornamental. The longer people are inclined to stay on your website, the more likely they are to acquire your goods or services. (See Chapter 5 for some specific suggestions on generating compelling, useful content.)

A newsletter for next to nothing

It used to be said that the pen is mightier than the sword, but these days nothing beats a well-used mouse. No longer do you have to spend time and money to print a newsletter on actual paper and distribute it around the neighborhood. Now that you're online, you can say what you want — as often as you want — with your own publication. Online newsletters also help meet your clients' customer service needs, as I discuss in Chapter 8.

Many of the suggestions in this section apply to an even easier way of getting the word out: creating a blog. With a blog, you don't have to worry about design, distribution, and organization issues, either; you just have to focus on putting out content that your readers actually find useful and that encourages them to return on a regular basis.

Publish or perish

The work of producing an online newsletter is offset by the benefits you get in return. You may obtain hundreds — even thousands — of subscribers who find out about you and your online business.

To run your publishing venture smoothly, however, consider these areas:

- ✔ **Topics:** If you run out of topics to write about, look to others for inspiration. Identify magazines in your field of business so that you can quote articles. Get on the mailing list for any press releases you can use.

- ✔ **Staff:** You don't have to do it all. Delegate the editing function to someone else, or line up colleagues to function as contributors.

✔ **Design:** You have two choices: Send a plain-text version that doesn't look pretty but that everyone can read easily, or send a formatted HTML version that looks like a web page but is readable only by people who can receive formatted e-mail. Keep in mind, though, that many users are on corporate e-mail systems that either discourage or prohibit HTML-formatted e-mail. Others don't like HTML e-mail because it takes longer to download the graphics files.

✔ **Audience:** Identify your readers and make sure that your content is useful to them. (This last item certainly applies to business blogs: Save the personal news about your trip to Ibiza or your new puppy for a personal blog; focus on your area of expertise and present news and tips for readers who are interested in them.)

Newsletters work only if they appear on a regular basis *and* they consistently maintain a high level of quality. Whether yours comes out every week, every month, or just once a year, your subscribers expect you to re-create your publication with every new issue. Keep your newsletter simple and make sure you have the resources to follow through.

Extra! Read all about it!

After you do your planning, the actual steps involved in creating your newsletter are pretty straightforward. Because you're just starting out, I suggest you concentrate on producing only a plain-text version of your newsletter. Later on, you can think about doing an HTML version as well.

People like receiving inside tips and suggestions in plain text; they're happy that they don't have to wait for graphics files to download. On the other hand, a simple layout with colors and small photos can work well. Figure 10-1 shows an example: The Chicago publishing house that published my book *Literary Chicago* uses a two-column arrangement for its user-friendly newsletter. It's a standard layout provided by the e-mail marketing service Constant Contact (www.constantcontact.com).

Before you do anything, check with your ISP to make sure that you're permitted to have a mailing-list publication. Even if your newsletter consists of a simple announcement that you send only once in a while (in contrast to a discussion list, which operates pretty much constantly), you'll be sending a *lot* more e-mail messages through your ISP's machines than you otherwise would.

Keep the size of your newsletters small; about 30KB is the biggest e-mail file you can comfortably send. If you absolutely must have a larger newsletter, break it into two or three separate e-mail messages. Reducing the file size of your newsletter keeps your readers from getting irritated about how long your message takes to download or open. And keeping your customers happy should be one of your highest business priorities.

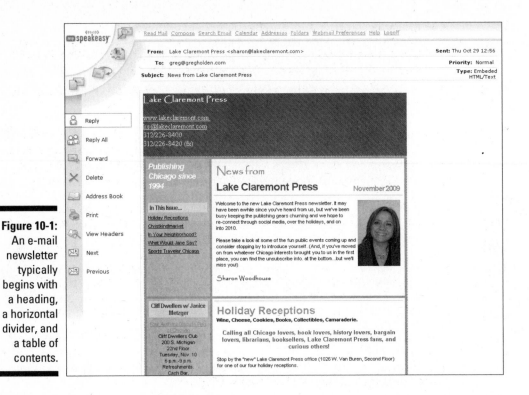

Figure 10-1:
An e-mail
newsletter
typically
begins with
a heading,
a horizontal
divider, and
a table of
contents.

When you're all set with the prep work, follow these general steps for an overview of how to create and distribute your publication:

1. **Open a plain-text editor, such as Notepad (Windows) or SimpleText (Mac).**

2. **Start typing.**

   Just because your newsletter is in plain text doesn't mean that you can't spice it up. Consider the following low-tech suggestions for emphasizing text or separating one section from another:

   - *All caps:* Using ALL CAPITAL LETTERS is always useful for distinguishing the name of the newsletter or heads from subheads.

   - *Rules:* You can create horizontal rules by typing a row of equal signs, hyphens, or asterisks to separate sections.

   - *Blank spaces:* Used carefully, that lowly spacebar on your keyboard can help you center plain text or divide it into columns.

Be sure to proofread the whole newsletter before sending it. Better yet, ask an objective viewer to read the text for you. Ask him or her to make suggestions on content, organization, and format, as well as to look for typos.

3. **Save your file.**

4. **Open your e-mail program's address book, select the mailing list of recipients, and compose a new message to them.**

5. **Attach your newsletter to the message or paste it into the body of the message, and click Send.**

If you're sending many e-mail messages simultaneously, be sure to do your mailing at a time when Internet traffic isn't heavy. Many popular newsletters, such as eWeek News, go out on weekends, for example. Other e-commerce providers, such as 1ShoppingCart.com (`www.1shoppingcart.com`).

Don't flood your Internet service provider's mail server with hundreds or thousands of messages at one time; you may crash the server. Break the list into smaller batches and send them at different times.

Be sure to mention your newsletter on your web page and provide an e-mail address where people can subscribe to it. In the beginning, you can ask people to send subscription requests to you. If your list swells to hundreds of members, consider automated mailing-list software or a mailing-list service to manage your list.

Participating in mailing lists and newsgroups

Many areas of the Internet can provide you with direct access to potential customers and let you interact with them. Two of the best places to market yourself directly to individuals are mailing lists and newsgroups. Both are highly targeted and offer unprecedented opportunities for niche marketing. Using them takes a little creativity and time on your part, but the returns can be significant.

Get started by developing a profile of your potential customer. Then join and participate in lists and newsgroups that may provide customers for your online business. For example, if you sell memorabilia of movie stars to fans online, you may want to join some newsgroups started by the fans themselves.

Where can you find these discussion forums? Topica (`lists.topica.com`) maintains a mailing-list directory that you can search by name or topic; it includes thousands of mailing lists. (Topica also helps you create your own e-mail newsletter, by the way.) Refdesk.com (`www.refdesk.com`) maintains links to websites, organized by category, that help you locate and participate in newsgroups, mailing lists, and web forums.

Managing your mailing list

When you decide to host and run your own mailing list, you assume the responsibility of processing requests to subscribe and unsubscribe from the list. This venture can eat into the time you need to spend on other business activities. When mailing lists get to be too much to handle yourself, you have a couple of options to make life easier:

✔ **Purchase special mailing-list software.** This type of program automatically adds or subtracts individuals from a mailing list in response to special e-mail messages that they send to you. You can usually manage the mailing list from your home computer. If you're a Windows user, check

out SendBlaster (www.sendblaster.com). Mac users can try Direct Mail (www.directmailmac.com).

✔ **Hire a company to run your mailing list for you.** Even though mailing-list software can help reduce the work involved in maintaining a list, you still have to install and use the software. So if you're really strapped for time, hiring a company to take care of your mailing list may be the way to go. Check out Constant Contact (www.constantcontact.com/index.jsp) or Lyris ListHosting (www.lyris.com/us-en/products) for pricing information.

A few newsgroups (in particular, the ones with biz at the beginning of their names) focus on small business issues and sales:

✔ misc.entrepreneurs

✔ biz.marketplace.discussion

✔ biz.marketplace.international.discussion

✔ biz.marketplace.services.discussion

✔ alt.business.home

✔ alt.business.consulting

✔ aol.commerce.general

The easiest way to access newsgroups is to use Google's web-based directory (groups.google.com). Each browser or newsgroup program has its own steps for enabling you to access discussion groups in an extensive network called Usenet. Use your browser's online help system to find out how you can access newsgroups.

Mailing lists

A *mailing list* is a group of individuals who receive communications by e-mail. Two kinds of mailing lists are common online:

✔ **Discussion lists:** These are lists of people interested in a particular topic. People subscribe to the list and have messages on the topic delivered by e-mail. Each message sent to the list goes to everyone in the group. Each person can reply either to the original sender or to everyone in the group. The resulting series of messages on a topic is called a *thread*.

✔ **Announcement lists:** These lists provide only one-way communication. Recipients get a single message from the list administrator, such as an attached e-mail newsletter.

Discussion lists are often more specific in topic than newsgroups. These lists vary from very small lists to lists that include thousands of people. An example of a discussion list is ROOTS-L, which is a mailing list for individuals who are researching family history. People on this list exchange inquiries about ancestors that they're seeking and announce family tree information they've posted online.

By making contributions to a mailing list, you establish a presence, so when members are looking to purchase the kind of goods or services you offer, they're likely to come to you rather than to a stranger. By participating in the lists that are right for you, you also find out invaluable information about your customers' needs and desires. Use this information to fine-tune your business so that it better meets those needs and desires.

Marketing through lists and newsgroups requires a low-key approach. Participating by answering questions or contributing your opinion to ongoing discussion topics is far more effective than blatant self-promotion.

Always read the welcome message and list guidelines that you receive upon joining a mailing list. Figure out the rules before you post. Lurk in the background for a few weeks to get a feel for the topics and participants before you contribute. Let your four-to-six-line signature file establish your identity without selling your wares directly. Also, don't forget to spell-check and proofread your messages before you send them.

Discussion groups

Discussion groups provide a different form of online group participation. On the Internet, you can find discussion groups in Usenet. America Online and CompuServe also have their own systems of discussion groups that are separate from Usenet. One of the easiest ways to access newsgroups, however, is with your web browser. Just point it to Google Groups (groups.google.com). Many large corporations and other organizations maintain their own internal discussion groups as well. In any case, you can also access discussion groups with your web browser's newsgroup or e-mail software. Microsoft Outlook Express can connect to newsgroup postings, for example.

You can promote yourself and your business in discussion groups in the same way that you use mailing lists: by participating in the group, providing helpful advice and comments, and answering questions. Don't forget that newsgroups are great for fun and recreation, too; they're a good way to solve problems, get support, and make new friends. For more information on newsgroups, see Chapter 3.

A contest in which everyone's a winner

In Chapter 13, I describe how Jason Bolt, the young owner of Society43, uses contests and other Facebook promotions to attract attention to his online sunglasses business. Remember that everyone loves to receive something for free. Holding a contest can attract visitors to your website, where they can find out about the rest of your offerings — the ones you offer for sale, that is.

You don't have to give away cars or trips around the world to get attention. Contests and giveaways are great ways to attract click-happy online shoppers. The floral site 1-800-Flowers.com, which has more than 670,000 "Likes" on Facebook, frequently holds contests there. So does Society43. Founder Jason Bolt knows it's a great way to build loyalty and keep shoppers returning to his website or Facebook page, especially since his fans love competition anyway.

"Product giveaways coupled with a competition are always our most popular promotions on Facebook," he comments. "Our fans are very passionate about sports and inherently competitive. Our most successful promotion to date involved a chance to win a pair of Limited Edition Oregon Chrome 43s. It was viewed by over 10,000 fans and shared 582 times."

Cybersurfers regularly take advantage of freebies online by downloading shareware or freeware programs. They get free advice from newsgroups, and they find free companionship from chat rooms and online forums. Having already paid for network access and computer equipment, they actually *expect* to get something for free.

Your customers will keep coming back if you devise as many promotions, giveaways, or sales as possible. You can also get people to interact through online forums or other tools, as I describe in Chapter 5.

A 16-year-old cartoonist named Gabe Martin put his cartoons on his website, called The Borderline. Virtually nothing happened. But when his dad put up some money for a contest, young Gabe started getting hundreds of visits and inquiries. He went on to create 11 *mirror sites* (sites that provide duplicated information) around the world, develop a base of devoted fans, contribute to newspapers such as *The San Diego Union-Tribune*, and sell his own cartoon book. (You can read a brief bio at www.care2.com/ecards/bio/1022.)

Waving a banner ad

I'm not as big a fan of traditional banner ads as I am of the other strategies that I discuss in this chapter — especially where small entrepreneurial businesses are concerned. But banner ads have hardly gone away. You see them on the free versions of mobile apps, and on popular sites such as YouTube (www.youtube.com). This venue reportedly attracts 790 million unique visitors per month, so it's a nearly irresistible place for advertisers. In general, though, banner ads are being used online less frequently than targeted ads — that is, ads that appear when specified keyword searches are conducted on sites such as Google (www.google.com) and Ask.com (www.ask.com).

Banner ads are like the traditional print ads you might take out in local newspapers. In limited cases, banner ads are free, as long as you or a designer can create one. Otherwise, you have to pay to place them on someone else's web page, the same way you pay to take out an ad in a newspaper or magazine.

Even these days, however, many commercial operations *do* use banner ads successfully on the web. Banner ads can be effective promotional tools under certain circumstances:

✔ If you pay enough money to keep them visible in cyberspace for a long period of time

✔ If you pay the high rates charged by the most successful websites, which can steer you the most traffic

Banner ads differ from other web-specific publicity tactics in one important respect: They publicize in a one-to-many rather than a one-to-one fashion. Banner ads broadcast the name of an organization indiscriminately, without requiring the viewer to click a link or in some respect choose to find out about the site.

Anteing up

You have to pay the piper to play the banner ad game. In general, websites have two methods of charging for banner ads:

✔ **CPM, or cost per thousand:** This is a way of charging for advertising based on the number of people who visit the web page on which your ad appears. The more visits the website gets, the higher the ad rates that site can charge. In this type of advertising, you have to pay depending on the number of times your ad is *viewed,* regardless of whether anyone clicks it to actually visit your site.

✔ **CTR, or clickthrough rate:** A *clickthrough* occurs when someone clicks a banner ad that links to your (the advertiser's) website. (Virtually all banner ads are linked this way.) In this case, you are billed after the ad has run for a while and the clicks have been tallied.

Say that 100,000 people visit the site on which your banner runs. If the site charges a flat $20 CPM rate, your banner ad costs $2,000 (100 × $20). If the same site charges a $1 per clickthrough rate, and 2 percent of the 100,000 visitors click through to your site (the approximate average for the industry), you pay the same: $2,000 (2,000 × $1).

Obviously, the more popular the site on which you advertise, the more your ad costs. Back in 1999, when Yahoo! was still publishing its advertising rates online, it charged a CPM rate of $20 to $50 for each 1,000 visits to the Yahoo! page on which the banner ad appeared. If the page on which your banner runs received 500,000 visits, such ads could cost $10,000 to $25,000. Not all advertising sites are so expensive, of course.

These days, many advertisers are following Google's lead and charging for ads with a cost per click (CPC) model, or some form of CPC. CPC is similar to CTR in that you, the advertiser, pay when someone clicks a link or graphic image that takes that person to your website. But the big difference is that in Google's CPC model, *you* determine how much you pay for each click; in traditional CTR, the advertisers set the rates. In this system, the advertiser pays only when someone actually clicks an ad. In the case of Google's AdWords program (adwords.google.com), the amount paid per click is one that the advertiser decides by placing a bid on keywords used to display the ad. See Chapter 11 for more information on AdWords.

CPM rates are difficult to calculate because of the number of repeat visitors a site typically receives. For example, a web page designer may visit the same site a hundred times in a day when testing scripts and creating content. If the site that hosts your ad charges a rate based on CPM, make sure the site weeds out such repeat visits. You're better off advertising on sites that charge on not only a CPM but also a clickthrough basis — or, better yet, *only* on a clickthrough basis. The combination of CPM and CTR is harder for the hosting site to calculate but ultimately fairer for you, the advertiser.

Positioning banner ads can be a substantial investment, so be sure that your ad appears on a page whose visitors are likely to be interested in your company. If your company sells automotive parts, for example, get on one of the Yahoo! automotive index pages.

Designing your ad

The standard "medium rectangle" and "large rectangle" banner ads are traditional. Some standard square configurations or small, button-like shapes are common, too. These days, ads appear on the side of a page (often on the right, as on Facebook) and they are relatively small. The measurements for ads usually appear in pixels. An inch contains roughly 72 pixels, so a 110-x-80-pixel ad (the size seen on Facebook) is less than 2 inches wide and about 1 inch high.

The rectangular ads appear most often at the top of a web page, so they load first while other page contents have yet to appear; smaller ads may appear anywhere on a page. (Ensuring that your ad appears at the top of a web page is always a good idea.)

Many banner ads combine photographic images, type, and color in a graphically sophisticated way. However, simple ads can be effective as well. You can create your ad yourself if you have some experience with a graphics program such as PaintShop Pro. (You can download a trial copy of PaintShop Pro at www.corel.com.)

Need some help creating your own banner ad? If you have only a simple, text-only ad in mind and you don't have a lot of money to spend on design, try a create-your-own-banner-ad service or software program. I've had mixed results with the online banner-ad services such as The Banner Generator, provided for free by Prescient Code Solutions (www.coder.com/creations/banner). See Figure 10-2 for an ad that I created in just a couple of minutes by using a shareware program called Banner Maker Pro (www.bannermaker pro.com).

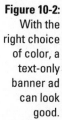

Figure 10-2:
With the right choice of color, a text-only banner ad can look good.

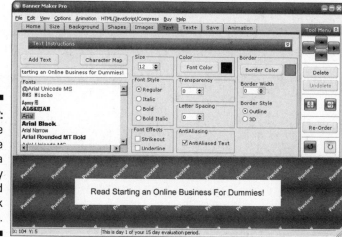

Profiting from someone else's banner ads

Banner ads may be out of favor, but they're not dead by any means. When used economically and targeted to the right audience, banner ads can help you achieve one of your goals: attracting visitors to your website. Attract enough visitors, and banner ads can help you achieve another, even more important goal: making money.

If you attract thousands or (if you're lucky) even millions of visitors to your site each month, you become an attractive commodity to advertisers looking to gain eye space for their own banner advertisements. By having another business pay you to display their ads, you can generate extra revenue with very little effort.

Of course, the effort involved in soliciting advertisers, placing ads, keeping track of how many visitors to your site actually click ads, and getting paid *is* considerable — but you don't have to manage ads yourself.

For John Moen, owner of a pair of map-related websites (including Graphic Maps), the move from marketing his own website to becoming an advertiser came when his WorldAtlas.com (`www.worldatlas.com`) site began to attract 3 million hits per month. He turned to advertising giant DoubleClick by Google (`www.doubleclick.com`) to serve the ads and handle the maintenance.

"We place DoubleClick's banner code on our pages, and DoubleClick pays us monthly for page impressions, direct clicks, page hits, and the like," says John. "DoubleClick also provides a daily report on site traffic. With [its] reports, I can tell which page gets the most hits and at what time of day. Banner advertising now pays very well."

Using Guerrilla Marketing Strategies

I didn't make up the term *guerilla marketing*. As you may already know, the term appears in the titles of a series of popular books by Jay Conrad Levinson and Michael McLaughlin. It appears to be a buzzword that encompasses many (actually sensible) marketing techniques — from providing good customer service to knowing what your competition is doing. It also means going beyond the passive placement of ads on web pages or other venues and taking a proactive, aggressive approach to getting your business name and brand in the marketplace. With competition growing all the time among online businesses, it pays to know all the options when dealing with online advertising — including the ones I describe in this section.

Pop-up (and under, and over) ads

You've probably experienced it: the moment you connect to a website, a window pops up on your computer with an ad. Other sites typically urge you to sign up for news alerts or subscribe to a newsletter. Anything you can do to induce your visitors to identify themselves and provide contact information, from an e-mail address to a street address, is to your advantage.

Many web surfers consider pop-up ads a bane, and some utilities — like the Google add-on browser toolbar and firewalls like Norton Internet Security, as well as browsers such as Internet Explorer and Firefox — can block them from appearing in the first place. But they can still get through to some individuals who don't have software configured to block them. And if your website becomes popular enough, a company will approach you about placing its ad on your page, either as a banner ad that is part of the page or as a window that does one of several things:

- ✔ **Pops up:** This type of ad window is probably the most common. It appears when a page is viewed and pops up atop the page you want to view. These ads work best when their content is related to the page you've opened: Subscribe to our newsletter, buy our book, attend our seminar, or other supplementary information.

- ✔ **Pops under:** When you open web pages on many sites that display ads, a new window opens. But this window, which contains an ad unrelated to the web page, opens underneath the primary window. Its content is visible only when the user specifically tries to close it, or closes or minimizes the other window(s) sitting on top of it.

- ✔ **Pops on top:** These ads, also called *interstitials,* totally replace the content you want to view. You are forced to look at them for a period of time and close them before you can view the page you want to see. I see these ads used on online magazines. When you click an article, a totally new window appears, with animated content, and big enough that it completely covers the article you want to read. You have to close the ad window to keep reading. You can read more about interstitials at `whatis.techtarget. com/definition/interstitial-in-between`.

John Moen told me that he has received criticism for pop-up and other ads on his clip-art site. But there's a trade-off here: The ad revenue makes it possible for him to keep creating the art and offering it for free. In the end, whether consumers realize it or not, they benefit from the ads because they get free art. All they have to do is click the close box to delete the window that pops up.

Adding life to your ads

Ads that appear on billboards, the sides of buildings, the sides of buses, the lights on top of cabs, and the pages of newspapers and magazines have one thing in common: They basically sit there and don't do anything. They can have lights pointed at them, and magazine ads for perfumes can be scented — but that's about it.

On the web, ads can be interactive in several different ways. The aim is to gain more attention from the hurried web surfer who is, after all, looking for something else on the current web page. You see several examples of interactive ads on the SteelHouse website (`www.steelhouse.com`). This company creates interactive ads for businesses. For example, go to the home page of SteelHouse client Mackenzie Limited (`www.mackenzieltd.com`) and you'll see a series of products for sale slide across the top of the page. These might include "interaction points" as well as YouTube videos, carousels, count-down timers, and social media icons.

Creating ads that appear to move around is easy, although you shouldn't expect them to look as elegant as those created by a professional designer. You need software that's used to create animated GIF images, such as GIF Construction Set Professional, a Windows-only program available for $24.99 (`www.mindworkshop.com/gifcon.html`), or the Mac application GIF.gIf. giF, available for $28 (`www.peda.com/ggg`). When you create the initial ad image and save it in GIF format, you create a series of variations and string them together to create the animation. The animation software leads you through the process.

Minding Your Ps and Qs (Puns and Quips)

What attracts shoppers to your business and encourages them to place orders from thousands of miles away? It's what you have to sell and how you present it. But how can customers understand what you're selling if they speak a different language? You must make your site accessible to *all* your potential customers.

Speaking their language

Put yourself in your customer's place. Suppose that you're from Spain. You speak a little English, but Spanish is your native tongue, and other Romance languages, such as French or Italian, are definitely easier for you to understand than English. You're surfing around an Internet shopping mall and you come across sentences such as

Hey, ratchet-jaws. Shoot me some e-mail with your handle, and steer clear of Smokeys with ears.

Whatever. All you home boys will be down with my superfly jive.

Like, this cable modem is totally awesome to the max.

Get the picture? Your use of slang and local dialect may have customers from your own hometown or region in stitches, but it can leave many more people scratching their heads and clicking to the next site. The first rule in making your site accessible to a worldwide audience is to keep your language simple so that people from all walks of life — and various places on the planet — can understand you.

Using the right salutations

First impressions mean a lot. The way you address someone can mean the difference between getting off on the right foot and stumbling over your shoelaces. The following useful tidbits are from the International Addresses and Salutations web page (`www.bspage.com/address.html`), which, in turn, borrowed them from *Merriam-Webster's Guide to International Business Communications:*

- ✔ In Austria, address a man as *Herr* and a woman as *Frau;* don't use *Fräulein* for business correspondence.

- ✔ In southern Belgium, use *Monsieur* or *Madame* to address someone, but the language spoken in northern Belgium is Flemish, so be sure to use *De heer* (Mr.) when addressing a man, or *Mevrouw,* abbreviated *Mevr.* (Mrs.) when addressing a woman.

- ✔ In India, use *Shri* (Mr.) or *Shrimati* (Mrs.). Don't use a given name unless you're a relative or close friend.

- ✔ In Japan, given names aren't used in business. Use the family name followed by the job title. Or add *-san* to the family name (for example, *Fujita-san)* or the even-more-respectful *-sama (Fujita-sama).*

Adding multilingual content to your website is a nice touch, particularly if you deal on a regular basis with customers or clients from a particular area. Regional differences abound, so it's prudent to find someone familiar with the area you're trying to target and ask that person to read your text before you put it up on the web. Let a friend — not the absence of orders for your goods — tell you that you've committed a cultural faux pas. That way, you can fix it before you put it out there.

Making your site multilingual

One of the best ways to expand your business to other countries is to provide alternative translations of your content. You can either hire someone to prepare the text in one or more selected languages or use a computer program to do the work for you. Then provide links to the web pages that contain the translated text right on your site's home page, like this:

```
Read this page in:
French
Spanish
German
```

One translation utility that's particularly easy to use — and free — is available from Microsoft's search service Bing. Just follow these steps to get your own instant translation:

1. **Connect to the Internet, launch your web browser, and go to** `www.bing.com/translator`.

   The Bing Translator page appears.

2. **If you have specific text you want to translate, type the text in the left box or copy and paste it from a word processing program; if you want the service to translate an entire web page, type or copy and paste the URL in the same text box.**

   Be sure to include the first part of the URL (for example, `www.mysite.com` rather than just `mysite.com`).

   Obviously, the shorter and simpler the text, the better your results.

3. **Choose the translation path (that is, *from* what language you want to translate) by clicking the Translate from or Translate to drop-down list.**

   At this writing, the service offers translation to or from 39 languages, including Chinese, Dutch, English, French, German, Greek, Italian, Japanese, Korean, Portuguese, Russian, and Spanish.

4. **Click the Translate button.**

   Almost as fast as you can say "Welcome to the new Tower of Babel," a new web page appears onscreen with the foreign-language version of your text. (If you selected a web page to translate, it appears in the new language. The title of the page, however, remains in the original language.)

A computer can never be as good as a human being when it comes to language translation. I once tried to translate my own web page into French, showed it to a friend who is a native speaker, and watched her laugh at the results. If you try a computer translation, attempt only the simplest of sentences. And get someone who *really* understands the language to proofread the results.

Instead of creating a foreign-language version of your web page, you can provide a link to the Yahoo! translation page on your own page. That way, your visitors can translate your text for themselves.

You can download the software behind the translation service, Systran Translator, from the SYSTRAN Software, Inc., website (`www.systransoft.com`).

The program costs anywhere from $69 to $749 depending on the number of languages you need. It is available for Windows only and requires at least a 1.2 Ghz processor, at least 1 to 2GB of RAM, and at least 500MB of hard drive space and 90MB of space per language pair during installation. If you need translation to or from Japanese, Chinese, or Korean (or from Russian to English), look into SYSTRAN Premium Translator, which starts at $899. This program has the same software requirements as the less expensive Personal package, as well as a driver for displaying Asian fonts, which is essential if you're translating into Asian languages.

You don't have to translate your entire website. Just providing an alternative version of your home page may be sufficient. The important thing is to give visitors an overview of your business and a brief description of your products and services in a language they can understand. Always include a `mailto` link (see Chapter 5) so that people can send mail to you. However, if you aren't prepared to receive a response in Kanji or Swahili, request that your guests send their message in a language you can read.

Although you probably don't have sufficient resources to pay for a slew of translation services, having someone translate your home page so that you can provide an alternative version may be worthwhile — especially if you sell products that are likely to be desirable to a particular market where a different language is the order of the day. Consider hiring a competent graduate student to do some translation for you. Plenty of translation services are available online. Yahoo! has an index of translation services at

```
dir.yahoo.com/Business_and_Economy/Business_to_Business/Translation_Services/
                      Website_Translation
```

Using the right terms

Sometimes communicating effectively with someone from another country is a matter of knowing the terms used to describe important items in that language. The names of the documents you use to draw up an agreement or pay a bill are often very different in other countries than they are in your own. For example, if you're an American merchant and someone from Europe asks you to provide a *pro forma invoice,* you may not know what the person wants. You're used to hearing the document in question called a *quote.*

When you and your European buyer have come to terms, a *commercial invoice* is an official form you may need to use for billing purposes. Many of these forms have to do with large-scale export/import trade, and you may never have to use them. But if you do undertake trade with people overseas, be aware that they may require you to use their own forms, not yours, to seal the deal. To avoid confusion later on, ask your overseas clients about any special requirements that pertain to business documents before you proceed too far with the transaction.

CASE STUDY

Marketing through global networking

Jeffrey Edelheit knows the potential for making connections around the world by taking advantage of the networking value of the World Wide Web. Edelheit, a business planning and development consultant based in Sebastopol, California, supports fledgling entrepreneurs' dreams of getting their businesses off the ground. You can find some of his advice for small business owners on the Bplans.com website, which is associated with the Business Plan Pro software product (`http://help.bplans.com/ask-bplans`). He also helps established businesspeople extend their reach by looking at ways of gaining greater market exposure — including going online. In addition, he works closely with management and staff to develop the internal systems necessary to build a strong operational base for the company.

Edelheit provides the following guidance:

- **Be deliberate in the creation of your website.** "I've worked with clients who are able to attract overseas customers and express themselves through creating their own websites," he says. A well-thought-out website can create a relationship between you and your customers; in other words, the stronger the relationship, the greater the opportunity for sales.

- **Know your market.** "The most important suggestion I can make," Edelheit says, "is to know the overseas market that you want to reach and be aware of the issues associated with doing business there. I recommend getting contact information for an international trade group from the country's consulate."

- **Research shipping costs and regulations.** Shipping costs and restrictions are among the most common problems new businesspeople encounter when dealing with foreign customers, he says. "Check with the U.S. Customs Service and find out what the duty charges are before you ship overseas. Once, in the '80s, a company I was working with shipped an IBM computer to Sweden, but because there were still restrictions on exporting high-tech equipment, I nearly got arrested by U.S. Customs for not having received the required special clearance."

- **Avoid being ethnocentric.** "Also be aware of how consumers in other cultures regard your products," he suggests. Make sure that nothing about your products would be considered offensive or bad luck to someone from another part of the world.

- **Be visible.** Edelheit emphasizes that after you figure out the inside tricks to the search engines and cooperative links, you have an unlimited potential to reach people. He believes that one of the keys to a successful website is providing information that your targeted market would find useful — and then providing product offerings as an attractive supplement.

You'll find tips for preparing a plan for a web-based business contributed by Edelheit and the founder of Business Plan Pro at `www.gregholden.com/appendix.htm`.

Chapter 11

Search Engine Optimization

• •

In This Chapter

▶ Analyzing how search engines find your site — so you can help them

▶ Focusing on ways to improve your coverage on Google

▶ Adding keywords and registering your site with search engines

▶ Making your website search engine–friendly

▶ Tracking referrals and visits to focus on the search services that count

• •

*I*f you can get your business mentioned in just the right place, customers can find you more easily. Consider my local electronics repair shop. The store has been in business for more than three decades but never seemed to be busy. When I asked, however, the owner told me he was overwhelmed with hundreds of back orders and couldn't get to my job for several weeks. His store had just been featured on a local public television show, and now people were driving long distances to bring him retro audio equipment to fix.

On the web, too, being found is the key to success. And search engines are the most important places to get yourself before the public. The key requirements for any business are to match its products or services with potential customers, to ensure that the company shows up in lots of search results, and to have the site near the top of the first page. *Search Engine Optimization* (SEO) is a set of practices designed to improve your site's placement in search results and is a cost-effective form of advertising that any website owner can tackle. SEO gives you a measure of control over the quality of your placement in search results, and this chapter describes strategies for improving it.

SEO has a bigger business impact than pay-per-click advertising or social media, according to the 2012 State of Digital Marketing Report conducted by webmarketing (http://go.webmarketing123.com/2012-State-of-Digital-Marketing-Report.html). For companies doing business-to-business (B2B) commerce, SEO generated the most leads, and for those doing business-to consumer (B2C) sales, it was most effective in promoting brand awareness.

Understanding How Search Engines Find You

Have you ever wondered why some companies manage to find their way to the top page of search engine results — and occasionally pop up several times on the same page — while others get buried deep within pages and pages of website listings? Ideally, search engines would rank e-commerce sites by how well designed they are and how responsive their owners are. But with so many millions of websites crowding the Internet, the job of processing searches and indexing website URLs and contents has to be automated. The process is computerized, so you can perform some magic with the way your web pages are written that can help you improve your placement in a set of search results.

Your site doesn't necessarily need to appear right at the top of the first search results page. But keep in mind that consumers on the web are in a rush, and if you can get your site on the first page of search results — if not at the top of that page — you get more attention. The important thing is to ensure that your site appears before that of your competition. To begin, you need to think like a searcher, which is probably easy because you do plenty of web-based searches yourself. How do you find the websites you want? Two things are of paramount importance: keywords and links.

Keywords are key

A *keyword* describes a subject that you enter in a search box to find information on a website or on the wider Internet. Suppose you're trying to find a source for an herbal sweetener called Stevia that low-carb dieters like. You'd naturally enter the term **Stevia** in the search box on your search service of choice, click a button — Search, Search Now, Go, or something similar — and then wait a few seconds for search results to gather.

When you send a keyword to a search service, you set a number of possible actions in motion. One thing that happens is that the keyword is processed by a script on a web server operated by the search service. The script makes a request (which in computerspeak is a *query*) to a database file. The database contains contents culled from millions (even billions, depending on the service) of web pages.

The database contents are gathered from two sources. In some cases, search services employ human editors who record selected contents of web pages and write descriptions for those pages. But web pages are so changeable that most of the work is actually done by computer programs that automatically scour the web. These programs don't record every word on every web page. Some take words from the headings; others index the first 50 or 100 words on a website. Accordingly, when I searched for *Stevia* on Google, the sites listed at the top of the first page of search results had two attributes:

- ✔ Some sites had the word *Stevia* in the URL, such as `www.stevia.net` or `www.stevia.com`.

- ✔ Other sites had the word *Stevia* mentioned several times at the top of the home page.

Observers agree that including the most relevant keywords in the titles and headings of the web page is essential. In addition, pages that are updated with fresh content on a regular basis and are thus re-indexed frequently get good search placement.

Wordtracker (`www.wordtracker.com`) does daily surveys of the keyword queries made to various search engines. It creates lists of the most popular search terms it finds. Those terms don't likely apply to your e-commerce site, of course. But if you want to maximize the number of visits to your site or just to make your site more prominent in a list of search results, you should know what's trendy and write your text accordingly.

Adding your site's most important keyword to the URL is one solution to better search placement. But you can't always do this. When it comes to keywords, your job is to load your website with as many words as you can find that are relevant to what you sell. You can do this by:

- ✔ Burying keywords in the `<meta>` tag in the HTML for your home page so they won't be visible to your visitors but do appear to the spider programs that index web pages (see the "Adding keywords to your HTML" section, later in this chapter).

- ✔ Adding keywords to the headings and initial body text on your pages. Check out the "Adding keywords to key pages" section, later in this chapter.

Adding keywords that are similar to your primary keywords helps with Microsoft's relatively new search engine Bing (`www.bing.com`). Bing categorizes its search results into a set of primary results and websites that are similar to the primary results. The latter results are presented in a column labeled Related Searches on the left side of a results page. By broadening the keywords you use on your pages, you increase your chances of turning up on Bing's Related Searches area on more people's search results. Find out more in Microsoft's white paper "Bing: New Features Relevant to Webmasters" (`http://www.microsoft.com/en-us/download/details.aspx?id=22140`).

A keyword doesn't have to be a single word. You can use a phrase containing two or more words. Think beyond single words to consider phrases people might enter when they're trying to find products or services you're offering.

Avoid piling a bunch of synonyms on the same page in an effort to boost page rank for your chosen keywords. For example, if your keywords are *Boston chop house,* don't place "Boston steaks, Boston chops, Boston chophouse, Boston chop house" all in the same sentence or paragraph. According to the blog of Google employee Matt Cutts (`www.mattcutts.com/blog/google-synonyms`), Google's algorithms are smart enough to identify this and nullify its effect.

Links help searchers connect to you

Keywords aren't the only things that point search services to websites. Services like Google keep track of the number of links that point to a site. The more links, the higher that site's ranking in a set of Google search listings. It's especially good if the URLs that form the links use your keywords. Suppose your ideal keywords are *Greg's Shoe Store.* The ideal URL choices would be `www.gregsshoestore.com`, `www.gregsshoestore.biz`, and so on. You could create the following HTML link to your e-commerce website on a personal web page, an eBay About Me page, or a Web Store on Amazon.com (see Chapter 14):

```
<a href="http://www.gregsshoestore.com"> Visit Greg's Shoe Store </a>
```

Such a link is doubly useful: A search service such as Google would find your desired keywords ("Greg's Shoe Store") in the visible, clickable link on your web page as well as in the HTML for the link.

Don't forget the human touch

Search engines don't work solely by means of computer programs that automatically scour web pages and by paid advertisements. Computer programs are perceived as the primary source, but the human factor still plays a role. Yahoo!, one of the oldest search engines around, originally compiled its directory of websites by means of live employees. These days, its directory (`dir.yahoo.com`) isn't as easy to find on Yahoo! as it once was. But editors still index sites and assign them to a New Additions category, which includes sites that are especially cool in someone's opinion.

There's almost no way to make sure that a human editor indexes your website. The only thing you can do is to make your site as unique and content-rich as possible. That helps your business not only show up in directories and search results, but also drum up more paying customers for you.

Having your site added to the Yahoo! Directory greatly increases your e-commerce site's visibility. But Yahoo! charges a $299 fee for businesses that want to be included. Focus on free directories, like Bing and Google, and try to improve your visibility that way before you put down the big bucks.

Taking the initiative: Paying for ads

You can't get much better placement than right at the top of the first page of a set of search results or in a column on the right side. It's even better if your site's name and URL are highlighted in color. The only way to get such preferred treatment is to pay for it. And that's just what a growing number of online businesses are doing — paying search engines to list their sites in a prominent location. See the "Paying for search listings can pay off" sidebar, later in this chapter, for more information.

Knowing who supplies the search results

Another important thing to remember about search engines is that they often gather results from *other* search services. You may be surprised to find that if you do a search of the web on America Online (AOL), your search results are primarily gathered from Google. That's because AOL has a contract with Google to supply such results. Not only that, many search services are owned by parent search services. Just what are the most popular search services, and where do they get their results? A rundown appears in Table 11-1. The services are presented in rank order, beginning in the first row with Google, which is number 1. Rankings of the top five were reported by comScore Media Metrix in November 2006.

Table 11-1		Internet Search Services		
Parent Company	**Its Search Services**	**URLs**	**Source (Search Results)**	**Source (Paid Listings)**
Google	Google	`www.google.com`	Google	Google
Microsoft	Bing	`www.bing.com`	Microsoft	Microsoft adCenter
Yahoo!	AltaVista, AllTheWeb	`www.yahoo.com`, `www.altavista.com`	Yahoo!	Yahoo!
Ask Network	Ask Jeeves, Teoma	`www.ask.com`, `www.teoma.com`	Teoma	Google
AOL	AOL Search, Netscape Search	`search.aol.com`	Google	Google

(continued)

Table 11-1 *(continued)*

Parent Company	Its Search Services	URLs	Source (Search Results)	Source (Paid Listings)
Excite (owned by Ask Jeeves)	Excite, iWon, MyWay.com	`www.excite.com`, `home.iwon.com`, `www.myway.com`	Google	Google
InfoSpace	Dogpile, WebCrawler	`www.dogpile.com`, `www.webcrawler.com`	Google, Yahoo!, MSN, Ask	Google, Yahoo!, MSN, Ask
Lycos	Lycos, HotBot	`www.lycos.com`, `www.hotbot.com`	LookSmart, Yahoo!	Google

The important thing to note is that many of the most popular search engines receive their listings not from their own database of websites but from other search services. If you pay for a listing with Google, your ad is likely to appear not only on Google, but also on HotBot, Lycos, Teoma, AOL Search, and other places. By getting your site in the Yahoo! database, you'll appear in Yahoo! search results as well as MSN Search.

These are by no means the only search services around. Other search engines focus on websites and Internet resources in specific countries. You can find more of them by going to Search Engine Watch (`searchenginewatch.com`) and clicking the Search Engine Listings link.

Going Gaga over Google

When it comes to search engines, Google is at the top of the heap. In fact, comScore Networks reports that approximately 67 percent of all search referrals are done by Google. The closest competitor, Yahoo!, has about 12 percent of the search market business.

Google is a runaway success thanks to its effectiveness. You're simply more likely to find something on Google, more quickly, than you are on its competitors. Any search engine placement strategy has to address Google first and foremost. But that doesn't mean you should ignore Google's competitors. Not long before this book was published, Microsoft came out with its own Internet search engine, Windows Live Search, which isn't as nearly as popular or as reliable as Google, though Microsoft would probably love to give Google some real competition.

Googling yourself

To evaluate the quality of your search results placement on Google, start by taking stock of where you currently stand. That's easily done: Just go to Google's home page (www.google.com) and do a search for your own name or your business's name (a pastime that's also been called *ego surfing*). See where your website turns up in the results and also make note of which other sites mention yours.

Next, click Advanced Search or go directly to www.google.com/advanced_search?hl=en. Under the heading Page-Specific Search, enter the URL for your e-commerce site in the Links text box and then click Search. The results that appear in a few seconds consist of websites that link to yours. The list suggests the kinds of sites you should approach to solicit links. It also suggests the kinds of informational websites you might create to steer business to your website. (See the "Maximizing links" section, later in this chapter, for an example.)

Playing Google's game to reach #1

Not long ago, some bloggers got together and decided to play a game called *Google bombing*. The game is simple: It consists of making links to a particular website in an attempt to get that site listed on Google. The more links the site has pointing to it, the higher that site appears in a set of search results. Of course, the links that are made all have to be connected with a particular keyword or phrase.

The Google game applies to your e-commerce website, too. Suppose you sell yo-yos, and your website URL is www.yoyoplay.com. (This is actually one of the sites run by Lars Hundley, the entrepreneur I profile in the "Paying for search listings can pay off" sidebar, later in this chapter.) The object is to get as many other websites as possible to link to this URL. The terms that a visitor clicks to get to this URL can be anything: *yo-yos, play yo-yos,* and so on. The more links you can make, the better your search results.

Getting started with Google AdWords

When most people think about search engine marketing, they immediately think about a single program: Google AdWords. AdWords revolutionized advertising on the web and, not incidentally, has made a fortune for Google as a company. What makes AdWords special is its do-it-yourself aspect, which puts a huge amount of control in the hands of individual businesspeople. You decide what programs to advertise; you specify how much you want to pay every time someone clicks one of your ads; you write the ads; you fine-tune your advertising programs to bid higher on those that are getting results and end the ones that aren't getting much attention.

This section presents an introduction on how to get started with AdWords. It isn't meant to be the last word on the subject. Entire books have been written about AdWords. Consult *Search Engine Optimization For Dummies,* 2nd Edition, by Peter Kent, or *Building Your Business with Google For Dummies* by Brad Hill.

Getting the big picture

AdWords is a service provided by Google that allows individuals and companies to take out ads that appear at the top or along the right-hand side of a page of Google search results. Do a search on Google right now, and you'll see what I mean: They're the ads enclosed in small boxes that contain links to websites. Perhaps you have clicked those ads yourself, perhaps not. The fact is that those ads are clicked hundreds of thousands — perhaps millions — of times every day. Every time someone clicks an ad, the person who placed the ad is charged a small fee by Google. (That's why they're called cost-per-click, or CPC, ads.)

If the "clicker" goes on to make a purchase on the website that is being advertised, or if he or she fills out a form or takes out a new membership, the person who took out the AdWords ad (for the purposes of this discussion, I'll call this person the affiliate) earns money in two possible ways. If your website is being advertised, you make money from the purchase. If you advertise someone else's site and that site pays affiliates, you earn a referral fee. The exact fee varies from site to site. On eBay, a purchase can earn the affiliate a sizeable fee of 40 percent or more. A new registration can earn the affiliate as much as $22. If that click cost 10 cents, that's a huge profit — even if it takes a hundred clicks before someone takes one of the actions that earn the affiliate a referral fee.

One thing that makes AdWords effective is that the ads are targeted; they appear only on search results that are similar to the product or service being advertised. The connection between the advertiser and search results is made by keywords that the affiliate associates with the ad. If the affiliate is advertising a site that sells dog and cat supplies and specifies keywords like "dog food," "cat collar," "flea spray," and the like, the ad appears when a web surfer searches for those terms. Another advantage is that you write the ad, and you specify how much you'll pay for each click: You're in control.

You might think that specifying common keywords is a good thing because it causes your advertised site to appear in its AdWords ad more often: More people likely search for "dog" or "cat" than "dog food" or "dog hip dysplasia," for example. But your goal is to target your search and find just those shoppers who are hunting for what the advertiser wants. If 100,000 people view your ad with the keyword "dog" and only 2 clicks are made, the ad is ineffective. If 100 people view the ad for "dog flea collars" but 30 clicks are made and they lead to 10 purchases, you have a far more effective ad.

Signing up for the service

Taking out an account with AdWords is the easy part. Before you start, you should decide what you want to advertise. For this example, I assume you're advertising your own website. You can also advertise for someone else, as long as you're willing to pay for the "clicks."

You also need to obtain a Google account with a username and password. To do this, go to Google's home page, click the Sign In link, and click the Create an Account Now link.

After you sign in, follow these steps:

1. **Go to the Google Advertising Programs page.**

   Click Advertising Programs at the bottom of the home page, or go directly to www.google.com/ads.

2. **Click Get Started beneath the Advertise on Google header to go to your page on the AdWords site.**

3. **Follow the steps shown on the screens that follow to finish creating your Google account.**

After you set up an account on AdWords, you can move to the next step: advertising your products.

Writing AdWords ads

After you create an AdWords account, as described in the previous steps, the Welcome to AdWords window automatically appears, open to the Campaigns tab. When the Google AdWords page appears, follow these steps:

1. **Click the green button labeled New Campaign.**

   A drop-down menu appears with options for where you want the ad to appear: Google's search network or its display network.

2. **Choose Search & Display Networks for the widest coverage.**

   The Search & Display Networks - Standard page appears, as shown in Figure 11-1.

3. **In the Campaign name box, enter the name of the business you are advertising.**

4. **Under Networks, make sure the networks where you want your ad to appear are checked.**

5. **Under Devices, all types of computer devices that could display your ad (mobile devices, tablets, and desktop computers) are chosen by default. If you don't want your ad to be seen by mobile devices, for instance, click Switch to Legacy Campaign Settings, twice.**

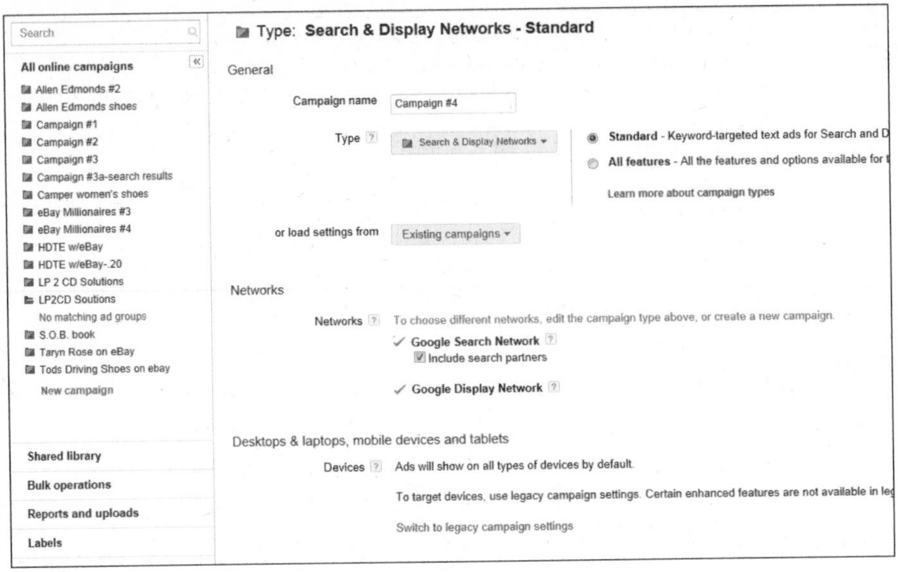

Figure 11-1: Name your ad campaign and ad group, even if you are creating only one ad.

6. **Under Locations, click the button next to the countries where you want your ad to appear.**

7. **Under Bidding and Budget, specify how much you want to pay whenever someone clicks your ad.**

   It's wise to set this amount low to begin with so you aren't surprised by high charges. To be conservative, you might choose 10 cents per click and a limit of $10 per day, for instance. Or click the button next to *AdWords will set my bids…* to let AdWords set a per-click price for you.

8. **Under Ad Extensions, check the box next to any additional information, such as your location or a phone number, that you want to add to your ad.**

9. **When you're done, click Save and Continue.**

10. **In the Ad Group Name box, enter a name that describes your ad.**

    This name is only for your convenience and can be something as simple as Website Ad.

11. **Under the Create an Ad heading shown in Figure 11-2, type an attention-grabbing, click-inducing, action-producing ad for this product.**

    You have only 35 characters for each of the four lines to do so; you'll see in a moment just how short a space that is.

12. **Type a heading (up to 35 characters including spaces) in the Headline box.**

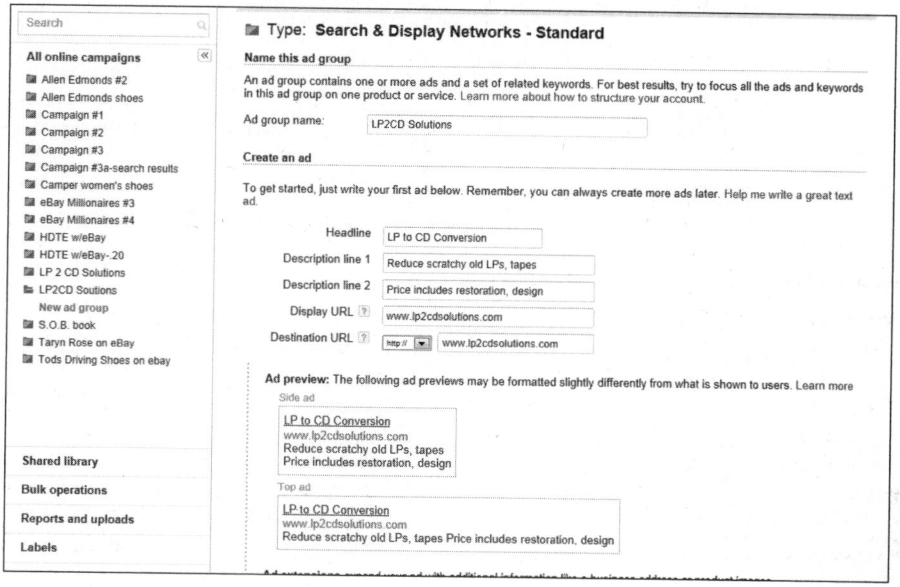

Figure 11-2:
Create a
short ad
that induces
clicks and
purchases.

13. **Write Description lines 1 and 2 (each up to 35 characters) in the boxes provided.**

14. **In the box next to Display URL, type the URL that will appear in the body of the ad.**

15. **In the Destination URL box, retype the same URL.**

    If you are advertising as an affiliate for a website like Amazon.com, this box will contain a complex link you need to obtain from Amazon.com. Here's an example of an ad I wrote:

    ```
    LP to CD Conversion
    Restore scratchy old LPs, tapes
    Price includes restoration, design
    www.lp2cdsolutions.com
    ```

16. **When you're done, scroll down to the Keywords section of the page, as shown in Figure 11-3.**

17. **Choose keywords to accompany your ad.**

    You can use Google's suggestions, which are presented on the Choose Keywords page. Or you can consult an online service such as Wordtracker (www.wordtracker.com) for suggested keywords.

18. **When you're done, click Save Ad Group.**

    You go to a page where you can review your ad and adjust your keywords, if needed.

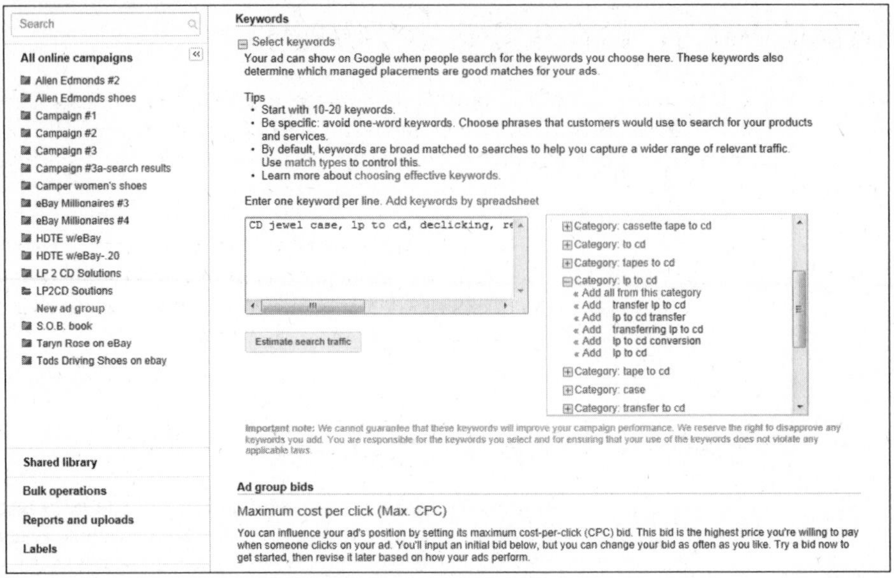

Figure 11-3:
Choose your
keywords.

Eventually, you launch your campaign, which goes online in a matter of min-utes if it meets Google's review standards. After your ad is online, you can create variations and see which ones get the best results. It can be quite an entertaining game to see which of your ads gets lots of page views and which attracts clicks. Figure 11-4 shows a group of ads I prepared as an affiliate for Amazon.com.

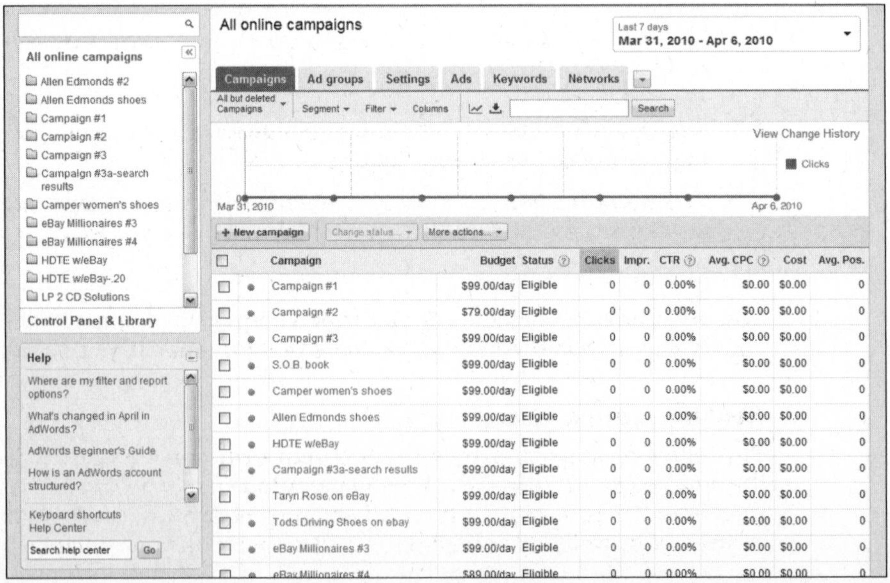

Figure 11-4:
Monitor
your ads
closely so
you don't
spend too
much on
"clicks" that
don't lead to
purchases.

Leaving a Trail of Crumbs

To improve your site's search placement, make it easy for searchers to find you. Leave a trail of digital crumbs, add keywords to the HTML for your web pages, and make sure that your site is included in the most popular services databases.

Most web surfers don't enter single words in search boxes. They tend to enter phrases. Combinations of keywords are especially effective. If you sell tools, don't just enter *tools* as a keyword. Enter keywords such as *tool box, power tool, tool caddy, pneumatic tool,* and *electric tool.*

Adding keywords to your HTML

What keywords should you add to your site? Take an old-fashioned pencil and paper and write all the words you can think of that are related to your site, your products, your services, or you — whatever you want to promote, in other words. You might also consult a printed thesaurus or use one supplied online at Dictionary.com (`www.dictionary.com`). Look up one term associated with your goods or services, and you're likely to find a number of similar terms.

Where to put the <meta> tag

Every web page is enclosed by two specific tags: `<html>` and `</html>`. These tags define the page as being an HTML document. The `<html>` tag goes at the beginning of the document, and `</html>` goes at the end.

Between the `<html>` and `</html>` tags reside two main subdivisions of a web page:

- ✔ **The header section:** This section, enclosed by the `<head>` and `</head>` tags, is where the `<meta>` tags go.
- ✔ **The body section:** This section, enclosed by the `<body>` and `</body>` tags, is where the contents of the web page — the part you actually see onscreen — go.

You don't have to include `<meta>` tags on every page on your site; in fact, your home page is the only page where doing so makes sense.

How to create a <meta> tag

The following steps show how to add your own `<meta>` tags from scratch to the source code of a web page by using Adobe Dreamweaver. These steps presume that you've already installed Internet Explorer and Dreamweaver, created your website's home page, and saved it on your computer with a name like `index.htm` or `index.html`. To add `<meta>` tags to your site's home page, start Dreamweaver and follow these steps:

1. **Click the Code button in the toolbar near the top of the screen.**

   The code for your web page displays.

2. **Scroll to the top of your page's source code, between the `<head>` and `</head>` tags, and enter your keywords and description.**

   Use the following format:

   ```
   <meta name="description" content="Your short Web site description goes
           here.">
   <meta name="keywords" content="keyword1, keyword2, keyword3, and so on">
   ```

   The output is shown in Figure 11-5.

3. **Click the Design button to return to the design view of your web page.**

   Your additions aren't visible on the web page because they're intended for search engines, not visitors to your site.

4. **You can now make more changes to your page, or you can save your web page and then close Dreamweaver.**

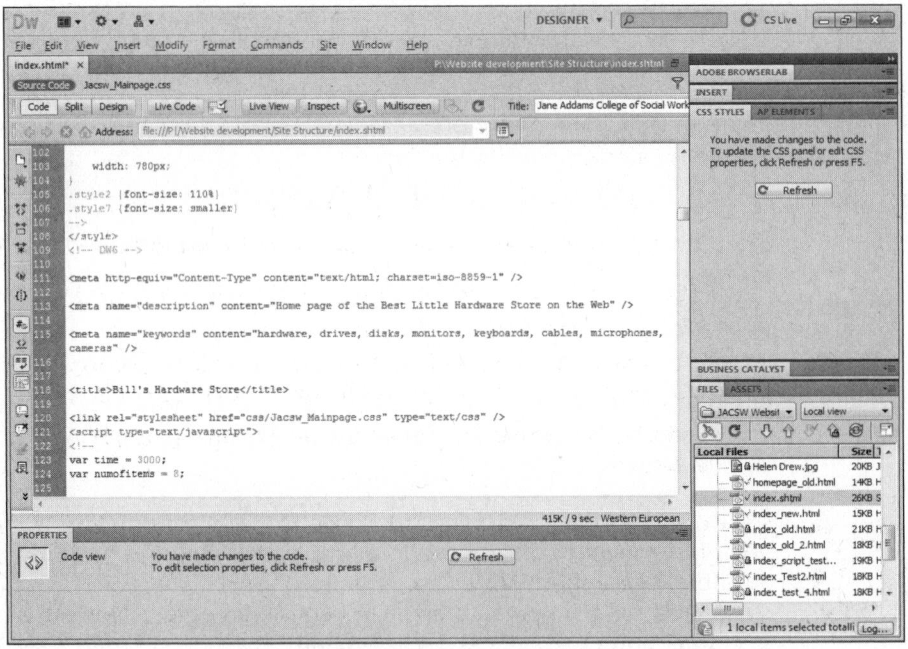

Figure 11-5: Insert your `<meta>` tags in the HEAD section of your HTML document.

Most web page editors make this user friendly for you: You can type your information in specially designated boxes. Figure 11-6 shows Expression Web's commands; open the page you want to edit by choosing File➪Properties, and type the words in the Keywords box. You can also type your official description in the Description box.

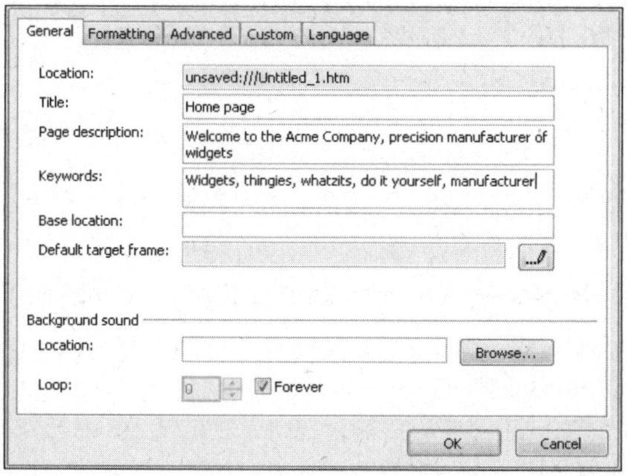

Figure 11-6:
Some web page editors make it easy to add keywords and descriptions for search services to find.

General	Formatting	Advanced	Custom	Language

Location: unsaved:///Untitled_1.htm

Title: Home page

Page description: Welcome to the Acme Company, precision manufacturer of widgets

Keywords: Widgets, thingies, whatzits, do it yourself, manufacturer

Base location:

Default target frame:

Background sound

Location: Browse...

Loop: 0 ☑ Forever

OK Cancel

You can also spy on your competitors' websites to see if they added any keywords to their web pages by following these steps:

1. **Go to your competitor's home page and choose View➪Source if you use Internet Explorer or right-click and choose View Page Source if you use Mozilla Firefox.**

   A new window opens, with the page source supplied.

2. **Scroll through the code, looking for the `<meta>` tags if they're present.**

   (Press Ctrl+F, enter **META**, and click the Find button if you can't find them on your own.)

   If the page's author used <meta> tags to enter keywords, you see them onscreen. They probably appear toward the top of the code.

3. **Note the keywords supplied and see if you can apply any to your website.**

Keywords, like web page addresses, are frequently misspelled. Make sure that you type several variations on keywords that might be subject to typos — for example, **Mississippi**, **Misissippi**, **Mississipi**. Don't worry about getting capitalization just right, however; most searchers simply enter all lowercase characters and don't bother with capital letters at all.

The <meta> tag is also important for the Description command, which enables you to create a description of your website that search engines can index and use in search results. Some search services also scan the description for keywords, so make sure you create a description at the same time you type your keywords in the <meta> tags.

Don't place too much importance on picking the ultimate, perfect keywords for use with your <meta> tags. They're not all that effective anymore — not with search placement on Google, for example. Keeping your content updated and promoting links to other websites are just as effective.

... and don't forget about Bing

The bulk of this chapter discusses SEO techniques that work with most search sites, especially Google. Google, after all, is still the "big dog" among search engines. But several reviews of Bing are very positive from the last few years, and when you're leaving a trail of crumbs for your prospective customers to find you, you should keep Microsoft's search service in mind, too.

A comparison of how Google and Bing handle SEO published on the blog SEOWizz.net finds that both take titles, keywords, links, and other factors into account when ranking websites in a set of search results. But two factors are considered more important by Bing: the age of your Internet domain (the .net or .com part of your URL) and the number of sites that link to you and that have your keywords in their title. (Google, in contrast, gives higher rank to sites that have your keywords in the body of their web pages.) So try to hold on to your domain, and cultivate links from sites that have titles with your favorite keywords in them. Find out more at www.seowizz.net/2009/06/bing-seo-how-does-it-differ-to-google.html.

Registering your site with Google

Google has a program — Googlebot — that automatically indexes web pages all over the Internet. However, you don't have to wait for Googlebot to find your site: You can fill out a simple form that adds your URL to the sites indexed by this program. Go to www.google.com/addurl.html, enter your URL and a few comments about your site, and click the Add URL button. That's all there is to it. Expect to wait a few weeks for your site to appear among Google's search results if it doesn't already appear there.

Getting listed on Yahoo!

If you want to get the most bang for your advertising buck, get your site listed on the most popular locations in cyberspace. For several years now, the many sites owned by Yahoo! have ranked in the top two or three most popular sites on the Internet in the Media Metrix Top 50 list of Web Properties published by comScore Media Metrix. Actually, Yahoo! was number two on the list in January 2013 (`www.comscore.com/Insights/Press_Releases/2013/2/comScore_Media_Metrix_Ranks_Top_50_U.S._Web_Properties_for_January_2013`). Although many people think of Yahoo! primarily as a search engine, it's also a categorical index to websites. Getting listed on Yahoo! means being included on one of its index pages. An *index page* is a list of websites grouped together by category, much like the traditional Yellow Pages.

Aside from its steadily increasing size and popularity, one thing that sets Yahoo! apart is the way it evaluates sites for inclusion on its index pages. For the most part, real human beings do the Yahoo! indexing; they read your site description and your suggested location, and then determine what category to list your site under. Usually, Yahoo! lists sites in only one or two categories, but if Yahoo! editors feel that a site deserves its own special category, they create one for it.

The Yahoo! editors don't even attempt to process all the thousands of site applications they receive each week. Reports continue to circulate on the web as to how long it takes to get listed on Yahoo! and how difficult it is to get listed at all. The process can take weeks, months, or even years. Danny Sullivan, editor of *Search Engine Watch,* estimates that only about a quarter of all sites that apply get listed. That's why Yahoo! has instituted an Express listing system — your business site is reviewed in exchange for a nonrefundable annual fee of $299 — although there's *still* no guarantee you'll get listed. Find out more at `http://help.yahoo.com/l/us/yahoo/helpcentral`.

Search Engine Watch (`searchenginewatch.com`) is a great place to go for tips on how search engines and indexes work and how to get listed on them.

Paying for Yahoo! Search Marketing

What *can* you do to get listed on Yahoo!? You can always sign up for Yahoo!'s paid search option (also called sponsored search), Yahoo! Search Marketing (`http://advertisingcentral.yahoo.com/searchmarketing/en_SG/index`). Paid search won't get you listed in the Yahoo! Directory, but it does ensure with some measure of certainty that you'll at least appear in search results on the site.

What sets Yahoo! Search Marketing apart is that an editorial team reviews your keywords and ads, much like the website listings at Yahoo!. Google AdWords listings are also reviewed thoroughly, but the results come back in a matter of seconds and appear to be automated. Yahoo! Search Marketing originally used Google's search technology but developed its search marketing system based on companies, like Inktomi and Overture, that it began purchasing after 2002. Yahoo! is a notable search engine because its search results mix organic results and paid listings, and the paid ads appear at the top, along the right, and at the bottom of a results page.

Listing in the Yahoo! index

If you want to appear in the Yahoo! Directory, I have a three-step suggestion:

1. **Make your site interesting, quirky, or somehow attention-grabbing.**

    You never know; you may just stand out from the sea of new websites and gain the attention of one of the Yahoo! editors.

2. **Go ahead and try applying to the main Yahoo! index.**

    You can at least say you tried!

    a. Go to `www.yahoo.com`, find the category page that you think should list your site, and click the Submit Your Site link at the bottom of the page.

        The Yahoo! Submit Your Site page appears.

    b. Click the Yahoo! Standard link.

    c. Verify that the Yahoo! category shown is the one in which you want to be included and then click Continue.

    d. On the form that appears, provide your URL and a description for your site.

        Make your description as interesting as possible while remaining within the content limit. (If you submit a description that's too long, Yahoo! asks you to revise it.)

3. **Try a local Yahoo! index.**

    Major areas around the country as well as in other parts of the world, have their own Yahoo! indexes. Go to `http://local.yahoo.com` to browse by city. Find the local index closest to you and apply it, as I describe in the preceding step. You have a much better chance of getting listed locally than on the main Yahoo! site.

Improve your listing on Yahoo! by shelling out anywhere from $25–$300 or more per year to become a sponsored website. Your site is listed in the Sponsored Sites box at the top of a Yahoo! category. The exact cost depends on the popularity of the category. There is life beyond Yahoo!, too. Several web-based services are trying to compete by providing their own way of organizing and evaluating websites. Try submitting a listing to Best of the Web (`http://botw.org`) or contact one of the guides employed by About.com (`www.about.com`).

Getting listed with other search services

Search services can steer lots of business to a commercial website, based on how often the site appears in the list of web pages that the user sees and how high the site appears on the list. Your goal is to maximize your site's chances of being found by the search service. But Google is hard to crack, and Yahoo!

charges for commercial sites that want to be listed. What about other search services?

Not so long ago, search services allowed you to list your site for free. After that, services adopted policies that guaranteed listings in their index only if you paid a subscription fee. These days, the preeminence of Google and Yahoo! has changed the playing field. Some services have consolidated; others "borrow" the search technology used by the competition. And only a few search services provide you with a Submit Your Site or an Add a URL link that enables you to include your site in their index.

Microsoft's Bing lets you submit your site by entering its URL at `www.bing.com/toolbox/submit-site-url`.

One of the few sites that allows individuals to submit personal or commercial websites for addition in its index is the Open Directory Project (`www.dmoz.org/add.html`). The advantage is that other well-known search services (AOL Search, Google, Netscape Search, and Yahoo! Search) use Open Directory data to update and augment their own databases. After you get your site in the Open Directory, anywhere from a few days to a few weeks later, you'll likely see it appear in other directories as well.

Follow these steps to submit your site to the Open Directory:

1. **Connect to the Internet, start your web browser, and go to the Open Directory home page at** `www.dmoz.org`.

   The ODP – Open Directory Project home page appears.

2. **Enter the name of the site you want to add in the box at the top of the page and click Search.**

   A set of search results appears.

3. **Check to see whether your site is already included in the directory.**

   If it isn't, scan the search results for the category "tree" that appears at the end of each listing, and find the category that fits your own site. A category tree looks like this:

   ```
   Regional: North America: United States: Business and Economy: Shopping:
        Sporting Goods
   ```

4. **Click the category tree.**

   The Category page on the Open Directory appears.

5. **Click the Suggest URL link near the top of the Category page.**

   The Submission form appears.

   Not all categories in the Open Directory include Suggest URL links. If you don't see one, that particular category doesn't allow submissions. But others will: Click a more specific subcategory to suggest your site.

6. **Type the URL and a brief but specific description for your site and then click Submit.**

   Your page is submitted to one of the Open Directory staff members who reviews it to decide whether the site is suitable for inclusion in the directory. It may take several weeks for your site to be added.

CASE STUDY

Paying for search listings can pay off

Listing with search sites is growing more complex all the time. Many sites are owned by other sites. On top of that, you can list your products on shopping aggregation sites. You can make the consolidation of search sites work to your advantage by choosing a few services carefully: You can then find your business listed with many other sites.

Lars Hundley, who in 1998 started his first online store, Clean Air Gardening, has received lots of publicity thanks to energetic marketing and good use of search engine resources. He's also had great success with a site that's not often

regarded as a search engine: YouTube. "I use Yahoo! Search Marketing and Google AdWords. I also sometimes use shopping aggregation sites, like Yahoo! Shopping, Shopzilla, and Shopping.com." Sales were down in 2009, so he is closely watching AdWords spending to make sure "we are generating a profit and not paying too much for each sale we generate." He hosts Clean Air Gardening (www.cleanair gardening.com) and other e-commerce sites with Yahoo! Small Business, a storefront solution I describe in Chapter 15. Other informational sites are hosted on his own web server.

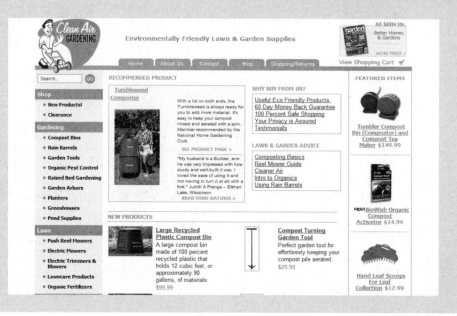

Hundley uses many of the search engine placement tools that I mention in this chapter. He says, "I also use tools, like Wordtracker to make sure that I use important keywords in all my product descriptions. I always try to name and describe things in the words that people are searching for, and I think that really pays off over time."

Hundley points out that YouTube is the fifth-most-popular website around, according to Hitwise (`www.experian.com/hitwise/online-trends.html`). "YouTube has been a phenomenal success for us and has been our most successful new marketing technique in the last two or three years," he comments. "We shoot short videos for all of our major products, demonstrating the product in action. We use a $600 Canon HD camcorder, and edit them on a Mac using iMovie or Final Cut Pro. Then we upload the movie to YouTube. We embed the YouTube video directly on our product page. So when someone is reading about the product, they can just click Play on the video and watch it." An example is shown below.

Hundley uses his journalism experience to write and distribute his own press releases and pitch articles to magazines, such as *U.S. News and World Report, The Wall Street Journal,* and *This Old House*. He also has an e-mail marketing campaign: "With Clean Air Gardening, I use Constant Contact to manage an e-mail newsletter that I send out every two weeks. I have approximately 25,000 subscribers. I use the newsletter to give gardening tips and promote my products at the same time — the tips are informational, but they also show how you can use Clean Air Gardening products for more successful gardening."

Hundley gives the following advice to budding entrepreneurs: "If you're thinking about starting your own Internet business, just do it! Start a small site and do it in your spare time to test the waters. I kept my day job for the first year when I started this business, until it started to take off and make money. Now, 11 years later, it is a multimillion-dollar-a-year company with 14 employees and a large 14,000-square-foot warehouse and office. You can do it too, if you try!" It's hard to argue with success: Hundley reports that Clean Air Gardening was named one of the 5,000 fastest-growing companies by *Inc.* magazine in 2008 and 2009.

Businesses on the web can get obsessed with how high their sites appear on the list of search results pages. If a web surfer enters the exact name of a site in the HotBot or WebCrawler search text box, for example, some people just can't understand why that site doesn't come back at the top — or even on the first page — of the list of returned sites. Of the millions of sites listed in a search service's database, the chances are good that at least one has the same name as yours (or something close to it), or that a page contains a combination of the same words that make up your organization's name. Don't be overly concerned with hitting the top of the search-hit charts. Concentrate on creating a top-notch website and making sales.

Adding keywords to key pages

Earlier in this chapter, I show you how to add keywords to the HTML for your web pages. Visitors don't normally see those keywords, unless they view the source code for your web page. Other keywords can be added to parts of your web page that are visible — parts of the page that programs called *crawlers* or *spiders* scan and index:

- ✔ **The title:** Be sure to create a title for your page. The title appears in the title bar at the top of the browser window. Many search engines index the contents of the title because it appears not only at the top of the browser window, but at the top of the HTML, too.

- ✔ **The headings:** Your web page's headings should be specific about what you sell and what you do.

- ✔ **The first line of text:** Some search services index every word on every page, but others limit the amount of text they index. So the first lines might be indexed, but others aren't. Get your message across quickly; pack your first sentences with nouns that list what you have for sale.

The best way to ensure that your site gets indexed is to pack it with useful content. I'm talking about textual content: Search programs can't view photos, animations, or sounds. Make sure your pages contain a significant amount of text as well as these other types of content.

Websites that specialize in SEO talk about *keyword density:* the number of keywords on your page, multiplied by the number of times each one is used. Keyword density is a way to gain a good search engine ranking. In other words, if you sell shoes and you use ten different terms once, you won't get as good a ranking as you would when using six or seven words twice or a handful of well-chosen keywords several times each.

Making your pages easy to index

Sometimes, the key to making things work is simply not putting roadblocks in the way of success. The way you format web pages can prevent search services from recording your text and the keywords you want your customers to enter. Avoid these obvious hindrances:

✔ **Your text begins too far down the page.** If you load the top of your page with images that can't be indexed, your text is indexed that much slower, and your rankings suffer.

✔ **Your pages are loaded with Java applets, animations, and other objects that can't be indexed.** Content that slows down the automatic indexing programs reduces your rankings, too.

✔ **Your pages don't actually include the ideal keyword phrase you want your searchers to use.** If you have a business converting LP records to CDs, you want the phrase *LP to CD* or *convert LPs to CDs* somewhere on your home page and on other pages as well.

Every image on your web page can and should be assigned a textual label (also known as *ALT text* because the `alt` element in HTML enables it to be used). The label tells visitors what the image depicts in case it can't be displayed in the browser window. (ALT text is actually required by the W3 Consortium to make sites more accessible; see `www.w3.org/TR/WAI-WEBCONTENT` for more information.) As a trick to produce more keyword density, you can assign keywords or keyword phrases to these names instead.

Maximizing links

Along with keywords, search engines use hyperlinks to index a site and include it in a database. By controlling two types of links, you can provide search services with more information about the contents of your site:

✔ The hyperlinks contained in your web pages

✔ The links that point to your site from other locations around the web

The "Links help searchers connect to you" section, earlier in this chapter, mentions the links in your own web pages. One of the most effective tricks for increasing the number of links that point to your online store is to create several different websites, each pointing to that store. That's just what Lars Hundley did with his main e-commerce site, Clean Air Gardening (`www.clean airgardening.com`). "Creating my own network of gardening sites that provide quality information helps me rise to the top of the search engines in many categories," he says. "People find the content sites sometimes and click through to Clean Air Gardening to buy related products."

It's true: Do an Advanced Search on Google for sites that link to `www.clean airgardening.com`. First, some sites, like the following, are just a sampling that link to Clean Air Gardening and that aren't run by Hundley:

- National Gardening Association (`www.garden.org`)
- Garden Tool Buyer's Resource (`www.gardentoolguide.com`)
- Master Composter (`www.mastercomposter.com`)
- Organic Gardening (`www.organicgardening.com`)

You might also find these sites farther down in the search results that *are* run by Hundley:

- Gardening Guide (`www.gardenplantcare.com`)
- Organic Pest Control (`www.organicgardenpests.com`)
- Reel Mower Guide (`www.reelmowerguide.com`)
- Organic Garden Tips (`www.organicgardentips.com`)
- CompostGuide.com (`www.compostguide.com`)
- Rain Barrel Guide (`www.rainbarrelguide.com`)

Hundley solicits links for the sites he doesn't run himself. "I also exchange links with other high-ranking related sites, both to improve my rankings and to provide quality links for my visitors. If you stick with quality links, you can never go wrong." For more about Hundley and how he uses the Overture search network to help users find him on the web, see the "Paying for search listings can pay off" sidebar, earlier in this chapter.

Monitoring Traffic: The Science of Web Analytics

How do you increase the number of times search engines find your site? One way is to analyze the traffic that comes to your site, a practice often called *web analytics*. When it comes to search engine placement, the type of research you need to perform is *log file analysis,* which can tell you exactly what keywords were used already to find your site. You can then combine those words into new keyword phrases, ideally helping even more people find your site. You can get software that does the analysis for you or you can do it yourself. I briefly describe each way in this section.

Software to improve SEO

Some software options are specifically designed to help improve SEO. Such programs can help you by counting the number of keywords on a web page. Others analyze the links that point at the page and helps you determine the best keywords, where to locate them, and what specific text can make the links rank higher in Google's search results. Another common feature is the ability to monitor competing web pages to see what they do for SEO that you don't. You'll find a good selection of programs under the heading SEO Software on the Mike's Marketing Tools website (`www.mikes-marketing-tools.com/directory/seo-software.html`).

Google Analytics (`www.google.com/analytics`) is one of the most useful tools you can have for studying who comes to your site and how they get there. Not only that, but it's free. Find out more in Chapter 14.

Do-it-yourself options

The other, more labor-intensive way to analyze what drives visitors to your website is through analysis of log files. A *log file* is an electronic document that a web server compiles as a record of every visit made to a web page, image, or other object on a site. Most web hosting services let you look at the log file for your website. The log file gives you a rough idea of where your visitors are from and which resources on your website are visited the most. By focusing on particular types of log file data, you can evaluate how visitors find your site and which search services are doing the best job of directing visitors to you.

If you look at log file information in its raw text form, you're probably mystified by page after page of numbers and techie gibberish. Log files typically record information, such as the IP address and the domain name of the computer that accesses a web page. They don't tell you the name and address of the person using the machine at the time. They give you an idea of where the computer is located geographically, based on the suffix at the end of a domain name (such as `.de` for Germany or `.fr` for France). You probably need to use a log file analyzer, Webtrends (`www.webtrends.com`), which presents the data in a format that is easy to interpret.

When you're viewing log files, one important thing to track is *referrer reporting,* which gives you the site the visitor was viewing just before coming to yours. This tells you what sites are directing visitors to yours. Note the search engines that appear most frequently; these are the ones you need to work on when it comes to improving your placement in sets of search results.

Chapter 12

Location, Location, Location Marketing

In This Chapter

▶ Listing your online business in essential local directories

▶ Optimizing your business for mobile GPS–enabled devices

▶ Advertising your products with locally oriented marketplaces

▶ Getting started with location-based marketing

*L*ocal is where most people still shop. Rather than reaching for their computing device, they walk or drive down the street or around the corner and go into a store near where they live.

If you have a local presence through a brick-and-mortar store, a mall space, or a market stall, you need to reach customers who take the time and effort to walk or drive to you and make a purchase. But as you've learned elsewhere in this book, more and more consumers are shopping using mobile devices. They're searching online rather than picking up the phone book or the ad supplement of the newspaper.

As a local businessperson, you need to reach your customers where they are. These days that's not always done by catching someone's eye as he or she is walking down the street. This chapter, which is primarily targeted at small businesses that have a brick-and-mortar presence, explores some of the exciting new options for enticing online shoppers to walk through the door and explore your real, live physical store.

Listing Yourself in All the Right Places

I don't know about you, but when the Yellow Pages is left on my doorstep (without my having asked for it), it goes straight into the recycling bin. I haven't looked at one in years. When I need to find a store (a real, local store with a street address), I whip out my smartphone and Google it. When the store shows up on Google, I can map it and then head out the door. When my wife and I need to choose a restaurant, we turn to Yelp and read the reviews (they also have maps and hours).

For you, the businessperson sitting behind the counter, this means you need to get on the right places where people like me can find you. Savvy store managers whose clients tend to be young and use smartphones put themselves in more than one location. In an article I wrote for EcommerceBytes on how to reach local buyers, I talked to Mike LoCarto, a web developer with Natural Body, Inc. (www.naturalbodyinc.com), which operates several brick-and-mortar stores in the New York City area. Mike makes sure his site is listed in all the places where fitness-conscious consumers look for vitamins and supplements online. Natural Body's Google+ page is shown in Figure 12-1. He also lists the site on several of the directories described later in this chapter.

The first group of places you need to know about is online directories where people are likely to search for and find you. You don't have to look far to find those places — just keep reading!

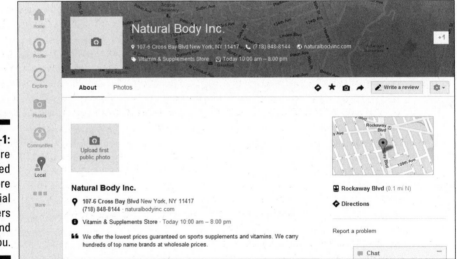

Figure 12-1:
Make sure you're listed where potential customers can find you.

Inviting Yelpers

You've probably used Yelp (www.yelp.com) as a consumer. It's a site that posts reviews and details about businesses located in metropolitan areas in the United States and other countries. You look for restaurants and other businesses by entering locations or keywords (for example, "downtown Thai restaurant") and read consumer reviews.

As a businessperson, you've got to make sure your store or physical location is listed on Yelp and that your listing contains accurate, basic information about you, starting with your address, hours, and contact information.

I've read both positive and negative comments about Yelp. Many comments are concerned with whether the reviews are genuine. In an effort to ensure that the reviews are posted by real consumers and not business owners or their friends or family, Yelp screens the reviews and rejects any that seem suspicious. When I set up a Yelp listing for my acupuncturist friend Allan Guilpain, several of his real-life customers, including me, had a tough time submitting reviews; several were "bounced" from the site for no clear reason.

If Yelp reviews are subjective and not always reliable, why should you go through the effort (and there is some effort involved) of getting listed on it? For one thing, Yelp attracts 100 million users around the world. For another, nearly half of its visitors are mobile users, according to Venture Beat (`venture. com/2012/11/01/yelp-mobile-searches`). Besides that, Yelp has become the most recognizable name in its field; it's so well known that many people automatically think of it when they are looking for a local business.

Yelp reviews can be unreliable; the company responded in fall 2012 to fraudulent reviews by "naming and shaming" the companies that paid for them. An article in *Ad Age* (`adage.com/article/digital/fake-reviews-rise-yelp-crack-fraudsters/237486`) estimated that as few as 20 percent of reviews submitted to the site actually get posted because of Yelp's stringent review policies.

Yelp makes money, in part, through advertising. Businesses can pay a fee to Yelp to show up higher in search results. Even if you have the most popular baseball card store in your area, you might not come out on top unless you pay for search placement in the manner of Google AdWords. You decide how much you want to pay every time someone clicks one of your ads.

To create a Yelp listing, you follow a process that you'll hear about a lot in this chapter. First, you find your business by doing a search on the site. Then you click a link labeled Claim This Site and fill out information about the business. The data you enter has to be reviewed and approved by Yelp, however. When you update your site by editing a form such as the one shown in Figure 12-2, you are also required to have the changes approved by Yelp before they go online.

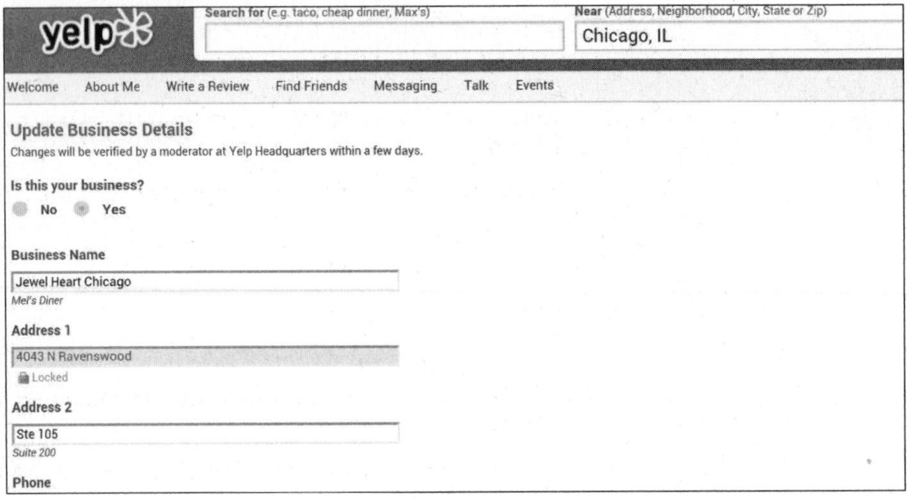

yelp	Search for (e.g. taco, cheap dinner, Max's)	Near (Address, Neighborhood, City, State or Zip)
		Chicago, IL

Welcome   About Me   Write a Review   Find Friends   Messaging   Talk   Events

Update Business Details
Changes will be verified by a moderator at Yelp Headquarters within a few days.

Is this your business?
○ No   ● Yes

Business Name

Jewel Heart Chicago

Mel's Diner

Address 1

4043 N Ravenswood

🔒 Locked

Address 2

Ste 105

Suite 200

Phone

Figure 12-2:
To ensure accuracy, Yelp approves all changes and reviews.

Once you have a listing on Yelp, you help customers to find you. You can give them an incentive to return to your Yelp listing (a process known as *checking in)* by offering gifts and deals. The notion of checking in and offering incentives takes on a whole new sense of importance when it comes to the next venue you need to exploit: Foursquare (which is discussed later in this chapter, in the "Marketing Yourself with Check-Ins and Offers" section).

Location-based services compete with one another for the most detailed listings, reviews, and tips of businesses in the geographical areas they cover. If your store has a street address, you probably already have a location on the service (often called a *page)* on those services. To do this kind of marketing, your job is to claim as many pages as possible.

Claiming your page on Google Places for Business

If you've ever Googled yourself, you know you already exist on Google. If you have a brick-and-mortar location, that's already on Google too. (It's likely the folks who take photos for Google Earth have even photographed your facility, too.)

Try it now. Do a search for your business so you can claim it as your own:

1. **Go to Google Maps (**`maps.google.com`**).**

2. **Type your business name in the search box and press Enter.**

   You may need to enter your street address and city to distinguish your business from others with similar names.

Suppose you don't find your business? I was unable to find my nonprofit meditation group because it's a new address, for example. If your business doesn't appear, go to Google Places at `www.google.com/business/placesforbusiness`. Search for the address rather than the business name; when the address turns up, continue with the steps.

3. **When your business (or your address) appears, click the red pin that represents it.**

   A window with information about the location pops up.

4. **Click More Info.**

   A Google Places page appears, with a description of your business.

5. **Click Manage This Page, which appears under Is This Your Business?, as shown in Figure 12-3.**

   A page appears with three options: Edit My Business Information, Suspend This Listing, and This Isn't My Listing.

6. **Click Edit My Business Information; then click Continue.**

7. **Select the method by which you want to confirm that you are the owner or manager of the business; then click Finish.**

8. **Make note of the PIN number and enter it in your Google Places dashboard, shown in Figure 12-4, to complete making your claim.**

Figure 12-3: Review your information to see if it's accurate; then click Manage This Page to edit or claim the page.

Click here to manage your business page

Any businesses you have submitted and claimed can now be marketed by you on Google. You can create Google AdWords ads so they get better placement in search results, for example.

See Chapter 11 for more on AdWords and search engine optimization (SEO).

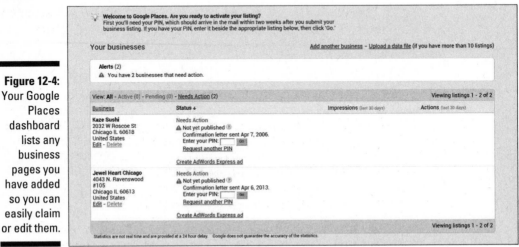

Figure 12-4:
Your Google
Places
dashboard
lists any
business
pages you
have added
so you can
easily claim
or edit them.

Yahoo! You're on Yahoo! Local

Yahoo! is one of the oldest indexes to the Internet, and it has always been a wonderful place to find businesses in your local area or across the sea. A Yahoo! Local listing gives you a chance to publish your business details and descriptions in the Yahoo! Directory. Listings can take one of two forms:

- ✔ **Basic Listings:** These are free and include your hours of operation, products sold, website URL, and other details.

- ✔ **Enhanced Listings:** These are paid listings (they cost $9.95 per month) that can include photos, a longer description, performance reports, and more.

To list your business on Yahoo! Local, go to the Local Listings Sign-up page (listings.local.yahoo.com/overview.php) and click the Sign Up button. Sign in with your Yahoo! ID and password (you'll need one to initiate the process) and follow the steps shown on subsequent screens.

Yahoo! Local is another place to get your business listed — and more importantly, found — on the Internet. Yahoo! is not as prominent as it once was, and not as widely used as Google, but if you want to maximize your coverage you should take the time to add your business there, at least with a Basic Listing.

Do a search for your business, or your type of business, in your local area on Google, Yahoo! Local, and Bing Local to compare their levels of coverage and to get an idea of who your competitors are.

In order for a business to be on Yahoo! Local, it must be located in the United States and the website must be in English. Check the Yahoo! Help pages (`help.yahoo.com`) for more requirements.

Reaching locals with Bing's help

In recent surveys of search engine use, Google remained the clear leader, but Microsoft's search engine, Bing, was a clear second on the list, so it's worth considering if you want online shoppers to find you. Bing currently has two ways for local businesses to be found: a Bing Local directory that resembles Yahoo!'s, and Bing Places for Business, which enables owners or managers to claim their businesses, like Google Places for Business.

At this writing, Bing Places for Business was labeled as being in "beta" or trial period. But all its features were working, and one of them was the ability to promote a business online by offering deals, including a loyalty program.

Getting listed on the Bing Local directory is free. Go to `www.bing.com/local/us`, click Add or Change Your Business Listing, and then follow the steps described in the "Offering 'punch-card' check-ins with Bing" section, later in this chapter.

Reaching your neighbors on Patch

Patch is a network of local news and information sites across the United States. If you live in a rural or suburban area, you might be covered by a local version of Patch; go to `www.patch.com`, and look through the list of states covered to see if your area or a nearby town is included.

If Patch does cover your area, it makes sense to make sure your business appears in the Patch Places directory. Patch Places isn't a website, but an app you can download for the iPhone and Android platforms.

You can download the Patch Places app from `www.patch.com/mobile`, from Google Play, or from iTunes.

To get started, search for your business on the app. Once you find it, click the Claim Your Listing link. Enter your business information in the form that appears. Submit the information to Patch and wait for Patch to contact you to verify that you are the business owner or manager. Once you are verified, you gain a Manage Your Listing button at the top of your listing page. Click this button to edit and update your business information.

If your business is not already listed on Patch Places, e-mail Patch at `directory support@patch.com` and ask to be added.

Marketing Yourself with Check-Ins and Offers

You've probably received one of those "punch cards" that give you a free coffee after you've made ten coffee purchases at the local cafe. It feels good to get that free coffee, doesn't it? If you're a member at Costco, you might receive a check once a year for cash back from purchases. It keeps you going to Costco, doesn't it, even though you still have to pay a yearly membership fee to get those rewards?

Customer loyalty is the ultimate goal for any business, whether online or off. A number of innovative web-based services bring loyalty and rewards programs within the reach of small brick-and-mortar businesses. They take such programs to a new level by adding the sophistication of GPS and smartphones. The system works like this.

You're walking down the street and, if you have configured your phone to do so, it notifies you that you're near the Fabulous Cupcakes bakery. You have checked in to Fabulous Cupcakes and are, in fact, considered a "mayor" of the site on Foursquare (which is described in the next section). You check in on your phone, and you can stop in for a free cupcake because of your past loyalty. The business has even provided you with a parking space because of your status as a "star" customer. Passersby see the parking sign and get to know that you're doing location-based marketing. This scenario can easily build you a steady stream of long-term walk-in customers. This section describes some venues that can help you market to a local clientele.

Tracking nearby shoppers with Foursquare

Consumers who routinely use mobile devices for searching and shopping will check in with you routinely if you give them an incentive to do so. The incentive takes the form of an offer that can benefit everyone; the more frequently you visit, the more benefits you get. Foursquare (www.foursquare.com), the most popular of the venues that do location-based marketing, is a perfect marketing venue for businesses whose clientele use smartphones on a regular basis.

Foursquare works like this:

1. People "check in" by telling Foursquare where they are. They might say they're at a particular coffee shop, hotel, museum, or restaurant.

2. Foursquare, in turn, tells those you have identified as your friends on the platform where you are, and recommends other places those friends might visit or things they can do nearby.

3. You and your friends can meet up if you're near one another.

4. Most important, from the standpoint of the brick-and-mortar business owner, you and your friends learn about what your favorite locations are and new places you might like to discover.

To get started with Foursquare, set up an account on its business page (business.foursquare.com). Click Learn More and then click Claim Your Business. Follow the steps on the Claim your business page.

Once you have an account on Foursquare, you can look around your current location to see other businesses that are taking advantage of the service and making offers. In my area, the historic Music Box Theatre is offering a free small popcorn to those who check in four times in one month, as shown in Figure 12-5.

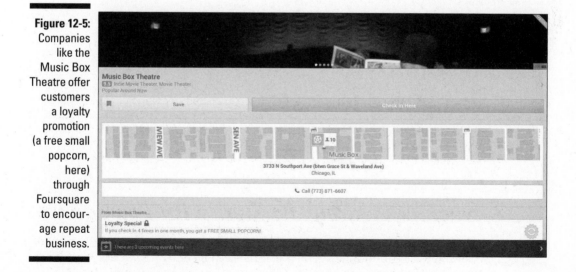

Figure 12-5: Companies like the Music Box Theatre offer customers a loyalty promotion (a free small popcorn, here) through Foursquare to encourage repeat business.

To get in the game and start developing your own loyalty programs, search on Foursquare for your business. If your business is already listed on Foursquare, click the link that allows you to claim it. If it's not, you need to add it. How do you add your business? I found this to be quite nonintuitive. I finally figured out how to do it on the Foursquare Android app:

1. **Click Check In.**

   A list of businesses in your current area where you can check in appears.

2. **Click the Search icon (the magnifying glass) and search for your business.**

   If your business doesn't appear, go to Step 3.

3. **Scroll to the bottom of the search results and click Not Listed? Add This Place to Check In Here.**

   The Add New Place screen appears, shown in Figure 12-6.

4. **Type in the basic details: the category and address.**

5. **Click Add New Place.**

Once you have added your business, do a search for it. When it turns up in the search results, click its hyperlinked name. A page with details appears. At the bottom of the right column, after "Do you manage this location?", click Claim Here. On the next page, enter information about yourself and provide your phone number. You'll receive a phone call from Foursquare and information on how to verify your position with the business.

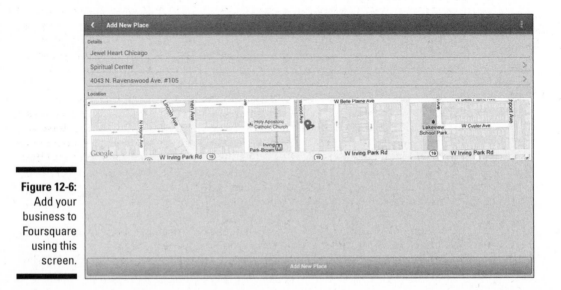

Figure 12-6:
Add your business to Foursquare using this screen.

After you have claimed your business, you can start offering promotions to those who check in to your business. To check in, they have to visit your facility in person and show you that they have checked in using the Foursquare app on their smartphone. But because they've walked through the door, the odds that they'll make a purchase go up dramatically. But at the very least, you should gain more attention as notifications about the check-ins spread through Foursquare — a form of free advertising.

This section only provides an introduction to Foursquare. For more detailed information on how this service can help your business, read *Location-Based Marketing For Dummies,* by Aaron Strout and Mike Schneider.

Don't worry if your store doesn't show up right away on Foursquare (or on other services mentioned in this chapter, for that matter). In many cases, the sites where visitors "check in" most frequently show up first in search results.

Checking in with customers at Facebook Places

Facebook is another big player in location-based marketing; if you have a Facebook presence for your business, it follows naturally that you should create a Facebook Place as well. Once you have claimed your location as a Place, you can do the kind of marketing described later in this chapter, in "Connecting with Locals with Interactive Content."

The process is similar to that for Google Places for Business: First you find your business's Facebook page, if it already exists, or create a new Facebook page for it if necessary. To create a new Facebook page for your business, go to www.facebook.com/pages/create/ and click the Local business or place option.

As you learn in Chapter 13, the Local business or place option is one of six different types of Facebook pages. After you create a page for your business in this form, you can claim it. Once you claim it, you can act as its administrator and track visits and comments or delete inappropriate posts. To claim your page, find it on Facebook and then click the icon that looks like a gear and that has a down arrow next to it. (It appears next to the Messages button.) Choose Is This Your Business? from the drop-down menu that appears. Follow the instructions on subsequent screens to claim your business.

One of the advantages of having a "Local business or place" page is that visitors can check in. But to enable check ins, you've got to specify a location. It's a good idea to add other general information, as well, so prospective customers can find out more about you. To add your location and information, first find your business page on Facebook. Either open the Facebook Home app on your tablet or mobile device, or go to the mobile version of Facebook at touch.facebook.com. Once there, do a search for your page. During the process, you'll add some basic information about your business — its name, the address, and a description (the description is optional, but a good idea).

Once you have claimed your business page, not only can others check in, but you can add or edit your business information at any time. Perhaps more importantly, you prevent your competitors or others from claiming the page and taking control of it, which occasionally happens.

Other location-based marketing services that serve niche audiences might be perfect depending on what you want to sell. These include Gowalla (www.gowalla.com), which encourages explorations and storytelling, and SCVNGR (www.scvngr.com), which lets businesses set up virtual scavenger hunts.

Offering "punch-card" check-ins with Bing

As mentioned in the preceding section, Microsoft's search engine, Bing, is getting in the location-based marketing game by giving businesses a chance to list themselves in the Bing Local business directory and by offering promotions.

Bing Places for Business is free and works just like Google Places for Business. One difference with Bing is that it offers customer support via live chat between 6 a.m. and 6 p.m. Pacific time Monday through Saturday. You can "talk" to a representative about claiming your listing or offering promotions.

Once you're listed on Bing Local, you can market your business with Microsoft adCenter (https://secure.bingads.microsoft.com), which is the rough equivalent of Google AdWords.

To get started, go to www.bingplaces.com/ and click Get Started. When the Find Your Listing page appears, search for your business. If it does not appear, click Add New Listing. You'll need to sign in with your Hotmail or Microsoft account, or create a new one if you don't already have one. After you sign in, you go to a page that functions as a dashboard and lists any businesses you have added to Bing, as shown in Figure 12-7.

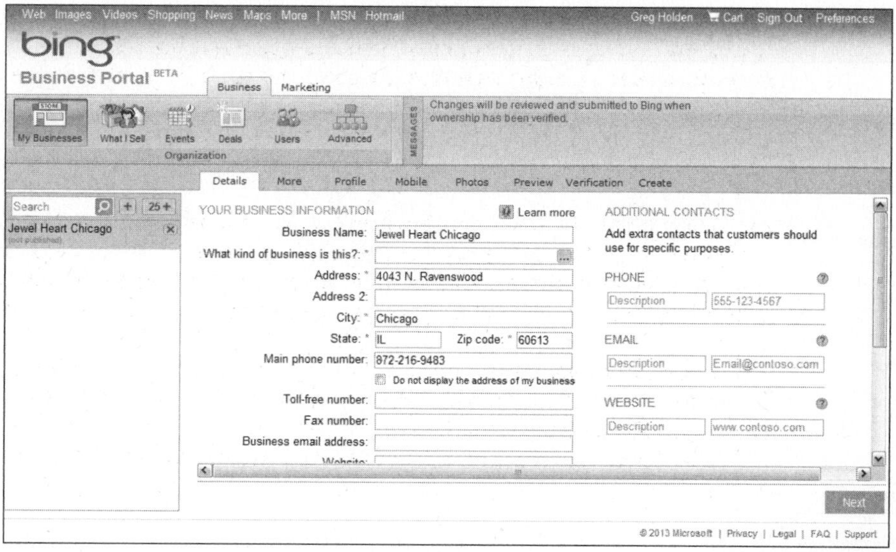

Figure 12-7:
This dashboard-style screen let you create and claim your business listing, and offer deals.

Adding your business is easy. Go to the dashboard page and make sure the My Businesses icon is selected. Then click the plus sign (+) next to the search box in the left column. Fill out the form with your business information and click Search. If your business is found, you're already in the Bing directory. If not, fill in the details in the dashboard and verify you are the owner to claim the business.

First, click your business name on the left side of the screen. A set of options appears: Details, More, Profile, Mobile, Photos, Preview, Verification, and Create. Click each of these options and fill in your business details to create a full Bing listing. In the Verification section, you verify that you are the owner of the business.

Once you have claimed your business, you can offer deals. Click the business you want to promote, and click the Deals icon in the dashboard. As you can see in Figure 12-8, you can offer either group deals or basic deals for a business. Group deals are Groupon-like promotions that take effect only if a certain number of consumers signs on to them. Basic deals can be promoted with a loyalty program. A mobile app is available that allows people to click a virtual "punch card" whenever they check in to your business. This enables you to offer promotions that take effect only when a certain level of loyalty has been reached: when someone has checked in five times, for example.

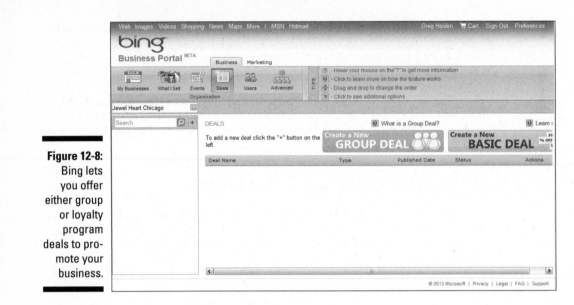

Figure 12-8:
Bing lets you offer either group or loyalty program deals to promote your business.

Connecting with Locals with Interactive Content

No matter where you list your business and claim your online page describing that business, you need to take advantage of the new exposure. Although you can certainly take the passive approach to marketing and wait for customers to find you organically by searching for you, you can entice them to visit (or encourage them to visit regularly) by making them some attractive offers.

Come up with a long-range plan for what you want to offer those who check in with you, not just once, but on a regular basis. You don't necessarily have to give price discounts; the point is to make your visitors feel valued. Some suggestions for offers that you can make on an ongoing basis follow.

Keep your customers coming back

You don't have to give something on a first check-in. A single visit doesn't necessarily give you income. Offers are more effective if they induce people to check in several times before they get something.

A theater might give a two-for-one ticket deal on someone's third or fifth visit, for example. If the Foursquare mayor checks in, he or she can be given free admission. These "down the road" promotions encourage people to visit you frequently.

If a customer or shopper does check in and your service gives you the ability to send a comment or greeting, by all means do so. That personal touch establishes a one-to-one connection between your business and the individual.

Make your offers well known

Part of location-based marketing boils down to good old-fashioned advertising. When you start connecting with your visitors through their mobile devices, make your offers known through signs in your store and on your website, Facebook page, and Twitter feed.

Make your offers tiered

In the preceding example, different levels of benefits were offered for different levels of visitors. Those who visit most often should naturally get the best deals. This sets up a spirit of competition among your regular customers, who might try to compete to see who can qualify for the best deals.

Chapter 13

Social Marketing: Facebook, Pinterest, Twitter, and Blogs

*W*hen I was working on this new edition, social networking remained a hot topic in e-commerce. No longer a novelty, sites like Facebook and Twitter are now a part of the daily lives of millions of people around the world. Facebook has gone public and is on the rebound after its stock initially plummeted. Pinterest is helping businesses improve visibility not by spreading the word but by spreading images. The idea that businesses can and should promote themselves through social media is a given.

But let's back up a moment. What exactly is "social networking"? If it's social rather than commercial, how can it help you and your online business? E-commerce, like more traditional kinds of business, is built on concepts such as trust, brands, and reputation. The better you can brand yourself and prove that you are either an authority in your field or someone who sells desirable merchandise, the more successful you'll be. By soliciting customers on social networking sites, you go out and actively find them rather than wait for them to find your storefront.

Social networking is simply the practice of connecting with people online at venues that have been specially created for that purpose. When the venues become especially popular, they become practical places to build a brand and spread the word about yourself and your business. You can even post items for sale through a social networking site or, at the very least, advertise them online. This chapter describes business uses for social networking sites like Facebook, Pinterest, and Twitter, and your own social networking venue: an online blog.

Developing a Business Presence on Facebook

Back in the early days of the Internet, the way to find customers was to create a website and then list your site on directories with names like Site of the Day. Then you sat back and hoped you would be noticed through your merchandise or your company name. As any established businessperson will tell you, the "sit back and wait" approach just won't fly these days. You've got to go out and find customers where they hang out — and increasingly, that's on social networking sites like Facebook.

As you may notice, I'm not writing about other social networking sites such as Friendster and MySpace. That's partly because I don't use those sites and partly because Facebook has some features that make it especially attractive. The best is its "opt in" nature. You get content from a person or an organization only if you decide to "friend" that person or indicate that you "like" an organization or a brand. You can set up seven different kinds of "pages" on Facebook:

- ✔ **A personal profile:** This is where you connect with family, friends, old school chums, and anyone who mutually agrees to be your Facebook "friend."

- ✔ **A page for a local business or place:** If you have a brick-and-mortar store in addition to an online business, choose this option.

- ✔ **A page for a company, organization or institution:** This is the best option for an online-only business, which doesn't have a physical presence.

- ✔ **A page promoting a brand or product:** Businesses that want to connect with customers regularly choose this option.

- ✔ **A page for an artist, band, or public figure:** Fans can connect, and performers or politicians can get the word out about what they're up to.

- ✔ **A page for entertainment:** This might be a book, a television show, a sporting event, a movie, and so on.

- ✔ **A cause or community page:** This can be a page about a cause, an organization, or a business. Individuals connect to such a page by clicking a link to show they "like" it. The organization can then communicate with those who "like" it by sending out announcements.

Because this is a book about online business, I'll assume you're interested in the third option. Starting a company or organization page is easy, as long as you have a Facebook account. First, go to the Facebook home page (www.facebook.com). If you don't have an account, fill out the form on the right side of the home page under the heading Sign Up. After you sign up, you create a business page by going to www.facebook.com/pages and clicking Create Page.

Do some prep work before creating your page. Decide on

- ✔ The name of your page.
- ✔ The purpose of your page.
- ✔ What thumbnail image you'll post along with your page. (If you have a business logo, this is the perfect place for it. If you are selling your professional services, include a thumbnail image of yourself.)
- ✔ A short (two- to three-paragraph) description of yourself, your business, or your place ready to post.

When you're ready, click Company, Organization or Institution. Fill out the form shown in Figure 13-1 and click Get Started.

Figure 13-1: Make the name of your Facebook page easy to remember.

You can also create a "local business or place" page on Facebook, of course. This might be a good option if you sell a particular product or service and you have a physical location. Check the categories in both the local business and company page options for a category that matches what you do.

Attracting "likers" to your Facebook page

As a businessperson, your job is to encourage Facebook members to "like" you. But first, they've got to find you on Facebook. You should definitely include a link to your Page on your website and as part of the signature file at the bottom of your e-mail messages.

See Chapter 8 for more on creating and using a signature file, a cost-effective form of marketing.

There are other ways to attract fans to your Page. One is shown in Figure 13-2. The venerable business 1-800-FLOWERS offers a discount: If you click the Fan Offer! link, a code appears that gives you a discount when you order flowers from the company.

Anything that keeps visitors on your site and gives them an incentive to return makes it more likely they'll purchase something.

Figure 13-2:
Give visitors a reason to return to your site, such as a discount, game, or freebie.

Getting personal with fans and customers

Society43 is a company that's very much in touch with its fan base. Founder Jason Bolt is careful to use the word "fans" as well as "customers" to describe those he seeks to reach through a website www.society43.com and a variety of social media presences such as a Facebook page (www.facebook.com/society43), a Twitter feed (https://twitter.com/Society43), and Pinterest pinboards (www.pinterest.com/society43).

By treating them as fans, Bolt and his employees can engage with them through social media events that don't necessarily involve direct selling. The point is to interact, build enthusiasm, and spread the word in an exciting and

entertaining way. On Society43's Facebook page, you get plenty of ideas for how to do this. There are contests, quizzes, and photos from campus parties at which students were wearing the company's colorful and school-branded sunglasses.

The promotions are in touch with what's happening right now, just like the Facebook news feed itself. As I was working on this chapter, it was Final Four weekend, so Society43 was offering free shipping on items purchased that weekend.

Earlier in the NCAA tournament, pairs of sunglasses were given away to those who choose the winners in various games. Another contest offered a free bike and a pair of sunglasses to 50 people who picked the eventual champion. Does giving away so many products help the company? You bet, says Bolt, who founded Society43 while he was a college student. He was still only 29 when I spoke to him recently for a story on EcommerceBytes (www.ecommercebytes.com/cab/abu/y212/m10/abu0321/s04).

"Being a company made up of young (average age of 25) ambitious team members definitely helps us to connect to our younger customers," said Bolt. "Our customers are looking for trendy exciting products that meet their fashion and fan needs at the same time." He mentioned these tips for social marketing newbies:

- ✔ **Keep it fresh:** Society43 team members make sure content on their website is always relevant and up to date, which draws repeat customers and improves rank on search results.

- ✔ **Use keywords:** The website, Facebook posts, and other content contain keywords that also improve SEO (see Chapter 11 for more on SEO).

- ✔ **Know your customers:** Society43 knows its customers are primarily sports-mad, cash-poor college students, which partly explains all the giveaways.

Having employees on staff who are the same age as the customer base also helps, Bolt adds. "R&D boils down to: If we wouldn't wear it, we won't make it," he says.

FREE SHIPPING!

In honor of Final Four weekend, we are offering FREE SHIPPING on all products purchased on www.Society43.com. Simply enter coupon code "FinalFour" at checkout.

Final Four Teams:
... See more

Society 43
THE ROAD NARROWS
WHO WOULD HAVE THOUGHT WE'D NEED WICHITA STATE?

Getting your customers excited

When you look at the 1-800-FLOWERS site, you immediately see another, perhaps even bigger benefit: You get to interact with individual customers and get feedback on how they deal with your site. On the Wall for the site, some leave comments about company postings, as they would about any information on Facebook; others simply indicate that they "like" a promotion or announcement. (On Facebook, "liking" is essentially a way of giving the thumbs-up gesture without actually saying anything.) Some of the comments are complaints, but the fact that they are on Facebook gives the staff person who is assigned to manage the fan page a chance to respond personally and perform some positive customer-relations work.

Other feedback on the page is enthusiastic: comments from people who are happy with the flowers they ordered and who are true "likers" of the company. Such interaction not only builds loyalty and lets customers feel empowered, but also gives 1-800-FLOWERS personal comments about packages that are well received and deals that generate interest. You would have to conduct expensive and time-consuming focus groups to get the same sort of feedback.

The Info tab, which is available on Facebook business pages, allows you to put out basic information about your company and make a link to your website. The Shop tab, which is not typically available on Facebook pages, lets customers shop for and purchase floral arrangements. Such a utility requires a programmer to create a Facebook storefront using the Facebook application programming interface. Unless you have a programmer on hand, you can't create such a sales tab yourself — that is, unless you sign up for an account with the marketplace ArtFire or another shopping cart that provides you with a Facebook storefront.

Creating a Facebook "kiosk"

An innovative marketplace called ArtFire (www.artfire.com, profiled in Chapter 15) has developed a Facebook sales system for members who sign up and pay their monthly subscription fee.

The Facebook kiosk is available to all ArtFire members. At this writing, an account costs $12.95 per month.

After you create a storefront with ArtFire and list works of art or other items for sale in a catalog, you set up a page for your store on Facebook. Then you install the kiosk, which "grabs" your store logo and a selection of merchandise for sale and groups them in a format that those who "like" you will find easy to browse. You can also make purchases directly from the kiosk without ever having to log out of Facebook and go to another site.

Kharisma Ryantori, who sells handmade jewelry through an ArtFire store called Popnicute, has a page for her business on Facebook, shown in Figure 13-3. Click the down arrow next to ArtFireKiosk near the top of this page and you can access a selection of her items for sale. (You could still shop although she was on vacation when I visited.)

Click one of the items shown for sale in the kiosk to view a close-up image of the item. You can select it by clicking the Add To Cart button shown in Figure 13-4. You then click the Checkout Now button to complete the purchase.

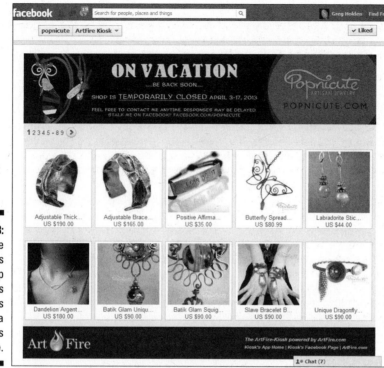

Figure 13-3:
ArtFire members set up a sales "kiosk" as part of a business page.

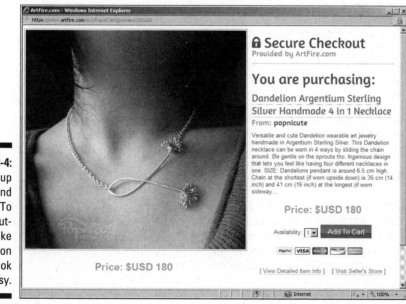

Figure 13-4:
Close-up photos and Add To Cart buttons make shopping on Facebook easy.

Sharing Your Images with Pinterest

You're used to sharing short messages with Twitter and Facebook; it's not a great leap to start sharing images as well. That's the purpose of Pinterest: It allows you to post content that your customers and fans can then repost around the Internet. Suppose you have a brand-new rhinestone dog leash that your pet supply business has just developed. After announcing it on Facebook, Twitter, your blog, and your website, "pin" it to your pinboard on Pinterest. Those of your customers who are already on Pinterest will see it and share it with their pet-loving friends. The result: viral marketing for free, with a positive personal endorsement included as a built-in extra.

Pinterest, a newcomer in the social marketing field, has grown by leaps and bounds since it was launched in 2010. That's probably because the Web is such a visual medium, not to mention the adage that a picture is worth a thousand words. Take a look at what Society43 (featured in the sidebar earlier in this chapter) does on Pinterest. In Figure 13-5, you can see that it has pinned 104 images, and that 55 individuals are "following" them on Pinterest. Best of all, from Society43's standpoint, three people have repinned its images and told their friends about them.

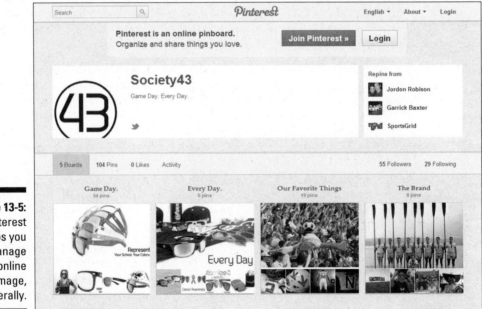

Figure 13-5:
Pinterest helps you manage your online image, literally.

To take advantage of Pinterest, make sure you do the following:

✔ Sign up for a business account with Pinterest (`business.pinterest.com`); it's free.

✔ Get a "Pin" button that you can add to your website next to your Facebook "Like" icon and Twitter "tweet" icon.

✔ Check out any businesses on Pinterest that are similar to yours for ideas about the sorts of images they pin.

One business I've profiled, Liberty Jane Clothing, has even found a way to sell products on Pinterest. Visit its site at `pinterest.com/libertyjaneco/express-checkout` or read about it at `www.ecommercebytes.com/cab/abu/y212/m11/abu0323/s03`.

Building a Fan Base with Twitter

Twitter (`www.twitter.com`) is one of those social networking sites that you hear about and then scratch your head, saying, "What's the purpose of *that*?" At first glance, you might not think a site that lets you post 140-character messages would have a business purpose. But look around at businesses that are using Twitter, and you realize that yes, Twitter can play a huge role in keeping up with customers, building brand visibility, and promoting your own identity or that of your organization.

Although lots of individuals use Twitter for fun, celebrities like Ashton Kutcher use it to make a point about a cause or issue. Big corporations such as the following use Twitter for a variety of business-related purposes:

✔ **Ford Motor Company:** Through its FordService Twitter feed (`twitter.com/FordService`), Ford fields complaints, spam, and occasional useful feedback from customers.

✔ **Popeyes Chicken:** The company (`twitter.com/popeyeschicken`) jokes with customers about its food selections, announces sales, and occasionally responds with offers to personally address customer concerns with comments like this:

> Sorry about your experience. Direct Mail me your e-mail & phone number and our Manager of Guest Relations will give you a call.

✔ **Starbucks:** The coffee giant has a Twitter site called MyStarbucksIdea (`twitter.com/mystarbucksidea`) where the company listens to customer suggestions and implements many of them. At this writing, one Twitter posting (known as a *tweet)* boasted that 50 suggestions originally voiced via Twitter had been implemented.

✔ **H & R Block:** The tax preparation service (`twitter.com/HRBlock`) responds to customer questions, either by e-mail or phone.

Of course, one social networking forum can be used to point to another one. The Kodak CB feed (twitter.com/kodakCB) is used to publicize new posts on the Kodak Corporate Blog. The blog, in turn (1000words.kodak.com), has links to the Kodak website, the Kodak Facebook page, the Kodak YouTube feed . . . get the idea?

For businesses small and large, Twitter plays a role in the overall online marketing effort. To build prominence on search engine results and word-of-mouth publicity, you need to set up a web of connections from one site to another. By chatting with your customers, even if it seems as though you are giving your knowledge away and answering questions that don't lead to immediate sales, you are building loyalty and good relations. Those benefits to others lead to sales for you.

Setting up a Twitter presence

It's easy to start posting on Twitter. As on Facebook, the challenge is to come up with a plan for promoting your business with Twitter postings *(tweets)*. Before you sign up, answer a few simple questions:

- ✔ What are your business goals for being on Twitter? Who will read your tweets?

- ✔ Do you have a cause or issue you want people to pay attention to?

- ✔ What action do you want people to take after reading a tweet? Do you want them to visit your website, read your blog, or shop in your sales catalog?

- ✔ How will people find you easily? What's a one- or two-word name that you can assign to your Twitter page?

- ✔ Who will post tweets? Should this be a team effort, to keep postings flowing to Twitter on a regular basis?

- ✔ Do you have special sales or promotions you can offer?

That last part is especially important if you sell items from a catalog. Twitter denizens are used to getting special details or notices of items on sale from sites like DellOutlet (www.twitter.com/delloutlet). According to Business Insider (www.businessinsider.com/henry-blodget-twitter-sells-3-million-of-computers-for-dell-2009-6), the Dell Twitter site generated $3 million worth of computer sales over a two-year period.

Signing up and posting

After you have a Twitter communications plan in place, you can sign up for the service and set up your Twitter feed. Go to www.twitter.com; enter a name, e-mail address, and password; and then click the Sign Up for Twitter button.

After filling out a simple form to create an account comes the real work: remembering to post, and updating your posts regularly. Being limited to 140 characters per tweet is a relief to many. But because tweets are so short, the convention is to keep them coming at least once a day or even several times a day.

Twitter is perfect if you have a smartphone with a keyboard and you like to type text messages. You can post on Twitter directly from your phone (m.twitter.com), as long as you do some setup beforehand. You can find a help forum called Twitter via SMS FAQs at https://support.twitter.com/articles/14014-twitter-via-sms-faqs.

Using Your Blog for Profit . . . and Fun

You are probably familiar with blogs as online diaries whose owners record thoughts and observations and share them with anyone who cares to read them. There are millions of blogs in the world; in fact, at the time it closed up shop in 2012, the site BlogPulse reported that there are more than 180 million blogs in the world.

According to a story from Technorati (technorati.com/social-media/article/state-of-the-blogosphere-2009-introduction), 28 percent of all people who responded to a questionnaire described themselves as "professional bloggers." Fully 17 percent reported that blogging is their primary source of income. Many blogs are just casual chatter. A few, though, make money for their creators. You, too, can use a blog to spread the word about you, your company, and what you sell, and make a few extra bucks as well.

Choosing a host with the most for your posts

One of the many nice things about blogging is that you don't have to invent the wheel. Some sites set you up with a graphic look and a mechanism for posting, editing your posts, and receiving comments. Two are especially popular:

- ✔ WordPress (www.wordpress.com)
- ✔ Blogger (www.blogger.com)

Of these two, WordPress is far more popular because it offers more features than Blogger. For its part, Blogger (which is owned by Google) has been around a while and is free. WordPress is also free, but it offers a Premium version that adds features such as a custom domain, extra storage, and the ability to add a feature called VideoPress to your postings. You can also buy premium themes to give your site a professional-looking design; such themes typically cost $30 to $100.

If you are more technically minded and like to control your website and your blog, consider Movable Type (www.movabletype.org). Instead of hosting your blog on someone else's site, you post this blogging software on a server that you either own or on which you rent space. Movable Type is free for individuals but costs $395 for a five-user license.

Adding ads to your blog

The most obvious and common way to make money from a blog is to sell ads on it. This becomes practical, however, only if you are already attracting a substantial number of visitors to your blog. Advertisers aren't going to pay to place ads on a blog that has only 300 visitors a month. One that has 3,000 visitors per month has a chance of gaining some ad revenue. The most common ad sources include the following:

- ✔ **AdSense:** This service from Google allows you to choose advertisers whose products and services are related to your own content.

- ✔ **BlogAds:** This service does the "matchmaking," pairing up bloggers with advertisers and taking a fee for its work.

- ✔ **Affiliate ads:** As an affiliate, you advertise someone else's products. You sign up for a program such as the popular affiliate program run by Amazon.com. Suppose you review a book on your blog and include a link to the book's description in the Amazon.com marketplace. If someone clicks your ad to Amazon and then buys the book, you get paid an affiliate fee.

A blog is essentially a website in its own right — one to which you add the primary content on a regular basis. Although many blogs generate income, they also provide financial benefits because they save money for their owners. You can set one up for no money at all, as long as you have it hosted for free and are willing to take photos and write content yourself.

An October 2009 article in Technorati (technorati.com/social-media/article/day-4-blogging-for-profit) reported that in a survey of active bloggers, the average income was $75,000 for those who had 100,000 or more unique visitors per month.

Asking for donations

You can simply ask people to donate to your blog. Sound crazy? It works. Add a PayPal button to your site. Visitors can then click the button and add money directly into your PayPal account. Follow these steps to add such a button:

1. **Go to the Buttons for Donations page on the PayPal website** (www.paypal.com/cgi-bin/webscr?cmd=donate-intro-outside).

2. **Click the Create Your Button Now link.**

   The Create a PayPal Payment Button page appears with a form to fill out.

3. **Fill out the form, describing your business and the purpose of the donations. Be sure to log in so that your payments can be directed to your PayPal account. Then click the Create Button button at the bottom of the form.**

   A page appears, with code that describes your button.

4. **Copy the code and paste it into the body of the web page where you want the button to appear.**

That's all you need to do. If you don't sell merchandise, donations can be a good way of keeping your effort going.

PayPal donation buttons aren't for your for-profit online business. They are intended primarily for fundraising or for nonprofits.

Achieving other business benefits

Blogs give customers and potential clients a place to gather so that they can find out more about you and your company. The more time they spend with you, the greater your chances of making a sale to them. A blog also gives you a forum for developing a credible reputation. Besides that, blogs are fun. They can take on a life of their own, especially when people start posting comments and you engage in dialog with them.

Marketing yourself

Many blogs exist to give the creator a place to demonstrate his or her knowledge and expertise in a chosen field. Even if your blog isn't specifically about you, consider including some biographical information so your visitors can find out something about your background, your knowledge of your field, and your trustworthiness. You might include the following:

✔ The basics about your qualifications: why you started your blog and why you went into business online

✔ Any certifications, honors, or titles related to your business

✔ Something about your business philosophy: your goals and objectives, and why you enjoy what you do

For many professionals, a blog is a place to promote and manage an image. As I wrote this, the famous golfer Tiger Woods was involved in legal controversy. He used his website (`web.tigerwoods.com`) to issue statements. The site includes a blog where he periodically posts about his tours and activities.

You don't have to include a photo with your blog if you want to maintain your privacy. A photo would make your blog seem more friendly and personal, however. Don't include your personal phone number or e-mail address unless you want to be especially open to your customers. Many CEOs do include e-mail addresses on their blogs and websites so that they can give personal attention to customer inquiries.

Selling your products instead of yourself

You don't have to get personal with your blog. Some of the most successful are roundups of software, gadgets, or other consumer goods. Some business-people advertise their products right within their blog.

Lars Hundley advertises through his Clean Air Gardening blog (`http://site.cleanairgardening.com/info`). You don't find much on the blog about Lars or his staff. Rather, you get product suggestions, gift ideas, and links to more detailed descriptions, as shown in Figure 13-6.

Lars Hundley has been very generous with sharing his business processes. You can find out more about how he sells online in Chapters 1 and 11.

Figure 13-6:
Many blogs function as advertise-ments for a line of products.

Part IV
Expanding Beyond Your Website

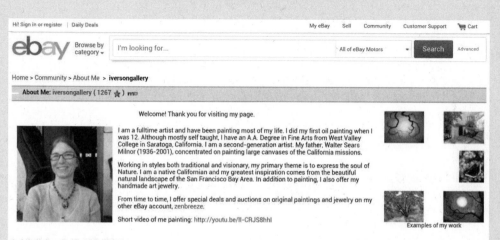

In this part . . .

✔ Explore options for selling merchandise on the biggest and best-travelled online marketplaces: eBay and Amazon.com.

✔ Take advantage of Fulfillment by Amazon (FBA), selling in the marketplace, opening an aStore, affiliate sales, and other Amazon.com offerings for sellers.

✔ Expanding your marketing and sales reach by opening stores on specialty marketplaces.

✔ Find out about services that can help multi-channel merchants manage multiple storefronts and work more efficiently.

Chapter 14

Selling on Amazon.com and eBay

● ●

In This Chapter

▶ Selling your items through Amazon.com's marketplace

▶ Becoming an Amazon.com marketing affiliate

▶ Exploring Amazon.com's other business options for entrepreneurs

▶ Selling on eBay

▶ Writing sales descriptions that attract buyers

▶ Giving your customers excellent service

▶ Opening an eBay Store

● ●

*W*hen it comes to making money online, the conventional notion is to think about creating a website or opening a storefront where you list many items for sale. You don't have to take such a structured approach, however. It's a lot of work to create a home page, set up a shopping cart, and establish a way to collect payments all by yourself. By listing individual items for sale on a well-established and well-known e-commerce venue, you can rack up sales without spending the big bucks on marketing and infrastructure. You can take advantage of the marketing tools the site gives you and the traffic the e-commerce venue already generates.

Amazon.com and eBay are among sites with the highest traffic in the marketplace. More and more often, when consumers are looking to purchase rare or unusual items or simply to save money, they automatically turn to these popular marketplaces. For sellers of all sorts, they are viable places to find customers and boost revenue. And both give merchants the ability to have their own storefronts hosted on their facilities.

With both Amazon and eBay, you don't necessarily have to create a website, develop your own shopping cart, or become a credit card merchant: The marketplace you choose handles those essential tasks for you. And you can sell outside of your store on both sites. On Amazon, you can add your items to those already in the marketplace, and on eBay, you can list items without having an eBay Store. Or if you already have a website that functions as an e-commerce store, expanding to these well-trafficked venues can help you build your brand and develop a multisite platform. Or you can focus solely on running a business in these marketplaces. You can achieve these goals with hard work and commitment, combined with the important business strategies I describe in this chapter.

Running a business on Amazon, eBay, or another site doesn't necessarily mean you depend on that site as the sole source of your income. It might mean that you sell on that site part time for some supplementary income each month. This chapter assumes that you want to sell regularly on Amazon, eBay, or another marketplace and build a system for successful sales that can provide you with extra money, bill-paying money, or "fun money."

Becoming an Amazon.com Seller

Over the years, Amazon.com has become known as "Earth's Biggest Bookseller" by selling books on the site all by itself. Having conquered the world of online bookselling, Amazon.com is attempting to give individual entrepreneurs different options for generating revenue. You'll find links leading to many of the options for selling with Amazon.com if you go to the home page and click the Selling on Amazon link below the various department headings.

Amazon.com gives entrepreneurs a variety of ways to sell through its existing marketplace. If you have an item to sell, you can list it on Amazon.com. You also get to place your ad alongside the listing for the same item that's being sold brand-new on the site. You can also make money by advertising someone else's product.

Becoming an Amazon.com Associate

You're probably already familiar with the idea of an affiliate program. The Amazon.com Associates program works as you would expect: When you become an Amazon.com Associate, you place a link to Amazon.com on your website. When someone makes a purchase after following the link from your site, you earn a referral fee.

Selling as an affiliate

If you've written or created books, CDs, or other materials that are sold on Amazon.com, you can create links to those items on your website and refer your visitors to the bookseller's site so that you can potentially earn the referral fee. I have a few books that are sold on Amazon.com, and I include images of several of these books on my website (www.gregholden.com). I already had several of the ingredients for generating referral income: a website, books to sell, and a need for extra revenue. All that remained was to sign up with the Amazon.com Associates program and create specially formatted links that I associate with each of the book images on my home page.

To get started with the program, just follow these steps:

1. **Go to the Amazon.com home page and, near the bottom of the page, click See All link under the Make Money with Us heading.**

2. **On the Make Money with Amazon page, scroll down and click the Learn More link under the Amazon Associates heading.**

3. **On the Amazon Associates page, click the Join Now for FREE! button on the right side.**

4. **Fill out the forms provided to become a member.**

   You have to tell Amazon.com all about your website and its content. When you're done, click Finish.

5. **Choose the type of content you want Amazon to add to your site. The first section is for the Associates program. Click Get Started Now under this section.**

   You have to set up a payment program by telling Amazon whether you want to receive a check or direct deposit into your bank account. I chose the direct deposit method, so I entered my bank account number and bank routing number.

6. **Click Get Started Now and then click Continue on subsequent pages to read about setting up links to Amazon.com products on your website.**

   You have to set up the Associates links according to Amazon.com's specifications so that it can track when the links are clicked and determine whether purchases are subsequently made.

7. **From the Associates Central welcome page, click either the Search for a Product or Browse for a Product tab, enter keywords or ASIN/ISBN numbers for the products you want to promote, and then click Go.**

   A list of products appears.

   A *keyword* is a word or phrase that describes the item you have for sale and that prospective buyers are likely to enter in their searches.

8. **Click the Get Link button next to the item you want to advertise.**

   The Customize and Get HTML page appears, displaying one version of an ad for the product. The results of my search are shown in Figure 14-1.

You can click one of the tabs above the product ad describing other types of ads you can display:

- *Text Only:* This is a text link to a specific book, movie, or CD you want to promote. If a graphic ad takes up too much space on your web pages, include a simple text link that points people to specific items on Amazon.com.

- *Image Only:* This is a graphic image you display on your site that displays a book or other product without text to save space.

- *Add to Widget:* Widgets are small-scale applications that automate the process whereby readers choose books, music, and other products from the Amazon.com catalog. You can include an Amazon.com search engine on your page, for example. You can also include your favorite books or music, among other things.

You can promote your friends' books and CDs, books or CDs that relate to your goods and services, or other books and CDs you admire. By spreading the word about such materials, you can earn a few cents or perhaps a few dollars. Because I have some specific books to promote, I chose the first option, Product Links.

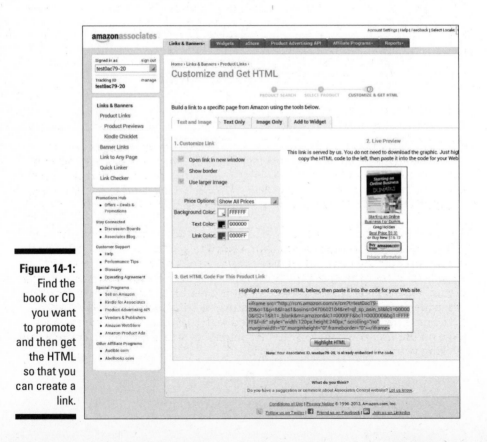

Figure 14-1:
Find the book or CD you want to promote and then get the HTML so that you can create a link.

9. **Scroll down the page and click Highlight HTML to highlight the code for the link; then press Ctrl+C.**

   The code is copied to your computer clipboard.

10. **Go to the web page where you want the ad to appear and paste the code into the page.**

    I pasted the HTML into my web page, which produced the link, as shown in Figure 14-2.

Figure 14-2:
You can turn a book cover into a clickable link that can earn you a referral fee.

Becoming a search marketer

Most people who earn affiliate sales fees by advertising Amazon.com products do so by posting links on their websites or blogs. A growing number of enterprising individuals are advertising by placing ads on search and content sites such as Google, Yahoo!, and Bing. They're taking products sold on one popular website and advertising on another well-traveled site.

The process works like this: You locate a product on Amazon.com that you want to sell. You become an Amazon Associate and create a link to the product on the Amazon.com website (see the previous section, "Selling as an affiliate"). Rather than post the link to the product on your own website, you create one of those paid search ads that appear off to one side or at the top of a page full of search results. You write an ad that attracts people's attention. Some people click the link included with the ad and go to the product page on the Amazon.com website. If someone makes a purchase as a result of clicking your ad, you earn a referral fee.

After you've signed up with Amazon.com, chosen a product to sell, and generated a link to it, sign up with Google's AdWords program (`www.google.com/adwords`). Start a campaign and write a short, three-line ad for the product. You identify keywords you want to associate with the ad and bid a certain amount on each one (10 cents per click is a reasonable amount). See the AdWords Help files for more instructions.

Search marketing through Google or other sites is an example of *pay-per-click* advertising: You're charged for placing an ad only when someone clicks it. You choose keywords that cause your ad to appear in a set of search results. You place a bid on the keyword; the bid indicates how much you're willing to pay if someone clicks your ad. The higher you bid, the better placement you have in ads (but the more you pay, too).

Here's an example: Suppose you want to place an affiliate ad for an iPod Nano. This is a popular item, so you can expect to have a lot of competition from other search marketers who want to promote the same product. Suppose you have five other marketers who bid on the keywords "iPod nano." How can you stand out from the crowd? One option is to be as specific as possible: If the other marketers bid on the keywords "iPod nano" and you bid on "16GB iPod nano," you distinguish yourself — and attract a more targeted audience. You'll get fewer clicks overall, but the chances are better that the people who see your ad will click it and purchase the iPod nano you're promoting. You bid 10 cents per click on these keywords. If one of your ads causes the ad to appear 1,000 times in one month and 100 people click the ad, you pay $10 for that keyword for that month. If none of those clicks leads to a purchase, you don't earn any money, either.

Along with signing up for an account with Amazon.com and with Google, you also need to sign up with an *affiliate network* — an organization that tracks how many clicks your ads have generated and issues commissions to you. Affiliate networks, such as Commission Junction, consolidate payments from many different advertisers and pay you in a single check. They're most useful when you have multiple payouts from different advertisers.

Creating an aStore page

If you enjoy making referrals in a particular area and find that some of the shoppers you've referred are subsequently making purchases on Amazon.com, you might want to present the items you recommend in an aStore. An *aStore* is an online store with a twist. An aStore isn't a site where you put your own merchandise up for sale; rather, you present your own selection of items from Amazon.com's merchandise on a web page. A sample store that's been set up to benefit a school is shown in Figure 14-3.

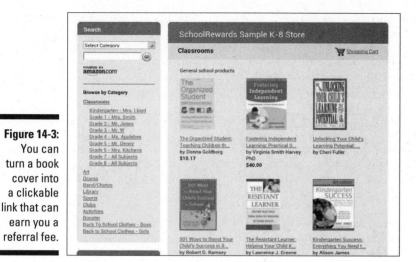

The aStore interface helps you set up your page full of links and product images; you can then publish the page as part of your own website. The theory is that by having a "dedicated shopping area" on your site, you'll keep visitors there longer (although if they want to investigate a link, they'll leave your site and go to Amazon's). Find out more about aStores at `affiliate-program.amazon.com/gp/associates/join/info6.html`.

You probably won't make a fortune from Amazon.com's referral fees. You earn on average 45 percent of the value of the items sold, depending on the number of items you sell. If you refer someone who purchases a book for $15, for instance, you earn about $0.75 for that purchase.

Joining the marketplace

Suppose you have a pile of recently published books or DVDs around (books or DVDs that are being sold on Amazon.com) and you need to sell them. You can sell those items yourself by adding them to Amazon.com's marketplace. Click the Sell on Amazon link at the bottom of any Amazon.com page, and you go to the Amazon Services part of the site, where you can find out how to add your inventory. It then shows up in individual product listings next to the price of the featured product in a small link such as "Used from $9.99" or "New from $19.99." And someone can buy it on a page like the one shown in Figure 14-4.

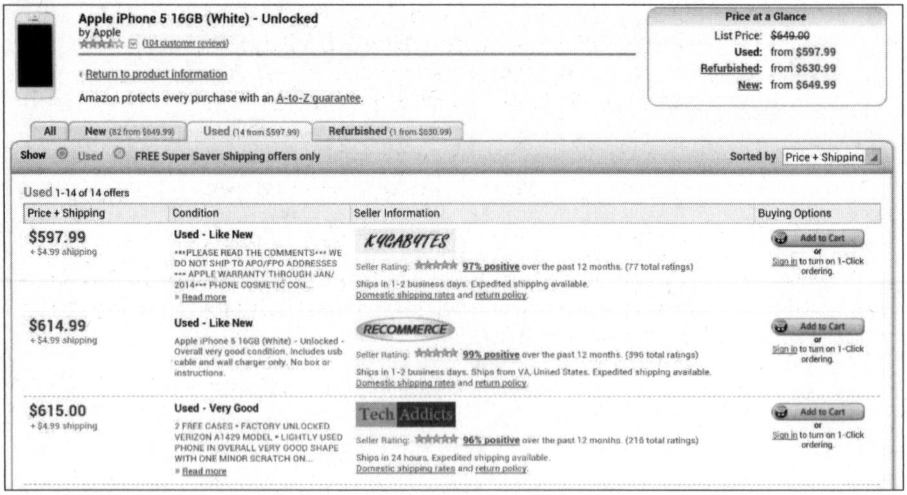

Figure 14-4:
Individual
sellers can
offer their
items for
sale on a
page like
this.

In this example, the featured product (the one that shows up in Amazon search results and has photos and product details) is known as the one with the "Buy Box." The products offered by other sellers are the same ones but they may or not be in new condition. For many sellers, adding to the Amazon marketplace in this way is easy to do and an excellent venue for those who sell mass-market items as opposed to one-of-a-kind handmade goods or other niche items.

Suppose you purchase a book and you're so happy with it that you just feel compelled to sell it so that others can share the wisdom contained within. Here's how you sell it:

1. **Go to the Amazon.com home page (**www.amazon.com**) and click the Sell on Amazon link (under the Make Money with Us heading in the middle of the screen, near the bottom of the home page).**

   The Sell On Amazon.com page appears.

2. **Click one of the two Start Selling buttons, depending on whether you want to be an individual or professional seller.**

   If you haven't yet signed in to your Amazon.com account, you will be prompted to do so and then asked to create a seller account.

   Individuals sell fewer than 40 items a month for $0.99 per sale plus other selling fees; professionals sell more than 40 items per month for $39.99 per month plus other selling fees.

3. **Choose the category you're interested in (in this example, the books category) and enter the name or ISBN (the number on the back cover, just above the "zebra stripe" code) of the specific item you want to see; then click the Start Selling button.**

   The sales page for the item (in this case, the book) appears.

4. **Click the Sell Yours Here button on the right side of that page.**

   The Sell Your Item - Select Condition page appears.

5. **Choose an option from the Condition drop-down list to describe the condition of your item; add some text that describes the condition, if you want, and then click Continue.**

   The Sell an Item - Enter Price page appears. This page includes the important information about Amazon.com's fees: You're charged $0.99 plus a 6–25 percent fee for each item you sell.

6. **Enter your price in the Price box and then click Continue.**

   Make sure that your price is at or below Amazon.com's own price.

   The Sign In page appears.

7. **Enter your Amazon.com e-mail address and password. (You can use the same password you use to make purchases or sell as an Associate.) Then click Continue.**

   The Registration page appears.

8. **Choose a credit card from the list (or enter a new card name and number) to identify you and then click Continue.**

   Another Registration page appears.

9. **Enter your nickname and a daytime phone number and then click Continue.**

   Optionally, you can enter checking account information so that Amazon.com can deposit purchase money into your account. You can skip this step for now.

   A Confirmation page appears.

10. **Click Submit Your Listing.**

    The Your Listing Is Complete page appears. In addition, Amazon.com sends an e-mail message confirming that your item is now up for sale.

If your item doesn't sell within 60 days, Amazon.com closes your listing, and you pay nothing. You receive an e-mail with details for relisting the item if you want.

When you list in the marketplace, Amazon collects the sales price and shipping costs from the buyer, deducts a "referral fee" of 6–25 percent of the sales price, a variable closing fee, and a per-item fee of $0.99, and then passes along the net proceeds along with a specified shipping credit based on the item you sold. The $0.99 per-item fee is waived for Pro Merchant Subscribers. You can become a Pro Merchant once you sell in volume on Amazon and it becomes worthwhile. You pay $39.99 per month, but you get access to software that helps you list in bulk, and you can compete for the Buy Box, which is described later in this chapter.

Taking out a Professional Subscription

If you have lots of items to sell, consider taking out a Professional Subscription. You have to pay a $39.99 monthly fee to be part of this Amazon. com program, but there are some big advantages:

- ✔ You don't have to pay the $0.99 fee.
- ✔ Your listings aren't closed after 60 days.

A Professional Subscription also allows you to use the powerful inventory reports to view orders, sold listings, and current open listings. You also get access to a bulk-listing tool so that you can create lots of descriptions simultaneously. You have to sell at least a few items each month to make back your subscription fee, but if you're a bookseller by trade and have a lot of inventory to unload, this is a good alternative.

You can find out more about the Professional merchant program at `services.` `amazon.com/content/sell-on-amazon.htm`.

Pricing your merchandise

Amazon isn't the most profitable venue, especially because of the "rush to the lowest price" trend on the marketplace, which can minimize your margin. Amazon's fees also cut into your margin. To make sales and generate profits, you have to ensure that

- ✔ You're selling items that people tend to buy on Amazon.
- ✔ Your prices are either lower than those of your competitors or at least close to the lowest.

Because sellers are constantly adding items to the Amazon marketplace, it's important to check your prices against those of your competitors. If ten people list the same item and yours is the highest price, you can't expect to make a sale. You can automate this process using a repricing tool — software that compares your price to others and makes sure yours is lowest. The tool I'm familiar with is Price Spectre (`www.pricespectre.com`). It works with both Amazon and eBay. You can configure it so that your price does not fall below a specified level, or that it stays a certain amount below others' prices.

Some Amazon sales categories are closed to individual sellers; that is, you can't add merchandise to those categories as described in preceding sections. Before you invest in a lot of inventory, confirm that you can sell those items in the category of your choice. Follow the steps described in the "Joining the marketplace" section, earlier in the chapter, and make sure you don't see a warning message when you get to Step 3 indicating you can't sell items in your chosen category. Verify that you can sell at least one item of the type you want to offer before you go through the effort of listing multiple items for sale.

Running a Webstore

On top of everything else it does, Amazon.com is becoming a web hosting service. Its Webstores program (`webstore.amazon.com`) gives you the ability to run your own branded store through the site. The difference between a conventional hosting service and a Webstore is that the latter makes use of Amazon.com's e-commerce technology, including its fraud security, shopping cart, and payment systems. One of the best advantages is that Webstore owners can use the Fulfillment By Amazon (FBA) system in which they send their merchandise to Amazon and let it do the shipping and handling as needed. See the following section, "Shipping with Fulfillment By Amazon," for more information on this intriguing fulfillment option.

Lots of successful businesses use the Webstores platform, from well-known retailers like Marks & Spencer (which runs an outlet site at `outlet.marks andspencer.com` as a Webstore, as a supplement to its primary website at `www.marksandspencer.com`) to lesser-known businesses like TexCynGoods (`www.texcyngoods.com`), which is run by Texas entrepreneur Cynthia Lozana. Another seller I have interviewed, Mimi Kriele, has about a dozen stores on Amazon.com Webstores. Her main business is called A Touch of Europe (`https://touchofeurope.net`). Such sites are transparent "white label" operations; there is no indication that they are hosted by Amazon. Customers also have the option of having `Service Provided by Amazon` indicated at the bottom of their website pages. This notice appears at the bottom of the Marks & Spencer outlet store's home page, shown in Figure 14-5.

Figure 14-5:
Merchants
can "white
label" their
stores or
display the
Amazon
brand
shown on
this site's
page.

Webstore customers pay $24.99 per month plus a 2 percent commission for a website only; merchants who sell on Amazon.com, in the Amazon marketplace, pay $14.99 per month, a 1 percent commission, and Selling on Amazon fees.

Webstore owners can also drive traffic to their sites by paying for integration with Amazon's ad platform, Amazon Product Ads (`http://services.amazon.com/content/product-ads-on-amazon.htm`). This platform enables businesses to advertise their products to Amazon's millions of customers.

Some companies set up shop on the Webstores platform temporarily to run a "daily deal" promotion. If you want to offer a special clearance or other sales event, you might consider doing the same. Jerlique, an Australian body cream merchant, once held a 24–48-hour promotion through a Webstore. After the event the site was taken down.

Shipping with Fulfillment By Amazon

One of Amazon's most attractive features for entrepreneurs is its ability to handle an online business's packing and shipping needs. Its Fulfillment By Amazon (FBA) program works like this:

1. You pack up your merchandise and send it to Amazon.

2. You pay a small storage fee so Amazon can store your stuff.

3. You list the items up for sale.

4. When the item sells, Amazon "picks and packs" it.

5. You pay a pick and pack fee.

6. You pay a per-pound shipping fee.

Discovering the hidden benefits of FBA

Some of FBA's benefits are obvious. You clean out your storage area and, in exchange for storage and fulfillment fees, let Amazon do the packing and shipping for you. But intrepid sellers have uncovered hidden ways to leverage FBA to make money. For example, some are doing arbitrage: buying items at retail stores and reselling them for a profit online. They let Amazon.com do the packing and shipping for them through FBA.

Then there's Chris Green. He not only sells a large volume of products using FBA, but he has created products and a web-based business based on it. He blogs and instructs sellers about how to use the service through his website FBAPower (`www.scanpower.com/fbapower`). As shown in the following figure, this site offers hardware that sellers like you can use to scan bar codes, gather sales data, and suggest pricing for products you may want to sell on Amazon and ship using FBA.

You can get all three in our FBAPower Pack for $59.95/month.
CLICK HERE to sign up for our free two week trial.

With FBA, Green can place an order at 5 p.m. and it can go out the same day, he says. Another advantage is the increased profit margin because of reduced shipping. For example, a non-FBA seller sells an item for $10 plus $3.99 shipping. An FBA seller can offer the same item for $13.99. Not only that, but the FBA item shows up ahead of the non-FBA item in Amazon's search results because Free Super Saver Shipping or similar discounted shipping status is used as a "tie-breaker." You show up first, you are more likely to get the purchase, and you get more profit — even after you subtract Amazon's storage and fulfillment fees.

"It's a way to compete," says Green. "I definitely get more profit per item for doing less work. It's like a double win. It's a margins game. I may not get all the sales, but I get two or three times the margin as other sellers."

This program is especially attractive to beginning sellers, who don't usually have the staff available to help them with fulfillment. With FBA, you can focus your energy on sourcing, selling, and customer service. You have the opportunity to build up your sales volume far higher than you could if you were doing all the sourcing, listing, selling, and shipping on your own. Even if your profit margin isn't big, you make up for it in volume.

To ship with FBA, your items must have an ISBN code or UPC bar code and be in good condition.

FBA is a form of *drop-shipping:* the practice of selling merchandise that you don't actually have on hand in your home, office, or store. You usually have to choose a drop-shipper with care; there is a risk of fraud, and you place a lot of trust in your shipper. But you can trust Amazon because it's so big and well known. The only risk is that your items won't sell or that you won't make more than a few cents in profit. But if you have, say, a lot of recent textbooks or DVDs to sell, FBA can be a very attractive option.

When you join FBA, your items become eligible for Amazon Prime reduced shipping costs on orders over $25 or free 2-Day Air shipping for Amazon Prime members. Because your fees are so low, you can raise your prices and still remain competitive compared to sellers who have to build, say, a $3 shipping fee into their price (that's a $3 shipping fee that a seller might pay to Amazon for an item that doesn't go through FBA).

Playing Amazon's game to win

To sum up, by following good business practices and taking advantage of a few special approaches, you can make a profit on Amazon:

- ✔ **Keep your prices competitive.** Use e-commerce management software to make sure your product is priced competitively compared to other Amazon.com sellers. Always know how your price ranks among other retailers selling the same product.

- ✔ **Make sure you have enough supply to meet demand.** You don't want to sell out of a product before your Amazon inventory updates.

- ✔ **Respond to customers quickly.** Amazon expects you to provide top-quality customer service. Respond to questions or comments quickly, and resolve problems so you don't get negative feedback.

- ✔ **Gather strong reviews.** Positive ratings and good comments mean a lot on any marketplace, but with so much competition, they're especially important on Amazon. They'll prompt Amazon to push buyers to you over your competition.

There's one more thing. If you sell on a regular basis on Amazon, it's to your advantage to do everything you can to get the Buy Box for as many items as you can.

You've seen the Buy Box before; it's the product listing you see first when you search for something. An example is shown in Figure 14-6.

ASUS TF700T-B1-GR 10.1-Inch Tablet (Gray)
by Asus
★★★★☆ ☑ (623 customer reviews)

List Price: ~~$499.99~~
Price: **$437.78** & eligible for **FREE Super Saver Shipping**. Details
You Save: $62.21 (12%)

In Stock.
Ships from and sold by Amazon.com.

Want it tomorrow, March 7? Order within 41 mins, and choose **One-Day Shipping** at checkout. Details

Size: **32 GB**

| 32 GB | 64 GB |

Color: **Amethyst Gray**

Roll over image to zoom in
See all 15 customer images
Share your own customer images

63 new from $409.99   15 used from $363.19   1 refurbished from $399.99

Quantity 1

Yes, I want FREE Two-Day Shipping with Amazon Pr...

Add to Cart

or
Sign in to turn on 1-Click ord...

Add Accessories
☐ Norton Anti-Theft $36.24
☐ Bamboo Stylus Pocket $23.43
☐ 2-Year Drops & Spills Warr $77.54

Add to Wish List

More Buying Choices
Adorama Camera $429.99 + Free Shipping   Add
HPP Enterprises $457.78 + $8.85 shipping   Add
Mobile Advance $457.00 + $10.00 shipping   Add
79 used & new from $363.19

IPS (In-Plane-Switching) is a new technology for LCD displays that offers users wider viewing angles and bolder colors by allowing more light to pass ... el. As a result, *IPS* panels can exhibit a slight glow around the edges and corners (also known as light bleed), which is entirely normal.

Figure 14-6:
The seller with the Buy Box is most likely to get the sale.

In this example, Amazon.com itself has the Buy Box — the blue highlighted box on the right side of the page. Others are selling the same item for a lower price, but the links leading to them are pretty unobtrusive. Amazon has the advantage.

Learning from Amazon's business strategy

Some of the things that Amazon.com does aren't direct sales opportunities for fledgling businesses like yours. They are, however, good examples of new ways to make money on the web — options that don't always involve catalogs, tangible items such as books, or retail or wholesale prices.

In 2006, for example, Amazon founder Jeff Bezos spoke on new initiatives the company was taking to promote its computing power. One service, Compute Cloud, has really taken off and has been replicated widely by Google and many other service providers. A "cloud" or online storage and work area lets businesses tap into the computing power of Amazon.com's own servers: They can use the servers for storage space and to perform computations. A company that makes virtual reality software

"borrowed" Amazon.com's computers to enable its customers to quickly download its new software version, for example.

It's all about making your business a resource that people turn to on a regular basis rather than a source of a single product or service. This wouldn't work if you're a childcare provider or a dentist — someone whose business requires personal contact. But if you help someone complete a dissertation, write essays to apply for college, provide legal advice, sell your home, or manage a condo association, the web can help you. More and more commerce on the web is taking the form of services that help businesses operate more efficiently. If Amazon.com and Google are putting their energy into web-based services, you should think about doing so, too.

Because multiple sellers are probably offering the same items you are, if you can earn the Buy Box from Amazon, you'll have a big advantage. There's no hard and fast formula for winning the box, but following Amazon's best practices go a long way, as well as keeping your pricing competitive and making sure your products are always available.

You can find Amazon's description of the Buy Box and some tips on how to win it at www.amazon.com/gp/help/customer/display.html?node Id=200401830.

Understanding eBay Auctions

In any contest, you have to know the ground rules. Anyone who has held a garage sale knows the ground rules for making a person-to-person sale. But eBay, the other big marketplace you can use, is different, and not just because auctions are the primary format. eBay gives its members many different ways to sell, and each sales format has its own set of rules and procedures. It pays to know something about the different sales so that you can choose the right format for the item you have.

This section assumes that you have some basic knowledge of eBay and that you have at least shopped for a few items and possibly won some auctions. When it comes to putting items up for sale, as opposed to simply buying items, eBay gets more complicated. You have the following sales options:

- **Standard auctions:** This is the most basic eBay auction: You put an item up for sale and specify a starting bid (usually, a low amount — from $1–$9.99). You don't have a reserve price, and the highest bidder at the end of the sale wins (if there is a highest bidder). Standard auctions and other auctions on eBay can last one, three, five, seven, or ten days. The ending time is precise: If you list something at 10:09 a.m. on a Sunday and you choose a seven-day format, the sale ends at 10:09 a.m. the following Sunday.

- **Reserve auctions:** A *reserve price* is a minimum price you specify for a successful purchase. Any bids placed on the item being offered must meet or exceed the reserve price; otherwise, the sale ends without the seller's being obligated to sell the item. You know if a reserve price is present by the message Reserve Not Yet Met next to the current high bid. When a bid is received that exceeds the reserve, this message changes to Reserve Met. The reserve price is concealed until the reserve is met.

Reserve prices aren't used as often on eBay as in the past; instead, you can set a starting bid that represents the minimum you want to receive.

✔ **Fixed-price Buy It Now (BIN) sales:** A *BIN price* is a fixed price that the seller specifies. Fixed prices are used in all eBay Stores: The seller specifies that you can purchase the item for, say, $10.99; you click the Buy It Now button, agree to pay $10.99 plus shipping, and you instantly win the item.

✔ **Mixed auction/fixed-price sales:** BIN prices can be offered in conjunction with standard or reserve auctions. In other words, even though bidders are placing bids on the item, if someone agrees to pay the fixed price, the item is immediately sold and the sale ends. If a BIN price is offered in conjunction with a standard auction, the BIN price is available until the first bid is placed; then the BIN price disappears. If a BIN price is offered in conjunction with a reserve auction, the BIN price is available until the reserve price is met. After the reserve price is met, the BIN price disappears and the item is sold to the highest bidder.

Those are the basic types of sales. You can also sell automobiles on eBay Motors. By knowing how eBay sales work and following the rules competently, you gradually develop a good reputation on the auction site.

How you sell is important, but the question of exactly *what* you should sell is one you should resolve well before you start your eBay business. Most people begin by cleaning out their closets and other storage areas, but that inventory doesn't last more than a few weeks. Start by selling something you love, something you don't mind spending hours shopping for, photographing, describing, and eventually packing up and shipping. Sell something that has a niche market of enthusiastic collectors or other customers. Do some research on eBay to make sure that a thousand people aren't already peddling the same things you hope to make available.

Building a Good Reputation

To run a business on eBay, you need a steady flow of repeat customers. Customer loyalty comes primarily from the trust that is produced by developing a good reputation. eBay's feedback system is the best indicator of how trustworthy and responsive a seller is, because past performance is a good indication of the kind of service a customer can expect in the future. Along with deciding what you want to sell and whether you want to sell on eBay on a part- or full-time basis, you need to develop a good reputation.

Learning from the pros: My own story

As part of the research for a book I was writing, I attended a convention in Atlanta of the Professional eBay Sellers Alliance (PeSA). PeSA members are among the elite of the eBay merchant association. Just to get into the group, you must meet two of three criteria: gross eBay sales income of $25,000 per month, eBay fees of $1,500 per month, or 500 positive feedback comments in the past 30 days. Today, PeSA is open to any eBay seller who has achieved PowerSeller status. (I give you all the PowerSeller details in the "Striving for PowerSeller status" section, later in this chapter.)

These are hard-working, enterprising, and successful individuals. But when I spoke to them and got to know them, I realized that they weren't very different from me: Other than a strong business sense and drive, most of them were normal folks with families who hadn't been selling professionally until they discovered eBay.

I left the convention inspired not only to write my book but also to start selling on my own. I have always collected antiques and other items, and I like "scrounging" for used items that are valuable. I am lucky enough to have a network of good resale shops in my area. I had already found some shoes at my local store that I knew cost $350 new. They weren't new but were in good condition and cost only a few dollars. I bought some shoes for myself and gave others to friends or relatives.

Now, I've started buying shoes to resell on eBay. At first, it felt strange to be shopping for "business" purposes at the store where I had previously shopped only for enjoyment and for my own benefit. It took me a few weeks to get over this, but it was easy to do so when I had made a few sales — of my own merchandise and some antiques sold on behalf of my mother — and realized that I was a legitimate businessperson.

Before too long, I easily achieved my initial goal of making $300 to $400 per month in sales. I decided to put into practice the most important lesson I gained from the PowerSellers I'd met: To make more money on eBay, you need to increase your volume. This sounds deceptively simple. But the tendency is to start slowly — perhaps putting ten items up for sale in a week. Putting up ten items for sale three, five, or even seven days a week is much more work. But the extra time and labor does pay off: The more you can put up for sale, the more you actually sell.

I became a PowerSeller in only about three months. I got a special icon next to my User ID. As a PowerSeller, I attracted more bids and more sales. After a year, I had raised my feedback rating to nearly 400. I found out a great deal about eBay and had some extra spending money besides. I got a debit card through eBay's payment service PayPal (www.paypal.com) and used the money I collected from my eBay sales to pay daily expenses and bills.

Getting good feedback

eBay's success is largely due to the network of trust it has established among its millions of members. The *feedback system,* through which members leave positive, negative, or neutral comments for the people with whom they conducted (or tried to conduct) transactions, is the foundation for that trust.

The system rewards users who accumulate significant numbers of positive feedback comments and penalizes those who have low or negative feedback numbers. By taking advantage of the feedback system, you can realize the highest possible profit on your online sales and help get your online business off the ground.

In recent years, eBay has refined its feedback system. Buyers have the chance to leave "detailed feedback" for sellers. One way of rating a seller on eBay is the Detailed Seller Rating (DSR). This new system makes it even more important to provide good service. Buyers can leave DSRs in four areas:

- ✔ How accurate was the item description?
- ✔ How satisfied were you with the seller's communication?
- ✔ How quickly did the seller ship the item?
- ✔ How reasonable were the shipping and handling charges?

Another seller rating system is the Top-Rated Seller designation, which depends on how rapidly you ship the item and what level of customer service you provide.

You can find out more about DSRs at `http://pages.ebay.com/help/feedback/detailed-seller-ratings.html`.

There probably aren't any scientific studies of how feedback numbers affect sales, but I've heard anecdotally from sellers that their sales figures increase when their feedback levels hit a certain number. The number varies, but it appears to be in the hundreds — perhaps 300 or so. The inference is that prospective buyers place more trust in sellers who have higher feedback numbers because they have more experience and are presumably more trustworthy. Those who have a PowerSeller icon are even more trustworthy (see the "Striving for PowerSeller status" section, later in this chapter).

eBay members take feedback seriously. You'll see this after you start selling. If you don't leave feedback for your buyers after the transaction has ended, they'll start reminding you to do so. You're in control of the feedback you leave; don't feel coerced to leave comments unless you want to. Otherwise, the feedback system won't be of value. To read someone's feedback, click the number in parentheses next to his or her User ID.

Developing a schedule

On eBay, timeliness can boost your reputation above all else. If you respond to e-mail inquiries within a few hours, or at most a day or two, and if you can ship merchandise quickly, you're virtually guaranteed to have satisfied customers who leave you positive feedback (that is, as long as the product they receive is in the condition you promised). You're more likely to be designated a Top-Rated Seller, too. The way to achieve a timely response is to observe a work schedule.

It's tedious and time consuming to take and retake photos, edit those photos, get sales descriptions online, and do the packing and shipping that's required at the end of a sale. The only way to come up with a sufficient number of sales every week is to come up with a system. A big part of coming up with a system is developing a weekly schedule that spells out when you need to do all your eBay activities. Table 14-1 shows a possible schedule.

Table 14-1	eBay Business Schedule	
Day of Week	*First Activity*	*Second Activity (Optional)*
Sunday	Get seven-day sales online	Send end-of-sale notices
Monday	Pack items	Respond to e-mails
Tuesday	Ship items	Respond to e-mails
Wednesday	Plan garage sales	Take photos
Thursday	Go to garage sales	Prepare descriptions
Friday	Find more sales	Prepare descriptions
Saturday	Respond to buyer inquiries	Get some sales online

You'll notice that something is conspicuously missing from this proposed schedule: a day of rest. You can certainly work in such a day on Sunday (or whatever day you prefer). If you sell on eBay part time, you can probably take much of the weekend off. But most full-time sellers (and full-time self-employed people in general) will tell you that it's difficult to find a day off, especially when it's so important to respond to customer e-mails within a day or two of their receipt. You don't have to do everything all by yourself, however. You can hire full- or part-time help, which can free up time for family responsibilities.

Sunday nights are traditionally considered the best times to end eBay auction sales (or sales on iOffer or other sites) because that's when most potential buyers are available. But if you have an item for sale that someone really wants, any night of the week attracts buyers. You can try starting a five-day sale on a Tuesday night so that it ends on the following Sunday night; that way, you won't have to work on Sunday.

Creating an About Me page

One of the best ways to build your reputation on eBay is to create a web page called About Me that eBay makes available to each member free of charge.

Your About Me page should describe who you are, why you collect or sell what you do, and why you're a reputable seller. You can also talk about an eBay Store, if you have one, and provide links to your current auction sales. Creating an About Me page takes only a few minutes (not much longer than filling out the Sell Your Item form to get a sale online, in fact). If you want to include a photo, take a digital image and edit it in an image-editing program, such as PaintShop Pro or Photoshop, just as you would any other image. A photo isn't absolutely necessary, though.

Laura Milnor Iverson, the eBay seller I profile in Chapter 15, has a simple About Me page, shown in Figure 14-7.

When you've decided what you want to say on your page, you need to save a digital photo if you want to include one. You then need to upload your photo to the web server where you usually store your photos. Note the URL that identifies the location of the photo (for example, www.*myphotohost*.com/ *mydirectory*/*photoname*.jpg).

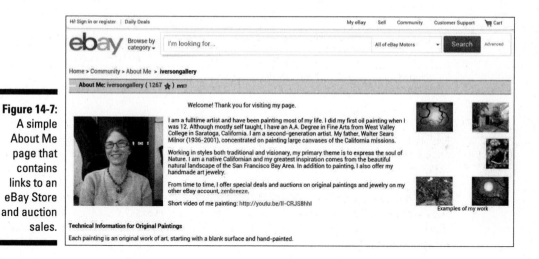

Figure 14-7: A simple About Me page that contains links to an eBay Store and auction sales.

Follow these steps to create your About Me page:

1. **Click My eBay on the navigation bar near the top-right corner of virtually any eBay page.**

   A login page appears.

2. **Type your User ID and password and then click Sign In Securely.**

   The My eBay page appears.

3. **Click the Account tab and select Personal Information from the drop-down list that appears.**

   The My eBay Account: Personal Information page appears.

4. **Scroll down to the About Me link and click Create or Edit (on the right side of the page).**

   The About Me welcome page appears.

5. **Scroll to the bottom of the page and click Create My Page.**

   The Choose Page Creation Option page appears.

6. **Leave the Use Our Easy Step-By-Step Process option selected and click Continue.**

   The About Me: Enter Page Content page appears.

7. **As indicated on the page, type a heading and text for your page.**

   a. *Label your photo and enter the URL for the photo in the Link to Your Picture text box.*

      You can also type links to favorite pages and your own web page, if you have one.

   b. *When you're done, click Continue.*

      The Preview and Submit page appears, as shown in Figure 14-8.

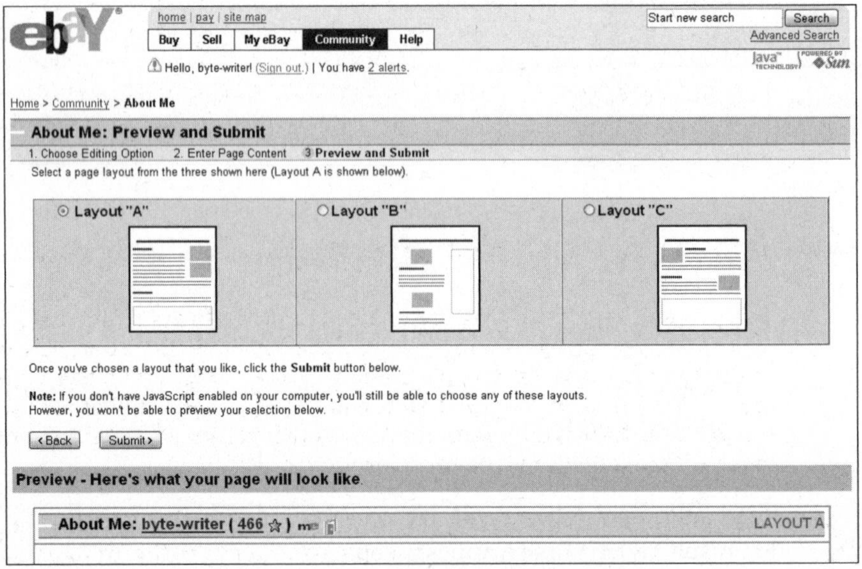

Figure 14-8:
Proofread
your About
Me page
before
you post it
online!

8. **Choose one of three possible layouts for your page, and preview your page content in the bottom half of the page.**

9. **When you're done, click Submit.**

   Your page goes online.

As with any web page, you can change your About Me page at any time by following the preceding steps.

Another way to ensure a good reputation as a seller is to actively participate in eBay's discussion boards. Pay special attention to boards that pertain to the type of merchandise you buy and sell. Responding to questions from new users and offering advice based on your experience boosts your standing within the user community.

Creating Sales Descriptions That Sell

How do you actually go about selling on eBay or another auction-based site, or a fixed-price marketplace? The aim is similar to other forms of e-commerce: You select some merchandise, take photos, type descriptions, and put the descriptions online in a catalog. But there are some critical differences. You don't have to specify a fixed price on eBay; you can set a starting bid and see how much the market will bear. All sales descriptions are not created equal, however. Many sellers argue that clear, sharp photos are the most important part of a description, and that if you show the item in its best light, it practically sells itself. I believe a good heading and descriptions that include critical keywords are just as important as good photos. Learn the art of creating descriptions by inspecting other people's sales listings; the essentials are described in the sections that follow.

Focusing on the details

The primary way of getting your sales online is eBay's Sell Your Item form. You can access it by clicking Sell on the eBay navigation bar, which appears at the top of just about any page on the eBay website. The Sell Your Item form is easy to use, so I don't step you through every nuance and option. In this section, however, I do point out a few features you might overlook that can help you get more attention for your sales.

The Sell Your Item form is by no means the only way to get eBay sales online. Many full- or part-time businesspeople use special software to upload multiple images simultaneously or schedule multiple sales so that they all start and end at the same time. The auction services Vendio (www.vendio.com) and inkFrog (`https://www.inkfrog.com`) offer eBay auction-listing tools. In addition, eBay offers two programs you might find helpful:

- ✔ **Turbo Lister** (`http://pages.ebay.com/sellerinformation/ sellingresources/turbolister.html`) is a free program that provides sellers with design templates they can use to add graphic interest to their sales descriptions. This is the program I use. It takes a lot of memory and is sometimes slow to run but, as shown in Figure 14-9, Turbo Lister enables you to format auctions quickly and reuse standard elements such as your shipping or return policies.

- ✔ **Selling Manager** (`pages.ebay.com/selling_manager/index.html`) is a monthly subscription service that uses sales and management software. It gives you convenient lists that let you track what you have up for sale, which sales have ended, which items have been purchased, and what tasks you have yet to do — for example, sending e-mails to winning bidders or relisting items that didn't sell the first time.

Figure 14-9: Prepare sales descriptions with the Sell Your Item form or with software like Turbo Lister.

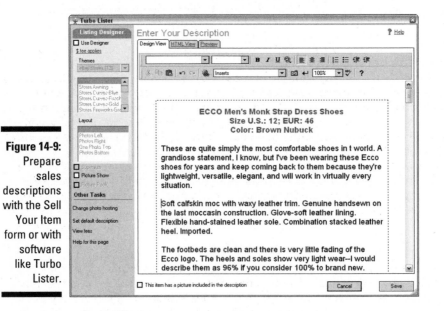

Choosing a second category

One of the first things you do in the Sell Your Item form is choose a sales category in which to list your item. I highly recommend using the search box at the top of the Select Category page. When you enter a keyword and click Find, a detailed list of sales categories appears. The best thing about the list is that it's ranked in order of categories most likely to sell items matching your desired keywords. Choose the categories near the top of the list.

I also recommend paying an extra dollar or so (when you choose a second category, your listing fee is doubled) and listing the item in a second category — especially if the second category has a percentage ranking that's almost as high as the first.

Focusing on your auction heading

The *heading* of an eBay sales description is the six or seven words that appear in a set of search results or in a set of listings in a category. These are the words a potential customer initially sees when he or she is deciding whether to investigate a sale and possibly bid on it. Keep your heading short and specific. Include dates, colors, or model numbers if applicable. Try to pick one word or short phrase that might attract a buyer, such as "rare," "hard-to-find," "mint," or "new."

Be sure to work keywords into your auction title — brand names or phrases that shoppers might search for on eBay. Your sale is more likely to turn up in search results with desirable brand names such as Gucci or Versace. Be as specific as you can; include sizes, colors, and original retail prices in your headings, too.

Choosing a good ending time for your sale

With eBay, the starting time isn't what counts; it's the ending time that makes a difference. The more attention you can get at the end of a sale, the more likely you are to make a profit. Most sales get attention on weekends, when the majority of shoppers aren't working. In my experience, the optimal time is to have the sale end some time on a Saturday afternoon or Sunday evening (though Wednesday evenings are also good — I'm not sure why).

Of course, bidders can come from all over the world, and what's Sunday afternoon in California is Monday morning in Australia. But don't worry too much about such distinctions. Pick an ending time that's convenient for eBay shoppers in your own country — not in the middle of a workday, but on the weekend.

In eBay's early days, if you wanted a sale to end at a particular time (say, 7 on a Sunday evening, when lots of bidders are available), you had to physically be present to create the description at a certain time. For example, if you wanted a sale to last seven days, you had to list it at precisely 7 p.m. the preceding Sunday. Now you don't have to be physically present exactly a week, five days, three days, or one day before you want your sale to end. Instead, you can specify an ending time when you fill out the Sell Your Item form or with Turbo Lister, although you'll have to pay an extra listing fee of 10 cents for each sale you schedule.

Adding keywords

You don't have to make your auction description overly lengthy. The length isn't what counts; it's the number of keywords you include. If your description contains a keyword that someone enters, your sale might show up in search results. And just appearing in the search results is half the battle: If a buyer can find your item, he or she can follow through with the purchase.

The more keywords you can add to your description, the more frequently searchers find the sale. It's to your advantage, then, to think of all the terms that someone would use when looking for your item and add as many of those keywords to the heading as well as to the body of the description as you can. If you're selling an electric drill, for example, use keywords — such as "cordless," "electric," "3/8-inch," "Black & Decker," or anything else a likely buyer might enter.

Upgrading your listings

Near the end of the Sell Your Item form, a series of items gives you the option to specify whether you want to upgrade your listings. *Upgrade,* in this case, is adding graphic highlights that help your listing stand out from those around it, either in search results or on category pages. You can choose from the options shown in Table 14-2.

Table 14-2	Listing Upgrades for Auction Sales	
Upgrade	*Description*	*Cost*
Subtitle	You can insert another 80 characters of text to appear below the Title as buyers are searching.	$0.50
Bold	The auction title is formatted in bold type.	$2.00
Gallery Plus	Displays a larger image when users roll their mouse over the gallery thumbnail image.	$0.35

Note: Although it's free to register for an account on eBay and free to fill out the Sell Your Item form, eBay sometimes charges an Insertion Fee when you actually put an item up for sale. The Insertion Fee is based on the starting price of the auction. The fee is not charged for the first 50 auctions, and then you're charged only $0.25 for a starting bid of $9.99 or less, which explains why most starting bids are less than $10. A Final Value Fee is also charged at the end of the auction, and it depends on the sale price and category of item that sold. On a sale of $100, the Final Value Fee is 9 percent or $9; at $5,000, it is $250 because the maximum Final Value Fee is $250. For a detailed explanation of the formula used to calculate fees, go to http://pages.ebay.com/help/sell/fees.html.

Including clear images

No matter how well written your auction's headings and description are, all your work can quickly be undone by digital images that are dark or blurry or that load too slowly because they're too large in either physical (length and width) or file size. The same principles you use when capturing digital images for your e-commerce website apply to eBay images: Make sure you have clear, even lighting (consider taking your photos outdoors); use your camera's auto-focus setting; crop your images so they focus on the merchandise being sold; and keep the file size small by adjusting the resolution with your digital camera or your image-editing software.

Some aspects of posting images along with auction descriptions are unique to eBay:

- ✔ **Image hosting:** If you run a business on eBay and have dozens or even hundreds of sales items online at any one time, you can potentially have hundreds of image files to upload and store on a server. If you use eBay Picture Services as your photo host, your images are hosted free for 90 days, except in eBay Motors, where you get four free images with each subsequent one costing $0.15. There is a 12-photo limit for each listing. If you need more flexibility, consider an economical photo-hosting service such as PixHost (www.pixhost.com) or Photobucket (www.photobucket.com).

- ✔ **Close-ups:** If what you're selling has important details, such as brand names, dates, or maker's marks, you need to have a camera that has *macro capability* — that is, the ability to get clear close-ups. Virtually all digital cameras have a macro setting, but it can be tricky to hold the camera still enough to get a clear image (you may need to mount the camera on a tripod). If you use a conventional film camera, invest in a macro lens.

- ✔ **Multiple images:** You never hear an eBay shopper complaining that you included too many images with your auction listings. As long as you have the time and patience as well as an affordable image host, you can include five, six, or more views of your item. (For big objects such as automobiles and other vehicles, multiple images are especially important.)

Be sure to crop and adjust the brightness and contrast of your images after you take them, using a program such as PaintShop Pro by Corel (www.corel.com) or Adobe Photoshop Elements (www.adobe.com).

 If you want to find out more about creating sales descriptions (and practically every aspect of buying or selling on eBay, for that matter) take a look at my book *eBay PowerUser's Bible* (John Wiley & Sons, Inc.).

Being flexible with payment options

In the past, payments have been the most nerve-racking part of a transaction on eBay. These days, eBay provides more safeguards for its customers. That doesn't mean you won't run into the occasional bidder who doesn't respond after winning your auction, or whose check bounces. But as a seller, you have plenty of protection: If someone doesn't respond, you can relist your item; if someone's check bounces, you don't lose your sales item because you hold on to it while the check clears.

You can enable your customers to pay with a credit card, either by using your merchant credit card account if you have one (see Chapter 7) or eBay's own PayPal payment service (www.paypal.com). PayPal is by far the most popular option; you're charged a nominal fee (2.2–2.9 percent of the amount plus a 30-cent fee) when a buyer transfers money electronically to your account.

Don't accept other forms of payment from buyers. Occasionally, a buyer insists on sending you cash in an envelope; you should in turn insist that the buyer join PayPal or use a credit card instead. C.O.D. (Collect on Delivery) is expensive and cumbersome; it makes the delivery service responsible for collecting your money, and if the buyer isn't home when the delivery people arrive, you might have to wait a long time to get paid. Western Union wire transfers are notorious for being used by scam artists — although I have used Western Union money order payments with no problem.

Providing Good Customer Service

When you sell on eBay on a regular basis, you need to develop a good reputation. One way to achieve that goal is to provide a high level of customer service to your buyers. The best way to do that is to be responsive to all e-mail. This means checking your e-mail at least once a day and spending lots of time typing messages. If you take days to get back to someone who asks you about the color or condition of an item you have for sale, it might just be too late for that person to bid. A slow response to a high bidder or buyer after the sale can make the buyer nervous and result in neutral feedback — not a complaint about fraud or dishonesty, but a note about poor service. On eBay, such feedback is considered as bad as a negative comment.

Setting terms of sale

One aspect of good customer service is getting back to people quickly and communicating clearly and with courtesy. When you receive inquiries, always thank prospective customers for approaching you and considering the sale; even if they don't end up placing bids, you'll have spread goodwill.

Another way to be good to your customers is to be clear about how you plan to ship your merchandise and how much it will cost. When you fill out the Sell Your Item form (which I discuss in the "Focusing on the details" section, earlier in this chapter), you can specify either an actual *shipping cost* (a cost based on weight and the buyer's residence) or a *flat shipping fee* (a shipping fee you charge for all your items).

The moment you specify a shipping charge in the Sell Your Item form, you set eBay's automated Checkout system in motion. The Checkout system enables buyers to calculate their own shipping charges. The advantage to you, the seller, is that you don't have to send your buyers a message stating how much they need to pay you.

Packing and shipping safely

One of the aspects of selling on eBay that is often overlooked (not by *buyers)* is the practice of packing and shipping. Sellers need to keep in mind that, after sending out payment for something, buyers often wait on pins and needles, eagerly hoping to receive their items while dreading an unresponsive seller who refuses to ship their purchases. There's also the danger that the item you send will be damaged in transit.

Be sure to use sturdy boxes when you ship and take care to adequately cushion your merchandise within those boxes. I've received boxes from sellers who stuffed the insides with bubble wrap and newspaper, and I was happy for the trouble. If you're shipping something particularly fragile, consider double-boxing it: Put it in a box, place the box in a larger one, and put cushioning material between the two. Your customers will be pleased to receive the merchandise undamaged, and you'll get good feedback as a result.

Place a thank-you note, business card, or even a small gift inside the box with your shipment. It spreads good feelings and reminds buyers how to get in touch with you in the future.

Moving from Auctioneer to eBay Businessperson

Most eBay sellers don't start out saying, "I'm going to be a PowerSeller, and I'm going to sell full time on eBay for a living!" Rather, they typically start out on a whim. They find an object lying in a box, in the attic, or on a shelf, and they wonder: Will anyone pay money for this?

That's what happened to Kimberly King, a housewife living in Longmont, Colorado. In March 2000, she was cleaning the house when she found an old purse. She says, "I thought, 'Gee, should I sell this?' I didn't have enough stuff to hold a garage sale. I'd heard about eBay, so I thought I would see what it was like to sell something. I found out just how easy it was to set up an ID and to register. I ended up getting $20 for the purse, which was much more than I would have at a garage sale. I was hooked."

After she felt comfortable selling on eBay, things fell into place: "You start thinking, 'Let's see, that thing sold, what else do we have that we can sell?' When I really saw that I could do this on a regular basis, I thought, 'I can do this all the time; I can have some fun money.'"

Opening an eBay Store

An *eBay Store* is a website within eBay's own voluminous web empire. It's a place where sellers can post items for sale at fixed prices. The great advantage of having a store is that it enables a seller to keep merchandise available for purchase for 30, 60, 90, or even an unlimited number of days at a time. It gives customers another way to buy from you, and it can significantly increase your sales in other venues or of items you sell at auction on eBay, too.

Starting an eBay Store is a big undertaking and therefore something you should do only when you have a proven system for selling items on eBay at auction. You should also have a ready source of inventory with which you can stock your store. The problem with stores is that they cost $15.95 and up per month, depending on the package you choose, and you have to sell that much just to break even every month. For sellers who have a small profit margin, it can be a struggle to make back that monthly payment, especially in the slow post-holiday months.

When you know what you want to sell and have good-quality inventory to offer (not just castoffs that went unsold at auction), go to the eBay Stores home page (`stores.ebay.com`) and click the Open a Store link. You need to decide on a name for your store and organize your merchandise into sales categories. You also need to attend to and update your store to make it a success. But having a store can be a key step toward making an eBay business work, and if you're serious about making eBay a regular source of income, I encourage you to give the store option a try.

A 2008 article on the AuctionBytes website describes how eBay gets your items listed on Google and contains links to eBay tutorials on search engine optimization. You can read the article at `www.ecommercebytes.com/cab/abu/y208/m11/abu0227/s02`.

Striving for PowerSeller status

PowerSellers are among the elite on eBay. Those members who have the coveted icon next to their names can feel justifiably proud of their accomplishments. They have met the stringent requirements for PowerSellers, which emphasize consistent sales, a high and regular number of completed sales, and excellent customer service. Moving from occasional seller to PowerSeller is a substantial change — and quite a thrill, I assure you. Requirements include

- ✔ At least 100 unique transactions and a minimum of $3,000 in gross sales in the past 12 months

- ✔ Positive feedback results of 98 percent in the past three months

- ✔ Minimum average Detailed Seller Ratings (DSRs) of 4.60 or higher for all four DSR categories: item is as described, communication, shipping time, and shipping and handling charges

- ✔ A good standing record — achieved by complying with eBay Listing Policies

- ✔ A current account — achieved by contacting bidders within three business days and upholding the eBay Community Values

In return for the hard work required to meet these standards, PowerSellers get a number of benefits, including discounts on eBay final value fees, merchandise with a special logo on it, customer support via telephone, and a special discussion board just for PowerSellers. The biggest benefit is that the number of bids and purchases goes up because buyers have more confidence in you.

The PowerSeller program isn't something you apply for. eBay reviews your sales statistics and invites you to join the program when you meet the requirements. You can find out more about the requirements and benefits of the PowerSeller program at `http://pages.ebay.com/sellerinformation/ sellingresources/powerseller.html`.

Chapter 15

Moving to Specialty Marketplaces

• •

In This Chapter

▶ Selling big items on Craigslist the smart way

▶ Choosing options for auctioning your creative work

▶ Finding marketplaces that let you buy and sell affordably

▶ Locating places where you can buy or sell for free

▶ Merchandising your creative work with CafePress

• •

A single website isn't enough anymore. The newest entrepreneurs focus on branding themselves and gain as much exposure as possible through cost-effective marketing methods including multiple marketplaces. *Omni-channel commerce* is the buzzword you hear about.

By signing up with a niche marketplace, you can set up a storefront, communicate with customers, accept payments, and socialize with other sellers who deal in the same kinds of merchandise you do. You might have to pay a modest hosting fee — or you might not, because many of the sites are totally free to their members. This chapter collects a variety of small, innovative, full-featured marketplaces that are attractive alternatives to the big e-commerce hosts. Consider opening storefronts in one or more venues to increase your visibility and, with luck, put some extra cash in your pocket.

Even if you have a commercial site, you might still want to sell specialty items on venues that are set up to handle them — such as Craigslist for big items that are difficult to ship, Amazon.com for used books, and CafePress or other sites for artwork. In fact, the more places you "pop up" as a web merchant, the better. Your stores can sell different products and link to one another, which boosts your business overall. This chapter examines some of the best-known alternatives for making money with hosting services.

 The marketplaces profiled here are only a selection of many. You can find more listed on AuctionBytes beneath the article about eBay alternatives at www.ecommercebytes.com/cab/cab/abu/y209/m01/abu0230/s03 An article on SmartMoney entitled "eBay's Allure Is Going, Going, Gone" describes how eBay began losing its popularity as many sellers started exploring alternatives (www.smartmoney.com/spend/family-money/ebay-allure-going-going-gone).

Sellers reach customers on multiple sales venues

When I wrote previous editions of this book, eBay was the marketplace of choice for enterprising entrepreneurs wanting to sell antiques, consumer goods, handicrafts, and just about any other kind of merchandise. As of this writing, the atmosphere is different. I have profiled a number of sites that either compete directly with eBay or provide a niche alternative to the auction giant. Experienced sellers no longer focus solely on eBay. Rather, eBay is just one of a number of venues for them. For some sellers who are fed up with eBay's listing and final value fees, eBay doesn't play any role at all; they sell through their own websites and other marketplaces.

Laura Milnor Iverson has been selling her original artwork online since 2002 through her Zen Breeze Art Gallery website (www.zenbreeze.com). She also sells on eBay (User ID: iversongallery) where she is currently a Top-Rated Seller. Another successful venue is her store on CafePress (http://shop.cafepress.com/zenbreeze.com). You can also find Laura on the following sites:

✔ Bonanza (www.bonanza.com/booths/ZenBreeze)

✔ eCRATER (http://zenbreeze.ecrater.com/)

✔ Etsy (www.etsy.com/shop/laurali)

"I have a bunch of basic (free) stores, linked together by using a search tag — my website name: zenbreeze," she says. She sells her art online full time.

Laura has been online long enough that much of her business comes from referrals made by satisfied customers who perform "viral marketing." In other cases, when she sells a painting or print, she sends an e-mail with a link to her sales items on CafePress. This free marketing brings her more business.

Sometimes, she even gets commissions. "I often get requests from buyers to get a painting on some item or another." She marks up her artwork modestly, making a profit of only about 15 percent.

"In this economy, I find that you have to spend more time online listing on a variety of venues," she comments. "There's no single one that's going to generate enough income."

Researching the Right Sales Venues

Once you start looking beyond your own website, eBay, or Amazon, you've got lots of options. The challenge is to pick the best venue for your needs. You don't want to open eight or ten storefronts just because you can, only to find that you aren't getting many new customers. Make sure you choose a host that fills the criteria listed in the sections that follow.

How much does it cost?

If you're a lone entrepreneur or the owner or a small business, this is probably your first question. You already pay fees for Internet access, inventory, a shopping cart, and other business services. You can't afford high fees. In that case you might opt for a free marketplace such as eCRATER (www.ecrater.com), Storenvy (www.storenvy.com), or Wensy (www.wensy.com).

Also pay attention to the fees charged for putting items up for sale. If you plan to have hundreds or even thousands of pieces of merchandise to sell, such fees can eat into your profits, especially if the items *don't* sell.

How many customers does it attract?

Lack of customers is the most common complaint voiced with regard to small niche marketplaces. The fact is, you can't depend totally on a marketplace to do your marketing for you. No matter where you are, you need to make your site visible on Google and other search engines and do SEO (see Chapter 11).

That said, it's still worth reading each marketplace's FAQs and discussion forums to see what strategies the marketplace follows to boost its visibility and market its customers' storefronts, and to get an idea how successful it is.

 If you sell specialty items of a particular type, consider a marketplace that isn't necessarily free but that can bring you customers who are looking specifically for what you have to sell. Sites like Etsy and ArtFire aren't free, but they're great for artists. If you sell books, consider sites like Alibris (www.alibris.com) and ABEBooks (www.abebooks.com).

Scanning EcommerceBytes' Seller Survey

When you're researching e-commerce marketplaces, be sure to take advantage of ratings and comments provided by sellers who have experience with them. Each year, the website EcommerceBytes surveys its readers, who are primarily small online businesses and lone entrepreneurs. The Sellers' Choice survey ranks marketplaces both big and small. The 2013 survey is at www.ecommercebytes.com/cab/abu/y213/m02/abu0328/s02, and its opening page is shown in Figure 15-1.

Figure 15-1:
Research
how cur-
rent sellers
evaluate
their
market-
places.

If you drill in to each marketplace, you get a page full of quotes from sellers that can be quite revealing. You find out, for example, that eCRATER has no fees but one seller finds that it needs more exposure and more customers (a common complaint voiced about many, if not most, marketplaces). "Sales are slow, but when you make them it is usually 100 percent profit!" one says. You learn that Webstore.com (`www.webstore.com`) is "geared for the U.S. only" while eBid (`www.ebid.net`) is better for UK sellers because it's based in the United Kingdom. The fact that such comments are anonymous makes them that much more believable. The 2013 seller survey lists these venues as the top ten:

1. **Etsy.** It's the preeminent site for handmade arts and crafts.

2. **Ruby Lane.** This long-standing antiques site gets high marks for customer service and communication.

3. **Amazon.** It's easy to use and brings you lots of potential customers.

4. **Bonanza.** It got the highest marks of all sites for being easy to use.

5. **eBay.** This site is easy to use with lots of traffic, but customer service gets low marks.

6. **eBid.** It gets higher marks than eBay for customer service, but lower marks for profitability.

7. **Addoway.** This site is built with social networking in mind and traffic is said to be growing.

8. **Webstore.com.** One seller calls it the best of the no-fee sites.

9. **ArtFire.** This site no longer has a free stores option, but it charges a flat monthly fee regardless of how many items you sell.

10. **eCRATER.** It has strong store hosting features, but needs more traffic, sellers say.

The number of free options means that you can open more than one store and give each outlet its own graphic identity and product line, as other energetic sellers have done.

Branching Out to Other Marketplaces

For many online sellers, an eBay or Amazon.com storefront or a standalone website is only a starting point. Sellers also set up storefronts on similar but much smaller marketplaces. Having multiple venues lets you reach a wider customer base, and your sites can link to one another, which improves their placement on Google.

Selling the smart way: Craigslist

Craigslist, the classified ad service started in the mid-1990s by Craig Newmark, has become an institution on the web and beyond. It's so popular that it's cutting into the business of traditional print newspapers, which depend in part on their own classified ad postings for revenue. It's also popular enough that it's become a target for scam artists who try to trick sellers out of their money.

For entrepreneurs, Craigslist is a good way to sell merchandise locally. Sometimes, you just have big-ticket items that don't work well on eBay or another site because the cost of shipping is prohibitive. Craigslist is perfect for furniture, major appliances, motor vehicles, and other items that need to be picked up by the buyer. I recently sold a trailer for my father, and most of the experience went smoothly. It's important, though, to be aware of some of the quirks and unique features of selling on Craigslist so that you don't end up with a bad experience.

eBay also has an extensive marketplace designated especially for motor vehicles and related items such as parts. eBay Motors (www.ebay.com/motors) includes extensive protections for both buyers and sellers. That makes it a good alternative to Craigslist if you are looking to sell a car.

To illustrate the Craigslist sales system, I run through the process of listing items online, using two examples from my own experience. My father asked me to sell a trailer and a motorized chair lift. Some parts of the sales went well and some parts were alarming.

Gather details

On Craigslist, just as on eBay and other auction sites, the more details you have about an item, the better. Details sell: Sizes, colors, and serial numbers are all good to gather beforehand. Don't be surprised if you are asked about them. I did field some amazingly detailed questions. Get out a tape measure and measure your item. Get the exact model number and serial number. In your description, be sure to play up any desirable features.

Take photos

Take good, clear JPEG images of your item. If the item is especially large (such as a motor vehicle), be sure to photograph it from all sides. (Buyers want to make sure that you aren't concealing scratches or dings on a side you aren't showing.) Save the images in a graphics program, if necessary, so that each image is 72 dots per inch (dpi) in resolution. The ideal file size for an image is 50–100KB.

List the item

Find the version of Craigslist that is closest to you geographically by searching the list on the site's home page `www.craigslist.org`. Go to the local site and search for objects that are similar to yours. See where they are sold and list your item in the same category. To list the trailer, I went to the North Chicagoland page, marked All for Sale (`chicago.craigslist.org/nch/sss`) and clicked the Post link in the upper-right corner. When a page full of more specific categories appeared, I clicked General for Sale. A list of items for sale appeared. Next, I clicked North Chicagoland and got a shorter list of items for sale located on the north side of Chicago and the surrounding suburbs, which is where the items were located. I typed the description shown in Figure 15-2.

As you can see, I added the sentence "Cash or PayPal only" at the end of the description. I did this for a reason. Craigslist, in its guidelines for sellers, warns against scams involving fraudulent buyers buying items with forged cashier's checks. When the checks bounce, the seller has lost the merchandise and is out the value of the check as well.

Be wary of buyers who offer to have a shipper pick up the item and who say they'll pay with a cashier's check. Buyers should pick up in person and either pay cash or via PayPal. Be especially wary of buyers who offer to pay more than you advertise and then ask you to reimburse the shipper for the difference. This is an age-old scam designed to take even more from you than the merchandise — you'll lose the money, too.

Figure 15-2:
Be specific
with your
Craigslist
descrip-
tion, and
be careful
about what
payment
you accept.

After you have written the description, click Add/Edit Images. Choose up to four images to include with the listing. (You can post no more than four.) Click Continue and preview your listing, as shown in Figure 15-3. Read carefully for any mistakes. If you need to make revisions, click Edit. If everything looks OK, click Continue.

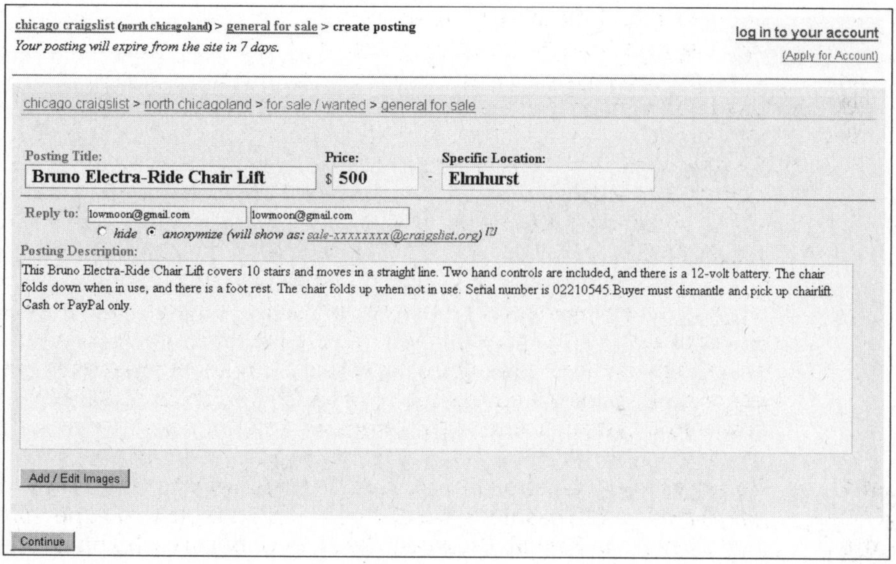

Figure 15-3:
Review
your posting
carefully
before you
put it online.

After you click Continue, accept the terms of use, and read the e-mail that Craigslist sends to you. Click the link supplied in the e-mail, which takes you back to Craigslist to approve your listing. After you click the Publish button, your listing goes online. Be aware that the sale is online for only seven days. After that, it is removed, and you have to list it again. Keep the description and photos handy should you need to relist.

When you receive e-mail responses, be selective. Respond only to those e-mails from people who seem eager to pick up your item themselves and who will pay you either by cash or PayPal. I received plenty of responses from people who would not pick up in person but insisted on sending a "shipper." One e-mail read as follows (I am leaving misspellings intact):

> *Thanks for your prompt reply. Well, i must say you ve got a nice item and as a matter of fact, In a transaction like this, i will appreciate it if we can put trust first so that the transaction can go smoothly. I would have love to come by with cash and pick it up but at the moment am a kinda of too busy to come over, so i think i can send you a cashier check via Fedex Or UPS overnight and my shipping company could come pick it up once payment is cleared. The Check will be excess and all what you will need to do is to just send the remaining balance to my Shipper for pick up after deducting your money, if you are ok with this pls do get back to me with your full name, address and phone number so i can proceed with the payment and pls do keep this item for me and inform other interested party that its been sold..ok*

Needless to say, I told the buyer that I was insisting on cash or PayPal and that the item must be picked up in person. I never heard back from him. Craigslist can be a great place to sell, but remember that you're in charge. Don't be rushed by people who claim to be in a big hurry and who don't want to meet your terms. There will be others after them who will be more compliant.

Making your own product line: Etsy.com

If the merchandise you sell includes items you have designed or crafted yourself, consider selling them on Etsy.com. Rob Kalin, who was then a 27-year-old painter, carpenter, and photographer, started Etsy in 2005. It has since grown into a hugely successful marketplace for crafts and artwork of all kinds. In June 2008, the site announced its millionth registered user. Etsy reports that $895.1 million worth of items were sold on Etsy in 2012. The site currently has more than 22 million members and 850,000 sellers.

Etsy has been featured on Martha Stewart's TV show, and AuctionBytes editor Ina Steiner found that on a visit to the company's Brooklyn, New York, headquarters, the offices are decorated with many of the crafts sold on the site. (You can read her report at www.ecommercebytes.com/cab/abu/y209/m04/abu0236/s02.) Selling on Etsy makes for a personal experience that brings to mind the "old days" of the web when buyers and sellers got to know one another personally and sent out personal notes and freebies with items they sold.

Etsy, like other marketplaces, requires you to sign up for membership and gives sellers a user-friendly way to create an online storefront and list items for sale. As part of your storefront, you can describe what you make and talk about artists or craftspeople who have influenced you. You pay nothing for a storefront, but you are charged 20 cents per item and 3.5 percent of the final sales price of each item you sell (this does not include shipping). The 3.5 percent is much lower than eBay's final value fees, which start at 9 percent for auction items that sell for up to $50.

The Internet offers plenty of alternatives to Etsy in the field of selling arts, crafts, jewelry, and other handmade products. Etsy is just the best-known marketplace of its type. Also consider Zazzle (www.zazzle.com) and ArtFire (www.artfire.com); I describe ArtFire later in this chapter.

Going beyond listing fees: OnlineAuction.com

Like many online marketplaces, OnlineAuction.com (www.onlineauction.com) was founded when an antiques and collectibles dealer who started out selling on eBay became disenchanted with the site. Founder Chris Fain sold both on eBay and in brick-and-mortar businesses near Grants Pass, Oregon. When I interviewed Fain in 2008, the site had 50,000 users.

One big difference between OnlineAuction.com and other sites, including eBay, is the fee structure. At OnlineAuction.com, sellers don't pay listing fees or final value fees. They can sell as many items as they want, and in place of per-item fees, they pay annual or monthly memberships. New sellers can open a basic storefront called My OLA House for $8 per month. (The service is free to founding members.) Sellers can also list and sell as many items as they want for $10 per month.

Avoiding hosting fees: eCRATER

Dimitar Slavov got the idea for eCRATER when he ordered a book from Amazon.com. He found the Amazon site difficult to navigate. Because he is a programmer, he decided to create his own online marketplace, one that would be marked by simplicity. eCRATER (www.ecrater.com) charges no fees for buying or selling items. You are charged only if you want to have your store featured on the site and given premium placement.

Also, sellers are allowed to host their own websites on the site. Through a process called *URL masking,* you use your own web address, not eCRATER's, which makes it seem as though you operate a completely independent site rather than one that is part of eCRATER Sellers also get access to an administrative tool that allows them to manage their online stores. All products are advertised on Google, and Google Checkout, as well as PayPal, are accepted forms of online payment.

See Chapter 7 for more on Google Checkout, PayPal, and other payment options.

Reversing the sales process: iOffer

If you are looking for a truly different buying and selling experience, check out iOffer (www.ioffer.com). This site turns two basic principles of online auctions on their heads. First, there's the idea that the seller either sets a starting price, a reserve price, or a fixed price for the sale. Instead, iOffer puts buyers in charge by giving them a system through which they make an offer and then bargain with the seller until a price is agreed on.

Second, there's the notion that auction sales end at a fixed time. On eBay, this encourages buyers to wait until the last minute, or even the last second or two, to place a bid. On iOffer, there is no fixed ending time. It's free to set up a store, and sellers are charged fees only when they sell an item. Fees tend to be lower than on eBay; for items that sell for $10 to $24.99, the fee is $1.25, for example.

Evaluating your items: WorthPoint/GoAntiques

Knowledge sells. That maxim applies on the web, where shoppers are used to digging around for specifications and all the information they can find about items they seek. WorthPoint (www.worthpoint.com), which also owns the venerable online auction site GoAntiques, makes knowledge a big asset for anyone who wants to sell online.

Don't know what that antique lamp with the clock in the middle of the woman's stomach is worth? You can look up similar items on WorthPoint's database and get a good idea. Or you can ask an expert, called a "Worthologist," who is there to answer questions and provide advice just for registered sellers. You have to be a member to gain access to this wealth of information. Memberships start at $14.99 per month, which gives you full access to the "Worthopedia" database.

Chatting it up: Bonanza

If you want to forget about the suspense of auction sales and simply offer merchandise at a fixed price, just as in a garage sale, take a look at Bonanza (`www.bonanza.com`). Lots of entrepreneurs have already taken a look. Bonanza (formerly known as Bonanzle) was only launched in June 2008, but by August 2009, it had 100,000 registered users. In March 2013, EcommerceBytes reported that the site was expecting its one millionth user (`www.ecommerce bytes.com/cab/abn/y13/m03/i08/s03`). The most popular areas on the site are collectibles, shoes, books, records, and jewelry.

At a garage sale, buyers are apt to haggle and chat with sellers, and the same applies at Bonanza. If you like some social networking along with your selling, this is the place for you. Sellers offer their merchandise in a sales "booth," which is the equivalent of a store on other sites. The site charges merchants a flat 3.5 percent fee for each item sold. Each booth has a chat window incorporated into it. The seller can use it to say "Hi" or engage buyers in conversation. Bonanza also has discussion boards, just as other sites do. But the fact that chat goes on in the midst of sales descriptions sets Bonanza apart.

The interaction extends to management as well. Customers can add to a "wish list" of features they want to see on the site. Founder Bill Harding reviews the list and often responds personally to requests.

Hosting your store for free: Highwire

Highwire Commerce (`www.highwire.com`), formerly BuyItSellIt.com, is more than an auction or fixed-price sales marketplace. It's a free e-commerce hosting service. It costs nothing to create a storefront that allows you to sell on eBay, Facebook, and Bonanza. For $19.95 per month, you can have your own webstore and add your own domain name. (Otherwise, your storefront's domain name takes the form `www.mystorefrontname.mybisi.com`.)

Highwire's $19.95 option lets you sell up to $1,500 of merchandise per month; any higher, and you are automatically upgraded to the $39.95 per month hosting option. The emphasis here is on features that make a full-featured e-commerce site run, including bulk uploading of multiple items, the ability to offer sales coupons, a customer account manager, and a customizable checkout process.

Finding the features you need: ArtFire

If you sell handmade jewelry, art, or other handcrafts, ArtFire (www.artfire. com) is an option worth considering. Many of the site's features used to be available for free; some ArtFire sellers were angered when free hosting and sales were discontinued. On the other hand, ArtFire is still in business.

After a 14-day trial period, you are charged $12.95 per month for membership. (There are no listing or final value fees.) For this, you get access to a long list of features including the ability to create discount sales, the option to establish a Facebook store called a *kiosk,* and coupon codes you can issue to shoppers. You can list an unlimited number of items, too. A seller named Dotoly's store, based in Hong Kong, has a sale page and advertises other features such as coupons and a newsletter, as shown in Figure 15-4.

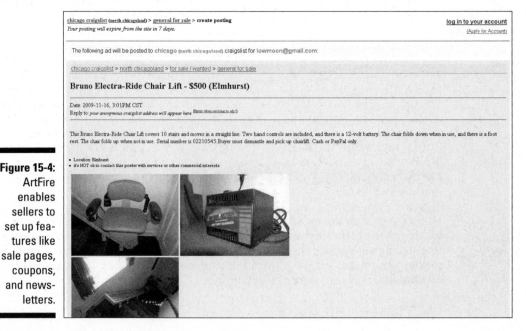

Figure 15-4: ArtFire enables sellers to set up features like sale pages, coupons, and news- letters.

Joining Robin Hood: Webstore.com

Julio Pereda, who founded Webstore.com (www.webstore.com), likes to think of his site as being the Robin Hood of online marketplaces. Webstore focuses on the "Daily Deal," the practice of listing one item per day and making it available at a deep discount for a limited amount of time. It's an approach that has worked well on sites like Woot.com and on home shopping networks on television.

For sellers and buyers alike, the big advantage of Webstore.com is that no fees are charged, period. It's absolutely free to buy and sell. The site makes money from display ads posted on the side of many pages. Even though it's free, Webstore.com offers some nice features: Sellers can design their stores using customizable templates, and buyers can shop for items in their local area if they want to pick up something in person.

Taking a personal approach: Wensy.com

Remember the days when every neighborhood had a corner store? You knew the people who ran the store, and they greeted you by name when you came in. For the most part, those days are gone. But in the online world, you occasionally find a site that is run by a true "lone entrepreneur," a do-it-yourselfer who doesn't have help and doesn't have to report to anyone else.

That's the story with Wensy.com (www.wensy.com), a site created and managed by Darren Bock, a man who has a day job as director of a hospital intensive care unit. In his spare time, after taking care of heart patients, he relaxes by responding to messages and managing his site. Although he manages a staff of 71 during his day job, his website staff is just one: himself. (He occasionally pays programmers to make technical changes.) The 12,000-plus registered users don't pay a penny in fees to either list items or sell them. Bock does include some ads on the site and gets donations from some users. But he's in it for the personal contact with his user community. He checks e-mails every 12 hours and responds personally to all of them. "It's a lot of fun," he told me.

On top of everything else it does, Amazon.com is trying to be a web hosting service as well. The Webstores program gives you the ability to run your own branded store through the site. The difference between a conventional hosting service and a webstore is that the latter uses Amazon.com's own e-commerce technology. Find out more in Chapter 14.

Selling your creative work: CafePress

If you're a creative artist and you just want to sell a few examples of your work to family and friends, CafePress might be just what you need. If you already have an account with PayPal and regularly use its payment services for sales on eBay, it makes sense to open a PayPal store. If you use Microsoft products, such as Expression Web, to create your web pages, Microsoft Small Business Center is a good option for creating an online sales catalog and storefront. It's all a matter of deciding what you need.

Creative people aren't always the best at marketing and selling their own work. Millions of amateur artists out there are probably hoping to become professionals. They have great ideas for cartoons, logos, and drawings, but the prospect of getting them printed and sold in stores is a big obstacle.

It's easy enough to start your own CafePress store. (Figure 15-5 shows an example of a CafePress store.) Follow these steps:

1. **Connect to the Internet, start up your web browser, and go to the CafePress Free Store page (**`www.cafepress.com/cp/info/sell`**).**

   The Sell Online: Introduction page appears in your browser window.

2. **Click the Create My Shop link or the Start Selling Now! button.**

   The Join CafePress.com! page appears. Before creating a store, you need to register with CafePress.

Figure 15-5:
A CafePress. com storefront enables you to print and sell your original artwork.

3. **Assign yourself a username and password (if you haven't done so already). When you're done, click Join Now.**

   The New Member Survey page appears.

4. **Fill out the survey and click Open Your Shop!**

   The Open a Shop page appears.

5. **Click Open a Basic Shop.**

   The Welcome to CafePress.com Basic Shops! page appears.

6. **Under the Shop Information heading, enter a short ID that will be included in your store's URL and enter a name for your store. Fill out the rest of the options on the page if necessary, and click Submit when you're done.**

   The Welcome to CafePress.com Basic Shops! page appears. Click the URL supplied for your new store so that you can see that although it's empty, it really exists, as shown in Figure 15-6.

7. **Click the Build Your Shop button.**

   The Products page appears.

8. **Under the Storefront Contents tab, select Add a Product.**

   The Choose a Product page appears, with a set of products you can personalize and sell in your store, as shown in Figure 15-7.

Figure 15-6:
Presto!
You've
opened your
store, which
you can
now fill with
merchandise.

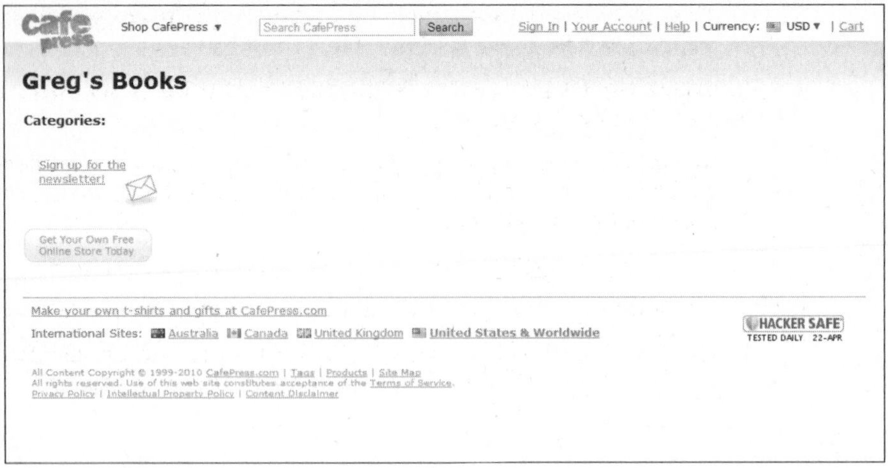

cafe press
Shop CafePress ▾
Search CafePress
Search
Sign In | Your Account | Help | Currency: USD ▾ | Cart
Greg's Books
Categories:
Sign up for the newsletter!
Get Your Own Free Online Store Today
Make your own t-shirts and gifts at CafePress.com
International Sites: Australia Canada United Kingdom United States & Worldwide
HACKER SAFE
TESTED DAILY 22-APR
All Content Copyright © 1999-2010 CafePress.com | Tags | Products | Site Map
All rights reserved. Use of this web site constitutes acceptance of the Terms of Service.
Privacy Policy | Intellectual Property Policy | Content Disclaimer

Figure 15-7: CafePress.com gives you a selection of items that you can personalize and sell online.

9. **Close the new browser window that opened so that you could inspect your page and return to the Welcome to CafePress.com Basic Shops! page. Click the Add These Products button at the bottom of the page.**

   The Your Account page appears.

   REMEMBER: If you want to sell something other than a tote bag, license plate frame, book, or other products shown on the Choose a Product page, you should open a site with another web host. But if you're just beginning with e-commerce and aren't sure what to sell, a CafePress.com store is a good starting point.

10. **Select the box that contains the type of item you want to sell and then click the Edit button.**

    The Product Designer page appears.

11. **Click Select Image.**

    The Media Basket page appears. This page is intended as a storage area — a place where you can store product images so that you can add them later when you want to put items up for sale.

12. **Click Add Image.**

    The Upload Image page appears, with an explanation you should read that describes the acceptable file formats.

13. **Click Browse.**

    The Choose File dialog box appears.

14. **Select the file you want to place on the front of the object and click Open.**

The path leading to the location of the image file on your computer appears in the Image file box.

15. **Check the I Agree to the Terms and Conditions Described Above box and then click Upload.**

    An Uploading dialog box appears with a progress bar that describes the progress of the file transfer. When the transfer is complete, the image appears in your Media Basket.

16. **Click Add image.**

    The image is added to the front of your product, as shown in Figure 15-8.

17. **Click Next and follow Steps 11 through 16 to add images to the back of the object and to add more objects to your online store.**

Figure 15-8:
You save the items you want to print in a holding area called the Media Basket.

Make sure your logo or other image meets the height and other requirements for a CafePress.com store. Images must be 200 pixels in height (1 inch equals approximately 72 pixels). Find out more by clicking the Need More Image Help? link, which appears on the product design pages as you're creating your store.

Visit your new site by entering your web address, which takes the form www.cafepress.com/*storename* (where *storename* is the name you choose in Step 6).

CafePress.com sets a base price for each object. For example, a set of six greeting cards has a base price of $10.99. If you charge $14.99 for the cards, CafePress.com collects the base price, but you get the $4.00 profit. You don't have to do the printing or shipping; CafePress.com handles all of that for you.

Connecting All Your Outlets

You can advertise your sites on EveryPlaceISell, a site run by my colleagues Ina and David Steiner (see Chapter 20 for details). This site lets sellers collect links to all their storefronts on one convenient page. For example, Figure 15-9 shows links to 12 venues where you can purchase photos by nature photographer Skye Ryan-Evans, who sells her work through her website, Rustic Moon Crafts (www.rusticmooncrafts.com).

Figure 15-9:
You can open multiple storefronts and link them to one another.

Chapter 16

Managing and Growing Your Online Business

*T*he preceding two chapters focus on some of the most popular marketplaces for establishing one or more online storefronts. Having more than one venue to attract sellers helps you do cross-marketing and boosts your visibility; it's the strategy more and more small businesses are using to compete online with the big players. But the more storefronts you have, the more difficult it is to manage them at all. Suppose you have a single item listed for sale in two of your stores. If someone clicks the Buy button on an item in one of your stores and you can't ship it because someone else just purchased the same item from another store, your reputation takes a big hit. Repeat such problems and all your hard work can be undone.

This chapter focuses on good practices and useful tools for keeping track of inventory, sales, and payments among multiple stores to keep your online business running smoothly. As you might expect, service providers are eager to help entrepreneurs just like you with management interfaces that can provide you with a complete "back office" so you can focus on selling and marketing. But there are also some basic approaches to search visibility, analysis, and business applications that you can check out on your own for little or no cost. You find out more about them in the second half of this chapter.

Choosing Channel Management Software

A special kind of service provider is designed specifically for businesses that maintain multiple sales channels — online, brick-and-mortar, flea markets, arts-and-crafts shows — to help maintain their stores' very different inventories.

For example, Brad Owens sells T-shirts and other merchandise at his Rock Shop Music and Comics store in the Mall of Georgia in Buford, Georgia. When a shirt is sold from that location, it needs to be removed from the inventory of Owens's online store (www.rockshopmusicandcomics.com) or from his inventory on eBay, Amazon, or BigCommerce. Owens's store and website are shown in Figure 16-1.

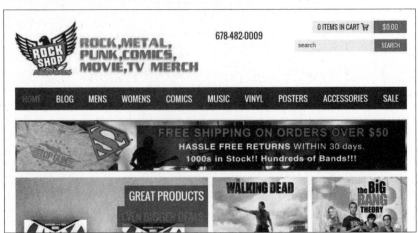

Figure 16-1: Rock Shop Music and Comics has a brick-and-mortar store in a mall. The store's website sells some of the same merchandise online.

Owens, who has been selling online for several years, doesn't have the same selection of merchandise in his stores. He needed an automated solution for adjusting inventory.

"We had to have a solution that not only would work with Amazon, eBay, and our BigCommerce store, but could also manage inventory for our size variations among the three," he says. "Instead of manually going into each channel and adjusting our inventory when an item is sold, it does that automatically. We can also manage orders within one interface. It's also very easy to add items to a different channel."

Owens is talking about ChannelGrabber (www.channelgrabber.com), a UK-based service provider that specializes in managing multiple sales channels for businesses. ChannelGrabber's interface presents a business with all of its stores and products in a single spreadsheet-type grid (see Figure 16-2): Stores are arranged in columns, products in rows. A seller who manages multiple online stores can keep track of it all by looking at a single screen.

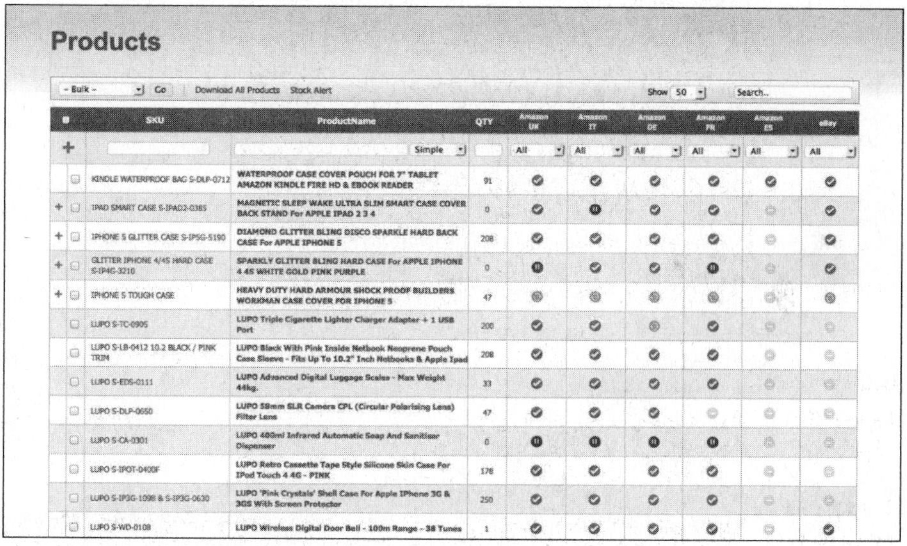

Figure 16-2: Channel Grabber and similar products help you manage inventory listed in several stores.

You pay a monthly fee to have such services handle your business. That's on top of your Internet access fees, your store hosting fees, and other fees. ChannelGrabber, for example, costs 60 British pounds per month for its least expensive Standard package, which lets businesses sell up to 5,000 products per month. Here are some other channel management offerings you might consider:

- ✔ **ChannelAdvisor** (www.channeladvisor.com) has been helping businesses manage their inventory for years. The price you pay this service provider depends on the features you want, so e-mail them for a quote.

- ✔ **Volusion** (www.volusion.com) is a store provider and a shopping cart and payment service provider as well as a resource for managing more than one store. You get a website, mobile store, and Facebook store, plus a 10 percent discount on any additional stores you open. Plans range from $15 to $195 per month.

- ✔ **Monsoon Pro** (www.monsooncommerce.com/e-commerce-products/monsoon-pro), part of Monsoon Commerce, lets businesses list products in multiple storefronts and track inventory. Fees vary depending on the number of products being sold, but they start at around $500 per month.

- ✔ **Stone Edge** (www.stoneedge.com) isn't a channel management service per se, but a specialty back-end software provider, also part of Monsoon Commerce. Stone Edge enables businesses with multiple presences manage their fulfillment needs. Pricing is different than with other services; you purchase a license for multiple workstations. Plans start at $4,000 per year for up to five workstations.

Each of these services represents an investment, to be sure. But if your business is your livelihood and you aren't able to maintain a large staff or IT department, a management package might make sense.

Make sure you get a return on investment (ROI) before investing in a channel management solution. When I asked ChannelGrabber CEO Daniel Williams at what point services like his make sense for small businesses, he said: "Don't take on an expense unless you intend to receive a return on investment. Multi-channel solutions like ChannelGrabber allow for you to realize ROI very early on by saving you time on simple but necessary tasks. ChannelGrabber should be used as an aid to the businesses wanting to automate as much as possible but also sell effectively without risking their feedback."

Spreading the Word with Google

Mimi Kriele, who is featured in the preceding sidebar, emphasized the role of SEO in growing the visibility of her website and sales to her online business. When you look at *Search Engine Optimization* (SEO), the practice of optimizing your content to get the best placement in search results, you need to look first at Google.

CASE STUDY

Sellers with multiple stores reach more customers

When I wrote previous editions of this book, eBay was the marketplace of choice for enterprising entrepreneurs. These days, Amazon.com is the big player. You can read more about Amazon.com's advantages as a store host and a shipping service in Chapter 14. Here, I focus on how one seller uses Amazon and Stone Edge to run a dozen online stores.

Mimi and Peter Kriele operate those Amazon-based stores as well as their own website (https://.touchofeurope.net) from their home in Marietta, Georgia. Mimi says she could never keep track of it all without the help of her online management services.

"We don't need to do anything special with managing our stores," says Mimi. "We use the same management interface as an Amazon Seller Central account. All the orders come in to the same place. The interface tells us which web store the order is coming from. Because we have a broad inventory and we carry so many types of products, we decided to divide them into 'microsites.' One offers only chocolate, for example. But the orders are pulled out of the same Amazon inventory." The Krieles' primary website is shown below.

A Touch of Europe offers products the Krieles grew up with and that were missing when they moved to the United States. "We know European products, and it turned out we weren't the only ones missing things," Mimi says.

Stone Edge is worth the expense, Mimi adds. "They have an amazing program. They integrate the store and Amazon.com. They handle inventory, order management, order confirmations for Amazon, and a lot of our shipping. I don't know how we would be able to grow otherwise."

She advises sellers to focus on developing their own websites and work on search engine optimization — and diversify their service providers. "As far as I am concerned, don't put all your eggs in one basket," she says.

Google started as a *search engine* — a website that organizes the contents of the entire Internet and makes information easy to find. It turns out that the same approaches that apply to organizing content and presenting search results apply to merchants as well as their goods and services. Google now makes millions by giving online businesspeople the ability to pay for ads that steer consumers to their websites. The site has branched out to supply a variety of new services, including free e-mail, web hosting, and business applications.

You owe it to yourself to pay attention to what Google has to offer and take advantage of its services. The sections that follow summarize the basics of using Google for marketing and publicity, two of the most important ways in which Google can help small businesses.

The practice of SEO is such an important and cost-effective marketing strategy for small businesses that Chapter 11 examines it in depth.

Getting yourself listed in the Google Directory

The Holy Grail for many online businesspeople is a ranking right at the top of Google's search results — or at least on the first page of search results. I write a good deal about my brother's website in this book not just because I want to give him free publicity, but also because he's done some smart things to market his site and protect himself in a field in which he could get into legal trouble: copying and restoring records and other recordings.

When you do a search for "transfer LP to CD" on Google (at least at the time I wrote this chapter) and scan the search results, you find my brother's web-site (`www.lp2cdsolutions.com`) listed third on the first page of ten search results. (His site ranked number eight when I checked a couple years ago; he has been improving his search placement steadily.) He has done a lot of work to get to this point. He has submitted his site to Google and other search engines, updates his site frequently, asks other sites to exchange links with him, and more.

Following all of those steps is a good idea, but at the very least make sure you submit your site for inclusion in the Google Directory, exchange links with other websites, and maintain high-quality content on your pages.

Submitting your site for inclusion

Perhaps the simplest and most practical approach all businesses can take is to add the business's URL to Google. I mention how to do this — by accessing

Google's form for submitting a web page URL to the Directory (www.google. com/addurl) — in Chapter 11. But I don't mention one thing you should do when you fill out this form: Create your own description of your website. The description you type appears in Google's search results. For example, with the www.lp2cdsolutions.com site, the Google search result description looks like this:

```
Transfer your LP collection (also 78, 45, 8-track, reel-to-reel . . .
Audio restoration and transfer to CD of recordings (LP, 33, 78, 45,
        8-tracks, reel, cassette)" Drastically improve the sound of the
        original recording to . . .
```

The ellipses (. . .) are shown because the descriptions are too long to fit in the search results. Nevertheless, what does appear gets the message across. By taking the time to submit your own description instead of waiting for Google's automated content-scouring programs called spiders to index your site, you can control exactly what appears in the search results and in the Directory as well. (A longer description you type appears in Google's web directory.)

The *Google Directory* is a Yahoo!-style index to the contents of the Internet, arranged by category. Most people access the Google database of websites by using its well-known search page, which is also the site's home page. To find the Directory, you have to burrow into the site: Go to the home page, click More, click Even More, and when the More Google Products page appears, click Directory under the Search heading.

Exchanging links with other websites

Google's engine is smart enough that it doesn't necessarily give a good ranking to websites that have added keywords and descriptions to their web pages. The search engine favors sites that are popular and frequently updated. A sign of popularity, from the search index program's point of view, is the number of links made to a page. Another is the *quality* of the links— the more links you have to pages that are rich in content that is frequently updated, the more valuable your page must be, and the higher the ranking Google gives it.

One of the best ways to get better visibility in search results is to get other sites to link to you. How do you do it? You might automatically think of programs or technological shortcuts that can create links for you on other people's websites. There are such tools, but the best way is to roll up your sleeves and create links the old-fashioned, time-consuming, human way: Look for sites that have products and services that complement yours, approach the owners of those sites, and ask to exchange links ("I'll publicize your site if you publicize mine"). You find some examples of such links in Chapter 11.

Link exchanges are networks of online businesspeople who are specifically looking to increase their links to other sites. But Google discourages the use of such exchanges. At the very least, check out the sites you link to and make sure they are full of interesting content, not just "placeholder" pages or pages full of links.

Optimizing your site for better search results

For just about all online businesses, it's important to get a good ranking in Google search results. Google's exact formula for determining search result rankings is a well-kept secret. But again, you can take some simple and practical approaches to better your chances of getting placed near the top of the first page. Chapter 11 describes such strategies in more detail; I cover two other tips in the following sections.

Keeping it fresh

When you submit your site for inclusion in the Google Directory, you read the following instructional note: "Google updates its index on a regular basis, so updated or outdated link submissions are not necessary. Dead links will 'fade out' of our index on our next crawl when we update our entire index."

In other words, Google continually re-indexes the Web and ignores sites that are considered dead. A *dead site* is one that hasn't been updated for a long time and that doesn't receive many (or any) visits. To avoid becoming one of these cobweb sites, update some of your content on a regular basis.

You don't have to update your whole site. If you have a blog online, you only have to make an entry every week (or better yet, every day) to keep your site fresh. Otherwise, make a commitment to change something — anything — on your site every week or so. This can be something as insignificant as the "last updated" date at the bottom of your web page or as significant as the page title. Just add a bit of information as often as you can; this practice not only improves your search results but also keeps your visitors coming back to you on a regular basis.

Some sites (for example, Google Guide, at www.googleguide.com) claim that popular web pages are re-indexed as often as they're updated. I don't know whether this is true. A post on Webmasterworld (www.webmasterworld.com/forum10003/1015.htm) estimates that the index is updated several times a month, but Google employee Matt Cutts has been quoted as saying that the index is "incrementally updated every day (or faster)." On his blog, he reports that his own site has had more than 430 pages indexed in a day (www.mattcutts.com/blog/more-webmaster-console-goodness). All of this means that you have another incentive to update your site as often as you can.

How does your site rank? A peek behind the scenes

Google keeps its algorithm for ranking pages secret. But it's generally known that Google assigns a web page a score called a PageRank. A patent request filed with the U.S. Patent and Trademark Office in 2010 indicates that PageRank might depend, in part, on how a user navigates based on a link. But PageRank is based on lots of different and complex factors. Although it dates back to December 2003 and the formulas for calculating PageRank have certainly evolved, an earlier patent application gives you plenty of clues for how the Google PageRank system operates. More recent comments on Google employee Matt Cutts' blog (for example, www.mattcutts.com/blog/pagerank-sculpting) indicate that freshness of content, good organization, good use of keywords, and the speed with which pages load all play a role in calculating PageRank. Here are some tidbits from the 2003 patent application, which are still applicable today:

- The history of the web page is important. This includes the date the page was first discovered by a search engine.

- The frequency with which the content of the web page changes is also important. This includes an average time between the changes, a number of changes in a time period, and a comparison of a rate of change in a current time period with a rate of change in a previous time period.

- The number of new pages associated with the document matters as well.

- The amount of content that changes in proportion to the amount of content in the entire document matters, too.

- How frequently the document is associated with search queries is taken into account.

These are just a few of the 63 separate claims listed in the patent request. You can read a detailed and more recent interpretation of PageRank at www.webworkshop.net/pagerank.html. The claims all boil down to making your page worthwhile, keeping it up to date, and promoting as many links as you can to other websites and from those sites to yours.

Building in keywords

When Google's automated indexing programs scour web pages, they ignore common words such as *the, at, is, a,* and *how*. What do they pay attention to? *Keywords* — nouns and verbs individuals might enter into Google's search box when they're looking for your site.

To determine what keywords your customers are likely to enter into the Google search box when they're looking for you or your services, use a service such as Wordtracker (www.wordtracker.com), which suggests likely terms for you based on the name and content of your website.

Keywords do make a difference — especially if you place them in strategic locations such as the title of your page, the headings, and the first 50 or so words of text on a page. Sprinkle your web page text with key terms and don't worry about repeating them from page to page. The more frequently they appear, the better your chances of ending up number one.

Having Google's spider programs crawling through your web pages isn't always a good idea. Some webmasters don't like to give all their content (such as newspaper or magazine articles) away for free. However, you can block indexing programs such as Google's from including your pages in their index. Include a simple text file named `robots.txt` and identify the automated program you want to block or the pages on your site that you don't want indexed. Then post this text file on your website. Google provides instructions for people who want to block indexing programs at `support.google.com/webmasters/bin/answer.py?hl=en&answer=156449`.

Adding Google Apps to Your Business

Website hosting and business applications are particularly important to small organizations that don't have in-house information technology (IT) staff. Google has created a set of similar services, called Google Apps (`www.google.com/apps`).

After December 6, 2012, the Standard (or free) version of Google Apps, which is recommended for personal use, was discontinued. If you signed up for Google Apps Standard before that date, you can continue to use it now. Otherwise, you need to sign up for Google Apps for Business, which cost $5 per user per month or $50 per user per year. For that price, you get 25GB of storage space for Gmail and 5GB of space for files. If you need more space, you can buy more. For an additional $4 per month, you get 20GB of additional space, for example. With either version, you pay a $12 per year fee to register a `.com` domain name. If you're frustrated with login problems and slow performance of similar applications such as Microsoft's Office 365 service, Google Apps might be just the ticket.

For more information on Google Apps for Business pricing and features, see the Google Apps for Business page (`www.google.com/enterprise/apps/business/pricing.html`).

Becoming master of a domain

Like Yahoo! Small Business and other hosting services, Google gives small businesses the ability to register a domain name. Google offer services in a wide variety of names, including the `.com`, `.org`, `.biz`, and `.info` domains. This is a somewhat wider range of options than other services offer.

It's often a good idea to "lock down" the same domain name in many different domains; for example, I paid an extra fee to GoDaddy to register not only gregholden.com but also gregholden.net and gregholden.org so that others couldn't purchase them.

You don't have to obtain a brand-new domain to take advantage of Google Apps. If you already own a domain, you can associate Google Apps with it. Whether you already have a domain or want to get one through Google, and whether you have the Standard or Business edition, the initial steps are the same. The following steps illustrate how to get started with Business edition:

1. **Go to the Google Apps for Business Welcome page at** www.google.com/apps/intl/en/group/index.html **and click the Get Started Now button.**

   The first signup page appears.

2. **Enter your personal information and click Next.**

   A domain name signup page appears.

3. **Enter the domain you want to use with Google Apps or purchase a new one.**

   If you don't already own a domain name, click the I would like to Buy a new Domain now link on the right half of the page, select the domain (such as .com) from the drop-down list, and then click Check Availability. When you have a domain, your browser displays a page stating that your domain is available, and you can register a .com name with Google for one year for $12. Other domains have different prices.

4. **Click Next.**

5. **Enter information about your organization and click Continue.**

6. **Create a username and password to create your Google Apps account, and type the characters seen in the box to prove you're not an automated indexing program called a "robot."**

7. **Review the terms of service, and then click the Accept and signup button.**

   A page appears, asking you to verify your account.

Verifying ownership

After you obtain a domain and sign up for the service, you need to verify that you own the site. After you complete verification, one option you have is to identify your domain name registrar (the company from which you purchased your domain name). You choose the registrar from a list and sign in to it with your username and password for that company (not Google Apps, but your registrar). Then follow the steps provided; they vary depending on your registrar.

One other option is to change the CNAME record for your domain registration. If you have an existing website, you already know how to upload a file to it, so you should choose that option. If you don't have a website (for example, if you registered your domain name but haven't created any pages for it), choose the CNAME option. The following steps assume that you already have a business website and want to upload a file:

1. **Create a web page HTML file and name the file** `googlehosted service.html`**.**

   You have to insert a string of characters, which Google gives you.

2. **Upload the file to your website.**

   Make sure the file is in the same directory as your home page.

3. **Click the I've Completed the Steps Above button.**

   Google Apps offers you the chance to launch its Setup guide. If you click Skip this Guide, the Dashboard page, shown in Figure 16-3, appears.

When you first sign up for Google Apps, you go to your Dashboard page. You use this page to access all the apps for which you signed up. Simply signing up for a service isn't enough to start working on it. You need to activate it from the Dashboard.

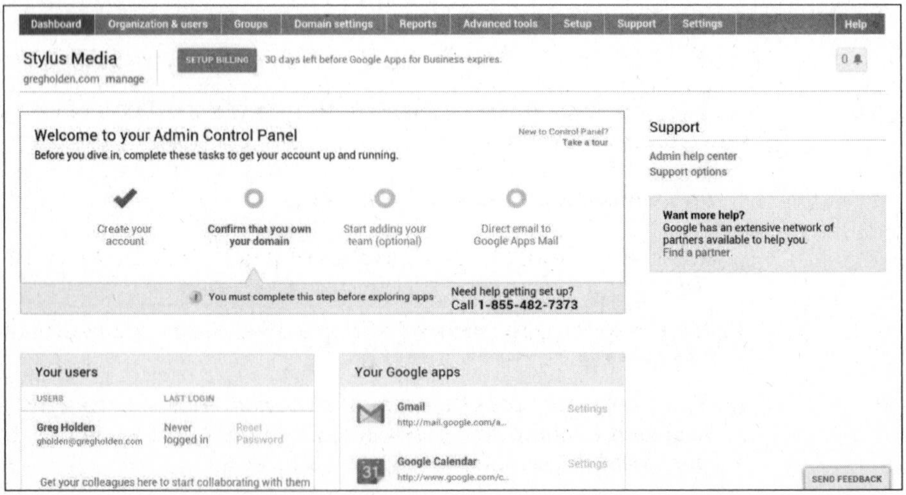

Figure 16-3: You can add Google Apps to an existing domain you own or one you obtain through Google.

The details on creating a web page and uploading it to the server that hosts your site vary, depending on the type of software you use to create web pages. Creating a web page is as simple as opening a text editor (such as Notepad), adding the <html>, <head>, <title>, and <body> tags that define a web page, and saving the document with the .htm or .html file extension. If you use a program such as Dreamweaver to create your web pages, the process is even easier. You can upload the file using a file transfer program, such as WS FTP or CuteFTP, or a web editor that has FTP capabilities. See Chapter 5 for details on working with web editors.

The Dashboard page allows you to add new services (Google Apps, in other words) to your domain. You also use the Dashboard page to create new user accounts for your colleagues (see the following section, "Creating user accounts)."

After verifying ownership and accessing your Dashboard, you'll want to create a Start page for your Google Apps domain. The Start page is where you and your small business co-workers can check your Gmail inboxes, see shared calendars, and view links that you provide for them. Your Start page takes the form http://partnerpage.google.com/*domain*. For example, if your domain were gregholden.com, your Start page would be http://partnerpage.google.com/gregholden.com.

Creating user accounts

Google Apps isn't really intended for a lone user working in isolation. If you're a one-person shop, you can obtain a Gmail account for yourself and create your web pages through the web page creation service or application of your choice. Google Apps excels (to use a Microsoft pun) in giving a group of users an easy and free way to share information. To allow others into your Google Apps–powered domain, create user accounts. You have room for 50 separate accounts in your domain in the Standard Edition of Google Apps, so there's plenty of room to grow.

To add user accounts, follow these steps:

1. **From your Google Apps Dashboard page, click the Create a New User link.**

2. **On the next page (shown in Figure 16-4), enter the username of the new user.**

   The username takes the form of *username@domainname*. You're assigned a temporary password; when the user logs in with this password, he or she can create a new one.

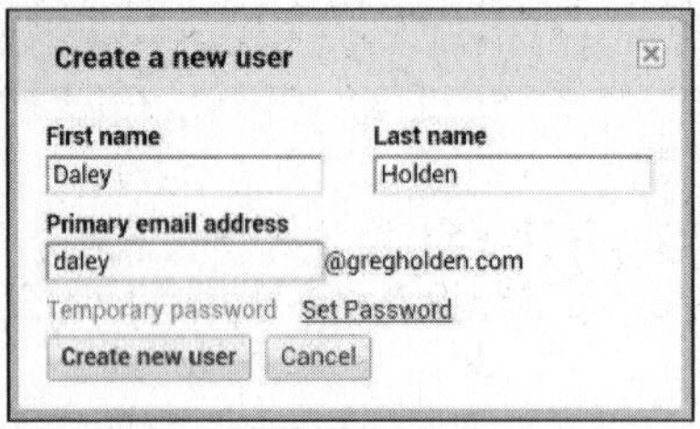

Figure 16-4:
Google
Apps is
primarily
intended for
workgroups
that need to
share infor-
mation.

Create a new user   ⊠

First name   Last name
Daley   Holden

Primary email address
daley   @gregholden.com

Temporary password   Set Password

Create new user   Cancel

3. **Click Create New User to create the account.**

4. **When you're done, click the Create Another User button and repeat Steps 2 and 3 to create accounts for everyone in your workgroup.**

   Be sure to write down the temporary password for each account you create and send it to the account holder.

   Click the User Accounts link to view the list of all the accounts in your domain and to track when users logged in most recently.

5. **Send an announcement to all users in your workgroup, telling them that the Google Apps service has been added to your domain.**

   On the Dashboard page, click the Create Email List link and assign the mailing list with its own e-mail address, such as `mailings@mydomain.com`. Then add users in your domain to a domain mailing list. When you want to communicate with everyone simultaneously, you or other users can simply send a single message to the mailing list's e-mail list, and all the members on the list receive that message.

Even if you're the administrator for your domain and plan to use the administrator account, create an account for your personal use so that you can keep e-mail and other information separate.

Part V
Keeping Your Business Legal and Fiscally Responsible

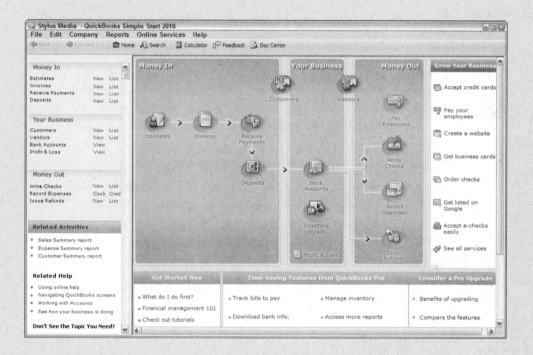

In this part . . .

- ✔ Protecting your business's identity — your trade name, trademarks, and domain name.

- ✔ Being aware of local regulations and restrictions you need to observe.

- ✔ Choosing an accounting method and keeping track of your business records to streamline the tax return process.

Chapter 17

Keeping It All Legal

• •

• •

A s the field of e-commerce becomes more competitive and enterprising businesspeople find new ways to produce content online, e-litigation, e-patents, e-trademarks, and other means of legal protection multiply correspondingly. The courts are increasingly called upon to resolve smaller e-squabbles and, literally, lay down the e-law.

Many of the recent legal cases in the news concern the proliferation of content on popular file-sharing sites and other web resources. For example, in 2006, the Chicago Lawyers' Committee for Civil Rights Under Law sued the classified ad service Craigslist for violating the Federal Fair Housing Act because of real estate postings that contained discriminating messages, such as "No Minorities." In 2009, the Cook County Sheriff in Illinois went after Craigslist, alleging that the site abets prostitution through ads in the "erotic services" area of its website. Craigslist prevailed on both lawsuits by having each dismissed by the courts under a safe harbor provision of federal law.

Obviously, there is some built-in protection for sites like Craigslist that publish user-generated content (UGC). (YouTube and eBay are two other prominent UGC websites, of course.) But it is clear that those who publish their own information online can be liable if they break the law. A Florida woman was awarded $11.3 million in a defamation lawsuit filed against a Louisiana woman who posted messages on the Internet calling her a "crook," a "con artist," and a "fraud." The case was seen as a warning to bloggers and other website owners. The point: Be sure that what you publish doesn't break the law.

In previous years, big e-commerce players, such as Microsoft and Google, were involved in patent and trademark disputes. In 2007, a company called

Savvysoft ended a dispute with Microsoft when it changed the name of its TurboExcel product to Calc4Web. Microsoft had charged that intellectual property rights associated with its trademark Excel (a spreadsheet program) had been violated. In the summer of 2004, Microsoft decided to settle a lawsuit it filed in the U.S. courts by paying $20 million to stop a company — Lindows.com — from infringing on its trademarked name Windows.

The message for you as a new business owner is ignorance isn't an excuse. This area may well make you nervous because you lack experience in business law and you don't have a lot of money to hire lawyers and accountants. You don't want to be discovering for the first time about copyright law or the concept of intellectual property when you're in the midst of a dispute. In this chapter, I give you a snapshot of legal issues you can't afford to ignore. With luck, this information can help you head off trouble before it occurs.

Note: David M. Adler of the Chicago law firm David M. Adler, Esq. & Associates, PC (www.ecommerceattorney.com), reviewed the original draft of this chapter for accuracy. Adler and his firm specialize in legal issues facing businesses that want to conduct e-commerce. Adler advises: "This chapter is a good starting point. But it cannot begin to explain all the issues in all their complexity, and [it] should be regarded as just the beginning of a discussion with a competent lawyer who will look in detail at your individual facts and situation."

Understanding Trade Names and Trademarks

A *trade name* is the name by which a business is known in the marketplace. A trade name can also be a *trademark,* even though it hasn't been registered as such. The U.S. Patent and Trademark Office (USPTO) defines a trademark as "a word, phrase, symbol, or design, or a combination of words, phrases, symbols, or designs, that identifies and distinguishes the source of the goods of one party from those of others." Big corporations protect their trade names and trademarks jealously, and sometimes court battles erupt over who can legally use a name.

Although you may never get in a trademark battle and you may never register a trademark, be careful which trade name you pick and how you use it. Choose a trade name that's easy to remember so that people can associate it with your company and return to you often when they're looking for the products or services. Also, as part of taking your new business seriously and planning for success, you may want to protect your right to use your name by registering it as a trademark. You may do this at the federal level through the USPTO or register it in your state or the states in which you conduct business.

You can use as a trademark any visual element that accompanies a particular tangible product or line of goods and serves to identify and distinguish it from products sold by other sources. In other words, a trademark isn't necessarily just your business's trade name. In fact, you can use as a trademark letters, words, names, phrases, slogans, numbers, colors, symbols, designs, or shapes. Take a look at the cover of this book. Look closely and see how many ™ or ® symbols you see. The same trademarked items are shown on the For Dummies website, which is shown in Figure 17-1.

Figure 17-1:
You don't have to use special symbols to designate logos or phrases on your website, but you may want to.

You can use the ™ symbol with anything you deem to be your trademark and that would be protected by common law rights. However, you must only use trademarks that have passed the requirements imposed by the federal government and become registered through the USPTO. Your trademark may carry the ® symbol and in addition to any common law rights, would be protected by the rights gained through USPTO registration.

For most small businesses, the problem with trademarks isn't so much protecting your own; rather, it is avoiding infringing the trademark rights of others. As a prudent businessperson, you should exercise due diligence to research the name you want to use to make sure that you don't run into trouble.

Determining whether a trademark is up for grabs

To avoid getting sued for trademark infringement and possibly suffering through its consequences (the cost of litigation, having to change your trade name or trademark, or paying damages), conduct a trademark search before you settle on a trade name. You want to find out if there are any potential conflicts between your trade name and someone else's. Ideally, you conduct the search before you actually use your trade name or register for an official trademark.

"If you don't have a registered trademark, your trade name becomes very difficult to protect," comments David Adler, the attorney quoted in the introduction to this chapter. "It's a good idea to do a basic search on the Internet. But keep in mind that just because you don't find a name on the Internet doesn't mean it doesn't exist. Follow that up with a trademark search. You don't want to spend all the money required to develop a brand name only to find that it isn't yours."

There are three ways you can do a trademark search:

- ✔ **Search the old-fashioned, manual way by visiting one of the Patent and Trademark Depository Libraries.** They're listed online at www.uspto.gov/products/library/ptdl/locations/index.jsp. Although time-consuming, this approach doesn't cost anything.

- ✔ **Pay a professional search firm to do the research for you.** Look for professional search firms in the Yellow Pages under Trademark Consultants or Information Brokers. (You can also try SuperPages.com at www.superpages.com/yellowpages/C-Trademark+Consultants+&+Searches.) You can expect to pay $25–$50 per trademark searched. More complete searches that cover registered and unregistered marks that are similar to the one you want to use can cost several hundred dollars.

- ✔ **Conduct a search online.** You can use the web to help you conduct a trademark search. The best place to go is TESS, the U.S. Patent and Trademark Office's federal trademark database. It's convenient and free. Just go to www.uspto.gov and click Search for Trademarks.

Cyberspace goes beyond national boundaries. A trademark search in your own country may not be enough. Most industrialized countries, including the United States, have signed international treaties that enable trademark owners in one country to enforce their rights against infringement by individuals in another country. Conducting an international trademark search is difficult to do yourself, so you may want to pay someone to do the searching for you.

The consequences of failing to conduct a reasonably thorough trademark search can be severe. In part, the consequences depend on how widely you distribute the protected item. For example, on the Internet, one may determine that you have distributed it worldwide. If you attempt to use a trademark that's been federally registered by someone else, you could go to court and be prevented from using the trademark again. You may even be liable for damages and attorney's fees. So it's best to be careful.

Protecting your trade name

The legal standard is that you get the rights to your trade name when you begin using it. You get the right to exclude others from using it when you register. But when you apply to register a trademark, you record the date of its first use. Effectively, then, the day you start using a name is when you actually obtain the rights to use it for trade.

In addition to a federal trademark law, each state has its own set of laws establishing when and how trademarks can be protected. You can obtain trademark rights in the states in which the mark is actually used, but attorney Adler says a federally registered trademark can trump such rights. It's important to also file an application with the U.S. Patent and Trademark Office, but only if your trademark will be used beyond your state's borders. You are eligible to apply for national registration of your trademark only if you plan to use your trademark in interstate commerce.

After researching your trade name against existing trademarks, you can file an application with the Patent and Trademark Office online by following these steps:

1. **Go to the Trademark Electronic Application System (TEAS) home page (**www.uspto.gov/trademarks/teas/index.jsp**), as shown in Figure 17-2.**

   This page includes links to forms and instructions on how to fill out your application online.

2. **Click the Initial Application Form link, which is on the page under the Forms heading.**

   A page with a list of application forms appears.

3. **Click the Trademark/Servicemark Application, Principal Register link.**

   The Selection of Application Type page appears.

4. **Choose the type of form that applies to you and click Continue.**

   The Trademark/Servicemark Application Form Wizard page appears.

5. **Fill out the Applicant Information form and click Continue.**

   The Mark Information page appears.

6. **Enter the trademark in the box provided and click Continue.**

   The Goods and/or Services Information page appears.

7. **Click the Add Goods/Services button, enter any goods or services you provide that are associated with your trademark, and click Continue.**

   A form entitled Correspondence Information appears.

8. **Review the correspondence information, make any corrections needed, and click Continue.**

   The Signature Information page appears.

9. **Type your signature, date, and position, and click the Validate button at the bottom of the form.**

   If you filled out all the fields correctly, a Validation screen appears. If not, you return to the original form page so that you can correct it.

10. **Print the special declaration to support the adoption of the electronic signature and retain it for your records; then click the Submit button.**

    You receive a confirmation screen if your transmission is successful. Later, you receive an e-mail acknowledgment of your submission.

Generally, each state has its own trademark laws, which apply only to trademarks that are used within a single state. Products that are sold in more than one state (such as those sold on the Internet) can be protected under the federal Lanham Act, which provides for protection of registered trademarks. To comply with the Lanham Act, register your trademark, as I describe in the preceding steps.

Trademark registration can take 18–24 months. It's not uncommon to have an application returned. Often, an applicant receives a correspondence called an *Office Action* that either rejects part of the application or raises a question about it. If you receive such a letter, don't panic. You need to go to a lawyer who specializes in or is familiar with trademark law and who can help you respond to the correspondence. In the meantime, you can still operate your business with your trade name. You can also fill out and submit a form that communicates your intent to use a trademark, which enables you to use a trademark before it's registered.

Trademarks listed in the USPTO register can last indefinitely provided you follow all of the maintenance requirements. You don't have to use the ™ or ® symbol when you publish your trademark, but doing so not only impresses upon people how seriously you take your business and its identity, but affords you certain remedies should someone else infringe your trademark.

Making sure your domain name stays yours

The practice of choosing a domain name for an online business is related to the concept of trade names and trademarks. By now, with cybersquatters and other businesspeople snapping up domain names since 1994 or so, it's unlikely that your ideal name is available in the popular .com domain. Here are two common problems:

- ✔ Someone else has already taken the domain name related to the name of your existing business.

- ✔ The domain name you choose is close to one that already exists or to another company with a similar name. (Remember the Microsoft Windows/Lindows.com dispute that I mention early in this chapter.)

If a domain name is already taken, you have some options. You can contact the owner of the domain name and offer to buy it. Alternatively, you can choose a domain name with another suffix. If a dot-com name isn't available, try the old standby alternatives, .org (which, in theory at least, is for non-profit organizations) and .net (which is for network providers).

You can also choose one of the newer *Top-Level Domains* (TLDs), a second set of domain name suffixes that were made available a few years ago, which include .biz for businesses, .info for general use, and .name for personal names. You can find out more about the more recent TLDs at the InterNIC website (www.internic.net/faqs/new-tlds.html).

You can always get around the fact that your perfect domain name isn't available by changing the name slightly. For example, rather than `treesurgeon.com`, you might choose `tree-surgeon.com` or `treesurgery.com`. But be careful lest you violate someone else's trademark and get into a dispute with the holder of the other domain name. A court may order you to stop using the name and pay damages to the other domain name's owner.

On the other hand, if you've been doing business for a while and have a trademark you feel has superior rights, you may find that someone else owns the domain name. You can assert your rights and raise a dispute yourself. To resolve the dispute, you could go to a group such as the WIPO Arbitration and Mediation Center (`arbiter.wipo.int/center/index.html`) or ICANN, the Internet Corporation for Assigned Names and Numbers (`www.icann.org`). But first, find out more about what constitutes trademark infringement and how to enforce a trademark. Go to Nolo.com's Legal Encyclopedia (`www.nolo.com/legal-encyclopedia`); scroll down and click the Intellectual Property Law: Patent, Copyright & Trademark section; click the Trademark Law link; click After You Register Your Trademark; and then click Enforcing Your Trademark Rights rather than Practicing Safe Copyright.

What's the difference between a trademark and a copyright? *Trademarks* are covered by trademark law and are distinctive words, symbols, slogans, or other things that serve to identify products or services in the marketplace. *Copyright* refers to the creator's ownership of creative works, such as writing, art, software, video, or cinema (but not names, titles, or short phrases). Copyright also provides the owner with redress in case someone copies the work without the owner's permission. Copyright is a legal device that enables the creator of a work to control how the work is used.

Although copyright protects the way ideas, systems, and processes are embodied in the book, record, photo, or whatever, it doesn't protect the idea, system, or process itself. In other words, if Abraham Lincoln were writing the Gettysburg Address today, his exact words could be copyrighted, but the general ideas he expressed couldn't be.

Even if nobody ever called you a nerd, as a businessperson who produces goods and services of economic value, you may be the owner of intellectual property. *Intellectual property* is a broad descriptor and not only can refer to works of authorship, but also includes trademarks, inventions, trade secrets, and other proprietary information. Because intellectual property can be owned, bought, and sold just like other types of property, it's important that you know something about the laws governing intellectual property. Having this information maximizes the value of your products and keeps you from throwing away potentially valuable assets or finding yourself at the wrong end of an expensive lawsuit.

Fair use . . . and how not to abuse it

Copyright law doesn't cover everything. One of the major limitations is the doctrine of *fair use,* which is described in Section 107 of the U.S. Copyright Act. The law states that fair use of a work is use that doesn't infringe copyright "for purposes such as criticism, comment, news reporting, teaching (including multiple copies for classroom use), scholarship, or research." You can't copy text from online magazines or newsletters and call it fair use because the text was originally news reporting.

Fair use has some big gray areas that can be traps for people who provide information on the Internet. Don't fall into one of these traps. Shooting off a quick e-mail asking someone for permission to reproduce his or her work isn't difficult. Chances are that person will be flattered and let you make a copy as long as you give him or her credit on your site. Fair use depends entirely on the unique circumstances of each case, and this is an area in which, if you have any questions, you should consult with an attorney.

Counting on copyright

These days, the controversy regarding copyright on the web centers on the Digital Millennium Copyright Act (DMCA), which covers all forms of digital content on the Internet. Among other things, the DMCA calls for Internet radio stations to pay high royalty fees to record labels for music they play. The DMCA contains at least one provision that has implications for all online businesses: Internet service providers (ISPs) are expected to remove material from any customer websites that appears to constitute copyright infringement. So it pays to know something about copyright.

Everything you see on the Internet is copyrighted, whether or not a copyright notice actually appears. Copyright exists from the moment a work is fixed in a tangible medium, including a web page. For example, plenty of art is available for the taking on the web, but look before you grab. Unless an image on the web is specified as being copyright free, you violate copyright law if you take it. HTML tags themselves aren't copyrighted, but the content of the HTML-formatted page is. General techniques for designing web pages aren't copyrighted, but certain elements (such as logos, which are essentially trademarks) are.

It's okay to use a work for criticism, comment, news reporting, teaching, scholarship, or research. That comes under the fair use limitation. (See the next sidebar, "Fair use . . . and how not to abuse it," for more information.) However, I still contend that it's best to get permission or cite your source in these cases, just to be safe.

Making copyright work for you

A copyright — which protects original works of authorship — costs nothing, applies automatically, and lasts more than 50 years. When you affix a copyright notice to your newsletter or website, you make your readers think twice about unauthorized copying and put them on notice that you take copyright seriously. You can go a step farther and register your work with the U.S. Copyright Office.

Creating a good copyright notice

Even though any work you do is protected automatically by copyright, having some sort of notice expresses your copyright authority in a more official way. Copyright notices identify the author of a given work (such as writing or software) and then spell out the terms by which that author grants others the right (or the *license*) to copy that work to their computer and read it (or use it). The usual copyright notice is pretty simple and takes this form:

```
Copyright 2013 [Your Name]. All rights reserved.
```

You don't have to use the © symbol, but it does make your notice look more official. In order to create a copyright symbol that appears on a web page, you have to enter a special series of characters in the HTML source code for your page. For example, web browsers translate the characters `&copy;` as the copyright symbol, which is displayed as © in the web browser window. Most web page creation tools provide menu options for inserting special symbols such as this one.

Copyright notices can also be more informal, and a personal message can have extra impact. ESA/Hubble, which operates the Hubble space telescope, has a web page devoted to how others can reproduce its incredible images of the universe (www.spacetelescope.org/copyright).

Creative Commons has extensive information about how to make your work available to others either on a "fair use" basis or for commercial use. See `wiki.creativecommons.org/Main_Page` for more information.

Protecting your products with digital watermarks

In traditional offset printing, a *watermark* is a faint image embedded in stationery or other paper. The watermark usually bears the name of the paper manufacturer, but it can also identify an organization for which the stationery was made.

Watermarking has its equivalent in the online world. Graphic artists sometimes use *digital watermarking* to protect images they create. This process involves adding copyright or other information about the image's owner to the digital image file. This information may or may not be visible. (Some images have copyright information added; it's not visible in the body of the web page but in the image file itself.) Other images have a watermark pasted right into the visible area, which makes it difficult for others to copy and reuse them. Digimarc (www.digimarc.com), which functions as a plug-in application with the popular graphics tools Adobe Photoshop (www.adobe.com) and PaintShop Pro (www.corel.com), is one of the most widely used watermarking tools.

Doing the paperwork on your copyright

You have copyright over the materials you publish on the web, but there's a difference between having a copyright and having a *registered copyright*. Registering your copyright is something I recommend for small businesses because it's inexpensive, easy to do, and affords you an extra degree of protection. Having registered your copyright gives your case more weight in the event of a copyright dispute. It enables you to claim statutory damages of $150,000 if you can prove that an infringement occurred. You don't need to register, but doing so shows a court how serious you are about obtaining protection for your work.

Registering copyright is a breeze compared to the process of registering a trademark. To register your work, you can download a short application form from the U.S. Copyright Office website at www.copyright.gov/forms. This form is in Adobe Acrobat PDF format, so you need Acrobat Reader to view it. (Adobe Acrobat Reader is a free application that you can download at www.adobe.com.) You can then send the form by snail mail, along with a check for $65 and a printed copy of the work you're protecting, to Library of Congress, Copyright Office, 101 Independence Ave., S.E., Washington, DC 20559-6000. (You can also file online for $35.)

Licensing and Other Restrictions

Another set of legal concerns that you must be aware of when you start an online business involves any license fees or restrictions that are levied by local agencies. Some fees are specific to businesses that have incorporated, which brings up the question of whether you should consider incorporation for your own small business. (I discuss the legal concerns and pros and cons of incorporation in the "Deciding on a Legal Form for Your Business" section, later in this chapter.)

Heeding local regulations

Before you get too far along with your online business, make sure that you've met any local licensing requirements that apply. For example, in my county in the state of Illinois, I had to pay a $10 fee to register my sole proprietorship. In return, I received a nice certificate that made everything feel official.

Other localities may have more stringent requirements, however. Check with your city, county, and state licensing and/or zoning offices. Trade associations for your profession often have a wealth of information about local regulations as well. Also, check with your local chamber of commerce. If you fail to apply for a permit or license, you may find yourself paying substantial fines.

The kinds of local regulations to which a small business may be susceptible include the following:

- ✔ **Zoning:** Your city or town government may have *zoning ordinances* that prevent you from conducting business in an area that is zoned for residential use, or it may charge you a fee to operate a business out of your home. This policy varies by community; even if your web host resides in another state, your local government may still consider your home the location of your business. Check with your local zoning department.

- ✔ **Doing Business As:** If your business name is different from your own name, you may have to file a Doing Business As (DBA) certificate and publish a notice of the filing in the local newspaper. Check with your city or county clerk's office for more information.

- ✔ **Taxes:** Some states and cities levy taxes on small businesses, and some even levy property tax on business assets, such as office furniture and computer equipment.

Knowing what restrictions may affect your trade

If you're planning to sell your goods and services overseas, be aware of any trade restrictions that may apply to your business. In particular, you need to be careful if any of the following applies:

- ✔ You trade in foodstuffs or agricultural products.
- ✔ You sell software that uses some form of encryption.
- ✔ Your clients live in countries with which your home country has imposed trade restrictions.

Avoiding Conflicts with Your Customers

There are several ways you can get into legal trouble with the very people you rely on for your business success:

✔ **You fail to deliver something that a customer purchased.** The customer can seek a refund from the marketplace through which you sell (eBay, for example). Organizations such as eBay have dispute resolution processes available to resolve customer disputes. If you are found liable, you must issue a refund or you'll be blocked from using the marketplace again.

✔ **You deliver late, or the merchandise isn't what you described.** The customer can complain to the marketplace and leave bad feedback for you, which can damage your reputation.

✔ **You send out "spam," or unsolicited e-mail.** In severe cases, the government can go after you and arrest you. This has happened with spammers found guilty of sending out millions of unwanted e-mail messages (see www.msnbc.msn.com/id/18955115 for an example).

✔ **You fail to safeguard your customers' personal information.** Hackers can rifle through unsecured computers and steal credit card numbers. Depending on the type of business you run, a number of government agencies can come after you for allowing identify theft to happen. As an example, you can see the list of financial consumer alerts from the State of Washington's Department of Financial Institutions at www.dfi. wa.gov/consumers/alerts.htm.

Offending your customers can have consequences for your business that go beyond legal trouble. People who aren't happy with you can leave comments on message boards that hurt your reputation. In some cases, disgruntled consumers sometimes go to the effort of creating web pages such as I Hate Starbucks (www.ihatestarbucks.com) to voice their anger at a merchant.

Deciding on a Legal Form for Your Business

Picking a legal form for your online business enables you to describe it to city and county agencies as well as to the financial institutions you deal with. A legal type of business is one that is recognized by taxing and licensing agencies. You have a number of options to choose among, and the choice can affect the amount of taxes you pay and your liability in case of loss. The following sections describe your alternatives.

If you're looking for more information, Eric Tyson and Jim Schell explore the legal and financial aspects of starting and operating a small business in *Small Business For Dummies,* 4th Edition.

Sole proprietorship

In a *sole proprietorship,* you're the only boss. You make all the decisions and get all the benefits. You take all the risk, too. This is the simplest and least expensive type of business because you can run it yourself. You don't need an accountant or lawyer to help you form the business, and you don't have to answer to partners or stockholders, either. To declare a sole proprietorship, you may have to file an application with your county clerk.

Partnership

In a *partnership,* you share the risk and profit with at least one other person. Ideally, your partners bring skills to the endeavor that complement your own. One obvious advantage to a partnership is that you can discuss decisions and problems with your partners. All partners are held personally liable for losses. The rate of taxes each partner pays is based on his or her percentage of income from the partnership.

If you decide to strike up a partnership with someone, drawing up a *partnership agreement* is a good idea. Although you aren't legally required to do so, such an agreement clearly spells out the duration of the partnership and the responsibilities of each person involved. Without such an agreement, the division of liabilities and assets is considered to be equal, regardless of how much more effort one person has put into the business than the other.

Advantages of a statutory business entity

A *statutory business entity* is a business whose form is created by statute, such as a corporation or a limited liability company (LLC). If sole proprietorships and partnerships are so simple to start and operate, why would you consider incorporating? After all, you almost certainly need a lawyer to help you incorporate. Plus, you have to comply with the regulations made by federal and state agencies that oversee corporations. Besides that, you may undergo a type of *double taxation:* If your corporation earns profits, those profits are taxed at the corporate rate, and any shareholders have to pay income tax at the personal rate.

Despite these downsides, you may consider incorporation for the following reasons:

- ✔ If you have employees, you can deduct any health and disability insurance premiums you pay for them. (As a sole proprietor, you can deduct your own health insurance premiums.)
- ✔ You can raise capital by offering stock for sale.

✔ It's easier to transfer ownership from one shareholder to another.

✔ The company's principals are shielded from liability in case of lawsuits.

If you offer services that may be susceptible to costly lawsuits, incorporation or forming an LLC may be the way to go. If you choose a corporation, you then have two options: a subchapter S corporation or a C corporation. Although it depends on many factors, the LLC is a good choice for many small businesses. Because there can be only one shareholder/owner— you— it may give you more flexibility in the structure and formalities the LLC may be required to keep over incorporation.

Subchapter S corporations

One benefit of forming a subchapter S corporation is liability protection. This form of incorporation enables startup businesses that encounter losses early on to offset those losses against their personal income. Subchapter S is intended for businesses with fewer than 75 shareholders. The income gained by an S corporation is subject only to personal tax, not to corporate tax.

You might designate that you're the president, your cousin Nick is the secretary, and other relatives serve as your shareholders and officers. Many corporations that are run by one or two people have only one shareholder(s) meeting a year, which may be simply a document signed by all of the shareholders stating that the meeting took place and reporting on what happened. While an experienced attorney can make this procedure painless (of course, it comes with attorney fees), it can be accomplished by the business principals as well.

Sounds great, doesn't it? Before you start looking for a lawyer to get you started, consider the following:

✔ Incorporation typically costs several hundred dollars.

✔ Depending on your state, corporations may have to pay an annual fee or tax.

✔ Attorneys' fees can be expensive.

✔ It can take weeks or months for your filing for S corporation status to be received and approved. (You need to meet your state's requirements for setting up a corporation and then file IRS tax Form 2553 to elect S corporation status.)

All these facts can be daunting for a lone entrepreneur who's just starting out and has only a few customers. But my brother Mike, who owns an audio restoration business called lp2cdsolutions (`www.lp2cdsolutions.com`), did create an S corporation, so his liability is limited: In case of a lawsuit, assuming that no illegal conduct occurs on the part of the owner, the corporation is sued, not him personally. I recommend that you wait until you have enough income to hire an attorney and pay incorporation fees before you seriously consider incorporating, even as an S corporation.

C corporations

Any small business that incorporates is considered a C corporation unless it files to be considered an S corporation. Given the double taxation I mention earlier, you need to be sure you intend to be a C corporation (for various reasons) or make the appropriate filings with the IRS, which is a time-sensitive matter. Being a C corporation is probably not right for your small entrepreneurial business, but if you neglect to follow the appropriate procedure, you may become one whether you meant to or not.

Most C corporations tend to be large and have lots of shareholders. To incorporate, all stockholders and shareholders must agree on the name of the corporation, the people who will manage it, and many other issues. Because of the double taxation in connection with C corporations, contact a tax professional if you have questions about this business entity or are thinking of creating one.

Limited liability companies

The limited liability company (LLC) has been around for some time now but compared with the corporation, it is a relatively new type of entity structure that combines aspects of both partnerships and corporations. The government fees required to create an LLC vary depending on your state and that doesn't include an attorney's fees should you choose to hire one to form your LLC. You may also (like the corporate form) have to pay a yearly fee to maintain your LLC. And you may need to have yearly meetings at which you report on the state of the corporation. However, LLCs have some attractive options that make them good candidates for small businesses:

- ✔ Members have limited liability for debts and obligations of the LLC.
- ✔ LLCs are not double taxed.
- ✔ The individual investors, or *members,* share income and losses.

When an LLC is comprised of more than one owner, the responsibilities of the LLC members are spelled out in an *operating agreement,* an often-complex document that should be prepared by a knowledgeable attorney. If the LLC is comprised of a single member, such responsibilities are embodied in an *operating declaration.*

AllBusiness.com has published an article titled "How Much Does It Cost to Incorporate?" that details more costs related to incorporation. Check it out at www.allbusiness.com/legal/contracts-agreements-incorporation/ 2531-1.html.

Chapter 18

Online Business Accounting Tools

*I*n tough economic times, it's more important than ever to keep track of expenses, record financial information, and perform other fiscal functions. It's even more important to know some basic accounting procedures, especially those that relate to an online business.

Without having at least some minimal records of your day-to-day operations, you won't have any way — other than the proverbial "gut feeling" — of knowing whether your business is truly successful. Besides that, banks and taxing authorities don't put much stock in gut feelings. When you have to ask for a loan or pay taxes, you'll regret not having records close at hand. Even if you sell on eBay, you can't rely on the auction site to keep all your business records for you, and PayPal doesn't record payments by check or money order. And accurate record keeping is essential when revenues dwindle and expenses must be reduced.

In this chapter, I introduce you to some simple, straightforward ways to handle your online business's financial information. Read on to discover the most important accounting practices and software that can help you tackle the essential fiscal tasks you need to undertake to keep your new business viable.

ABCs: Accounting Basics for Commerce

The most important accounting practices for your online business are the following:

- ✔ **Deciding what type of business you are:** Will you be a sole proprietorship, partnership, or corporation? (See Chapter 17 for more about determining the legal status of your business.)

- ✔ **Establishing good record-keeping practices:** Record expenses and income in ways that can help you at tax time.

- ✔ **Obtaining financing when you need it:** Although getting started in an online business doesn't cost a lot, you may want to expand someday, and good accounting can help you do it.

There's nothing sexy about accounting (unless, of course, you're married to an accountant; in that case, you have a financial expert at hand and can skip this chapter!). Then again, unexpected cash shortages or other problems that can result from bad record keeping are no fun, either.

Good accounting is the key to managing your business. How else can you know how you're doing? Yet many new businesspeople are intimidated by the numbers game. Use the tool at hand — your computer — to help you overcome your fear: Start keeping those books!

Choosing an accounting method

Accepting that you have to keep track of your business's accounting is only half the battle; next, you need to decide how to do it. How and when you record your business transactions make a difference not only to your accountant but also to agencies such as the Internal Revenue Service (IRS). Even if you hire someone to keep the books for you, it's good to know what your options are.

You don't have to take my word for all this. Consult the Internal Revenue Service Publication 334, Tax Guide for Small Business (www.irs.gov/pub/irs-pdf/p334.pdf). Review Section 2, Accounting Periods and Methods, which explains how to do everything right when tax time comes. Also check out the Accounting System section of the CCH Business Owner's Toolkit site (www.toolkit.cch.com/text/P06_1300.asp).

Using cash-basis versus accrual-basis accounting

Don't be intimidated by these terms: They're simply two methods of totaling income and expenses. Exactly where and how you do the recording is up to you. You can take a piece of paper, divide it into two columns labeled Income and Expenses, and do it that way. (I describe some higher-tech tools later in this chapter.) Here are two standard ways of reporting income and expenses:

- ✔ **Cash-basis accounting:** You report income when you actually receive it and write off expenses when you pay them. This is the easy way to report income and expenses, and probably the way most new small businesses do it.

- ✔ **Accrual-basis accounting:** This method is more complicated than the cash-basis method, but if your online business maintains an inventory, you must use the accrual method. You report income when you actually receive the payment; you write down expenses *when services are rendered* (even though you may not have made the cash payment yet). For example, if a payment is due on December 1, but you send the check on December 8, you record the bill as being paid on December 1, when the payment was originally due.

Accrual-basis accounting creates a more accurate picture of a business's financial situation. If a business has cash-flow problems and is extending payments on some of its bills, cash-basis accounting provides an unduly rosy financial picture, whereas the accrual-basis method is more accurate.

Choosing an accounting period

The other choice you need to make when deciding how to keep your books is the accounting period you intend to use. Here again, you have two choices:

- ✔ **Calendar year:** The calendar year ends December 31. This is the period you're probably most familiar with and the one most small or home-based businesses choose because it's the easiest to work with.

- ✔ **Fiscal year:** In this case, the business picks a date other than December 31 to function as the end of its fiscal year. Many large organizations pick a date that coincides with the end of their business cycle. Some pick March 31 as the end, others June 30, and still others September 30.

If you use the fiscal-year method of accounting, you must file your tax return three and a half months after the end of the fiscal year. If the fiscal year ends on June 30, for example, you must file by October 15.

Knowing what records to keep

When you run your own business, it pays to be meticulous about recording everything that pertains to your commercial activities. The more you understand what you have to record, the more accurate your records will be — and the more deductions you can take, too. Go to an office supply store and get a bookkeeping record book that's set up with columns for income and expenses.

I know what you're thinking: printed record books? Who uses those anymore? As an alternative, search your app store. Apple's JustAddMoney Expense Tracker helps you set up accounts and record expenses. For Android users, Easy Money - Expense Manager is available in Google Play.

Tracking income

You need to keep track of your company's income (or, as it's sometimes called, your *gross receipts*) carefully. Not all the income your business receives is taxable. What you receive as a result of sales (your *revenue*) is taxable, but loans that you receive aren't. Be sure to separate the two and pay tax only on the sales income. But keep good records: If you can't accurately report the source of income that you didn't pay taxes on, the IRS labels it *unreported income,* and you have to pay taxes and possibly fines and penalties on it.

Just how should you record your revenue? For each item you sell, write down a brief, informal statement on a slip of paper or even on the back of a canceled check. Be sure to include the following information:

- ✔ Amount received
- ✔ Type of payment (credit card, electronic cash, or check)
- ✔ Date of the transaction
- ✔ Name and description of the item purchased, including model number or other applicable information
- ✔ Name of client or customer
- ✔ Goods or services you provided in exchange for the payment

Collect all your check stubs and revenue statements in a folder labeled Income so that you can find them easily at tax time.

Assessing your assets

Assets are resources that your business owns, such as your office and computer equipment. *Equity* is your remaining assets after you pay your creditors.

Any equipment you have that contributes to your business activities constitutes your assets. Equipment that has a life span of more than a year is expected to help you generate income over its useful life; therefore, you must spread out (or *expense)* the original cost of the equipment over its life span. Expensing the cost of an asset over the period of its useful life is *depreciation.* To depreciate an item, estimate how many years you're going to use it and then divide the original cost by the number of years. The result is the amount that you report in any given year. For example, if you purchase a computer that costs $3,000 and you expect to use it in your business for five years, you expense $600 of the cost each year.

Keep records of your assets that include the following information:

- Name, model number, and description
- Purchase date
- Purchase price, including fees
- Date the item went into service
- Amount of time the item is put to personal (as opposed to business) use

File these records in a safe location along with your other tax-related information.

Recording payments

Even a lone entrepreneur doesn't work in a vacuum. An online business owner needs to pay a web host, an ISP, and possibly web page designers as well as other consultants. If you take on partners or employees, things get more complicated. But in general, you need to record all payments such as these in detail as well.

Your accountant is likely to ask how you pay the people who work for you. You have two options: You can treat them either as full- or part-time employees or as independent contractors. The IRS uses a stringent series of guidelines to determine who is a contractor and who is a full-time employee. Refer to IRS Publication 15A (`www.irs.gov/pub/irs-pdf/p15a.pdf`), which discusses the employee/independent contractor subject in detail.

Hiring independent contractors rather than salaried workers is far simpler for you: You don't have to pay benefits to independent contractors, and you don't have to withhold federal and state taxes. Just be sure to get invoices from any independent contractor who works for you. If you have full-time employees whom you pay an hourly wage, consult an accountant to help you set up the salary payments.

Listing expenses

When you break down business expenses on Schedule C (Profit or Loss from Business) of your federal tax return, you need to keep track of two kinds of expenses:

- The first type of expenses (simply dubbed Expenses in Part II of Schedule C) includes travel, business meals, advertisements, postage, and other costs that you incur in order to *produce revenue*.
- The second kind of expenses (grouped under Other Expenses in Part V of Schedule C) includes instances when you're just exchanging one asset (cash) for another (a printer or modem, for example).

The difference between Expenses and Other Expenses lies in how close the relationship is between the expense and revenue produced. In the case of Part II Expenses, your expenditure is directly related; you wouldn't take out an advertisement or take a business trip if you didn't expect it to produce revenue. In the second case, the act of spending money doesn't directly result in more revenue for you. You would purchase a modem, for example, to help you communicate and get information online, not just to boost your bottom line. You do *hope,* though, that the equipment being purchased does *eventually* help you produce revenue.

Get a big folder and use it to hold any receipts, contracts, canceled checks, credit card statements, or invoices that represent expenses. It's also a great idea to maintain a record of expenses that includes the following information:

- ✔ Date the expense occurred
- ✔ Name of the person or company that received payment from you
- ✔ Type of expense incurred (equipment, utilities, supplies, and so on)

It's often difficult to recall what some receipts were for a year or even a month after the fact. Be sure to jot down a quick note on all canceled checks and copies of receipts to remind you what the expense involved.

Understanding the Ps and Qs of P&Ls

You're likely to hear the term *profit and loss statement* (also called a P&L) thrown around when discussing your online business with financial people. A P&L is a report that measures the operation of a business over a given period of time, such as a week, a month, or a year. The person who prepares the P&L (either you or your accountant) adds up your business revenues and subtracts the operating expenses. What's left are either the profits or the losses.

Most of the accounting programs I discuss in the following sections include some way of presenting profit and loss statements and enable you to customize the statements to fit your needs.

Accounting Software for Your Business

After rummaging through piles of receipts and records stuffed into a big manila envelope, my tax preparer gently but firmly urged me to start using some accounting software so that the records could be retrieved more easily next time. Ever since, I've been happy that I took his advice. I urge you to do the same. These days, you have lots of options for software that can help you record and organize your financial information. The programs break into four general categories:

 ✔ Simple, small-scale programs such as Owl Simple Business Accounting

 ✔ Bigger, full-featured programs such as Quicken, QuickBooks, and MYOB

 ✔ Online versions of the bigger, full-featured programs

 ✔ Apps that perform basic accounting tasks on mobile devices

The online versions are ones that you use on the web; you don't have to install any software on your computer. On the other hand, you do have to store your financial information on another website (not yours) when you use an online program. But all these options have one thing in common: They give you a user-friendly way to store your information and perform calculations on it. I present some examples in the rest of this section.

Easy-to-use, full-featured software: OWL Simple Business Accounting

The well-known, commercial accounting packages, such as Quicken, QuickBooks, and MYOB, let you prepare statements and reports and even tie into a tax preparation system. Stick with these programs if you like setting up systems, such as databases, on your computer. Otherwise, go for a simpler method and hire an accountant to help you.

Whatever program you choose, make sure you can keep accurate books and set up privacy as well as backup schemes that prevent your kids from accessing and possibly even deleting your business records.

If your business is a relatively simple sole proprietorship, you can record expenses and income by hand and add them up at tax time. Then carry them through to Schedule C or IRS Form 1040. Alternatively, you can record your entries and turn them over to a tax advisor who prepares a profit and loss statement and tells you the balance due on your tax payment.

If you're looking to save a few dollars and want an extra-simple accounting program that you can set up right now, a good option is Owl Simple Business Accounting 4 (www.owlsoftware.com/sba.htm), available for Windows 95 through Windows 8. Mac users can try FinanceToGo by Bert Torfs (www.rocketdownload.com/query.php?q=double-entry).

Keeping it simple: QuickBooks Simple Start

One of the big commercial accounting software programs, Intuit, has released a "simple" version of its popular QuickBooks software. The package is called Intuit QuickBooks Simple Start, and you can register for it at http://quickbooks.intuit.com. The program works through your web browser, so it's compatible with any operating system that has an Internet browser, whether it's PC-, Mac-, or Linux-based. It's free for 30 days, and as of this writing, costs $12.95 per month after that.

The following steps illustrate how easy it is to start keeping books with Simple Start:

1. **Point your web browser to** `http://quickbooks.intuit.com` **and click the Try It Free button.**

   A page appears that prompts you to register with an e-mail address and password.

2. **Type your e-mail address and password and then click Go.**

   Follow the steps presented on the next three screens to complete your registration (which is free):

   a. *Choose the simplest version of the software, QuickBooks Online Simple Start.*

   b. *Read the instructions and click the Sign In button included in the e-mail sent by Intuit when you're ready to start.*

   c. *Sign in with the User ID and password you just created.*

   If you're using a desktop computer, the window shown in Figure 18-1 appears. (The mobile version is simpler and is shown later in these steps.)

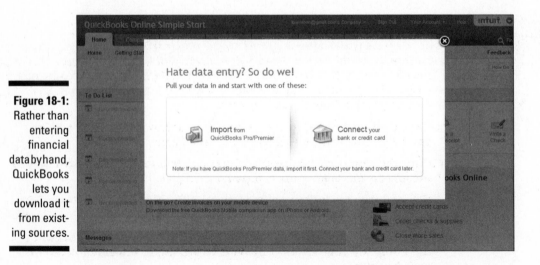

Figure 18-1: Rather than entering financial data by hand, QuickBooks lets you download it from existing sources.

3. **If you want to download existing information, such as your credit card records, into QuickBooks Online, click either the Import or Connect button and follow the prompts.**

   (If you don't want to download your existing data, click the X in the upper-right corner to close the window.)

   The QuickBooks Online Simple Start home page shown in Figure 18-2 opens and explains the different options.

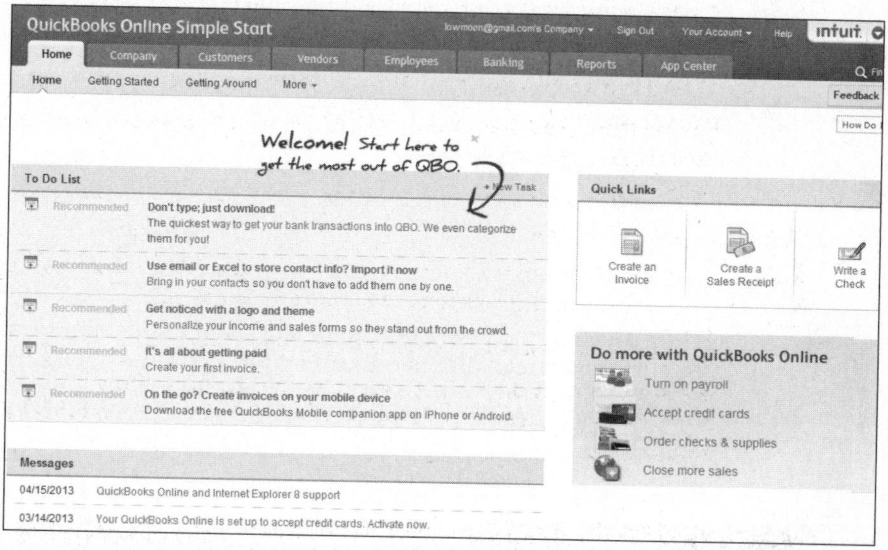

Figure 18-2: QuickBooks Online Simple Start gives you a variety of options to get started.

Simple Start comes with extensive Help files to get you accustomed to its features. Click Help or How Do I? near the right side of the home page to get a jump start on using the program. Or click Getting Started to find out more about how to keep records.

4. **Click Getting Around to get a visual map of how this online service can help you keep financial records (see Figure 18-3).**

5. **Click the Company tab, next to the Home tab, to view the expense and income accounts for your company.**

   You can click the buttons at the bottom of the Company tab (New, Edit, Delete, and so on) to change the list of the accounts.

6. **Click any of the rows and then click the Edit button at the bottom of the Company page to enter income, expenses, or information about your business.**

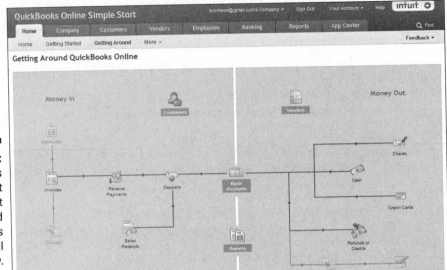

Figure 18-3:
QuickBooks
Simple Start
helps get
you started
with this
visual
overview.

7. **When you are ready to enter data such as a cash expenditure for supplies, for instance, click the Banking tab and then click Cash Expense.**

   The Cash Expense window appears, as shown in Figure 18-4.

8. **Click the down arrow next to Cash Account.**

   A dialog box appears that prompts you to choose the type of bank account to create.

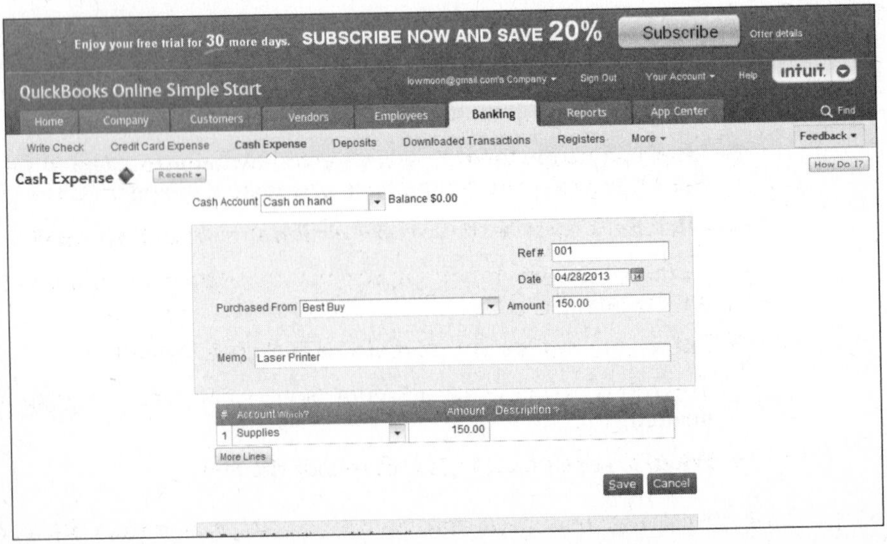

Figure 18-4:
Use a dialog
box like this
to record
expenses
and vendors
and to track
cash on
hand.

9. **For this example, click Cash on Hand and then click Next.**

    A window appears with the message What do you want to call this account?

10. **Enter a description of the account and then click Finish.**

    The window closes and you return to the Cash Expense window.

11. **Enter the information about your expense and then click Save (refer to Figure 18-4).**

12. **To record a new customer, click the Customer tab; then either click Import to import customer data from a file or click New Customer.**

    This example assumes you click New Customer.

    The Customer Information dialog box appears.

13. **Enter the contact information for the customer and click Save.**

    The customer's information is added to your business file. You can now choose that customer when performing subsequent tasks.

14. **To send a customer an invoice, click Invoice on the Customers tab.**

    The Invoice dialog box appears.

15. **Click the down arrow next to Customer and choose the name of the customer you just added.**

    The customer's name appears in the Customer box at the top of the Invoice dialog box.

16. **Under New Charges, in Row 1, click in the boxes underneath Product/ Service and Description and enter the type of item for which you want to bill your customer.**

    If you haven't yet defined the item, a dialog box appears, prompting you to add a description of the work and the amount.

17. **Fill out the item information as required.**

    After you define the item and choose the item from the drop-down list, the description and amount are automatically added to the invoice.

18. **Click Save to save the invoice or Send to send it by email.**

    A dialog box appears, prompting you to set up your company information for the invoice.

19. **Enter your company information and click Submit.**

    You return to the Invoice window so you can create another invoice if needed.

20. **When you're done, Sign Out to exit the site.**

After entering some data, you can click the Reports menu option and choose from among several reports that you can generate and print. As shown in

Figure 18-5, you can track customer activity, all expenses, all transactions, or product tax or accountant reports. When running the reports, be sure to select a reporting period within the current calendar year.

Accounting from anywhere: There's an app for that

For recording expenses while on a business trip or when visiting a supplier or store, you'll likely need a mobile solution. In those cases, seek out and download a mobile app for your smartphone or tablet. You can use a mobile app with these devices to record data while you're on the road and then view and analyze the full financial picture when you connect to a website with your desktop or laptop computer.

You can download an iPad/iPhone version of the QuickBooks program (described in the preceding section) from the App Store. The Finance41 mobile app syncs your data with the website application Finance41.com (`https://finance41.com`). Because I'm an Android user, I tried a free app called T2 Expense - Money Manager. The interface is exceptionally clear. After you type your name and your currency into the welcome screen, the screen shown in Figure 18-6 appears. Choose Income or Expense from the top drop-down menu, describe the expense, add a dollar amount and other information, and then click Save.

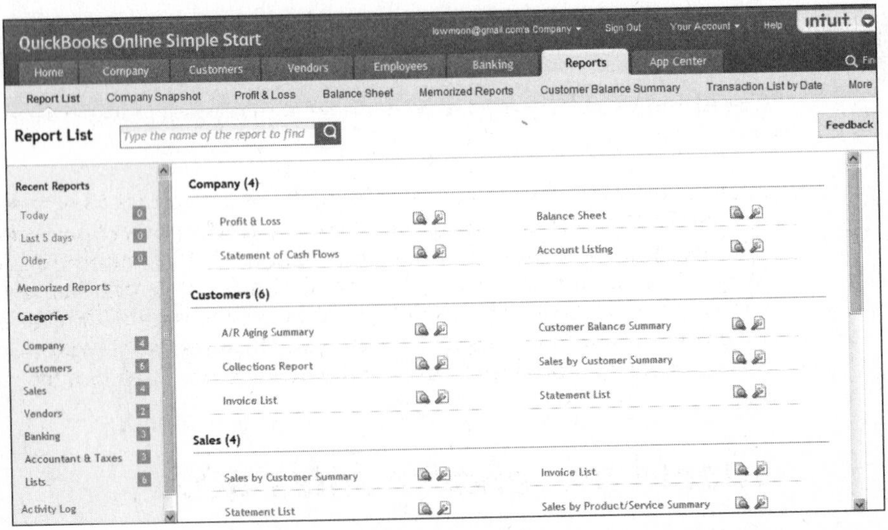

Figure 18-5: Use the Reports feature to get an idea of your business's financial health.

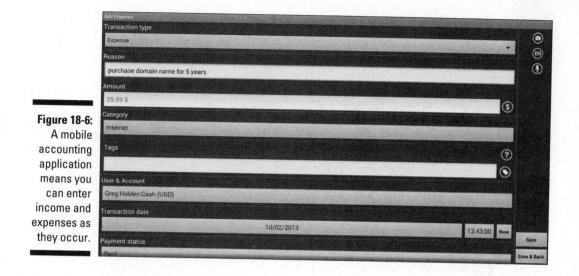

Figure 18-6:
A mobile
accounting
application
means you
can enter
income and
expenses as
they occur.

At any time, you can see a summary and run analyses on income or expenses by categories.

The Taxman Cometh: Concerns for Small Business

After you make it through the startup phase of your business, it's time to be concerned with taxes. Here, too, a little preparation can save you lots of headaches down the road. But as a hard-working entrepreneur, your biggest obstacle is time.

In an American Express survey, 26 percent reported that they wait until the last minute to start preparing their taxes, and 13.9 percent said that they usually ask for an extension. Yet advance planning is truly important for taxes. In fact, Internal Revenue Code Section 6001 mandates that businesses must keep records appropriate to their trade or business. The IRS has the right to view these records if it wants to audit your business's (or your personal) tax return. If your records don't satisfy the IRS, the penalties can be serious.

Should you charge sales tax?

This is one of the most frequently asked questions I receive from readers: Should I charge sales tax for what I sell online? The short answer is, it depends on whether your state collects sales tax at all. No single regulation applies to all states equally.

If your state doesn't collect sales tax (at this writing, five states — Montana, Alaska, Delaware, New Hampshire, and Oregon — do not), you don't need to, either. However, if your state requires it, yes, you need to collect sales tax from customers who live in the same state where your company has a "physical presence." In recent years, the pattern has been that a state's tax laws apply only within its own borders. If you're located in Ohio, for example, your business is subject to Ohio sales tax regulations, but only for transactions that are completed in Ohio.

The nature of what constitutes a "physical presence" varies. Some states define it as an office or warehouse. If you take orders only by phone or online, you don't have to collect sales tax. But again, check the regulations for your state. Also, most states require that their merchants charge sales tax on shipping and handling charges as well as the purchase price.

But things are changing. For example, if you are located outside of California and you sell to someone in that state, yes, you *do* need to collect sales tax from that California resident. In June 2011 a state law went into effect that required out-of state businesses to collect sales tax from California residents who make online purchases from them. Here are some other recent developments:

✔ In Washington, online businesses have to collect sales tax, and consumers need to pay sales tax on out-of-state purchases.

✔ New York requires its residents to calculate how much they should pay in sales tax on Internet purchases.

Because tax laws change frequently, check with your state's department of revenue to make sure.

NOLO.com maintains a page that keeps up with the latest Internet sales tax changes across the country. You can look up each state's laws by starting at `www.nolo.com/legal-encyclopedia/50-state-guide-internet-sales-tax-laws.html`. President George W. Bush signed the Internet Tax Freedom Act Amendments Act of 2007 into law on October 31, 2007. It extends the prohibitions against new taxes on Internet access and e-commerce until November 1, 2014. But as of this writing, several states have proposed state tax on Internet sales, so keep an eye on the news for further developments.

The Internet Tax Freedom Act does *not* mean that Internet sales are free from sales tax. It means only that states can't impose any new sales tax requirements on Internet merchants over and above what other merchants already have to collect in sales tax. To deal with this supposed loophole, most states charge a "use" tax in addition to a sales tax: If a resident of the state makes a purchase from another state, the transaction is still subject to use tax. But one state can't compel a merchant in another state to collect its use tax; only merchants located within the state's own borders must do so.

Sales tax varies from state to state, city to city, and county to county. Some states tax only sales of tangible personal property; others tax services as well. Not only that, but some counties and municipalities levy local taxes on sales. In my state, Illinois, I have to report my sales tax income from my eBay sales and pay it on a monthly basis, even if it amounts to only a few dollars a month. Make sure that any buyers in your state are charged the correct sales tax and that you keep records of how much you charged. Check with your local comptroller or department of revenue to find out what your requirements are.

Federal and state taxes

Although operating a business does complicate your tax return, it's something you can handle if your business is a simple one-person operation, if you're willing to spend the time and keep the proper business records.

If you have a sole proprietorship, you need to file IRS form Schedule C along with your regular form 1040 tax return. If your sole proprietorship has net income, you're also required to file Schedule SE to determine any Social Security and FICA taxes that are due.

State taxes vary depending on where you live. You most likely need to file sales tax and income tax. If you have employees, you also need to pay employee withholding tax. Contact a local accountant to find out what you have to file, or contact the state tax department yourself. Most state tax offices provide guidebooks to help you understand state tax requirements.

When you start making money for yourself independently, rather than depending on a regular paycheck from an employer, you have to start doing something you've probably never done before: estimating the tax you'll have to pay based on the income from your business. You're then required to pay this tax on a quarterly basis, both to the IRS and to your state taxing agency. Estimating and paying quarterly taxes is an important part of meeting your tax obligations as a self-employed person.

A page full of links to state tax agencies is available at www.tannedfeet.com/state_tax_agencies.htm.

Deducing your business deductions

One of the benefits of starting a new business, even if the business isn't profitable in the beginning, is the opportunity to take business deductions and reduce your tax payments. Always keep receipts from any purchases or expenses associated with your business activities. Make sure you're taking all the deductions you're eligible for. I mention some of these deductions in the following sections.

Your home office

If you work at home (and I'm assuming that as an entrepreneur, you probably do), set aside some space for a home office. This isn't just a territorial thing. It can result in some nifty business deductions, too.

Taking a home office deduction used to be difficult because a 1993 Supreme Court decision stated that unless you met with clients, customers, or patients on a regular basis in your home office, you couldn't claim the home-office deduction. However, the 1997 tax law eliminates the client requirement and requires only that the office be used "regularly and exclusively" for business.

What you deduct depends on the amount of space in your home that's used for your business. If your office consumes 96 square feet of a house with 960 square feet of living/working space, you can deduct 10 percent of your utilities, for example. However, if you have a separate phone line or cell phone that's solely for business use, you can deduct 100 percent of that expense.

Your computer equipment

Computer equipment is probably the biggest expense related to your online business. But taking tax deductions can help offset the cost substantially. The key is showing the IRS (by reporting your income from your online business on your tax return) that you used your PC and related items, such as modems or printers, for business purposes. You track what you spend on computer equipment in the Other Expenses section, which is Part V of Schedule C in your federal tax return.

In case you're ever audited, be sure to keep some sort of record detailing all the ways you use your computer equipment for business purposes.

Other common business deductions

Many of the business-related expenses you can deduct are listed on IRS form Schedule C. The following is a brief list of some of the deductions you can look for:

- Advertising fees
- Internet access charges
- Computer supplies
- Shipping and delivery
- Office supplies

Part VI
The Part of Tens

Learn more about developing a mobile business presence and ways to develop a platform at www.dummies.com/extras/startinganonlinebusiness.

In this part . . .

✔ Gain a better understanding of how to present your store or website so potential customers and clients can navigate it on mobile devices.

✔ Discover specialized services designed specifically for mobile merchants — payment systems, mobile app creators, and shopping carts.

✔ Learn what a "platform" is and how to create one via your website, social marketing, and other customer/fan base connections.

✔ Listen to my comments on my own experience selling online, misconceptions about e-commerce, and advice for new online business owners at `http://youtu.be/XqoRFhuikXo ?t=1m16s`.

Chapter 19

Ten Ways to Reach Mobile Shoppers

• •

As I write this, I just covered eBay's annual Analyst Day meeting. Its CEO spent a good portion of his opening remarks discussing not auctions, not eBay stores, but the rise of mobile commerce. If eBay realizes that a key to increasing its business in the coming years is the number of individuals around the world who use tablets and smartphones to go online, you should, too.

In this Part of Tens chapter, you get ten suggestions for making your online store just as effective with mobile shoppers as with those who are sitting at a desktop. Think about some of these things when choosing a host or designing a store; you can implement other suggestions any time to expand your customer base.

Make Your Online Store Mobile-Friendly

You've probably seen websites that look exactly the same as their big-screen counterparts. Chances are they appear slowly and are difficult to read. You've probably also seen sites that look totally different on a mobile device than they do on a desktop computer. Those are simplified, with rows of easy-to-find and easy-to-click links, few graphics, and a rudimentary layout. These appear quickly and it's easy to tap what you need.

The question is, how do you get one of those sites or storefronts that is tailored to appear easily and simply on the small screen? You can hire a programmer (an option also mentioned in the "Create an App" section, later in this chapter) or you can choose a shopping cart program or e-commerce host that does the conversion for you automatically.

A growing number of e-commerce hosts create a mobile-friendly version for you for no extra cost. They include Jimdo (www.jimdo.com), Magento (www.magento.com), Shopify (www.shopify.com), and Pinnacle Cart (www.pinnaclecart.com), to name a few. If it's important to you to have a mobile site as well as a conventional one, make sure the e-commerce host you choose does this for you as part of your hosting package.

A service called Mobify (www.mobify.com) converts your website to a format that can easily be viewed and navigated on a mobile device. You can also use an online utility called Onbile (www.grovo.com/onbile) to create your own mobile site.

Keep Your Presentation Ultra-Simple

Your conventional website or storefront might have a Flash animation as an introduction; it might feature video clips and content arranged in multiple columns. That's all well and good, but you need to keep all these flashy elements off your mobile site.

Shoppers just want to find what they're looking for quickly and be able to pay for it with a few mouse clicks. If they have to wait too long for a page to load because it's too complicated, they'll simply give up and go elsewhere. With that harsh fact in mind, it's wise to adhere to the following rules of mobile simplicity:

- ✔ **Invite shoppers to explore.** Less is more when it comes to shopping. Your initial screen should include just the most important links to your catalog or website. This allows visitors to decide quickly where to click.

- ✔ **Make purchases simple.** In Chapter 6 you learn about organizing a website to keep shopping simple. On a mobile site, it's essential to be able to add an item to a shopping cart and then make a purchase with a minimum of mouse clicks.

Smartphones and mobile devices are all about convenience, so your mobile commerce site should echo what mobile users already want and expect from an online shopping experience.

Enable Mobile Device Payments

If, like many online businesspeople, you also operate a brick-and-mortar store or sell at flea markets or art fairs, it pays to sign up with a mobile payment service so people can pay you wherever you are. The best-known such service is called Square Payments (www.square.com).

Other companies have created payment systems that work with mobile devices. Check out PayPal Here (www.paypal.com/webapps/mpp/credit-card-reader) and Intuit GoPayment (http://payments.intuit.com/mobile_credit_card_processing). All these services work by means of a device called a *dongle* that plugs into a smartphone and enables it to connect to a payment network.

Create an App

The ultimate way to give your store a functional presence on a smartphone or tablet is to create an app for it. An app performs lots of essential business functions:

- **It's embedded into the device.** Once a user downloads and installs an app, it's there in the device. It is assigned a shortcut, and the user can place that shortcut right on his or her home screen for the ultimate in convenience.

- **It promotes your products.** If you have Groupon's popular app, you know that the daily deal site uses the app as a promotional tool; you see today's special deals the moment you open it up.

- **It makes your site easy to use.** The app can be configured to store user information so it doesn't have to be entered at checkout; a purchase might take just one or two clicks.

If creating an app is beyond the reach of your small business, you can hire a programmer to create an app just for you, with the features you want. That, at least, is the ultimate goal. But hiring such a programmer might be beyond the reach of those businesses on a shoestring budget. Still, you might consider a simple app; it makes your business look legitimate and cutting-edge, and gives you added credibility.

Sites like Intellectsoft (`www.intellectsoft.co.uk/iphone_applications_development.html`) give you an estimate on how much your own app might cost.

Offer a Coupon Deal They Can't Refuse

Coupons are highly effective promotional tools that attract devoted (and on occasion, deal-obsessed) shoppers. The latest trend is to have coupons delivered to consumers' smartphones; they don't necessarily have to appear in print at all.

With a little effort, you can create coupons that you post on your website or in your store so that customers can download them to their phones. The free service Keypons (`www.keypons.net`) makes it easy for you to assign a name to your offer, enter the specifics in a form (whether the coupon is for 10 percent off, for example) and enter instructions on how the shopper should redeem it ("Text 'save cleaning' to 42424," for example). One advantage of using a coupon creation service is that you can track the effectiveness of the promotion. You get reports on how many people saw your coupon, how many used it, how many passed it on to their friends, and so on.

Consider a Mobile-Only Shopping Cart Provider

Some shopping cart/e-commerce hosting services give their customers a mobile version of their online storefronts. That version is probably good enough for most small business owners. But if most of your customers use mobile devices, or if you are just starting out and want to focus exclusively on mobile commerce, create your store especially for the "small screen" with a mobile shopping cart.

Service providers like 2ergo (www.2ergo.com) and asknet (www.asknet.com) work from the ground up with mobile sites, so they are familiar with what platforms to work with, what size constraints they have to meet, and so on, as well as features like mobile coupons, which are described in the preceding section.

Go Beyond "Mobile" to Include "Social"

Social marketing is a natural activity on mobile devices. Your e-commerce presentation can feed into this by making it easy for mobile shoppers to connect with their friends and online acquaintances and spread the word about your products and services. Here are some suggestions:

- **Take advantage of mobile reviews.** Give your visitors a chance to post reviews of your store or your products; mobile web surfers love reviews and seek them out.

- **Help shoppers "pin" your products.** Provide a button that enables visitors to quickly "pin" items they like to the social marketing site Pinterest.

- **Help reviews share their views.** Provide one-touch buttons so those who leave reviews for you can share those reviews with their friends on Facebook and Twitter.

Your mobile site should be a place that encourages shoppers to return; enabling interaction with the site gets them involved and gives them a reason to check back on a regular basis.

Keep Your Mobile Site Cross-Platform

It's always important to make sure your web content appears the way you want no matter what computer platform or browser your visitor uses. It's even more important when the content appears on a tablet or smartphone.

Be sure to test your site to make sure the appearance is accurate on the most popular (iPhone, Android) platforms and on browsers such as Chrome, Safari, and Android's built-in browser.

Focus on Shoppers Who Are Likely Buyers

A study by Apsalar (apsalar.com/blog/2012/09/apsalar-more-mobile-apps-lead-to-engagement-deficit-disorder) indicates that mobile shoppers are not necessarily engaged buyers. The sheer number of apps they have installed and the number of things demanding their attention on their smartphones mean they tend not to follow through with transactions on their mobile devices.

But there's good news. You already have a set of engaged customers — shoppers who have already purchased from you, who "Like" you on Facebook, who have chosen to subscribe to your newsletter if you have one. These are customers you can drive to your mobile site. Offer them special promotions and rewards, and encourage them to tell their friends on Facebook and Twitter.

Contact Customers in Your Area with a Geofence

This advanced tip combines the location-based marketing described in Chapter 12 with mobile devices. A *geofence* is a location that you specify using a service such as Thumbvista (www.thumbvista.com). Logically, this would be the location of your brick-and-mortar store if you have one. It could also be an art fair or another event in which you are participating.

When someone nears or passes by the geofence, the service sends a text message to the mobile devices of individuals who have already opted in to receive such messages. The text message might say "50 percent off pottery today only!" For customers who have already made purchases from you and who have opted in as part of one of your e-mail campaigns, this can be a welcome alert that might well result in a purchase.

Chapter 20

Ten Ways to Develop a Platform

• •

*N*ot so long ago, starting an online business primarily meant creating a website or selling on a marketplace such as eBay. The landscape has shifted as I write the seventh edition of this book. Yes, websites are still important. But the notion of what constitutes a "website" has expanded to include a blog, a storefront on eBay, or a site hosted by any of a number of intriguing niche marketplaces.

The ultimate result of this combination of online sales and marketing efforts is a *platform*. The term should be familiar to anyone involved in publishing. In the world of book writing and marketing, an *author platform* is all-important. This is a base of readers who are already familiar with and like your work or your services and to whom you can market future books. An author who gives seminars and who has thousands of followers on Facebook and Twitter has a platform of devoted fans eager to hear about new books or seminars.

The same principle can apply to e-commerce. Your ultimate goal is to develop a *seller platform*. You want to have repeat customers, subscribers to your newsletter, readers of your blog, and followers on social media. You become the "go-to" person when it comes to widgets, or what's-its, or whatever you sell or create. It's a matter of branding yourself, and it's something that's easier than ever to do online. You find ten options for developing a brand and a platform in this chapter.

Following Wilco's Example

It's always helpful to find an example to follow when it comes to sales or marketing. You might know a seller in your field who seems to do everything right and who has developed a recognizable brand. If you need a suggestion, consider the well-known rock band Wilco, based in my own hometown of Chicago.

Wilco (`www.wilcoworld.net`) made headlines in 2002 when its record publisher rejected its album *Yankee Hotel Foxtrot.* The record company gave the band all the rights to the album; they started streaming it online to their fans. It turned out to be the band's most successful album to date, selling 670,000 copies. In addition to having an online store, Wilco has more than 500,000

"Likes" on Facebook and 92,000 followers on Twitter. Followers on Facebook can listen to concerts online; they let people listen to their music online before they sell it on CD in their online store. It's all about driving fans to their various locations online and building a community to sustain long-term sales. The community page on their website (`http://wilcoworld.net/community`) points visitors to many online forums where they can connect with like-minded fans.

Creating a Logo

A logo is like a storefront sign. It gives people, in one glance, a visual representation of what your business is and what you sell. Is it really necessary to have a logo? No. Does it hurt your business if you don't have one? I would argue yes. The web became popular in the 1990s because it was visual; suddenly you could see images and colors, not just text links. A logo can go a long way toward making a business seem "for real" in the minds of your customers, and your own mind, too.

A good logo is professional-looking. It represents who you are, what service you provide, or what you sell. But it can be simple, almost homemade-looking, like the logo for the Enchanted Hen website (`www.enchantedhen.com`).

Even if you have no artistic ability, you can still make a logo yourself that consists of only type. There are some really good precedents for this. The logo shown in Figure 20-1 is an example; so are Google's and eBay's logos.

Although simpler is better when it comes to logos, if you are creating a business or a brand that you want to promote for years to come, it's really worth your effort to spend some money on a professional designer. You can find one on the online employment site Elance (`www.elance.com`).

See Chapter 5 for more on creating a logo and how it can help your business.

Listing on EveryPlaceISell

A business with multiple storefronts and points of entry benefits by having a single location where all those venues are brought together under a single virtual "roof." A website called EveryPlaceISell (`www.everyplaceisell.com`) provides such a home base for free.

A typical EveryPlaceISell listing not only lists the various storefronts operated by a single individual or company, but also includes background information about the owner, something that customers might not be able to find elsewhere. There's no reason not to list on this site; you gain another place to reach customers and another page to link to (which should improve SEO).

You can put a link to your EveryPlaceISell page everywhere you appear online, including Facebook and Twitter. It might be especially effective to include this link as part of your e-mail signature file as well.

Being a Social Marketing Maven

Social marketing can serve many purposes that go beyond keeping up with friends and family and sharing news stories that you find interesting. It can meet some of your business goals as well. Keeping up with your customers and sharing stories about your company or your field of business is the same kind of activity but with a different emphasis.

E-commerce, like more traditional kinds of business, is built on concepts like trust, brands, and reputation. The better you can brand yourself and prove that you are either an authority in your field or someone who has desirable merchandise, the more successful you'll be. Social networking is simply the practice of connecting with people online to build loyalty, establish a one-to-one relationship with your customers, build a sense of community, and let people know about your products and business.

You can go beyond sharing to offer freebies, conduct contests, and even post items for sale through a social networking site or, at the very least, advertise them online. See Chapter 13 for more.

Developing an E-Mail Campaign

I'm involved in an e-mail marketing campaign as I write this chapter. My non-profit spiritual community is promoting a visit by our teacher, who is coming to our center in Chicago. We're conducting a planned series of mailings using the e-mail service Constant Contact (www.constantcontact.com).

That's the first thing you should consider when you think about progressing from occasional e-mail sender to organized e-mail campaign conductor: Pay a modest monthly fee for an e-mail service provider (ESP). An ESP doesn't just help you keep track of mailing lists. It streamlines the process whereby individuals can subscribe or unsubscribe from those lists, which is required by law.

ESPs also help you with designing and revising e-mails so you don't have to create them from scratch each time. You can save an e-mail as a draft before it goes out; you can resend e-mails with a single click; you can copy e-mails and revise them with new content as needed. But among the best features is the report function: You can keep track of how many people opened your e-mail and how many clicked links in the message, for example.

Posting on Your Blog

Over the years, I've seen one business principle play out over and over again: The more generous you are with your knowledge, the more business you'll get. For many people, a blog provides a way to share your knowledge, experience, and interests, as well as news about your products or services.

A business blog has a special purpose. It shares news and the views of a businessperson who's knowledgeable about a particular area of commerce and who wants to connect with people who are interested in the same subject. Setting up a blog isn't difficult thanks to tools like WordPress; putting substantive posts on it regularly is the challenge.

A blog is another way of building your platform. By inviting comments from readers and responding to them, you give your customers another reason to visit you. And people who are impressed with your knowledge may well check out your store.

One of the biggest benefits of having a blog and updating it regularly is that you improve your search engine placement. Google, for example, likes pages that are updated frequently; it ranks those pages higher in search results, as I discuss in Chapter 11. To find out more about blogs, see Chapter 13.

Giving Something Back to Your Supporters

There's a business I'm familiar with, a small Chicago company that sells organic and heirloom food products, called The Scrumptious Pantry (www.scrumptiouspantry.com). When they were just getting started, the owners went on the revolutionary fundraising site Kickstarter, where anyone can raise money from sympathetic individuals for a personal project or a cause, trying to raise $12,000, and they reached their goal and then some.

Look up this business on Kickstarter (www.kickstarter.com/projects/61608863/tasty-packaged-food-from-small-sustainable-farms), and in the right column you see all the things The Scrumptious Pantry is doing to keep up with its donors and give something back, including providing donors with a recipe a day for a year. This, of course, is a great way to market and expand one's customer base and build a brand.

On their website, the owners invite visitors to join an heirloom club, and they provide recipes as well. They're putting it all together with a newsletter, an online store, a blog, Facebook and Twitter links, and all the tools to help them assemble a platform of dedicated supporters and customers.

Popping Up on Other People's Websites

One of the most effective ways to build a name for yourself (and, by extension, a platform) is to spread your name around the web as widely as possible. Luckily, the proliferation of blogs and discussion areas means it's easy to do so.

Look for sites that sell items that complement the things you sell. Ask if you can trade advertisements or links: I'll place a link (or ad) to your site on mine, if you do the same for my site. Because the other site isn't a direct competitor, the owner should be receptive.

Look for blogs that discuss topics or areas of business that relate to what you do, or that focus on your own area of expertise. Ask if you can write a guest blog post. If the response is yes, write a useful post that (ideally) provokes discussion.

Be available to people like me, who write about online business. If someone asks you for an interview, jump at the chance. Having your name and the URL of your website in an article on a well-traveled venue is like business gold. It can be available in Google search results for months, even years; a half-hour of answering questions can lead customers to your site for a far longer period of time.

Publishing Your Own Newsletter

Your main goal as an online businessperson should be to make sales. But at the same time, you need to gather names and e-mail addresses, and one of the best ways to do this is by creating a newsletter. A newsletter doesn't have to contain a series of detailed stories and photos. It can be a set of announcements, too. Here are some ideas of what a newsletter might contain:

- ✔ **Announcements of special sales and promotions:** "Check out our spring cleaning sale this weekend," for instance, or "Half Off All Fishing Tackle This Saturday!"

- ✔ **New products:** When you introduce new merchandise, feature it with photos, a short article, and suggestions of how the reader might use it or benefit from it.

- ✔ **Instructions on how to use your products:** If you sell shelving or organizational products, for example, create a special report showing how to use your products to organize a home or garage.

- ✔ **Keepsakes:** Offer a recipe book, for example.

- ✔ **A bonus:** If someone subscribes, offer a 33 percent discount on his or her next purchase, for example.

Once you sell to someone, put his or her name on a mailing list. It's easy to do so. Record the information in a word processing or spreadsheet file. The spreadsheet option is especially good because the contents can be easily exported to a mailing list service.

Send that person a newsletter or e-mail that tells about your new products or that simply describes what you're up to.

Before you start gathering your customers' contact information, check with your marketplace to make sure you know their policy on e-mail marketing. Some venues (notably, Amazon.com) prohibit the use of customer e-mail addresses for marketing.

Keeping Your Content Fresh and Up to Date

Do you have a favorite blog, comic strip, or newspaper columnist website that you like to visit each day? I certainly do. With luck, your customers will want to visit your site, eBay Store, or other sales venue every day as well. Of course, that won't be the case unless you come up with new material on a regular basis.

I know what you're thinking: You have so many things to do that you can't possibly revisit your website every day and change headings or put new sales online. You have to get the kids off to school, pack up some merchandise, run to the post office, clean up the house — the list goes on and on. You can't be in two places at the same time. Two people can be, though. Consider hiring a student or friend to help run your site and suggest new content for you.

Index

About the Author

Greg Holden started the small business Stylus Media, which is a group of editorial, design, and computer professionals who produce both print and electronic publications. Greg has been a freelance writer since 1996, and is also a novelist. A former PowerSeller on eBay, he is now embarking on a new hobby — beekeeping. (Visit Greg's blog, www.gregholden.com, for more about his activities and for links to his fiction.)

The first edition of *Starting an Online Business For Dummies* was the ninth of Greg's more than 45 computer books, and he authored *eBay PowerUser's Bible* for Wiley Publishing. Over the years, he has been a regular contributor to CNET (www.cnet.com) and to EcommerceBytes (www.ecommercebytes.com). Greg balances his technical expertise and his entrepreneurial experience with his love of literature. He received a Master of Arts degree in English from the University of Illinois at Chicago, and he writes general-interest books, short stories, and poetry.

Greg translated his experiences raising two daughters into the book *Karma Kids: Answering Everyday Parenting Questions with Buddhist Wisdom*. He lives with his wife and their Corgi in a Victorian rowhouse in Chicago. He is a longtime member of Jewel Heart, a Tibetan Buddhist meditation and study group based in Ann Arbor, Michigan.

Dedication

To my father, who taught me all about being innovative, working independently, and working hard.

Author's Acknowledgments

The most successful entrepreneurs tend to be the most generous with their time and experience. I want to thank everyone who was profiled as a case study: Dean Pettit of Space Coast Outdoors; Ryan Hatfield of PriceSpectre; Lucky Boyd of MyTexasMusic.com; Paula Slof of Paula and Chlo; Mike Holden of lp2cdsolutions; Nanette Thorell of Enchanted Hen Productions; Mimi Kriele of A Touch of Europe; Eva Kertesz; John Moen of Graphic Maps; Mike LoCarto of Natural Body Inc.; Jason Bolt of Society43; John Counsel of The Profit Clinic; Jeffrey E. Edelheit; Lars Hundley of Clean Air Gardening; Laura Milnor Iverson; Chris Green of FBAPower; Brad Owens of Rock Shop Music and Comics; Doug Laughter of The Silver Connection; Skye Ryan-Evans; Kharisma Ryantori; Sarah-Lou Morris of Alfresco; Judy Vorfeld of Office Support Services; Marques Vickers; and Scott Wills. Special recognition also goes to attorney David Adler (www.ecommerce attorney.com) for his assistance with Chapter 16.

I would also like to acknowledge my wife, Peggy, who has supported and encouraged me in all areas of life. And thanks to Ina Steiner at EcommerceBytes for allowing me to write interesting articles about online businesses of all sorts.

For editing and technical assignments, I was lucky to be in the capable hands of the folks at Wiley Publishing: my project editor, Brian Walls; my copy editor, Lynn Northrup; and my technical editor, Joel Elad.

Thanks also to Neil Salkind of Studio B, and to Kyle Looper of Wiley Publishing, for helping me to add this book to the list of those I've authored and, in the process, broadening my expertise as a writer.

Last but certainly not least, the future is in the hands of the generation of my two daughters, Zosia and Lucy, who allow me to learn from the curiosity and joy with which they approach life.

Publisher's Acknowledgments

Acquisitions Editor: Kyle Looper

Project Editor: Brian Walls

Copy Editor: Lynn Northrup

Technical Editor: Joel Elad

Editorial Assistant: Annie Sullivan

Sr. Editorial Assistant: Cherie Case

Project Coordinator: Katherine Crocker

Cover Image: © John Lund/Marc Romanelli/ Jupiter Images